POWER

Police Officer Wellness, Ethics, and Resilience

Edited by

Konstantinos Papazoglou

Daniel M. Blumberg

Forewords by

John M. Violanti

Tracie Keesee

ELSEVIER

ACADEMIC PRESS

An imprint of Elsevier

Academic Press is an imprint of Elsevier
125 London Wall, London EC2Y 5AS, United Kingdom
525 B Street, Suite 1650, San Diego, CA 92101, United States
50 Hampshire Street, 5th Floor, Cambridge, MA 02139, United States
The Boulevard, Langford Lane, Kidlington, Oxford OX5 1GB, United Kingdom

Notices
Knowledge and best practice in this field are constantly changing. As new research and experience broaden our understanding, changes in research methods, professional practices, or medical treatment may become necessary.

Practitioners and researchers must always rely on their own experience and knowledge in evaluating and using any information, methods, compounds, or experiments described herein. In using such information or methods they should be mindful of their own safety and the safety of others, including parties for whom they have a professional responsibility.

To the fullest extent of the law, neither the Publisher nor the authors, contributors, or editors, assume any liability for any injury and/or damage to persons or property as a matter of products liability, negligence or otherwise, or from any use or operation of any methods, products, instructions, or ideas contained in the material herein.

Library of Congress Cataloging-in-Publication Data
A catalog record for this book is available from the Library of Congress

British Library Cataloguing-in-Publication Data
A catalogue record for this book is available from the British Library

ISBN: 978-0-12-817872-0

For information on all Academic Press publications visit our website at https://www.elsevier.com/books-and-journals

Publisher: Stacy Masucci
Acquisition Editor: Elizabeth Brown
Editorial Project Manager: Fernanda A. Oliveira
Production Project Manager: Bharatwaj Varatharajan
Cover Designer: Miles Hitchen

Typeset by TNQ Technologies

Transferred to Digital Printing in 2019

Working together to grow libraries in developing countries

www.elsevier.com • www.bookaid.org

*We would like to dedicate this book to all law enforcement officers who put
their lives on the line every day to help keep us safe.
Drs. Papazoglou & Blumberg*

*And, I would also like to dedicate the book to my beautiful little flower,
my daughter Dominiki, who makes me smile every day.
Dr. Konstantinos Papazoglou*

Contents

Contributors

Prashant Aukhojee University of Toronto, Toronto, ON, Canada

Daniel M. Blumberg Department of Undergraduate Psychology, California School of Professional Psychology, Alliant International University, San Diego, CA, United States

Kimberly C. Burke Center for Policing Equity, UC, Berkeley, CA, United States

Brian A. Chopko Criminology and Justice Studies program, Department of Sociology, Kent State University at Stark, North Canton, OH, United States

Lisa M.Z. Couperthwaite Department of Psychiatry, University of Toronto — St. George Campus, Toronto, Ontario, Canada

Sarah Creighton Assistant Chief (Retired), San Diego Police Department, San Diego, CA, United States

Mark Davies BC Counselling, Surrey, BC, Canada

Andrew L. Eagle East Lansing, MI, United States

Breanne Faulkner Centre for Addiction and Mental Health, Toronto, Ontario, Canada

Samantha Fuss Centre for Addiction and Mental Health, Toronto, Ontario, Canada; Department of Psychological Science, University of Toronto — Scarborough Campus, Scarborough, Ontario, Canada

Olivia Johnson Blue Wall Institute, Belleville, IL, United States

Katy Kamkar Centre for Addiction and Mental Health, University of Toronto, Department of Psychiatry, Toronto, ON, Canada

Chuck Kaye Chief of Police, City of Coronado Police Department, Coronado, CA United States

Tracie Keesee   Tracie Keesee Vice President of Law Enforcement and Social Justice Initiatives for the Center for Policing Equity; Former Deputy Commissioner of Equity and Inclusion for New York Police Department (NYPD); Former Deputy Commissioner of Training for NYPD; Graduate of the 203rd Session of the FBI National Academy

Christine C. Kwiatkowski   Michigan State University, Neuroscience Program, East Lansing, MI, United States;   Michigan State University, School of Criminal Justice, East Lansing, MI, United States

Claire E. Manning   East Lansing, MI, United States

Detective Beth Milliard   York Regional Police, Aurora, ON, Canada

Konstantinos Papazoglou   Yale School of Medicine, New Haven, CT, United States

Alfred J. Robison   Michigan State University, Department of Physiology, East Lansing, MI, United States

Felipe Rubim   Munich Center for Mathematical Philosophy, LMU Munich, Munich, Germany

Lucas Rubim   Department of Psychology, University of Toronto, Toronto, Ontario, Canada

Chuck Russo   American Military University/American Public University, Charles Town, WV, United States

Mike Schlosser   Police Training Institute of the State of Illinois, Champaign, IL, United States

Alex R. Thornton   Kelley School of Business, Indiana University, Bloomington, Indiana, United States

Brooke McQuerrey Tuttle   Center for Family Resilience Department of Human Development and Family Science, Oklahoma State University, Tulsa, OK, United States

John M. Violanti   Research Professor of Epidemiology and Environmental Health, University at Buffalo, School of Public Health and Health Professions

Testimonials

"Trauma exposure within the policing and first responder environments can lead to real, de-habilitating psychological injuries if left untreated. Although there are no slings, crutches or bandages for such operational stress injuries the end consequences may lead to suicide ideation, attempts or actual completion contributing to disastrous consequences for the involved member, their family and loved ones, along with their colleagues and the community in which they serve. The authors of the book, POWER, provide an extensive collection of education, awareness, research and accessibility to evidence-based techniques that can provide members, their family and loved ones with the information, skills and coping strategies necessary for enjoying an exciting career armed with the knowledge by promoting wellness and healthy strategies that can be implemented via individuals and their respective organizations. This book will become required take home literature for ALL First Responders participating in our future Badge of Life Canada programming focusing on topics, such as moral injury, sanctuary trauma and perceived injustice."

Sgt. Bill Rusk (Ret.) Executive Director, Badge of Life Canada

"Written by a powerful line up of experts in the field, many with years of hands-on experience, this book is a must read for anyone with a professional or personal interest in law enforcement. Offering an impressive breadth of coverage on topics related to police wellness, the editors and contributors present a comprehensive view of the many ways law enforcement personnel can be affected by the realities of the job. The authors also provide valuable insight and key strategies designed to promote a culture of individual and organizational wellness. This publication is a very welcome and important contribution to our field."

Dr. Carolyn Burns, Registered Psychologist
Over 30 years of experience working with first responders

"This is a very important book brought to us by very compassionate people who've dedicated their careers to serving the law enforcement community. Through their sworn duty to serve, police officers and their families make sacrifices to protect the community at large. As a society we have failed to treat them with the respect and appreciation for these sacrifices that they deserve. In my work in the field of police wellness I hear from officers again and again 'it's been a long time coming' that their wellness is something that's being prioritized. They deeply appreciate knowing someone sees the ways in which they suffer, and they respond to this compassion. The topics covered in this book are exactly where the light needs to be shone in order for compassionate, comprehensive, effective, programs and policies to be developed and established."

Chris Checkett, MSW, LISW-S, Founder of Cleveland Mindfulness Center, Co-creator of the Mindfulness Training Program for the City of Cleveland, Division of Police.

"With traumatic incidents, routine stressors and the toxic nature of police work, *POWER: Police Officer Wellness, Ethics, and Resilience* dives into the psychological wounds created by this environment and how departments and officers can promote wellness. Now, more than ever, departments need to make wellness a top priority. Dr.'s Papazoglou and Blumberg, use evidence-based strategies to build strong and positive peace officers and a department culture of wellness."

Brian R. Marvel, President
Peace Officers Research Association of California (PORAC)

"POWER is an essential resource for those engaged in the high-stress, high-stakes law enforcement profession, and for those who support them. The authors distill science into practical, actionable approaches that support departments and officers to not only survive the job, but also to improve their performance, their health, and their connection to family and loved ones. A must read for those who want to dedicate their careers to service."

Diana M. Concannon, PsyD
Dean, California School of Forensic Studies
Alliant International University

"For over thirty years people asked me, 'Why are cops so angry?' In most circumstances, this was not anger they were experiencing but the toll of constant conflict, suffering, tragedy, and frustration. The research presented here can be what changes the paradigm. The book reveals the hidden truth of policing: there are consequences to the officer beyond the physical injuries. The authors look into the multi-faceted elements of policing's impact on the officers' mental well-being and offer methods to mitigate the effects. This work is desperately needed and answers the question as to why cops become so detached from the people they serve. Finally, a comprehensive and objective look into the issues that plague law enforcement and hinder successful police-community relations."

Glen A. Haas, Police Commander (Ret)
President/CEO
Operant Learning Systems, Inc.

"As a 30-year veteran of the San Diego Police Department, I can attest to the emotional toll this profession can take on the men and women who protect and serve. Any individual who performs this role, day in and day out, has to deal with these conditions one way or another. Taking this in depth and comprehensive look at the effects of stressors that are present while on and off duty, is long overdue. In order for our law enforcement professionals to continue to perform at the high levels our communities demand, addressing physical and emotional wellness is essential."

Detective Jack Schaeffer
San Diego Police Department
President, San Diego Police Officers Association

"It is exciting to see a book that offers a wide ranging approach to promoting well-being of police officers in a multidisciplinary context. Covered is not only the potential impact of police work on the officer, and the recover from trauma, but also the grounding that needs to be set in the policy programs for this important work to take place. Included are also prevention and resilience aspects of wellbeing. POWER to this book!"

Dr. Mari Koskelainen, Senior Advisor, Clinical Psychologist,
National Bureau of Investigation, Finland

"With the contribution of many established scholars and experts in the field of law enforcement, the editors are successfully shedding light upon the multifaceted nature of police wellness and resilience. Diving deep into the reality of police work and the psychological trauma officers are often confronted with, the book goes a step further in providing valuable evidence-based techniques in an effort to counteract the consequences of daily stressors and improve police officers' personal and professional well-being!"

Stavroula Soukara PhD
Associate Professor of Forensic Psychology
University of Nicosia, Cyprus

"Drs. Papazoglou and Blumberg address the issues all too familiar with our law enforcement officers policing the country in this day and age. The stressors have become more significant and the battles are not just on the streets but within the departments and society itself. This book brilliantly addresses the stressors current day policing holds as well as the repercussions for ignoring them. This book looks at the problems but more importantly the solutions to many of the psychosocial stressors impacting officers. Gaining insight into the need for mental health programs and the destigmatizing of such lends a much needed positive perspective on the importance of selfcare and the normalization of seeking help to achieve it. Resiliency is only achieved through traumatic experiences and survival and this population is the epitome of both."

Stephanie Samuels, Founder and President, Copline, Inc

"From within the world of lived experience there is a struggle to not only get people to understand our pain, but to understand it ourselves. In our weakest moments' words and pathways to recovery elude us. We oftentimes find ourselves getting into more difficulties simply by the ill-informed ways in which we choose to heal ourselves than by the root injury itself. We know, as we share our stories that our wounds are as diverse as there are experiences. We each have our own reactions to the event or series of events that have wounded us. There is no one cookie-cutter template to assist us in our recovery and in dealing within our families, our workplace and our society. So, it is imperative for our mental health leaders and specialists to share as much as they can to better understand the complexities of our reactions. For far too long those of us with lived experience have said that we can excuse the lack of support or the damage done because we as a society as a whole did not know better. Now we do know better and these authors are helping by lifting the fog of ignorance from our world."

Staff Sergeants (ret'd.) Sylvio (Syd) A. Gravel, M.O.M., and Brad McKay, C.T.S.S.
Co-Authors of "Walk the Talk — First Responder Peer Support — A
Boots-on-the-Ground Peer & Trauma Support Systems Guide"
Co-Leads of the lived experience "Peer and Trauma Support Systems Team"
Senior Police Advisors, Badge of Life Canada.

Foreword by John M. Violanti

The issue of wellness in policing has begun to permeate the long held notion that police work is only dangerous because of chasing criminals and facing uncontrollable crime. While this may be the case in some police jurisdictions, another danger lurks beneath-that of psychological and health survival in this high stress occupation. Law enforcement candidates come into police work with the purpose of helping others. While this is an admirable goal, time and exposure to stress, trauma and human misery soon takes a toll on officers. Seeing incidents involving death, severe assaults, traffic accidents, and abused children can dampen even the strongest will to help others.

It is well past time to focus on this hidden danger within, this unwarranted stress, this cancer of the police spirit that eats away at those who serve. Officers stretch their compassion for others to a point of fatigue, leaving them torn between helping and at times giving up. In my twenty-three years of police service, I have seen and at times felt these things happen.

The present writing offers good evidence and suggestions to help officers psychologically survive a term of service, often lasting 25—30 years. Drs. Konstantinos Papazoglou and Daniel Blumberg have brought together both academic and law enforcement stakeholders to offer their research and experience concerning this important issue. The forward progress of wellness will substantially benefit from their contributions.

In my view, the process of wellness begins in the mind and the body just keeps score (Van der Kolk, 2014). It is essential that those in command pay close attention to the pathologic outcomes of chronic stress and trauma-those contributing factors along the pathway to poor physical health.

The first chapters discuss the erosion process of wellness among police officers - the idea that both person and occupation experience a deterioration of mental and physical well-being. There are many threats to personal wellness, both social and biological. In this edition, Drs. Kwiatkowski and Robison discuss the probable neurobiological threats to well-being. In our own work, we found that police officers with high levels of PTSD symptomatology had significantly more difficult time in making decisions in a lab experiment. Measures of neural activity demonstrated that PTSD essentially compromised functions in the brain which impeded decision processes (Covey et al. 2013).

As Dr. Faulkner and colleagues point out in this edition, Posttraumatic Stress Disorder PTSD may affect physical wellness. Data from the National Comorbidity Survey indicates that 60% of men and 50% of women are exposed to a traumatic event at some time in their lives (Kessler, Sonnega, Bromet, Hughes, & Nelson, 1995). Such exposure may involve actual or threatened death, serious injury, threat to one's physical integrity, or witnessing such events occurring to other persons or significant others. Symptoms such as re-experiencing the event, avoidance of stimuli associated with the trauma, numbing of general responsiveness, and symptoms of increased arousal, and mood changes are all part of this disorder (DSM-5, American Psychiatric Association, 2013).

Recent studies describe a positive relationship between PTSD and cardiovascular problems, including higher rates of angina, lower cardiovascular effort tolerance on a treadmill test, and electrocardiogram abnormalities (Freedman, Brandes, Peri & Shalev,

1999). Evidence linking cardiovascular disease (CVD) and exposure to trauma has been found across different populations and stressor events. Military veterans diagnosed with PTSD, for example, were significantly more likely to have had abnormal electrocardiographic results (Boscarino, 2004). Civilian populations exposed to traumatic events also have reported increased cardiovascular health problems (Buckley et al., 2004).

In our own research on police officers, we have found that differing levels of PTSD symptoms had an impact on differing levels of subclinical cardiovascular biomarkers such as artery health. Impaired artery regulation may lead to cardiovascular abnormalities during mental stress. Officers with severe PTSD symptoms were approximately three times more likely to have the metabolic syndrome-a complex of five different cardiovascular risk factors (Violanti, et al. 2006).

Physiological outcomes are not the only consequences of wellness erosion. In section two, Dr. Russo and colleagues point out the impact of compassion fatigue. Compassion fatigue has been associated with the psychological "cost of caring" for others (Figley, 1999). Figley's (1999) model argues that there will be a residual of stress in police officers from being compassionate that may develop fatigue. If personal or organizational efforts are insufficient to eliminate compassion stress, there is a buildup of distressing, unprocessed memories and sensations that requires discharging. Moreover, if there are unprocessed traumatic memories from the officers personal life that have not been dealt with and desensitized, this could lead more quickly to police compassion fatigue.

One of the major contributors to compassion fatigue is the experiencing of traumatic events. Our conjecture is that police officers exposed to certain types and frequencies of traumatic events will be at higher risk for developing PTSD. Compassion fatigue may indirectly be a function of the type and frequency of exposure to traumatic events in police work and resultant symptoms. This may be especially relevant in cases involving victimization of the officer's peers or victims of crime. The role of compassion fatigue as secondary trauma is complex. Precisely at what point in the trauma process and whom compassion fatigue may affect is still unknown. We also do not yet fully understand to a full extent the additive effect of multiple traumas on police officers. Police work is a helping profession. Caring for others is an admirable quality for police officers, but caring without knowledge of result, perceived effectiveness, the possibility of prevention, and departmental support can lead to debilitating results. This is the pressing psychological dilemma for the police officer.

In section three, Dr. Thornton and colleagues develop ideas to create a culture of wellness. I would add to their excellent coverage of this topic that there are several dimensions to this admirable and sorely needed goal. The first is one of blockage. Within the culture of police work, there is an ethos that one does not report or display any form of weakness. Mental health problems fall into the category of "weakness." Many officers are in fear of admitting to mental difficulties because they perceive that they will be mistrusted by peers and supervision to do the job. Others feel that they will lose opportunities for promotion or even their job.

All of this fear likely finds its roots in stigma. Stigma is one of the most frequently identified barriers to mental health care and is prevalent among the police. A meta-analysis by Haugen et al. (2017) found that that the most frequently endorsed items by police and first responders were fears regarding confidentiality and negative career impact. Results from this meta-analysis indicated that on average, about one in three first responders (33.1 %) experienced stigma regarding mental health. The most commonly reported barriers to care were difficulty scheduling an appointment and not knowing where to get help (Haugen et al., 2017).

One possible solution is a peer support program. This will allow distressed officers to initially talk with other officers first and then possibly seek professional help. An assumption underlying peer support is that police peers trained in basic listening techniques are more trusted by officers in distress (Landers & Zhou, 2011). Peer supporters draw on their shared experiences in order to provide empathic understanding, information, and advice. Davidson, Chinman, Sells, & Rowe, 2006) reported that peer support reduced symptoms for participants and increased their social integration; an important factor in suicide prevention. Another recent suggestion is a "health and well-being check-in," where officers can (voluntarily) annually meet with a peer support officer or health professional on a confidential basis to discuss any problems. Lastly, and as important, there is a need for more education for police concerning mental health and effective treatment.

The second suggested dimension of a culture of wellness is grounded in positive psychology. This involves salutary influences which can help officers become more resistant to the impact of stress. The development of socially and individually based resiliency can make this possible. Resiliency is a concept that captures the idea of overcoming and adapting to negative experiences (Southwick, Bonanno, Masten, Panter-Brick, & Yehuda, 2014). Self-esteem, coping skills, hardiness, and social support are positively associated with individual resilience. Evidence suggests that resilience has a moderating influence on stress (Armeli, Gunthert, & Cohen, 2001).

There are specific characteristics that make individuals or organizations more or less resilient to stress (Maddi, 2002; Maddi & Khosaba, 2005). Taken together, these factors suggest that resilience is not so much a trait as it is a process of integration of available resources such as groups or organizations. In a social and supportive sense, it is appropriate to expand the scope of resiliency to the police organization (Klein, Nicholls, & Thomalla, 2003). Police officers respond to stressful incidents as members of agencies whose climate influences their thoughts and actions (Paton, Smith Ramsay, & Akande, 1999). Higgins (1994) and Sledge, Boydstun and Rahe (1980) also suggest that coping style and social cohesion could act to cognitively integrate the stressful experience. The effects of resilience and social integration suggests that the group can facilitate the active process of self-righting and growth. Leadership is critical for building individual and organizational resilience. Leaders who are resilient are crucial in creating a culture of resilience in an organization. Managers and supervisors are uniquely positioned to create a healthy and safe workplace by creating a wellness culture and supporting staff who want to achieve and/or maintain healthy lifestyles. The benefits of having healthy employees are numerous, from improved health and productivity to lower healthcare costs and risks.

In sum, witnessing death, human misery, abused children, and violence at work weigh heavily as precipitants to PTSD, depression, alcohol use, and suicide among police (O'Hara, Violanti, Levenson & Clark, 2013). Such exposure can have profound impacts on officers. However, with support from the organization and the strengthening of both personal and social resiliency, pathological outcomes may not necessarily be the norm. Those in the police field and academic research need to seek proactive ways to stop the erosion of wellness among police and reinforce the positive aspects of good health. The present edition provides a good starting point.

John M. Violanti, PhD
Research Professor of Epidemiology and Environmental Health
University at Buffalo
School of Public Health and Health Professions

References

American Psychiatric Association. (2013). *Diagnostic and Statistical Manual of Mental Disorders* (Fifth Edition). Washington, DC: American Psychiatric Association.

Armeli, S., Gunthhert, K. C., & Cohen, L. H. (2001). Stressor Appraisals, Coping, and Post-Event Outcomes: The Dimensionality and Antecedents of Stress-Related Growth. *Journal of Social and Clinical Psychology, 20*(3), 366–395. https://doi.org/10.1521/jscp.20.3.366.22304.

Boscarino, J. A. (2004). Posttraumatic stress disorder and physical illness: results from clinical and epidemiological studies. *Annals of the New York Academy of Science, 1032*, 141–153.

Buckley, B., Nugent, N., Sledjeski, E., Raimonde, A. J., Spoonster, E., Bogart, L. M., & Delahanty, D. L. (2004). Evaluation of initial posttrauma cardiovascular levels in association with acute PTSD symptoms following a serious motor vehicle accident. *Journal of Trauma Stress, 17*, 317–324.

Covey, T. J., Shucard, J. L., Violanti, J. M., Lee, J., & Shucard, D. W. (2013). The effects of exposure to traumatic stressors on inhibitory control in police officers: A dense electrode array study using a Go/NoGo continuous performance task. *International Journal of Psychophysiology, 87*, 363–375.

Davidson, L., Chinman, M., Sells, D., & Rowe, M. (2006). Peer support among adults with serious mental illness: A report from the field. *Schizophrenia Bulletin, 32*, 443–445.

Kessler, R. C., Sonnega, A., Bromet, E., Hughes, M., & Nelson, C. B. (1995). Posttraumatic disorder in the National Comorbidity Survey. *Archives of General Psychiatry, 52*, 1048–1060.

Figley, C. R. (1999). Police compassion fatigue (PFC): Theory, research, assessment, treatment, and prevention. In J. M. Violanti, & D. Paton (Eds.), *Police trauma: Psychological impact of civilian combat* (pp. 37–53). Springfiled, IL: Charles C. Thomas.

Freedman, S. A., Brandes, D., Peri, T., & Shalev, A. (1999). Predictors of chronic post-traumatic stress disorder. A prospective study. *British Journal of Psychiatry, 174*, 353–359.

Haugen, P. T., McCrillis, A. M., Smid, G. E., & Nijdam, M. J. (2017). Mental health stigma and barriers to mental health care for first responders: A systematic review and meta-analysis. *Journal of Psychiatric Research, 94*, 218–229.

Higgins, G. O. (1994). *Resilient adults: Overcoming a cruel past*. San Francisco: Jossey-Bass.

Klein, R., Nicholls, R., & Thomalla, F. (2003). Resilience to natural hazards: How useful is this concept? *Environmental Hazards, 5*, 35–45.

Landers, G. M., & Zhou, M. (2011). An analysis of relationships among peer support psychiatric hospitalization, and crisis stabilization. *Community Mental Health, 47*, 106–112.

Maddi, S. R. (2002). The story of hardiness: Twenty years of theorizing, research, and practice. *Consulting Psychology Journal: Practice and Research, 54*(3), 173–185. https://doi.org/10.1037/1061-4087.54.3.173.

Maddi, S. R., & Khoshaba, D. M. (2005). *Resilience at Work: How to Succeed No Matter What Life Throws at You*. New York: AMACOM.

Ohara, A. F., Violanti, J. M., Levenson, R. L., & Clark, R. G. Sr. (2013). National police suicide estimates: web surveillance study III. *International Journal of Emergency Mental Health, 15*(1), 31–38.

Paton, D., Smith, L. M., Ramsay, R., & Akande, D. (1999). A structural re-assessment of the Impact of Event Scale: The influence of occupational and cultural contexts. In R. Gist, & B. Lubin (Eds.), *Response to Disaster*. Philadelphia: Taylor & Francis.

Sledge, W. H., Boydstun, J. A., & Rahe, A. J. (1980). Self-concept changes related to war captivity. *Archives of General Psychiatry, 37*, 430–443.

Southwick, S. M., Bonanno, G. A., Masten, A. S., Panter-Brick, C., & Yehuda, R. (2014). Resilience definitions, theory, and challenges: interdisciplinary perspectives. *European Journal of Psychotraumatology, 5*, 1–14.

van der Kolk, B. A. (2014). *The body keeps the score: Brain, mind, and body in the healing of trauma.* New York, NY, US: Viking.

Violanti, J. M., Fekedulgen, D., Hartley, T. A., Andrew, M. E., Charles, L. E., Mnatsakanova, A., & Burchfiel, C. M. (2006). Police trauma and cardiovascular disease: Association between PTSD symptoms and metabolic syndrome. *International Journal of Emergency Mental Health, 4*, 227–238.

Foreword by Tracie Keesee

As a 25-year law enforcement veteran, former New York Police Department (NYPD) Deputy Commissioner, and co-founder of the Center for Policing Equity, I realized that prevailing issues in public safety and effective strategies are vital to catalyze positive, sustaining change between law enforcement and the communities they serve. In reference to Elinor Ostrom's theoy of co-production, I share the need for an immersive, trusting, police-community relationship. The process of co-production is the means to improve communication, combine knowledge, and develop understanding based on experiences of everyday life among citizens and law enforcement officers. Reminiscing about the days early on in my career, I can easily recall painful moments in history that gave rise to the fragile relationship of mistrust between the African-American community and the police. I believe this shared realization by scholars and government has produced a myriad of studies dedicated to improving public safety and to restoring trust in our communities.

In the city of New York, the NYPD encourages its citizens to attend neighborhood meetings where ideas and concerns are shared by the public and neighborhood coordinating officers (NCOs). This is accomplished via an online site (e.g., buildtheblock. nyc) where community members can search for upcoming meetings relevant to their block. This valuable communication between the public and officers has led to the development of new knowledge, where outdated policies (e.g., stop, question and frisk) can be replaced or improved upon based on the shared input of the meeting attendees.

Given that co-production is a collaborative effort between the community and law enforcement officials, officers are in charge of recognizing risks when having to make split-second decisions. At the organizational and departmental level, it is imperative to have readily available resources that address mental health concerns, such as, training modules that help officers to recognize risky situations as well as peer support and other police wellness programs that assure officers they are cared for. Additionally, by understanding and acknowledging that community members may be reluctant to having a conversation and that few may instead want to cause harm, officers must demonstrate that they care and understand that there are historical threads that are still present today, and they have a profound impact not only shared safety but community and officer health.

POWER is one of the tangible tools available in the law enforcement community as a way to promote health, wellness, and resilience amongst officers. When officers are healthy, well, and resilient they can better cope with challenges of police work and they are better capable of maintaining close ties with community members. This book is available to help all police officers who may want to get a deeper understanding of situations and moments that "bruise their badges." In addition, POWER supports law enforcement professionals in overcoming any potential stereotypes in regards to police and the mental health community by realizing that it is beneficial and "ok to ask for help." As well, this book highlights the plethora of studies that demonstrate techniques and strategies, which can help officers not only cope with police challenges but also prevent the impact of stress and trauma on officers' health and wellbeing.

I personally reiterate three fundamental ideologies: the first is that in order for the community to grow and prosper, we must begin to address the, "us versus them" narrative; secondly, we must learn from the past, but it should not keep us from moving forward. Instead, we should acknowledge, and embrace, the different lived experiences and lessons learned; lastly, we need to acknowledge when we are presented with various truths, the acceptance process is often painful, but that no action is unacceptable. By understanding and applying the three fundamental ideologies, we can ensure that progress is being made in the co-production of public safety. I appreciate that the POWER book incorporates those three ideologies throughout the chapters presented.

Tracie Keesee
Vice President of Law Enforcement and Social Justice Initiatives
for the Center for Policing Equity
Former Deputy Commissioner of Equity and Inclusion for
New York Police Department (NYPD)
Former Deputy Commissioner of Training for NYPD
Graduate of the 203rd Session of the FBI National Academy

Foundation

1

Introduction & statement of the problem

Daniel M. Blumberg[a], Konstantinos Papazoglou[b]

[a]DEPARTMENT OF UNDERGRADUATE PSYCHOLOGY, CALIFORNIA SCHOOL OF PROFESSIONAL PSYCHOLOGY, ALLIANT INTERNATIONAL UNIVERSITY, SAN DIEGO, CA, UNITED STATES; [b]YALE SCHOOL OF MEDICINE, NEW HAVEN, CT, UNITED STATES

In recent years, growing attention has been focused on the roles that wellness and the lack thereof play in the job performance of police officers. In addition to the bourgeoning overall emphasis on occupational health, trends in positive psychology have shifted the focus of police executives, police psychologists, and police officers themselves toward efforts at job satisfaction and retention, career development and enhancement, and life-work balance. Nevertheless, the job continues to be one of the most physically and psychologically challenging and poses numerous threats to officers' wellbeing. The present volume is intended to provide the reader with a greater understanding of the risks of police work and the ways in which these risks can be mitigated. In addition, this book showcases a variety of innovative protective factors, which can be utilized by police officers to promote their health and resilience.

Certainly, the media tend to focus on the overt dangers of police work. In the first eleven months of 2018, for example, there were 144 line-of-duty deaths of local, state, and federal officers in the US, which is a 12% increase from the previous year (Tucker, 2018). Most of these officers died from injuries sustained from gunshots (52) or vehicular accidents (50). The remaining 42 deaths were from "heart attacks, strokes, drownings and cancer and other illnesses among those who responded to the 9/11 World Trade Center attack" (Tucker, 2018). It can be argued that some of these duty-related deaths (e.g., heart attacks and strokes) may be attributed directly to police officers' lack of attention to maintaining their health.

At the same time, less consideration has been given to the more insidious dangers of police work. For example, the incidence rates of suicide among police officers far exceed the rates of on-duty deaths. In 2017, despite a tendency to under-report this cause of death, 140 police officers committed suicide, which is 67% more than those who were fatally shot that year (Hayes, 2018). Law enforcement agencies, as well as the media, tend not to focus as much on these psychological risks of the job as they do on the physical dangers. Due to concern for officers' physical safety (and, of course, risk management),

Power. https://doi.org/10.1016/B978-0-12-817872-0.00001-X

most law enforcement agencies mandate body armor for officers working patrol assignments. However, less than 5% of departments have suicide prevention programs (Hayes, 2018). Furthermore, it can be assumed that far more police officers experience depression, anxiety, and other psychological symptoms associated with the stressors of the job than those who decide to take their own life. Therefore, it is of utmost importance for police executives to increase their commitment to officers' psychological safety.

This book examines police wellness from a variety of perspectives. The collection of esteemed contributors represents scholars, practitioners, and current and former police executives. The book is organized into three sections. The first section defines officer wellness and presents specific threats that jeopardize wellness. These threats are cognitive, emotional, neurobiological, physical, social, and spiritual in nature. The second section presents various consequences faced by police officers when their wellness is compromised. The consequences include compassion fatigue, burnout, post-traumatic stress disorder, moral injury, and, more generally, moral risks associated with routine police practices. The final section emphasizes prevention and intervention. This is approached organizationally and individually, because police wellness requires both an agency-wide commitment to promoting employee health and the officers' dedication to maintaining optimal functioning.

A discussion of police officers' optimal functioning serves several purposes. Fundamentally, a healthy workforce benefits the communities in which police officers serve. Therefore, keeping officers healthy and intervening supportively at the earliest sign of distress should be of paramount importance to police executives. This becomes operationally feasible when police wellness is conceptualized as a perishable skill, which requires organizational programs and initiatives to strengthen and maintain officers' overall health. The result of such a culture of wellness for the individual is being supported by the organization for the active, ongoing utilization of various self-care, preventative, and intervention strategies.

With or without the opportunities that can be provided by the organization, police officers, ultimately, are responsible for maintaining their own health. They can learn how to navigate the various risks associated with the job. Specific techniques can be utilized to inoculate police officers against some of the most deleterious effects of the job. Likewise, resilience training can facilitate officers' psychological recovery from exposure to traumatic events. Much like other perishable police skills, which require ongoing practice and, in some cases, periodic recertification (i.e., firearms requalification), preserving optimal functioning takes effort. Officers' dedication to exert this effort, however, depends in large part on the extent to which the organization reinforces the importance of practicing these skills and provides opportunities for officers to do so. Additionally, the organization's wellness culture destigmatizes and promotes officers' decisions to seek help when aspects of the job begin to take a toll. In the end, police officers' power to successfully cope with and overcome the various risks associated with the job stems, in large part, to their ability to develop and exhibit resilience.

The present volume offers a comprehensive look at the importance of resilience in police officers. Through this lens, the stressors associated with police work can be viewed as surmountable. Moreover, although not everyone is suited for a career in law enforcement, a wellness perspective enables police executives to broaden recruiting, hiring, and retention efforts; procedures can be implemented, which are aimed at strengthening officers' ability to cope with and adapt well to adversity and the challenges of police work. At the same time, resilience does not imply that police officers simply rebound to pre-stressor levels of functioning. As the contributors in this book will explain, police work changes those who serve. Within a culture of wellness, however, those changes can reflect positive growth throughout a fulfilling career.

References

Hayes, C. (April 11, 2018). *'Silence can be deadly': 46 officers were fatally shot last year. More than triple that — 140 — committed suicide*. USA Today. Retrieved from https://www.usatoday.com/story/news/2018/04/11/officers-firefighters-suicides- study/503735002/.

Tucker, E. (December 27, 2018). *Deaths of police officers on duty on the rise in US*. Retrieved from https://www.yahoo.com/news/deaths-police-officers-duty-rise-us-150816873.html.

2

Police officer wellness

Alex R. Thornton

KELLEY SCHOOL OF BUSINESS, INDIANA UNIVERSITY, BLOOMINGTON, INDIANA, UNITED STATES

Officer Mitch Kajzer

On the evening of May 1, 1992, two days into the Rodney King riots in Los Angeles, South Bend, Indiana, Patrol Officer Mitch Kajzer and his trainee pulled a car over for a minor traffic violation (M. Kajzer, personal communication, December 1, 2015). In the background of this traffic stop was an apartment complex where two suspects were determined to get retribution against the police for an incident that took place more than two thousand miles away. While standing outside the stopped vehicle talking with the driver and passenger, Officer Kajzer simultaneously saw a muzzle flash out of the corner of his eye and heard a gunshot. The bullet ripped through his body and, as he fell, he pulled his pistol and returned fire. In less than 5 s, the suspect fired at Mitch ten times and Mitch returned fire with equal momentum.

The events of that night changed Mitch Kajzer's life. He underwent numerous surgeries addressing each of the four gunshot wounds sustained and still lives today with physical pain that cannot be resolved. He remained on the police force until 2000, and then retired for medical reasons directly related to the shooting. Mitch's experience is, for many reasons, considered one of the worst case scenarios police officers face. He was targeted for the uniform he wore. He was shot without warning, by a well-hidden suspect. He returned fire — not only to protect his own life but the lives of the two civilians in a nearby vehicle and the new patrol officer under his tutelage. His injuries plague him today, acting as a constant reminder of what he lived through. His body never fully recovered and he was forced to retire early from a profession he loved dearly.

What kind of life does this leave Officer Kajzer? He is no longer physically capable of doing the job, so how will he provide for his family? If most of his friends are cops, do you suppose they will remain close even after his retirement? What kind of lingering and intrusive memories plague Mitch's thoughts and dreams? Could his marriage fall apart after he is no longer the strong, protective police officer who his wife promised to love until death do they part? Was it just luck that he is still alive or would he have preferred — knowing now what he knows — to have been a little slower on the draw and simply fallen victim to his attacker?

Power. https://doi.org/10.1016/B978-0-12-817872-0.00002-1

These are examples of the quiet questions that creep into the subconscious when a true evaluation of a life-and-death event occurs. They feel wrong, but they are practical. Each speaks to the potential results of doing nothing more than is asked of police officers every single day. There was no way to predict that Mitch would be shot that night. There was no way to gauge the long arm of influence that events taking place across the country would have on the attempted murder of police officers in South Bend, Indiana. Yet, there are very specific reasons why Mitch not only lived through the shooting, the numerous surgeries that followed, and the disappointing loss of his patrol job. There are also very specific reasons for his current profession, his healthy marriage, and his social interactions today. Mitch recognized early in his career that being a police officer carries with it risk of injury … not only to the body but to the mind, spirit, and family as well. He intentionally sought opportunities to enhance his psychological skills, preparing himself and his family, just in case he ever faced a truly life-altering situation. Early in his career, Mitch took it upon himself to build the kind of wellness capital he knew he would need if he ever faced a truly critical incident. Mitch is an anomaly, but he does not have to be.

Problem statement

For far too long, wellness has been defined in deficit terms. Conversations about wellness follow the negativity pattern of mental illness represented by depression, anxiety, posttraumatic stress disorder, substance abuse issues, anger-management issues, and more. To focus on the negative is actually a direct reflection of the problem with wellness initiatives. They are reactive, waiting for officers to present troubling symptoms to be activated. They are half-hearted, sometimes being used to provide after-action debriefing following a critical incident. They are stigmatized, frequently viewed as a last resort for their danger to the career of the one seeking help. Any wellness initiative rooted in a reactive response to the daily stressors of policing is misrepresenting itself. What it actually is, is an illness tool. A method of last resort. Perhaps that is why it is difficult to find evidence supporting the efficacy of reactionary methods to establish and support individual wellbeing.

In *Positive Psychology: An Introduction,* (2000) Seligman and Csikszentmihalyi challenged organizational psychologists to change perspective when approaching organizational behavior. Rather than focusing on what was dysfunctional and wrong with people, Seligman and Csikszentmihalyi encouraged an approach based on finding what was good and right about them. The shift in focus uncovered the notion of engagement or a person's involvement in organizational goal attainment, resulting in individual goal alignment with that of the greater good (Luthans, Luthans, & Luthans, 2004).

As an individual becomes more engaged with organizational outcomes and begins to gauge personal success as it pertains to a company's performance, levels of psychological capital increase. Initially, psychological capital encompassed such characteristics as hope, wisdom, future-mindedness, creativity, spirituality, courage, responsibility, and perseverance. In 2004, researchers Fred Luthans, Kyle Luthans, and Bret Luthans dove into Seligman and Csikszentmihalyi's challenge with gusto and used Stajkovic's (2003) study of organizational motivation to determine what four core constructs of positive psychological capital and organizational behavior are most essential to uncovering a person's best self.

Wellness is not reflected by something that is lacking. Rather, it is a positive expression of a multitude of behaviors that are rooted in way the brain is educated to respond to stimuli. As such, it should be approached as an ongoing journey. It is fine to acknowledge that there are negative forces at play, particularly for police officers, that can erode wellness and cause negative mental, emotional, and behavioral problems. It is not fine to focus solely on trying to solve those problems because a focus on problems promotes tunnel vision, excluding the mind from a broader, solution-oriented experience. Organizational support of the pursuit of wellness is one that begins upon recruitment and should extend along the officer's life cycle. It is a unique experience, defined at an individual level and encouraged professionally.

Traditional wellness: the foundation

Hedonism

The Greek philosopher, Aristippus, believed that the goal of living is to experience as much pleasure as possible and that the experience of happiness is the sum total of hedonic moments (Brulde, 2014). His followers furthered the development of the hedonistic philosophy to include appetites for physical pleasure and a focus on self-interest (Huta, Park, Peterson, & Seligman, 2006). Early psychological views of happiness stemmed from this very individualistic definition, but broadened to include the desires of the mind in addition to the body (Kubovy, 1999). As a hedonic psychological concept, wellness is subjective and viewed comparatively as either pleasure or displeasure with the various good and bad aspects of life. Happiness, then, is much more than physical hedonism, and is experienced through achieving goals or positive outcomes in a variety of settings (Diener & Suh, 1998). This more refined perspective of hedonistic wellness partially ties in with current scholarship on positive psychology, which promotes the attainment of goals as a required element of a broader picture of wellness (Harms & Luthans, 2012).

Eudaimonia

While Aristippus was focused on physical hedonism in pursuit of happiness, Aristotle countered that such a singular perspective was vulgar, making people slaves to their selfish desires (Aristotle, 2000). Aristotle believed that wellness could only be experienced through virtuous behavior that challenged individual growth. Such growth meant the ability to distinguish between subjective *desires* rooted in momentary pleasure and *needs* conducive to human growth (Fromm, 1981). For the first time in the journey to providing a full picture of what well-being is, researchers expanded on Aristotle's initial definition of eudaimonia to recognize that not all intended and desired consequences result in well-being. In essence, just because something feels good does not mean it results in happiness. Eudaimonic living is now represented by six aspects of self-actualization: life purpose, autonomy, personal growth, acceptance of self, mastery, and the ability to positively relate to others (Ryff & Keyes, 1995).

Systems influencing traditional wellness

Wellness as a combination of hedonic and eudaimonic living does not allow for a broader understanding of how the pursuit of goals and pleasure are influenced by environmental and relationship factors. Stepping back from an individualistic perspective requires considering what wellness looks like as a person's choices influence and are influenced by the broader web of life. This macro view enhances prosaic definitions of wellness by considering individual well-being as a subset of a much larger, open system of environmental factors (Keeney, 1983). Wellness from this point of view is evidenced by the interpersonal exchanges between people as well as the intrapersonal goings on within each person (O'Connor & Lubin, 1990).

Moving from a selfish understanding of wellness to a systems understanding of wellness vastly increases the number of factors influencing individual well-being. Newtonian scientists approached this challenge by viewing the world as a large clock (Wilber, 2000). Understanding how the clock worked allowed a prediction for what was likely to happen at specific points in time. At the time, the focus was less on probabilities and more on certainties. However, a modern understanding of the chaos of life shows that causality is not universal but it is considered one of life's creative forces. From a developmental perspective, chaos is not a negative state reflecting incompetence or instability. Rather, chaos exists within limits and has a great deal of order to it (Henning & Cilliers, 2012) and is responsible for the variety and constant change that challenges individuals to enhance skills and overcome difficulty (Stacey, 2003). To understand wellness and the importance of hope as a positive psychological reflection of well-being, the use of chaos as a metaphor is helpful in describing the concept amidst the larger complex systems at play.

Historically, conversations and research into the notion of well-being have established wellness as a state of harmony or balance in the absence of mental illness (Cacioppo & Berntson, 1999). However, research in 2000 shifted away from a focus on the negative indicators associated with wellness and a fresh understanding emerged. The resulting scholarship challenged outdated perspectives of wellness and began defining what it means to be well (Ryan & Deci, 2001), what characteristics represent wellness (Luthans et al., 2004), how to build those psychological traits (Luthans, Avey, Avolio, & Peterson, 2010), and the expression of resilience as a reflection of what wellness looks like in action (Luthans, Vogelgesang, & Lester, 2006). With a fuller picture of wellness comes the understanding that, for police officers, a life well-lived is an individual endeavor influenced by the multifaceted reality of the profession.

Building upon wellness

When police departments decide to hire new officers, candidates are required to successfully pass a battery of physical, personality, and psychological tests. The goal of candidate assessment is to ensure that recruits possess the attitude, aptitude, and integrity necessary to handle the multifaceted stressors of the job and that they are a fit for the culture of the organization (Weiss & Inwald, 2018). This pre-employment testing speaks directly to the unique needs of police organizations and to the exceptional nature of police officers. The offer of employment is confirmation that the department finds the candidate extraordinary among his/her peers. Based on the results of the screening required to become an officer, it is safe to assume that — at the point of hire — cops express wellness behaviors.

While wellness is established at the onset of police careers, it has traditionally been treated as a stable characteristic with little to no focus on maintenance. Once officers enter the profession and are faced with compassion fatigue, moral distress, and challenges to their ethical principles, it should come as no surprise that wellness declines. To prevent this from occurring, wellness must not only be treated as perishable, it should be positioned as a priority investment at the individual and organizational level throughout the career-cycle of each officer. The most effective approach to a longitudinal perspective of wellness begins day one on the job.

Wellness is experienced amidst the active pursuit of goals in support of a sense of purpose while maintaining a positive growth attitude and building a social support system. This definition, based on decades of research from a multitude of disciplines, encompasses what it takes to experience a life well-lived, or put another way, the robust life. Wellness may seem fairly straightforward, but it actually requires taking proactive steps to build hope, efficacy, resilience, and optimism mentally, emotionally, physically, spiritually, and socially. Refining what wellness looks like holistically is largely an individual endeavor. However, organizational resources that enhance and require health maintenance will encourage individual pursuit of wellness and create an environment were being well is a primary expectation of a job well done.

The organizational investment involved in the hiring process establishes the psychological strengths necessary to succeed on the job. The next logical step is the professional development of each officer to ensure desirable workplace outcomes. Positive organizational behavior, a term coined by Luthans (2002a), refers to, "the study and application of positively oriented human resource strengths and psychological capacities that can be measured, developed, and effectively managed for performance improvement in today's workplace" (p. 59). Prior to research defining the characteristics that resulted in desirable workplace outcomes, the popularly-held belief was the employees with high levels of human capital (what you know), economic capital (what you have), and social capital (who you know) would rise to the top of any organization (Luthans, 2002b). Additionally, recent research into spiritual capital (what you believe) enhances decisions that align with ethical principles. However, none of these perspectives of capital provide a complete definition of wellness.

Human Capital, while essential to wellness, is not sufficient in and of itself to provide evidence of well-being. Knowledge advances wellness but does not define it. Economic Capital certainly has its benefits, but having financial security is only one part of the grander definition of wellness. Social Capital is another piece of the wellness puzzle, ensuring a healthy balance within social circles, but it does not encompass wellness. Spiritual Capital, an essential element of wellness, is focused on the culmination of beliefs of faith and a deep connection with a culture. Alone, it is one dimension of wellness but does not encompass it wholly. While each of the aforementioned strengths provides an integral piece of what wellness looks like, there remains a missing link. Psychological Capital (PsyCap) goes beyond the traditional definitions of capital and consists of who a person is and the potential inherent in the individual (Luthans et al., 2010).

Rooted in positive psychology and grounded in the need for organizations to develop positive organizational behaviors in the workforce, PsyCap has risen above all other types of measurable capital in determining the employee return on the organization's investment (Luthans et al., 2006). Psychological Capital is defined as:

> *An individual's positive psychological state of development characterized by: first, having confidence (self-efficacy) to take on and put in the necessary effort to succeed at challenging tasks; second, making a positive attribution (optimism) about succeeding now and in the future; third, persevering toward goals, and when necessary, redirecting paths to goals (hope) in order to succeed; and fourth, when beset by problems and adversity, sustaining and bouncing back and even beyond (resilience) to attain success*
>
> Luthans, Avolio, Avey, & Norman, p. 3.

When taken together, each type of capital plays a vital role in the full picture of what wellness is and the types of behaviors evidenced by healthy individuals.

Human Capital

The term human capital has long been considered the cumulation of the knowledge, skills, and abilities a person brings to a particular task (Becker, 1993; Schulz, 1977). Broken down into two constructs, human capital is operationalized as on-the-job training and formal education (Jollevet, 2008). Traditionally, human capital played an important role in compensation decisions, investments in training, and promotions (Combs, Liu, Hall, & Ketchen, 2006). However, police organizations do not take human capital into consideration the way other public and private entities do. Rather, when an officer is hired s/he is on an even playing field with all other new hires, regardless of experience, education, or skillset. Upward mobility, then, is not dependent upon an individual or an organizational dedication to enhancing human capital. This fact plays a significant role in the lack of dedication police officers exhibit to enhancing human capital through the pursuit of formal education and training along the career-cycle of the profession (Smith, 2015).

In 2011, the British Prime Minister challenged traditional police talent management strategies and opened the door to revolutionary change:

> *At the moment, the police system is too closed. There is only one point of entry into the force. There are too few, and arguably too similar, candidates for the top jobs. I want to see radical proposals for how we can open up our police force and bring in fresh leadership. Why should all police officers have to start at the same level? Why should not someone with a different skill set be able to join the police force in a senior rank? Why should not someone who has been a proven success overseas be able to help us to turn around a force here at home?*
>
> Cameron (2011).

Britain's direct entry program is in its infancy, and certainly opens the door for study into the effectiveness of bringing experts from outside the profession into leadership roles (Smith, 2015). However, it is a pioneering approach to raising the bar on human capital. If organizations explicitly seek leaders with a broad base of knowledge — stemming from formal education and experience — then obtaining a leadership role in the department becomes dependent upon the amount of human capital an internal or external applicant brings to the position. Candidates seeking professional growth and promotion will enter the profession understanding that an organizational priority is human capital. As such, the pursuit of opportunities to enhance formal education and training become an individual responsibility supported by organizational resources.

Economic capital

Economic capital, the amount of security a person feels in the financial stability of the household, plays an instrumental role in wellness (Clayton, Linares-Zegarra, & Wilson, 2015). Debt, as an indicator of financial instability, leads to anxiety and poor physical health which may worsen financial welfare (Berger, Collins, & Cuesta, 2013; Choi, 2009, pp. 120−122). The stress caused by financial woes leads to unhealthy behaviors such as alcohol and substance abuse and poor dietary habits (Gathergood, 2012). Police organizations focused on promoting officer wellness recognize that financial resilience counteracts stress and depression (Englert, 2019). Placing an organizational focus on financial stability enhances early employee awareness of the value of economic capital and provides officers with access to education and resources that build financial security.

At career onset, police officers are barely 21 years of age. Even with the advanced psychological, personality, and physical aptitude required of them, there exists plenty of opportunities for departments to support their financial stability. Indeed, the realities of policing and the dangers inherent in the profession make financial education a practical priority. No one knows better than officers who have been injured on the job the value of early, healthy financial decisions. Taking proactive measures to ensure economic capital for each employee establishes early on a keen awareness of the dangers implicit in the job and a protective stance over employee wellbeing.

Social capital

Social capital is broadly conceptualized to encompass the attributes expressed through the relationships and linkages made amidst an individual's social circle (Van Emmerik & Brenninkmeijer, 2009). Contrary to the common practice of law enforcement officers, keeping a tight social circle consisting primarily of fellow cops does not promote the kind of social capital that positively feeds wellness. Expanding one's social circle to include community members outside the profession enhances social stability. To measure the depth of a police officer's social capital, imagine a scenario where an officer is involved in a shooting incident. Policy dictates that officer-involved-shootings be investigated and, while under investigation, officers must not discuss the situation.

The order to remain silent is only one part of a much larger picture of the influential nature of social capital. Fellow officers require confirmation of innocence before feeling comfortable re-engaging their friend into their social circle. Such skepticism from the group of people who, just prior to the incident were considered close friends, takes a toll on officer wellness. Losing touch with close friends amidst an internal investigation leaves officers feeling isolated, vulnerable, and alone (Kosor, 2019).

Officers who expand their social circles well beyond the immediate influence of police open their lives up to perspectives outside the profession. Indeed, a broadened social circle allows for a focus on familial and cultural experiences. As officers move through the stages of life, (marriage, parenting) social capital should increase and broaden to support the health of the family unit. In the event of a professional incident that isolates an officer from h/her social support system, family and friends from the community at large are available to step in and provide support for the duration. A healthy balance of social capital is essential to a proactive wellness plan (Burt, 2000) and can be promoted by training officers, police peers, and leaders within the organization.

Spiritual capital

Unlike other kinds of capital, spiritual capital focuses on human authenticity – a required element of a rich society (Malloch, 2013). Spirituality is defined as a search for fulfillment and meaning and, through prayer, a cognitive connection with God (Malmin, 2013). The constructs of spiritual capital do not rely upon adherence to a specific religion, but do recognize that there is a battle between good and evil. For law enforcement officers, the biblical empowerment granted to those who protect and defend is not only motivating but supportive of the justice they seek to bring to the harmed (Patton, 2011). A secondary, yet essential element of human authenticity is a connection with where one comes from, or biological culture, and can also be expressed through the profession one chooses to dedicate oneself to. The culture of policing is both warrior and guardian, driven by the quest to fulfill a just destiny. Essentially, spiritual capital is found in the cross between a person's faith and legacy and is evidenced by the behaviors and practices that reflect core beliefs (Malloch, 2010).

For police officers, spiritual practice is essential to individual wellbeing (Charles, 2009). Officers enter the profession with a desire to do something meaningful and to help others. Many express a spiritual 'calling' tying the mission of law enforcement to their spiritually-held belief (Smith & Charles, 2010). Instrumental to their spiritual wellness is the knowledge that what police officers are called to do is in service of others. Officers with high levels of spiritual capital maintain the importance of moral and ethical behavior and are among the most resilient in the profession (Naz & Gavin, 2013). Those with active faith lives, tied to the traditions of spirituality (such as prayer, meditation, fellowship), experience positive physical benefits to the brain and body and have success rebounding from stress and pain (Polich, Polich, & Rael, 2006).

In conjunction with individual faith practices promoting officer wellness is the influence of the cultural legacy of policing and the subculture of the hiring organization (Malmin, 2013). Essential to the promotion of spiritual capital is a healthy organizational attitude about what it is to be well. For most, the stigma, distrust, fear, apprehension, and subcultural attitudes about accessing voluntary psychological resources are reason enough not to ask for help.

Unfortunately, law enforcement officers have been handed a legacy of silence and are taught to believe that behind the thin blue line, *taking care of their own* sometimes means turning a blind eye to the warning signs of distress in order to keep their peers' secrets. This attitude, while commendable in its protectiveness of colleagues, does little to protect the legacy of policing and can lead to behaviors that directly contradict its virtues.

Organizational support of spiritual capital is evidenced by the policies in place to provide care for officers involved in traumatic events. Specifically, if a department does not acknowledge the potentially negative impact of critical incidents, the message sent to new officers is that any expression of distress signals weakness. While most police officers are resilient and recover from trauma without missing a beat, some do not. For those who need assistance over the hump of posttraumatic stress, requiring them to ask for help reflects poorly on the organization. If, at such a fundamental level, departments lack employee assistance immediately following traumatic events, it does a disservice to the spiritual wellbeing of both the officers and the organization. The result of such toxicity is evidenced by inappropriate behavior including insubordination, citizen complaints, alcohol use, marital problems, and criminal social interactions (White & Kane, 2013).

Psychological capital

Establishing wellness requires focus on areas of the mind that enhance the characteristics that research has shown are most important in deflecting the impacts of trauma (Hetrick, Purcell, Garner, & Parslow, 2010). The development of PsyCap has been shown to elevate emotional intelligence, decrease stress levels, improve organizational commitment, and mediate anxiety for employees in constantly changing work environments (Newman, Ucbasaran, Zhu, & Hirst, 2014). Research on PsyCap's impact on employee performance focused on job performance ratings by supervisors

(Peterson, Luthans, Avolio, Walumbwa, & Zhang, 2010), a combatant to workplace stress, and employee intentions to quit (Avey, Luthans, & Jensen, 2009). For many people, feeling demoralized or experiencing helplessness, confusion, and hopelessness is the trigger for seeking help from medical doctors or counselors (Frank & Frank, 2002). According to the latest *Diagnostic and Statistical Manual of Mental Disorders* (DSM-V), feeling empty, sad, or hopeless is a key indicator of major depression (American Psychological Association, 2019). Combating this begins with the establishment of positive psychological characteristics that naturally ameliorate the stressors associated with the policing profession.

In a seminal work, Bandura (1977) introduced the concept of self-efficacy as one of the primary impact factors in the development of hope. Rather than follow fellow psychological behaviorists in the belief that humans are primarily a product of their environments, Bandura (2005) argued that people are agents of their environments, capable of responding and impacting others socially. Similar to Bandura, Seligman and Csikszentmihalyi (2000) emerged as a leader in the field of learned optimism due to opposition to the strict beliefs of behaviorists who viewed people as a product of their environment. Speaking specifically to the support of optimism in the development of hope, Seligman called optimistic explanatory style the "stuff of hope" (pp. 48–49). Rutter studied resilience in children and asserted that resilience can only be seen in the face of psychosocial risk experiences. The capacity for resilience, rather than originating internally as the other three constructs of PsyCap do, comes from outside the individual (Fleming & Ledogar, 2008). Resilience factors are found at the family, community, and cultural levels (Rutter, 2000). The cumulative influence of these core PsyCap constructs on wellness has empirical support at the individual, team, and organizational levels (Knaevelsrud & Maercker, 2007).

Efficacy

From the days of Albert Bandura's Social Cognitive Theory (1994, 1977, 2005), the construct with perhaps the most extensive research support is efficacy. Numerous studies have shown the positive impact self-efficacy has on performance (Sadri & Robertson, 1993; Stajkovic & Luthans, 1998). Stajkovic and Luthans define efficacy as it is applied to the workplace as "the individual's conviction or confidence about his or her abilities to mobilize the motivation, cognitive resources or courses of action needed to successfully execute a specific task within a given context" (1998b, p. 66).

Efficacy stands out from other constructs, particularly optimism, because of the focus on a specific task and context rather than a general belief in positive outcomes. A low level of efficacy indicates a belief that efforts to overcome difficulty are futile, hence the resulting increase in stress and anxiety (Bandura, 2005). Adversely, those with a well-developed efficacy approach believe that challenges are surmountable as long as the ability exists and the effort is put forth.

Strong links exist between performance outcomes at work and efficacy (Bandura & Locke, 2003; Stajkovic & Luthans, 1998). The development of efficacy has succeeded through the use of modeling, mastery experiences, physiological/psychological arousal, and social persuasion (Bandura, 1997). Recent studies of nurses specializing in cancer care (Fillion et al., 2007) and workers in Beijing and Hong Kong (Siu, Spector, & Cooper, 2005) link efficacy with lower levels of workplace stress. Retention studies show efficacy as a mediating factor in socialization, turnover intentions, and organizational commitment (Harris & Cameron, 2005).

Efficacy in the context of PsyCap is the combination of in-role confidence and mental acuity, both of which have extensive research supporting their positive impacts on performance (Sadri & Bowen, 2011). The key to establishing mental efficacy is confidence by task rather than a general belief in a positive outcome. By breaking down efficiency by task, it becomes a building block of critical self-awareness which opens the door for correction and improvement. For example, if mental efficacy is a generalized expectation of a positive outcome then increased effort is not required, creative problem solving is not necessary, and the end-result is dependent on some intangible force at play to influence a positive result. The single-event focus of confidence-building teaches critical decision-making as a process heavily influenced by the choices made throughout the event. Mastering this process requires practice and humble self-evaluation.

In 1964, military dogfighting strategist, John Boyd, began training American pilots with a tool he developed called the OODA Loop (Maccuish, 2012). This decision-making model in Fig. 2.1 below moves the strategic mind from Observation, to Orientation, to Decision, to Action, and then back to Observation again. In the Observe phase, trainees are taking in relevant information. For police officers, this includes details relevant to immediate safety issues: location of suspects, whether they exhibit aggressive behavior, the threat level, etc. Based on a quick assessment of danger, the officer then moves into the most valuable of the four stages: Orientation (Maccuish, 2012).

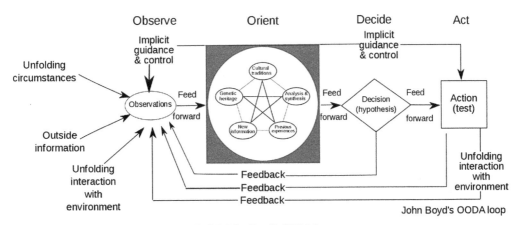

FIG. 2.1 John Boyd's OODA loop.

It is in the Orientation phase where all knowledge — from street smarts to book smarts — collides with implicit and explicit bias to form an assessment of the situation. If a bias is not acknowledged and becomes a prejudice, the decision that follows is likely to be based on faulty information. A powerful part of orienting is the ability to self-correct before deciding to take action. It is here where options formulate and the brain flips through them to find the most suitable few. The Decision step occurs when the brain has matched the option with its likeliest option for a positive outcome. Action quickly follows, testing the hypothesis. In the event the Action taken does not have the intended consequences, the loop begins again and the failure data is fed into the brain so that a new set of options is generated. This loop continues until the situation is resolved.

Because of the age of the OODA Loop philosophy and the problem-solving nature of the police profession, it is likely that cops are familiar with its tools. However, to truly master the mental-efficacy characteristic requires a great deal of practice processing through the four-steps of decision making so that when the danger is immediate the response to danger is automatic — and it is the correct response. This leads directly into the development of resilience because mastering mental efficacy demands an objective, unemotional analysis of performance. This analysis will bring to light actions that positively influenced resolution and actions that had a negative impact on resolving the problem — or, in some cases, caused a new problem. Because of the human brain's tendency to gloss over personal mistakes, recruiting a trusted and respected colleague to evaluate the same situation and provide objective feedback is the only way to ensure that future mental pathways are built based on (1) the intentional acknowledgment of mistakes and (2) the specification of what should be done differently in the future (Stajkovic & Luthans, 1998).

Resilience

Historically focused on at-risk youth dealing with adversity, resilience in positive psychology is defined as a person's ability to rebound from a failure, setback, conflict, or even increased responsibility, positive events, and progress, landing in a stronger strategic place than before (Block & Kremen, 1996; Luthans, 2002a; Masten, 2001). Positive emotions work to increase resilience in the face of negativity (Tugade, Fredrickson, & Barrett, 2004). Considered the most valuable positive resource in stressful, turbulent workplace environments, resilience prepares people to adjust, make transitions, and rebound during organizational restructuring and even downsizing (Makawatsakul & Kleiner, 2003).

Originally considered traitlike and not open to development, resilience has recently proven to fall into the statelike category on the continuum and is open to development (Youssef & Luthans, 2007). Methods used to build resilience include altering risk levels, using positive emotions, and fostering self-development and enhancement (Luthans, Vogelgesang, et al., 2006). The development of the resilient quality, characterized by a strong grip on realism (Coutu, 2002), utilizes the creation of coping strategies and realistic assessments during times of setbacks.

Tugade and Fredrickson (2004) report that resilient people are more capable of handling stress in a high-change environment, are flexible to shifting demands, are open to experiencing new and different things, and maintain emotional stability in the face of adversity. Employee performance (Luthans, Avolio, Avey, & Norman, 2007), job satisfaction, commitment to the organization, and happiness at work (Youssef & Luthans, 2007) as well as the ability to handle downsizing (Maddi, Bartone, & Puccetti, 1987) is also positively impacted by high levels of resilience. With the link between stress and avoidable turnover (Avey et al., 2009; Coomber & Louise Barriball, 2007), resilience is considered a key factor in predicting how people will respond in stressful working conditions.

Resilience occurs when a person establishes a certain comfort with ambiguous situations (Sharp, 2019). In order to do so, it is necessary to acknowledge what is outside the scope of control and what is beyond influence. Adaptation and mental flexibility when surrounded by chaotic, unpredictable environments is expressed in resilience (Masten & Reed, 2002, pp. 74−88). Popular thought on the meaning of resilience begins with an evaluation of a person, place, or culture *after* a traumatic experience occurs. The person before the trauma is compared with the person after the trauma to see if s/he is weaker, stronger, or the same. If the person is stronger, s/he is then considered resilient. Unfortunately, the social approach to resilience is not sufficient to meet the needs of a profession filled with ambiguity and change.

To ensure the development of resilience proactively, the process should begin before exposure to trauma occurs. As early as the first day on the job, police trainers are in the perfect position to establish a baseline for resilience development. By allowing new officers opportunities to make choices on their own, training officers grant them situational autonomy. When those choices merit immediate correction, training officers are available to explain what went wrong and how to adjust to meet expectations in the future. It is this evaluation, provided by a respected colleague, that builds the mental capacity for resilience. As new officers receive evaluation of their decisions, with a focus on professional development rather than criticism or punishment, they build an aptitude for analyzing their own behaviors through a similar lens. With time, they develop self-awareness within the context of the organizational mission.

It is here where the subculture of policing plays a vital role in officer resilience. If training officers provide feedback in relation to the values that support the mission, then new officers will gauge their performance accordingly over the long term. If, however, training officers correct procedural choices without an explanation of why the correction is necessary, they are missing an opportunity to tie choices to consequences (positive and negative). Answering the often unspoken question 'why' is a powerful motivator of positive behavior that aligns not only with organizational values, but the legacy of policing as a whole. The lesson learned is an invaluable one. Acknowledging mistakes or wrong decisions is not unforgivable unless such behavior continues uncorrected. In fact, resilience is found in the strength of the officers who are willing to accept and the advice and constructive correction of respected colleagues.

Hope

While hope is used frequently in everyday language, in this context it carries considerable theoretical support with a precise meaning. Snyder, Irving, and Anderson define hope as a "positive motivational state that is based on an interactively derived sense of successful agency (goal-directed energy) and pathways (planning to meet goals)" (1991, p. 287). The theory of hope begins with the assumption that people tend to be goal oriented through an empowered mentality (Snyder, 1994). Such goal-focus leads people to move toward accomplishment utilizing two hope components: agency and pathways (Snyder, 2000; Snyder, Rand, & Sigmon, 2002).

Agency includes a person's capacity or motivation to begin a task and to see that task through to completion (Snyder, 2000). This determination to achieve becomes essential when impediments, changes, or challenges arise. The use of positive self-talk, "I can do this" or "I will not quit" feeds into a person's continued forward movement (Snyder, Lapointe, Crowson, & Early, 1998). Willpower will drive a person ever forward while what has been deemed "waypower" is the bridge between thought and action (Avey et al., 2009).

Waypower, or pathways thinking, is a person's creation of contingency plans in the event something goes wrong. The proactive generation of multiple pathways is found in high-hope individuals (Snyder, 2002). The act of developing alternative routes from a starting point to the end goal creates a more flexible mind which helps decrease response times in critical situations. For instance, the high-hope leader faced with an unexpected challenge can quickly pull from potential solutions crafted in advance, losing fewer minutes of productivity and team focus.

Independent studies have demonstrated hope's positive impact on academic, health, and athletic outcomes as well as work performance levels (Luthans et al., 2007). A connection between hope and organizational commitment, job satisfaction, work unit performance, and retention rates has been found (Youssef & Luthans, 2007). In addition, stress and anxiety research has shown that hope has a significant negative correlation with anxiety and protects against feelings of vulnerability, unpredictability, and lack of control (Snyder, 1991, 2000, pp. 295–305). Utilizing a goals-based framework, hope has proven developable both in clinical psychology studies and short workplace training interventions (Luthans et al., 2010; Snyder, 2000).

Optimism

Seligman and Csikszentmihalyi (2000), the father of positive psychology, uses an attributional or explanatory approach to defining optimism as the positive attribution of events to permanent, pervasive, and personal causes and negative occurrences to temporary, situation-specific and external causes. Complementary to Seligman's approach is Carver and Scheier (2002), who explain optimists as people who expect positive things to occur while pessimists await the bad. Whether attributional or expectational, the optimistic process supports an employee's belief that a desirable outcome will be the result of increased effort (Luthans et al., 2010).

Schneider's (2001) method for developing optimism is a three-step process focusing on allowing leniency or forgiveness for the past, enjoyment of the present, and seeing opportunities in the future. Essential to the development of learned optimism is the separation of fact from perception and giving oneself and others the benefit of the doubt when uncontrollable misfortunes occur. Holding on to past mistakes, guilt, or shame hinders the learning process and stunts the desire to take risks.

Totterdell, Wood, and Wall (2006) found that optimism moderates the relationship between job strain and job characteristics. Higher levels of optimism add supplementary protection against stress in the workplace, increasing productivity and focus. Early studies of optimism indicated the characteristic as traitlike but Seligman and Csikszentmihalyi (2000) promoted its development. Optimists approach problems and challenges differently than pessimists and handle adversity in different fashions (Luthans et al., 2010). For the optimist, just knowing that a new approach or additional effort could change the outcome of a similar situation in the future increases the likelihood of tenacity.

Officer Mitch Kajzer

In 1992, Officer Kajzer's life changed trajectory (M. Kajzer, personal communication, December 1, 2015). Being shot in the line of duty did little to assuage his desire to serve, nor did it stop him from actively pursuing justice through law enforcement. He remained on the force for eight years after his shooting, overcoming the nerve damage and paralysis to his left leg to prove himself physically to his command staff so he could return to the streets. It was no small thing to withstand three surgeries and a permanent partial impairment to keep doing the job he was called to do, but it was his psychological resilience that paved the way toward a new life in the profession.

One of the first things Mitch did when he woke up was to ask to speak with a counselor. He had no idea what kind of mental fallout would attach itself to being shot, but he knew that his chances for living a healthy life greatly increased if he made the choice not to quietly battle the demons alone. He did not require long-term therapy, but what he received helped him meet his new normal head-on. Learning of his disability and the numerous roadblocks his paralysis would place in his path was made more manageable because he was not carrying traumatic baggage any longer.

Prior to the shooting, Officer Kajzer and his wife attended a training that required them to consider the worst-case scenario. During that training, they both signed a resolution statement confirming an intention to live. In the event that something happened to Mitch, by signing his name he made a conscious choice to fight for his life. When he talks about the hours he spent at the hospital immediately following the shooting, he shares that he was never faced with a doubt in his mind that he would live. His wife, a nurse at the hospital, recounted a similar feeling (L. Kajzer, personal communication, December 5, 2015). Their signatures were side-by-side on a living resolution and, that simple act of will, provided each of them with a certain amount of confidence.

The physical realities of the paralysis eventually caught up with Officer Kajzer. Even as one of the fittest men on the department, he had to acknowledge that the limitations forced upon him would eventually make it impossible to continue patrolling the streets (M. Kajzer, personal communication, December 1, 2015). Acknowledging his passion for policing and refusing to accept a life of unfulfilled goals, he went back to school and began studying cybercrimes. He still has friends in the department, but has expanded his social circle to include a healthy number of community members and academics. When asked about the man who shot him, Mitch has little to say. He forgave his shooter, not to relieve the man of his crime, but to release Mitch of the burden of a grudge. Today, he is the Director of the Cyber Crimes Unit in St. Joseph County, Indiana, and a professor at Notre Dame. He and his wife are still happily married and official retirement is nowhere on his radar.

Conclusion

The nature of law enforcement requires a great deal of training as a component of success in the job. However, current trends in police training focus too much attention on the physical aptitude required and not enough on the psychological. Building a culture of police wellness, evidenced by individual wellness plans and reinforced by policies and procedures that advance wellness as a priority is equally important. Treating wellness as a perishable skill promotes an elevated level of appreciation for what it means to be well and how invaluable wellness is along the career cycle. Making wellness an organizational priority can only enhance officer willingness to take seriously each type of wellness capital, prioritizing each from day one on the job.

For decades, reactive therapies have been used to alleviate the symptoms of distress in law enforcement officers, but proactive practices promoting wellness have not been widely instituted by police leaders. With so many positive organizational outcomes tied to the development of human, social, economic, spiritual, and psychological capital, wellness is a worthwhile investment. Not only do well employees meet performance requirements, they provide for organizational longevity. In a profession where experience is a highly-regarded resource, maintaining a deep bench of wisdom is essential to exceeding the expectations of the communities served.

References

American Psychological Association. (2019). Retrieved from http://www.apa.org.

Aristotle. (2000). *Nicomachean ethics. R. Crisp (trans.)*. Cambridge: Cambridge University, Press.

Avey, J., Luthans, F., & Jensen, S. (2009). Psychological capital: A positive resource for combating employee stress and turnover. *Human Resource Management, 48*(5), 677–693. https://doi.org/10.1002/hrm.20294.

Bandura, A. (1977). Self-efficacy: Toward a unifying theory of behavioral change. *Psychological Review, 84*, 191–215. https://doi.org/10.1037/0033-295x.84.2.191.

Bandura, A. (1994). Self-efficacy. In V. S. Ramachandran (Ed.), *Encyclopedia of human behavior* (pp. 71–81). New York, NY: Academic Press.

Bandura, A. (1997). *Self-efficacy: The exercise of control*. New York, NY: Freeman.

Bandura, A. (2005). The evolution of social cognitive theory. In K. G. Smith, & M. A. Hitt (Eds.), *Great minds in management: The process of theory development* (pp. 9–35). New York, NY: Oxford University Press.

Bandura, A., & Locke, E. (2003). Negative self-efficacy and goal effects revisited. *Journal of Applied Psychology, 88*(1), 87–99. https://doi.org/10.1037/0021-9010.88.1.87.

Becker, G. S. (1993). *Human capital: A theoretical and empirical analysis, with special reference to education*. Chicago: The University of Chicago Press.

Berger, L., Collins, J. M., & Cuesta, L. (2013). Household debt and adult depressive symptoms. *Journal of Family and Economic Issues, 37*(1), 42–57.

Block, J., & Kremen, A. M. (1996). IQ and ego-resiliency: Conceptual and empirical connections and separateness. *Journal of Personality and Social Psychology, 70*(2), 349–361. https://doi.org/10.1037/0022-3514.70.2.349.

Brulde, B. (2014). Hedonism. In A. C. michalos (Ed.), *Encyclopedia of quality of life and well-being research* (pp. 2837–2842). New York, NY: Springer. https://doi.org/10.1007/s10902-010-9214-x.

Burt, R. S. (2000). The network structure of social capital. In R. I. Sutton, & B. M. Staw's (Eds.), *Research in organizational behavior* (pp. 345–423). Greenwich, CT: JAI Press. Structural Holes. Cambridge, MA: Harvard University Press.

Cacioppo, J. T., & Berntson, G. G. (1999). The affect system architecture and operating characteristics. *Current Directions in Psychological Science, 8*, 133–137. https://doi.org/10.1111/1467-8721.00031.

Cameron, D. (July 20, 2011). *House of commons debate* (Vol. 531). col. 920. [Online] http://www.publications.parliament.uk/pa/cm201011/cmhansrd/cm110720/debtext/110720-0001.

Carver, C. S., & Scheier, M. F. (2002). Optimism. In C. R. Snyder, & S. J. Lopez (Eds.), *Handbook of positive psychology*. New York: Oxford University Press.

Charles, G. (2009). How spirituality is incorporated in police work: A qualitative study. *FBI Law Enforcement Bulletin, 78*(5), 22–25. Retrieved from https://libcatalog.atu.edu:443/login?url=https://libcatalog.atu.edu:2409/docview/204151069?accountid=8364.

Choi, L. (2009). *Financial stress and its physical effects on individuals and communities*. Community Development Investment Review.

Clayton, M., Linares-Zegarra, J., & Wilson, J. (2015). Cross country evidence on the debt-health nexus. *Social Science & Medicine, 130*, 51–58. https://doi.org/10.1016/j.socscimed.2015.02.002.

Combs, J., Liu, Y., Hall, A., & Ketchen, D. (2006). How much do high-performance work practices matter? A meta-analysis of their effects on organizational performance. *Personnel Psychology, 59*, 501–528. https://doi.org/10.1111/j.1744-6570.2006.00045.x.

Coomber, B., & Louise Barriball, K. (2007). Impact of job satisfaction components on intent to leave and turnover for hospital-based nurses: A review of the research literature. *International Journal of Nursing Studies, 44*(2), 297–314. https://doi.org/10.1016/j.ijnurstu.2006.02.004.

Coutu, D. (2002). How resilience works. *Harvard Business Review, 80*(5), 46–55. Retrieved from Google Scholar at http://nonprofitlearningpoint.org/wp-content/uploads/2010/03/Resilience-article.pdf.

Diener, E., & Suh, E. (1998). Age and subjective well-being: An international analysis. *Annual Review of Gerontology and Geriatrics, 17*, 304–324.

Englert, D. (January 2019). *Focus on officer wellness: Teaching financial resilience is essential to a successful wellness program*. Police Chief Magazine. Retrieved from http://www.policechiefmagazine.org/focus-on-officer-wellness-teaching-financial-resilience/.

Fillion, L., Tremblay, I., Manon, T., Cote, D., Struthers, C., & Dupuis, R. (2007). Job satisfaction and emotional distress among nurses providing palliative care: Empirical evidence for an integrative occupational stress model. *International Journal of Stress Management, 14*(1), 1−25. https://doi.org/10.1037/1072-5245.14.1.1.

Fleming, J., & Ledogar, R. J. (2008). Resilience, an evolving concept: A review of literature relevant to aboriginal research. *Pimatisiwin, 6*(2), 7−23. Retrieved from http://www.ncbi.nlm.nih.gov/pmc/articles/PMC2956753.

Frank, J. D., & Frank, J. B. (2002). *Persuasion and healing: A comparative study of psychotherapy.* Baltimore: Johns Hopkins University Press.

Fromm, E. (1981). *On disobedience and other essays.* New York: The Seabury Press.

Gathergood, J. (2012). Debt and depression: Causal links and social norm effects. *Economic Journal, 122,* 1094−1114.

Harms, P., & Luthans, F. (2012). Measuring implicit psychological constructs in organizational behavior: An example using psychological capital. *Journal of Organizational Behavior, 33*(4), 589−594.

Harris, G., & Cameron, J. (2005). Multiple dimensions of organizational identification and commitment as predictors of turnover intentions and psychological well-being. *Canadian Journal of Behavioural Science, 37*(3), 159−169. https://doi.org/10.1037/h0087253.

Henning, S., & Cilliers, F. (2012). Constructing a systems psychodynamic wellness model. *SA Journal of Industrial Psychology, 38*(2). https://doi.org/10.4102/sajip.v38i2.989.

Hetrick, S., Purcell, R., Garner, B., & Parslow, R. (2010). Combined pharmacotherapy and psychological therapies for post-traumatic stress disorder (PTSD). *Cochrane Database of Systematic Reviews, 7*(2), 1−36. https://doi.org/10.1002/14651858.CD007316.pub2.

Huta, V., Park, N., Peterson, C., & Seligman, M. (2006). *Pursuing pleasure versus eudaimonia: Links with different aspects of wellbeing* (Unpublished manuscript).

Jollevet, F., II (2008). African American police executive careers: Influences of human capital, social capital, and racial discrimination. *Police Practice and Research, 9*(1), 17−30. https://libcatalog.atu.edu:2217/10.1080/15614260801969904.

Keeny, B. P. (1983). *Aesthetics of change.* New York: Guilford.

Knaevelsrud, C., & Maercker, A. (2007). Internet-based treatment for PTSD reduces distress and facilitates the development of a strong therapeutic alliance: A randomized controlled clinical trial. *BMC Psychiatry, 7*(13). https://doi.org/10.1186/1471-244X-7-13.

Kosor, R. (2019). *Peer support instrumental to wellness* (2019, March 16). The command post [Audio podcast].

Kubovy, M. (1999). On the pleasures of the mind. In D. Kahneman, E. Diener, & N. Schwarz (Eds.), *Well-being: The foundations of hedonic psychology* (pp. 134−154). New York: Russell Sage Foundation.

Luthans, F. (2002a). The need for and meaning of positive organizational behavior. *Journal of Organizational Behavior, 23*(6), 695−706. https://doi.org/10.1002/job.165.

Luthans, F. (2002b). Positive organizational behavior: Developing and managing psychological strengths. *The Academy of Management Executive, 16*(1), 57−72. https://doi.org/10.5465/ame.2002.6640181.

Luthans, F., Avey, J., Avolio, B., Norman, S., & Combs, G. (2006). Psychological capital development: Toward a micro-intervention. *Journal of Organizational Behavior, 27*(3), 387−393. https://doi.org/10.1002/job.373.

Luthans, F., Avey, J., Avolio, B., & Peterson, S. (2010). The development and resulting performance impact of positive psychological capital. *Human Resource Development Quarterly, 21*(1), 41−67. https://doi.org/10.1002/hrdq.20034.

Luthans, F., Avolio, B., Avey, J., & Norman, S. (2007). Psychological capital: Measurement and relationship with performance and job satisfaction. *Personnel Psychology, 60*(3), 541−572. https://doi.org/10.1111/j.1744-6570.2007.00083.x.

Luthans, F., Luthans, K. W., & Luthans, B. C. (2004). Positive psychological capital beyond human and social capital. *Business Horizons, 47*, 45−50.

Luthans, F., Vogelgesang, G., & Lester, P. (2006). Developing the psychological capital of resiliency. *Human Resource Development Review, 5*(1), 25−44. https://doi.org/10.1177/1534484305285335.

Maccuish, D. A. (2012). Orientation: Key to the OODA loop − the culture factor. *Journal of Defense Resources Management, 3*(2), 67−74.

Maddi, S. R., Bartone, P. T., & Puccetti, M. C. (1987). Stressful events are indeed a factor in physical illness: Reply to Schroeder and Costa (1984). *Journal of Personality and Social Psychology, 52*(4), 833−843. https://doi.org/10.1037/0022-3514.52.4.833.

Makawatsakul, N., & Kleiner, B. (2003). The effect of downsizing on morale and attrition. *Management Research News, 26*, 52−62. https://doi.org/10.1108/01409170310783998.

Malloch, T. R. (2010). Spiritual capital and practical wisdom. *The Journal of Management Development, 29*(7), 755−759. http://libcatalog.atu.edu:2097/10.1108/02621711011059194.

Malloch, T. R. (2013). Spiritual capital: Spirituality in practice in Christian perspective. *Spiritus, 13*(1), 148−150, 161. Retrieved from https://libcatalog.atu.edu:443/login?url=https://libcatalog.atu.edu:2409/docview/1400483987?accountid=8364.

Malmin, M. (2013). Warrior culture, spirituality, and prayer. *Journal of Religion and Health, 52*(3), 740−758.

Masten, A. (2001). Ordinary magic: Resilience processes in development. *American Psychologist, 56*(3), 227−238. https://doi.org/10.1037/0003-066X.56.3.227.

Masten, A., & Reed, M. (2002). Resilience in development. In *Handbook of positive psychology*. Oxford: Oxford University Press.

Naz, S., & Gavin, H. (2013). Correlates of resilience in police officers from England and Pakistan: A cross national study. *Pakistan Journal of Criminology, 5*(2), 215−234. Retrieved from https://libcatalog.atu.edu:443/login?url=https://libcatalog.atu.edu:2409/docview/1630762683?accountid=8364.

Newman, A., Ucbasaran, D., Zhu, F., & Hirst, G. (2014). Psychological capital: A review and synthesis. *Journal of Organizational Behavior.* . https://doi.org/10.1002/job.1916, 35S120-S138.

O'Connor, W., & Lubin, B. (1990). *Ecological approaches to clinical and community psychology*. Miami: Robert Krieger.

Patton, G. L. (2011). *Coping with the career-a review of acquired life patterns of veteran officers. FBI Law Enforcement Bulletin*. Retrieved from http://www.fbi.gov/stats- services/publications/law-enforcement-bulletin/june_2011/research_forum.

Peterson, S. J., Luthans, F., Avolio, B. J., Walumbwa, F. O., & Zhang, Z. (2010). Psychological capital and employee performance: A latent growth modeling approach. *Personnel Psychology, 64*(2), 427−450. https://doi.org/10.1111/j.1744- 6570.2011.01215.x.

Polich, C., Polich, J., & Rael, B. (2006). Meditation states and traits: EEG, ERP, and neuroimaging studies. *Psychological Bulletin, 132*(2), 280-211.

Rutter, M. (2000). *Resilience re-considered: Conceptual considerations, empirical findings, and policy implications*. New York: Cambridge University Press.

Ryan, R. M., & Deci, E. L. (2001). On happiness and human potentials: A review of research on hedonic and eudaimonic well-being. *Annual Review of Psychology, 51*(1), 141−166.

Ryff, C. D., & Keyes, C. L. M. (1995). The structure of psychological well-being revisited. *Journal of Personality and Social Psychology, 69*(4), 719−727. https://doi.org/10.1037/0022-3514.69.4.719.

Sadri, G., & Bowen, R. (2011). Meeting employee requirements: Maslow's hierarchy of needs is still a reliable guide to motivating staff. *Industrial Engineer: IEEE, 43*(10), 44–48. Retrieved from https://www.highbeam.com/doc/1G1-270989759.html.

Sadri, G., & Robertson, I. T. (1993). Self-efficacy and work-related behaviour: A review and meta-analysis. *Applied Psychology: An International Review, 42*(2), 139–152. https://doi.org/10.1111/j.1464-0597.1993.tb00728.x.

Schneider, S. L. (2001). In search of realistic optimism: Meaning, knowledge, and warm fuzzies. *American Psychologist, 56*(3), 250–263. https://doi.org/10.1037/0003-066X.56.3.250.

Schulz, T. W. (1977). Investment in human capital. In J. Karabel, & A. H. Halsey (Eds.), *Power and ideology in education* (pp. 313–324). New York: Oxford University Press.

Seligman, M. E. P., & Csikszentmihalyi, M. (2000). Positive psychology: An introduction. *American Psychologist, 55*(1), 5–14. https://doi.org/10.1037/0003-066X.55.1.5.

Sharp, L. (2019). Resilience: Learning to bend but not break in the ebb and flow of life: I was extremely fortunate to hear the inspirational and witty Maiala Yousafzai speak in Melbourne last December. *Australian Nursing and Midwifery Journal, 26*(5), 6.

Siu, O., Spector, P. E., Cooper, C. L., & Lu, C. (2005). Work stress, self-efficacy, Chinese work values, and work well-being in Hong Kong and Beijing. *International Journal of Stress Management, 12*(3), 274–288. https://doi.org/10.1037/1072-5245.12.3.274.

Smith, R. (2015). Talent management: Building the case for direct entry into leadership roles in British policing. *Police Journal: Theory, Practice and Principles, 88*(2), 160–173. https://doi.org/10.1177/0032258X15579357.

Smith, J., & Charles, G. (2010). The relevance of spirituality in policing: A dual analysis. *International Journal of Police Science and Management, 12*(3), 320–338. https://libcatalog.atu.edu:2217/10.1350/ijps.2010.12.3.179.

Snyder, C. R. (1994). *The psychology of hope: You can get there from here.* New York: Free Press.

Snyder, C. R. (Ed.). (2000). *Handbook of hope: Theory, measures, and applications.* San Diego, CA: Academic Press.

Snyder, C. R. (2002). Hope theory: Rainbows in the mind. *Psychological Inquiry, 13*, 249–275. https://doi.org/10.1207/S15327965PLI1304_01.

Snyder, C., Irving, L., & Anderson, J. (1991). Hope and health. In *Handbook of social and clinical psychology.* Oxford: Oxford University Press.

Snyder, C. R., LaPointe, A. B., Jeffrey Crowson, J., & Early, S. (1998). Preferences of high- and low-hope people for self-referential input. *Cognition & Emotion, 12*(6), 807–823. https://doi.org/10.1080/026999398379448.

Stacey, R. D. (2003). *Strategic management and organisational dynamics: The challenge of complexity* (4th ed.). Harlow: Pearson Education.

Stajkovic, A. D. (2003). Behavioral management and task performance in organizations: Conceptual background, meta-analysis, and test of alternative models. *Personnel Psychology, 56*(1), 155–194. https://doi.org/10.1111/j.1744-6570.2003.tb00147.x.

Stajkovic, A. D., & Luthans, F. (1998). Self-efficacy and work-related performance: A meta-analysis. *Psychological Bulletin, 124*(2), 240–261. https://doi.org/10.1037/0033-2909.124.2.240.

Totterdell, P., Wood, S., & Wall, T. (2006). An intra-individual test of the demands- control model: A weekly diary study of psychological strain in portfolio workers. *Journal of Occupational and Organizational Psychology, 79*(1), 63–84. https://doi.org/10.1348/096317905x52616.

Tugade, M., & Fredrickson, B. (2004). Resilient individuals use positive emotions to bounce back from negative emotional experiences. *Journal of Personality and Social Psychology, 86*(2), 320–333. https://doi.org/10.1037/0022-3514.86.2.320.

Van Emmerik, I. J. H., & Brenninkmeijer, V. (2009). Deep-level similarity and group social capital: Associations with team functioning. *Small Group Research, 40,* 650−669.

Weiss, P., & Inwald, A. (2018). A brief history of personality assessment in police psychology: 1916−2008. *Journal of Police and Criminal Psychology, 33*(3), 189−200.

White, M. D., & Kane, R. J. (2013). Pathways to career-ending police misconduct: An examination of patterns, timing, and organizational responses to officer malfeasance in the NYPD. *Criminal Justice and Behavior, 40*(11), 1301−1325.

Wilber, K. (2000). *Sex, ecology, spirituality: The spirit of evolution.* London: Shambhala.

Youssef, C. M., & Luthans, F. (2007). Positive Organizational Behavior in the Workplace: The Impact of Hope, Optimism, and Resilience. *Management Department Faculty Publications, 36.* http://digitalcommons.unl.edu/managementfacpub/36.

3

Internal threats to police wellness

Christine C. Kwiatkowski[a, b], Alfred J. Robison[c]

[a]MICHIGAN STATE UNIVERSITY, NEUROSCIENCE PROGRAM, EAST LANSING, MI, UNITED STATES; [b]MICHIGAN STATE UNIVERSITY, SCHOOL OF CRIMINAL JUSTICE, EAST LANSING, MI, UNITED STATES; [c]MICHIGAN STATE UNIVERSITY, DEPARTMENT OF PHYSIOLOGY, EAST LANSING, MI, UNITED STATES

Introduction

The way an individual appraises and interacts with his/her environment is a major contributor to health and stress vulnerability. The ability of common psychosocial exposures to elicit differential attributions and responses is a reflection of the diverse experiences each observer possesses. For example, the severity of threat is subjective and depends upon previous social conditioning. Experience, both good and bad, shapes the way we subjectively understand our environment and how we physiologically respond to it. The brain is the primary mechanism through which humans perceive the environment and initiate responses to it, recruiting a multitude of neural circuits for complex processing of sensory input. Featured among these is the amygdala and prefrontal cortex (PFC), members of the cortico-amygdala loop, as well as the hippocampus and nucleus accumbens (NAc). These structures drive cognitive appraisal and the emotional valence of environmental stimuli, beginning with the perception of a stimulus.

Perception begins with a sensory experience that is transmitted throughout the brain to characterize the evoking stimulus. This permits the assessment of the level of threat present through activation of the cortico-amygdala loop to detect and engage in higher order processing of the stimulus. Emotional centers of the brain, such as the amygdala and NAc, further nuance stimulus processing with its emotional valence. In particular, the amygdala is a center for arousal and emotional processing, including fear, and the NAc is critical for perception and processing of reward and motivation. For example, the amygdala activates during times of fear, creating a protective aversion to the experience, while the NAc activates during pleasant experiences, like illicit drug use, driving motivation for repeating the behavior. Thus, these brain regions, along with other limbic regions, work together to guide approach and avoidance behavior via modulation of subjective negative experience and attenuated motivations toward rewarding aspects of a stimulus (Haines, 2013).

During a fear response, sensory information activates the amygdala, which in turn signals other regions of the brain, including the PFC, hypothalamus, and locus coeruleus

Power. https://doi.org/10.1016/B978-0-12-817872-0.00003-3

(LC) that a potential threat is present. Sufficient activation of the amygdala increases vigilance via LC-mediated catecholamines (e.g., epinephrine, norepinephrine) release and mobilizes innate survival behaviors by activating hypothalamic neurons that initiate the stress response (Davis & Whalen, 2001; Haines, 2013; Rodrigues, LeDoux, & Sapolsky, 2009). The PFC, the seat of executive planning and decision-making, also receives sensory information about the environment and synthesizes emotional, experiential, and contextual knowledge, drawing on hippocampal-mediated memory (Eichenbaum & Cohen, 2014), to appropriately respond to a stimulus. The PFC can either inhibit or enhance the fear and stress responses via reciprocal projections to the amygdala. Together, this system detects provocative stimuli and regulates emotional states to optimally respond to environmental stimuli. Aberrations in this system thus yield pathophysiological changes associated with emotional dysregulation, hyperreactivity of the stress response, and decrements in psychiatric health. Critically, experience shapes the structure and function of these systems, mediating the negative effects of external threats to police officer health and well-being.

At the onset of an acute social interaction, the actors and their biology arrive conditioned from their past. They import experience gained through development, socialization, and social learning (i.e., culture) as reference for appropriate behavior. Together, the actors' histories, social abilities, and other factors, such as current emotional and psychological state, frame each actor's perception of environmental and social cues, and shape the behavioral response (Crick & Dodge, 1994). As such, the role of biology is to simply enable an established propensity toward a conditioned behavioral pattern (Sapolsky, 2017). This biology, however, represents the host of internal threats to officer health and well-being.

Law enforcement officers are recruited to service from a variety of different backgrounds representing both positive and negative life experiences. A diversity of circumstance creates variation in the officer risk for negative health outcomes related to policing. Importantly, certain exposures, such as disadvantage, adversity, or abuse, are related to pathophysiological changes in the brain that may influence officer risk for negative health outcomes following work-related stress exposure.

Early life adversity

Traditional criminological research posits that neighborhood structural disadvantage and social disorganization create a common set of risk factors that affect psychological processes (Snedker & Herting, 2016), which can in turn affect health and behavior among residents of a given geographic area. Indeed, health disparities and crime are both non-randomly distributed in space with a tendency to cluster in disadvantaged neighborhoods (LaVeist, Pollack, Thorpe, Fesahazion, & Gaskin, 2011; Sampson, 2012). Furthermore, neighborhood characteristics have a known influence on parenting style (Zuberi, 2016), thereby modulating youth socialization. Moreover, environments riddled with the stressors inherent to disadvantage and adversity create conditions of chronic stress that can alter psychological status, basal arousal, and stress responsivity.

These factors may thus be important for understanding officer baseline risk for reactivity and stress vulnerability.

The combined effect of disadvantage and family disruption on brain development and emotional dysregulation has been explored in a series of natural experiments involving humans who had prolonged stays in overburdened Romanian orphanages during the 1980s. As adults, children reared separated from their mothers and in near social isolation demonstrated cognitive impairments, a high prevalence of mood disorders, severe social attachment deficits, and difficulty in emotional regulation. Imaging studies revealed striking neuroanatomical differences between subjects who had resided in overburdened orphanages and healthy controls. Specifically, subjects who had resided in overburdened orphanages showed overall reductions in brain size, fewer neuronal cell bodies, and reduced health of neuronal processes (i.e., less myelination) (Mehta et al., 2009; Sheridan, Fox, Zeanah, McLaughlin, & Nelson, 2012). Physiologically, these subjects showed decreased activity in frontal regions associated with executive function, including the PFC, and less connectivity between regions, indicating less circuit efficiency and regulatory control of the limbic system (Chugani et al., 2001; Eluvathingal et al., 2006). Importantly, the subjects' amygdalae were significantly enlarged and reactive compared to controls. This was associated with increased sensitivity to negative emotional content, heightened arousal and anxiety, difficulty regulating emotion, and increased aggression (Gee et al., 2013; Tottenham, 2012; Tottenham et al., 2010). Though this work represents a highly abnormal social environment, it is important to consider how early life conditions may affect the brain to create differential risk for stress vulnerability among incoming law enforcement trainees.

Importantly, environmental exposures and chronic stress associated with neighborhood disadvantage directly affect the cortico-amygdala loop, the neural circuitry responsible for understanding and engaging with the environment. Specifically, changes in the cortico-amygdala loop and related emotional behavior are widely attributed to exposure to socioeconomic disadvantage and unhealthy social relationships (e.g., abuse and neglect, trauma). For example, Noble et al. (2015) showed that individuals from low income families showed significant reductions in regional volumes in areas involved in executive function, an effect that became increasing pronounced as income decreased (Noble et al., 2015). Similarly, Liberzon et al. (2015) demonstrated that low socioeconomic status (SES) was associated with changes in emotional processing among adults with a history of childhood poverty. Researchers found that those exposed to childhood poverty showed less recruitment of the PFC during tasks of emotional regulation compared to mid-SES controls (Liberzon et al., 2015). Psychosocial factors, such as maternal health, family relationship quality, and a lack of stimulation in low SES contexts are implicated as drivers of the observed changes in executive function and associated neural circuitry (Hackman, Farah, & Meaney, 2010). Underlying these changes, however, are maladaptations that lead to increases in arousal and sensitivity to stress. Understanding such maladaptation is critical for understanding baseline stress vulnerability among police officers.

LC-NE system

The context in which an individual resides continues to shape the nervous system through early adulthood, ensuring that he or she will be optimally prepared for the challenges and demands most likely to occur in a unique environment (Sapolsky, 2017). As such, the stress system is flexible in its response to stressors to provide a competitive advantage. Under ordinary circumstances, a flexible, or adaptive, stress response aids in the development of adaptive strategies that increase the likelihood that an individual will successfully respond to stress or threat. In the presence of disadvantage, adversity, or abuse, however, chronic stress has deleterious consequences on the central nervous system (CNS) that are associated with changes in psychological status and the expression of maladaptive behavioral patterns. One such change in psychological status and reactivity to stress involves the brain's arousal system, a critical component for environmental monitoring and vigilance.

The locus coeruleus (LC) is a noradrenergic nucleus in the brainstem that delivers norepinephrine (also called noradrenaline) throughout the brain as part of the complex circuitry that initiates the body's stress response. The role of the LC is thus to act as an alarm and direct attention to the source of distress. As such, stressors that activate the autonomic nervous system and hypothalamus-pituitary-adrenal (HPA) axis also activate the LC, marshalling cognitive resources alongside the stress response. With projections to the amygdala, prefrontal cortex (PFC), and hippocampus, the LC participates in a feedback loop that perpetuates the stress response. Consider that detection of an environmental stimulus relies both on the brain's sensory systems and on emotional centers, such as the amygdala, to signal the threat associated with an observed stimulus or event. Reciprocal projections between the amygdala and LC thus both initiate and sustain the stress response following detection of a stimulus because the amygdala detects the threat and the LC amplifies that signal, thereby bolstering the stress response. For instance, a threat that is initially detected in the environment will engage attentional resources, but further appraisal of the threat and the environment permits ongoing assessment and escalation of responsivity, as might be the case when responding to a critical incident. Interestingly, prolonged LC activity inhibits activity of the PFC (Charney, 2004), impairing executive function and regulatory control over emotional reactivity driven by the amygdala. Altogether, this suggests that heightened activity of the LC promotes an exacerbated stress response with associated impairments in executive function and emotional regulation.

The LC is further affected by chronic stress via the HPA axis, the activation of which results in the release of corticotropin releasing hormone (CRH), a neuroendocrine chemical messenger with a primary role in initiating the stress response and suppressing non-essential physiological functions (e.g., reproduction) during acute stress (Chrousos, 2009). CRH binds receptors found in the amygdala, PFC, hippocampus, and LC. The LC, in particular, is rich in CRH-1 receptors whose activation drives increases in arousal and stimulatory input to the stress response system. Importantly, chronic stress is associated with upregulation of central CRH which increases action on CRH-1 receptors (Charney, 2004), promoting activity in the LC. Thus, chronic stress results in another mechanism that prolongs activity in the LC and maintains the stress response. Critically, individuals exposed to chronic stress during childhood exhibit elevated basal levels of CRH and hyperreactivity of the LC-norepinephrine system in adulthood (Wu et al., 2013), sensitizing the responsivity to stress and increasing risk for stress-related disorders (Feder, Nestler, & Charney, 2009).

Genetic predisposition to maladaptive stress responses

The response to chronic stress or trauma arises from a multitude of factors derived from life experience as described above, but also from inherent biological variability at the genetic and epigenetic levels. Examinations of the genetic contributions to stress-related disorders utilize both large-scale human data and a variety of animal models, some of which we will cover here. In general, these studies suggest that a substantial percentage of the variability in response to trauma or chronic stress is heritable, suggesting that an individual's biology interacts with their personal history and present circumstances to determine whether responses to stress will be maladaptive.

Twin studies and large-scale genetics-based heritability analyses have shown that around 50% of the variance in predicting post-traumatic stress disorder (PTSD) following trauma is heritable (Sharma & Ressler, 2019). Given that women are about twice as likely to be diagnosed with PTSD, as are men, it is possible that some of the genetic risk for this maladaptive response to traumatic stress is linked to genetic differences in the sexes; though, this is certainly complicated by differences between sexes in the nature of trauma exposure. In studies where trauma history was matched, the disparity in PTSD remains and is stable across trauma types (Breslau & Anthony, 2007; Breslau, Chilcoat, Kessler, Peterson, & Lucia, 1999), suggesting that stress vulnerability does indeed arise from biological (i.e., genetic) differences between the sexes. Such findings can be leveraged to better fit the needs of individual officers during training.

These findings indicate that there is a genetic cause to maladaptive responses to trauma that can be identified for use as a biomarker for predicting vulnerability and a leverage point for understanding etiology and developing novel treatments. However, a single genetic driver of vulnerability to stress has been elusive, likely because there is no single gene that contributes strongly enough to stress vulnerability to be identified in the limited screens of human populations so far performed (Sharma & Ressler, 2019). Nevertheless, both screening of the genome in human populations and the use of animal models of stress susceptibility and resilience have uncovered some targets that provide insight into adaptive and maladaptive stress responses. For instance, brain derived neurotrophic factor, or BDNF, is a neuronal signaling molecule associated with resilience to chronic social stress in rodent models such as mouse chronic social defeat (Krishnan et al., 2007), and BDNF has reduced expression in hippocampus in selectively bred rats that show exaggerated vulnerability to stress (Serra et al., 2017). In humans, functional variants in the BDNF gene are associated with susceptibility to PTSD (Felmingham, Dobson-Stone, Schofield, Quirk, & Bryant, 2013; Pitts et al., 2019), and drugs are currently under development to leverage BDNF in the treatment of stress-related disorders including PTSD (Ragen, Seidel, Chollak, Pietrzak, & Neumeister, 2015). Studies using chronic stress models in rodents have also uncovered a central role in stress resilience for the transcription factor ΔFosB (Robison et al., 2014; Vincent Vialou et al., 2010), an orchestrator of gene expression in the NAc, a critical brain center for processing reward and motivation. ΔFosB exerts its effects by regulating the expression of other genes that change neuron function (Robison & Nestler, 2011), and it is regulated in the brains of depression patients (Gajewski, Turecki, & Robison, 2016; Vincent Vialou et al., 2010), though it has not been examined in PTSD patients. Critically, this protein is also important for the function of neurons projecting from PFC to amygdala (Vialou et al., 2014), suggesting that it may regulate the cortico-amygdala loop that is central to maladaptive responses in PTSD.

Conclusions

This chapter describes the preexisting conditions that can contribute to the manner in which an individual physiologically responds to chronic or traumatic stress, including their childhood experiences, current condition, and their genetic makeup. Although all people will encounter stress of some kind, those in high-stress professions like law enforcement are more likely to encounter chronic or traumatic stress as part of their job. Understanding the mechanisms driving their appropriate or sometimes maladaptive responses to stress can help inform officers of their risks and empower them to prevent the noxious effects of stress by actively engaging in wellness practices. These findings also suggest a place for resilience training as a core component of officer education as primary prevention for stress vulnerability.

References

Breslau, N., & Anthony, J. C. (2007). Gender differences in the sensitivity to posttraumatic stress disorder: An epidemiological study of urban young adults. *Journal of Abnormal Psychology, 116*(3), 607–611. https://doi.org/10.1037/0021-843X.116.3.607.

Breslau, N., Chilcoat, H. D., Kessler, R. C., Peterson, E. L., & Lucia, V. C. (1999). Vulnerability to assaultive violence: Further specification of the sex difference in post-traumatic stress disorder. *Psychological Medicine, 29*(4), 813–821. https://doi.org/10.1017/S0033291799008612.

Charney, D. S. (2004). Psychobiological mechanisms of resilience and vulnerability: Implications for successful adaptation to extreme stress. *American Journal of Psychiatry, 161*(2), 195–216. https://doi.org/10.1176/appi.ajp.161.2.195.

Chrousos, G. P. (2009). Stress and disorders of the stress system. *Nature Reviews Endocrinology, 5*(7), 374–381. https://doi.org/10.1038/nrendo.2009.106.

Chugani, H. T., Behen, M. E., Muzik, O., Juhász, C., Nagy, F., & Chugani, D. C. (2001). Local brain functional activity following early deprivation: A study of postinstitutionalized Romanian orphans. *NeuroImage, 14*(6), 1290–1301. https://doi.org/10.1006/nimg.2001.0917.

Crick, N. R., & Dodge, K. A. (1994). A review and reformulation of social information-processing mechanisms in children's social adjustment. *Psychological Bulletin, 115*(1), 74−101. https://doi.org/10.1037/0033-2909.115.1.74.

Davis, M., & Whalen, P. J. (2001). The amygdala: Vigilance and emotion. *Molecular Psychiatry, 6*(1), 13−34. https://doi.org/10.1038/sj.mp.4000812.

Eichenbaum, H., & Cohen, N. J. (2014). Can we reconcile the declarative memory and spatial navigation views on hippocampal function? *Neuron, 83*(4), 764−770. https://doi.org/10.1016/j.neuron.2014.07.032.

Eluvathingal, T. J., Chugani, H. T., Behen, M. E., Juhász, C., Muzik, O., Maqbool, M., et al. (2006). Abnormal brain connectivity in children after early severe socioemotional deprivation: A diffusion tensor imaging study. *Pediatrics, 117*(6), 2093−2100. https://doi.org/10.1542/peds.2005-1727.

Feder, A., Nestler, E. J., & Charney, D. S. (2009). Psychobiology and molecular genetics of resilience. *Nature Reviews Neuroscience, 10*(6), 446−457. https://doi.org/10.1038/nrn2649.

Felmingham, K. L., Dobson-Stone, C., Schofield, P. R., Quirk, G. J., & Bryant, R. A. (2013). The brain-derived neurotrophic factor Val66Met polymorphism predicts response to exposure therapy in posttraumatic stress disorder. *Biological Psychiatry, 73*(11), 1059−1063. https://doi.org/10.1016/j.biopsych.2012.10.033.

Gajewski, P. A., Turecki, G., & Robison, A. J. (2016). Differential expression of FosB proteins and potential target genes in select brain regions of addiction and depression patients. *PLoS One, 11*(8), e0160355. https://doi.org/10.1371/journal.pone.0160355.

Gee, D. G., Gabard-Durnam, L. J., Flannery, J., Goff, B., Humphreys, K. L., Telzer, E. H., et al. (2013). Early developmental emergence of human amygdala-prefrontal connectivity after maternal deprivation. *Proceedings of the National Academy of Sciences of the United States of America, 110*(39), 15638−15643. https://doi.org/10.1073/pnas.1307893110.

Hackman, D. A., Farah, M. J., & Meaney, M. J. (2010). Socioeconomic status and the brain: Mechanistic insights from human and animal research. *Nature Reviews Neuroscience, 11*(9), 651−659. https://doi.org/10.1038/nrn2897.

Haines, D. E. (2013). *Fundamental neuroscience for basic and clinical applications* (4th ed.). Elsevier/Saunders.

Krishnan, V., Han, M.-H., Graham, D. L., Berton, O., Renthal, W., Russo, S. J., et al. (2007). Molecular adaptations underlying susceptibility and resistance to social defeat in brain reward regions. *Cell, 131*(2), 391−404. https://doi.org/10.1016/j.cell.2007.09.018.

LaVeist, T., Pollack, K., Thorpe, R., Fesahazion, R., & Gaskin, D. (2011). Place, not race: Disparities dissipate in southwest Baltimore when blacks and whites live under similar conditions. *Health Affairs, 30*(10), 1880−1887. https://doi.org/10.1377/hlthaff.2011.0640.

Liberzon, I., Ma, S. T., Okada, G., Shaun Ho, S., Swain, J. E., & Evans, G. W. (2015). Childhood poverty and recruitment of adult emotion regulatory neurocircuitry. *Social Cognitive and Affective Neuroscience, 10*(11), 1596−1606. https://doi.org/10.1093/scan/nsv045.

Mehta, M. A., Golembo, N. I., Nosarti, C., Colvert, E., Mota, A., Williams, S. C. R., et al. (2009). Amygdala, hippocampal and corpus callosum size following severe early institutional deprivation: The English and Romanian Adoptees Study Pilot. *Journal of Child Psychology and Psychiatry, 50*(8), 943−951. https://doi.org/10.1111/j.1469-7610.2009.02084.x.

Noble, K. G., Houston, S. M., Brito, N. H., Bartsch, H., Kan, E., Kuperman, J. M., et al. (2015). Family income, parental education and brain structure in children and adolescents. *Nature Neuroscience, 18*(5), 773−778. https://doi.org/10.1038/nn.3983.

Pitts, B. L., Whealin, J. M., Harpaz-Rotem, I., Duman, R. S., Krystal, J. H., Southwick, S. M., et al. (2019). BDNF Val66Met polymorphism and posttraumatic stress symptoms in U.S. military veterans: Protective effect of physical exercise. *Psychoneuroendocrinology, 100*, 198−202. https://doi.org/10.1016/j.psyneuen.2018.10.011.

Ragen, B. J., Seidel, J., Chollak, C., Pietrzak, R. H., & Neumeister, A. (2015). Investigational drugs under development for the treatment of PTSD. *Expert Opinion on Investigational Drugs, 24*(5), 659–672. https://doi.org/10.1517/13543784.2015.1020109.

Robison, A. J., & Nestler, E. J. (2011). Transcriptional and epigenetic mechanisms of addiction. *Nature Reviews Neuroscience, 12*(11), 623–637. https://doi.org/10.1038/nrn3111.

Robison, A. J., Vialou, V., Sun, H.-S., Labonte, B., A Golden, S., Dias, C., et al. (2014). Fluoxetine epigenetically alters the CaMKIIα promoter in nucleus accumbens to regulate ΔFosB binding and antidepressant effects. *Neuropsychopharmacology, 39*(5), 1178–1186. https://doi.org/10.1038/npp.2013.319.

Rodrigues, S. M., LeDoux, J. E., & Sapolsky, R. M. (2009). The influence of stress hormones on fear circuitry. *Annual Review of Neuroscience, 32*(1), 289–313. https://doi.org/10.1146/annurev.neuro.051508.135620.

Sampson, R. J. (2012). *Great American city: Chicago and the enduring neighborhood effect.* Chicago: The University of Chicago Press.

Sapolsky, R. M. (2017). *Behave: The biology of humans at our best and worst.* New York, NY: Penguin Press.

Serra, M. P., Poddighe, L., Boi, M., Sanna, F., Piludu, M. A., Corda, M. G., et al. (2017). Expression of BDNF and trkB in the hippocampus of a rat genetic model of vulnerability (Roman low-avoidance) and resistance (Roman high-avoidance) to stress-induced depression. *Brain and Behavior, 7*(10), e00861. https://doi.org/10.1002/brb3.861.

Sharma, S., & Ressler, K. J. (2019). Genomic updates in understanding PTSD. *Progress in Neuro-Psychopharmacology and Biological Psychiatry, 90,* 197–203. https://doi.org/10.1016/j.pnpbp.2018.11.010.

Sheridan, M. A., Fox, N. A., Zeanah, C. H., McLaughlin, K. A., & Nelson, C. A. (2012). Variation in neural development as a result of exposure to institutionalization early in childhood. *Proceedings of the National Academy of Sciences of the United States of America, 109*(32), 12927–12932. https://doi.org/10.1073/pnas.1200041109.

Snedker, K. A., & Herting, J. R. (2016). Adolescent mental health. *Youth and Society, 48*(5), 695–719. https://doi.org/10.1177/0044118X13512335.

Tottenham, N. (2012). Human amygdala development in the absence of species-expected caregiving. *Developmental Psychobiology, 54*(6), 598–611. https://doi.org/10.1002/dev.20531.

Tottenham, N., Hare, T. A., Quinn, B. T., McCarry, T. W., Nurse, M., Gilhooly, T., et al. (2010). Prolonged institutional rearing is associated with atypically large amygdala volume and difficulties in emotion regulation. *Developmental Science, 13*(1), 46–61. https://doi.org/10.1111/j.1467-7687.2009.00852.x.

Vialou, V., Bagot, R. C., Cahill, M. E., Ferguson, D., Robison, A. J., Dietz, D. M., et al. (2014). Prefrontal cortical circuit for depression- and anxiety-related behaviors mediated by cholecystokinin: Role of FosB. *Journal of Neuroscience, 34*(11), 3878–3887. https://doi.org/10.1523/JNEUROSCI.1787-13.2014.

Vialou, V., Robison, A. J., LaPlant, Q. C., Covington, H. E., Dietz, D. M., Ohnishi, Y. N., et al. (2010). DeltaFosB in brain reward circuits mediates resilience to stress and antidepressant responses. *Nature Neuroscience, 13*(6), 745–752. https://doi.org/10.1038/nn.2551.

Wu, G., Feder, A., Cohen, H., Kim, J. J., Calderon, S., Charney, D. S., et al. (2013). Understanding resilience. *Frontiers in Behavioral Neuroscience, 7,* 10. https://doi.org/10.3389/fnbeh.2013.00010.

Zuberi, A. (2016). Neighborhoods and parenting: Assessing the influence of neighborhood quality on the parental monitoring of youth. *Youth and Society, 48*(5), 599–627. https://doi.org/10.1177/0044118X13502365.

4

Implicit bias, officer wellness, and police training

Kimberly C. Burke

CENTER FOR POLICING EQUITY, UC, BERKELEY, CA, UNITED STATES

Introduction

In 2014, following a string of highly publicized police killings of unarmed Black people, the US Attorney General Eric Holder announced a $4.75 million grant to fund a project to address biased-based policing. The Office of the Attorney General turned to the scientific community with the question: Why are Black communities burdened by police so much more than their White counterparts? In response, the National Initiative for Building Community Trust and Justice ("The National Initiative," hereafter) was formed by a consortium of researchers from the Center for Policing Equity at John Jay College and UCLA (CPE), the National Network for Safe Communities at John Jay College, the Justice Collaboratory at Yale Law School, and the Urban Institute. The consortium developed a multi-pronged approach for diagnosing and treating racial inequities in law enforcement.

The training and policy interventions put forth by the National Initiative centered growing scientific evidence that unconscious, or implicit, biases are key drivers of racial discrimination. Contrary to the popular "bad apples" framing that suggests the racist attitudes of a handful of officers cause racially biased policing, the science of implicit bias demonstrates how pernicious stereotypes can influence perceptions and behaviors outside of an individual's conscious awareness. The National Initiative foregrounded the understanding that racially biased policing outcomes, like racial disparities in use of force, can occur in the absence of explicit or conscious racial animus (Correll, Park, Judd, & Wittenbrink, 2002; Cox, Devine, Plant, & Schwartz, 2014; Payne, 2006; Spencer, Charbonneau, & Glaser, 2016; Swencionis & Goff, 2017). Implicit bias provided a new point of entry for addressing the persistent problem of racial discrimination in US law enforcement.

The following will provide an empirical example of participatory action research within police and community stakeholder partnerships and highlight its utility in addressing implicit bias in policing. In my capacity as Project Director of the National Initiative and in collaboration with leading social psychologist and National Initiative

Power. https://doi.org/10.1016/B978-0-12-817872-0.00004-5

Co-Principal Investigator, Phillip Atiba Goff, I worked from 2015 to 2017 piloting an 8-hour training, titled "Tactical Perceptions"(Goff, 2016). *Tactical Perceptions* was designed to empower police officers to train their own in reducing bias-based policing practices in six police departments across the US. This chapter is a distillation of my experiences in the field supporting police trainers in the co-production and delivery of *Tactical Perceptions.*

First, I outline the scientific research on implicit bias in policing and the ways that bias impacts officer well-being and community safety. Then I summarize the theoretical and empirical literature on action research and police receptivity to research that guided my approach to curriculum development and implementation. Finally, drawing on self-reported examples of promising practices from the National Initiative training teams, I argue that police officers are increasingly willing to accept the role of implicit bias in policing when they are taught that implicit biases can negatively impact officer safety and well-being in ways that fundamentally reduce their ability to protect the most vulnerable communities they serve.

Implicit bias theory, community safety, and officer wellness

Social science research on implicit bias provides a contemporary basis for understanding the differences in police treatment of racial minorities and White people (Swencionis & Goff, 2017). Implicit bias is the psychological theory that human brains make unconscious associations about social groups and, that those associations can impact behavior (Greenwald & Banaji, 1995). Often, implicit cognition is benign and necessary for people to function efficiently and effectively. However, exposure to stereotypes through media, social interactions, and passive observations can permeate a person's mind and form the origins of implicit biases (Dasgupta, 2013; Kang, 2011). A growing body of evidence suggests that implicit associations can lead to negative decision-making and harmful behaviors due to pernicious group-based stereotypes that are present across society (Banaji & Greenwald, 1994; Eberhardt, Goff, Purdie, & Davies, 2004). These findings counter dominant conceptions of individual-derived racial discrimination by supporting the idea that biased behavior need not be a product of individual character or animus (Greenwald & Banaji, 1995).

Experimental studies have examined the specific ways that implicit biases can impact policing outcomes. For example, stereotypes about Black people as violent, hostile, and criminal have been linked to biases in police officer perception (Eberhardt et al., 2004) and decisions to shoot (Correll et al., 2002). Similarly, Smith and Alpert (2007) have shown that police officers may be vulnerable to unintentional stereotyping due to repeated contact with racial minorities involved in crime, which facilitates an over-estimation of the relationship between race and crime. Eberhardt and colleagues' (2004) laboratory results suggested that when officers were subliminally primed (or shown an image quickly enough to bypass the realm of conscious cognition) with phenotypically Black faces (compared to phenotypically White faces), that exposure prompted a faster identification of pictured weapons, even when the weapons were not displayed with a sharp focus. When subliminally primed with White faces, the unconscious exposure inhibited officers' ability to detect the imprecisely pictured weapon more than if the subjects had not been primed at all (Eberhardt et al., 2004). The data show that both Black and White police officers more quickly perceive (and misperceive) weapons with Black suspects than with White suspects, rendering the issue of implicit bias relevant for all police officers, regardless of race and ethnic identity. Importantly, bias in weapon detection and decisions to shoot likely "… reflect a much larger set of policing behaviors that are influenced by implicit biases, most of which (e.g., decisions to follow, stop, search, detain, etc.) would not be resisted as strenuously as shooting" (Spencer et al., 2016, p. 55). The stereotypes that exist in the world, whether consciously held or not, prove crucial to officer cognition. This research suggests that officers' unconscious beliefs can influence their professional understanding and decision-making practices, and even shape their split-second unconscious visual perceptions in ways that put police and the communities they are sworn to protect, at unnecessary risk.

The negative impact of implicit bias may also be compounded by experiences of intergroup interactions. Social psychological research shows that individuals often experience intergroup interactions as threatening and stressful (Mendes, Blascovich, Hunter, Lickel, & Jost, 2007; Trawalter, Richeson, & Shelton, 2009). A 2017 PEW Research Center study, relying on interview data collected from almost 8000 officers in over 50 departments across the United States, helps shed light on this issue. The study found that 87% of officers in large departments report more tense interactions between police and Black people as a result of high profile incidents involving Black people and police. Given these attitudes, officers that police predominantly Black neighborhoods may experience chronic stress, which has been shown to slow reaction times and weaken verbal memory thereby directly impacting their ability to perform their duties safely and effectively (Papazoglou & Andersen, 2014). Additionally, research has indicated that when officers are less psychologically and emotionally distressed, they report a stronger endorsement of democratic forms of policing that have been linked to improved outcomes for marginalized communities (Trinkner, Tyler, & Goff, 2016; Tyler & Fagan, 2008). These findings make explicit the inextricable relationship of officer and community wellness. The National Initiative's *Tactical Perceptions* training then, was developed as one mechanism to address the ways that bias negatively impacts not just community safety, but also officer well-being.

Action research, police training, and officer receptivity

Training teams were assembled to work with me and were charged with learning and delivering the *Tactical Perceptions* curriculum to all sworn officers in their respective departments. The teams included a mix of seasoned academy instructors and officers with little or no teaching history, but with the patrol experience necessary to lend credibility to the training efforts. Without exception, trainers across the six sites expressed concerns about facilitating a training that would overwhelmingly be seen by the rank and file as an accusation of wrongdoing and racism. Conversations with patrol officers revealed that the National Initiative, especially the training on implicit bias, was regarded as a punitive response by leadership to appease a "vocal minority" and as a capitulation to political pressures.

This climate of resistance was not unique to the National Initiative training context. Rather, this resistance is rooted in a persistent legacy of fraught researcher-police relationships and is consistent with officers' general skepticism of "outsiders," i.e. non-police actors (Lum, Telep, Koper, & Grieco, 2012). Too often, policing reform efforts do not take into account officers' concerns and fail to incorporate their experiences as valuable sources of knowledge. A fair proportion of police training curricula extend from the unidirectional position that research scientists possess all relevant expertise for practitioner consumption, and that "knowledge is produced by researchers, then transferred through dissemination processes to practitioners who apply it" (Nutley, Walter, & Davies, 2007, p. 111). The cynicism bred by these practices cannot be overstated. I learned from officers that trainings delivered in this way are referred to as "check the box" trainings where they attend and even participate in the sessions, but with very little buy-in or motivation to internalize the trainings' lessons. Essentially, officers described sitting through these kinds of trainings with crossed arms and closed minds to provide the department with a superficial display of compliance. "Check the box" trainings mimic other flawed and failed top-down pedagogies that treat the officers being trained as passive subjects, ignore their pre-existing and under-valued knowledge, and present them with pre-packaged solutions to pre-identified problems (Freire, 1972). This kind of approach would render meaningless an exceptional opportunity to nationally address bias in policing.

In order to avoid a "check the box" training approach, I forged partnerships with the National Initiative training teams, which were anchored by three commitments:

(1) they must engage as co-producers of the training,
(2) they must provide honest feedback to each other based on the diversity of their beliefs and experiences, and
(3) they must be as accountable to the most marginalized of communities they serve as they are to their fellow officers.

These partnerships reflect models of interactive research and participatory action research which emphasize exchanges between multiple actors within research, policy, and practice arenas (Nutley et al., 2007). Interactive models offer a nuanced understanding of the complex and dynamic factors shaping how research gets adopted, adapted, and blended with other sources of knowledge in particular contexts (Payne & Bryant, 2018). Thus, I engaged with the police trainers as active thought partners in each step of the training development, messaging, and delivery. This approach is consistent with a growing field of participatory action research (PAR) that eschews researcher/subject dichotomies and emphasizes collaborative research that engages communities nearest to the problems being addressed.

There are few empirical examples of researchers applying the principles of PAR in studies aimed at enhancing officer safety and well-being. One exception is recent work by Kerrison, Goff, Burbank, & Hyatt, (in press), who rely heavily on the application of participatory action research in contemporary policing data collection efforts. As they identified, PAR in policing science requires "an iterative problem-oriented and solution-driven methodological approach that involves joint input from researchers and those who are experiencing the problem, on diagnosing and solving the problem" (Kerrison et al., in press). In the context of my study sites, it is because I acknowledged that the patrol officers and their peer trainers are closest to uncovering and addressing the problem of police bias that the curriculum was necessarily shaped by their input and wisdoms.

With an additional commitment to "engaged pedagogy" (hooks, 2014) guiding my practice, I set out to facilitate trainers' development of the language and tools needed to translate the science of bias to their officer peers. Most importantly, they had to understand the concepts of the training before they could believe in their merit. I created a series of web-based curricula surveying the social science of bias. Each lesson contained assignments to help trainers to build customized language and exercises that identified both the problems of and solutions for bias in their departments. Many were shared across departments, while some were unique to local contexts, such as interactions with specific immigrant populations. I provided feedback and guidance based on my scientific expertise as the training teams worked together to generate content that best resonated with police officers. Through this interactive process and with the unifying framework of officer well-being, *Tactical Perceptions* began to crystallize.

Promising practices: linkages between implicit bias and officer and community wellness

One of the police trainers offered what continues to be one of the most referenced examples in the curriculum about the way that implicit bias can impede officer safety. It was an interview with a Las Vegas police officer featured on an episode of the *This American Life* podcast series titled, "Cops See It Differently" (Glass, 2015). In the interview, the officer discusses his experience responding to an active shooter situation in a Walmart. He talks about how he was socialized to think of active shooters as men, so much so that when he entered the Walmart and a woman pointed a gun at him, he hesitated just long enough that the woman fired her weapon at him. The shot proved non-fatal, and the officer retrospectively theorizes that his moment of hesitation was the product of implicit bias about gender, which slowed down his ability to perceive the threat posed by the armed female shooter. His reflections are consistent with the theory that implicit biases can create ways of "not seeing" (Poggi, 1965) or blind spots (Banaji & Greenwald, 2016). The officer received the "active shooter" radio call and immediately generated the profile of a White male shooter. This priming impeded his ability to detect a weapon when it was in the hands of someone, a woman, who did not match the stereotype in his mind. It was a real-life replication of the aforementioned Eberhardt et al. (2004) study findings. This story reveals how implicit bias made the officer less safe, and thereby also made him less effective at protecting those around him. The story presented a credentialed story from the perspective of a patrol-duty officer and provided a key example for understanding the harms of implicit bias in terms of officer safety. The inclusion of this media clip in *Tactical Perceptions* was pivotal to incorporating officer safety into conversations about bias and overcoming officers' pre-conceived notion that this would be another politically-driven and punitive "check the box" training done without any value for patrol officers.

Another important example generated by police trainers of how biases make officers and communities less safe was the "shared goals" exercise. At the beginning of the training, trainers ask class participants to generate a list of goals shared by officers in their department. Across sites, the goals of "go home safe" and "protect communities" topped the lists. Trainers return to the list of shared goals at the end of training by asking participants how biased policing interferes with each goal. Again, the idea of blind spots created by biases illustrates the interference of bias with the first goal of getting home safely at the end of every shift. They also show how biases inhibit officers' effectiveness in responding to certain situations that do not fit the stereotypical narrative, including domestic disputes in which the assailant is female. To demonstrate this point, the trainers ask participants to pretend that they have received a radio call for a domestic dispute. They then ask the officers to describe who they would anticipate the assailant and victim to be in this situation. Without fail the room responds: male assailant, female victim. The trainers ask the room if they have ever responded to a domestic that involved same sex couples, eliciting stories from officers who were caught off-guard and slower to process situations in which the perpetrator of violence and/or the victim of violence did not match the initial concepts that they had in their minds. These stories illustrated how blind spots created by biases made them and the people they were sworn to protect, less safe. Significantly, interventions based on shared values have been shown to increase receptivity to research, even if that intervention is critical of the organization (Lum et al., 2012).

Tactical Perceptions consists of four modules, and each module includes small group discussions in breakout teams that culminate with each team sharing a story or example to the entire class. When fellow officers share personal experiences of perpetuating or being subjected to biased behavior, it transforms the conversation from a "them" problem (i.e. civilians) to an "us" problem (i.e. officers). One particularly salient story came from a Black male officer who described showing up to court in casual clothes for his traffic court duty to attest to the traffic citations he had issued. The officer shared with the class that when he arrived in court, the judge had reprimanded him for his long list of traffic violations. The judge, also a Black man, had assumed that this officer was the offender rather than the cop. The defendant's lawyer spoke up to clarify that the White man standing next to him was the one in violation, not the Black police officer. He ended his story by admitting that, following that incident, he always wears his uniform to court so that he can avoid the embarrassment of being mistaken for a criminal defendant.

This example evidences the reality that implicit biases are universal, even when they are based on negative stereotypes about members of the group to which a person belongs. It also serves as an important reminder that non-White officers' face many of the racial biases being protested by activist organizations like Black Lives Matter (BLM). When these experiences are conveyed by fellow officers, they are less likely to be dismissed as the inflated concerns of a vocal minority epitomized by BLM, and more likely to make an impression on officers. The harsh implications of this officer's story are driven home by a 29-year study showing that of the 10 off-duty police officers mistaken for civilians and fatally shot by another police officer, eight were Black, one was Hispanic, and one was White (Charbonneau, Spencer, & Glaser, 2017). The *Tactical Perceptions* curriculum provides insight into why Black civilians and officers alike are more likely to be mistaken for criminals, and stories like this from officers deconstruct the false divide between the police and communities at large. The trainers used the curriculum to facilitate dialogues that fostered self-reflection among officers about the existence of bias, their role in perpetuating it, and their responsibility to address it. The success of these dialogues and their ability to impact and resonate with officers is reflected in outcome evaluations of the trainings, conducted by one of the National Initiative partners, The Urban Institute.

Outcome evaluations of the *Tactical Perceptions* curriculum were conducted immediately before and after trainings were administered. The evaluation findings, which represent more than 3400 officers across the six National Initiative agencies, show that in two-thirds of the agencies, officers reported a statistically significant increase in receptivity to the idea that implicit biases could impact their behavior following the training (Jannetta & Lynch, 2017). Two-thirds of departments also reported a statistically significant increase in their feeling empowered to address implicit biases and half of the agencies reported a significant increase in the idea that being self-reflective would improve their effectiveness as a police officer after the training (Jannetta & Lynch, 2017).

Conclusion

The challenge of overcoming police officers' resistance to research partnerships is compounded by the universal difficulties of teaching race-related content in intergroup settings (Maxwell, Nagda, & Thompson, 2012; Richeson & Shelton, 2007; Richeson & Trawalter, 2005; Stephan & Stephan, 1985). However, based on my experiences from the field detailed above and subsequent conversations with police trainers, I am confident that an effective learning climate can be cultivated through the deployment of a participatory action research approach. By focusing on the ways that implicit bias undermines officer well-being and diminishes community safety, the curriculum appealed to officers' primary goals and increased their receptivity to the learning objectives.

Tactical Perceptions was forged through an equal partnership from content design to delivery. I taught police trainers about the science of bias, and they generated salient examples about how implicit biases can create blind spots and hinder weapon detection in ways that reduce officer safety. I directed police trainers to research on how implicit biases can increase officer stress and threat perception in intergroup encounters, and they built dialogue between officers that made that science meaningful. The curriculum received overwhelmingly positive reviews from the National Initiative departments because it was co-produced by officers with support and guidance from social scientists rather than created and taught by researchers outside of those agencies.

The framework of *Tactical Perceptions* emphasizes that officer safety cannot be decoupled from community safety, and the development of the training highlights the need for officers to contribute to the curriculum to make the science of bias relevant to their experiences. Lastly, the delivery of its content reveals that a training that seriously incorporates police perspectives and values can overcome resistance to discussions of racial bias in order to better achieve learning objectives. Implicit bias trainings have the potential to affirm police officers' egalitarian values by unpacking how behaviors are influenced by cognition beyond their awareness or intention. Empowering officers in this way stands to decrease their experiences of threat and stress in intergroup interactions, which research suggests improves their job performance (Steele, 1988; Trawalter et al., 2009). However, not enough is known about officers' self-perceptions while policing Black and Latinx communities, or how those self-perceptions, particularly feelings of self-worth and legitimacy, impact their decisions to stop, search, or use force on members of these communities. Future studies should examine officers' self-perceptions and decision-making, the impact of implicit bias trainings on those self-perceptions over time, and take seriously the mutuality of officer-civilian safety by foregrounding concerns of officer wellness.

References

Banaji, M. R., & Greenwald, A. G. (1994). Implicit stereotyping and prejudice. *The psychology of prejudice: The Ontario symposium, 7*, 55–76.

Banaji, M. R., & Greenwald, A. G. (2016). *Blindspot: Hidden biases of good people*. New York, NY: Bantam.

Charbonneau, A., Spencer, K., & Glaser, J. (2017). Understanding racial disparities in police use of lethal force: Lessons from fatal police-on-police shootings. *Journal of Social Issues, 73*(4), 744–767. https://doi.org/10.1111/josi.12246.

Correll, J., Park, B., Judd, C. M., & Wittenbrink, B. (2002). The police officer's dilemma: Using ethnicity to disambiguate potentially threatening individuals. *Journal of Personality and Social Psychology, 83*(6), 1314–1329. https://doi.org/10.1037/0022-3514.83.6.1314.

Cox, W. T., Devine, P. G., Plant, E. A., & Schwartz, L. L. (2014). Toward a comprehensive understanding of officers' shooting decisions: No simple answers to this complex problem. *Basic and Applied Social Psychology, 36*(4), 356–364. https://doi.org/10.1080/01973533.2014.923312.

Dasgupta, N. (2013). Implicit attitudes and beliefs adapt to situations: A decade of research on the malleability of implicit prejudice, stereotypes, and the self-concept. *Advances in Experimental Social Psychology, 47*, 233−279. https://doi.org/10.1016/B978-0-12-4072367.00005-X.

Eberhardt, J. L., Goff, P. A., Purdie, V. J., & Davies, P. G. (2004). Seeing black: Race, crime, and visual processing. *Journal of Personality and Social Psychology, 87*(6), 876−893. https://doi.org/10.1037/0022-3514.87.6.876.

Freire, P. (1972). *Pedagogy of the oppressed.* New York, NY: Herder and Herder.

Glass, I. (February 13, 2015). *This American life: Cops see it differently- Part Two* ([Audio podcast]).

Goff, P. A. (2016). Identity traps: How to think about race & policing. *Behavioral Science & Policy, 2*(2), 10−22. https://doi.org/10.1353/bsp.2016.0012.

Greenwald, A. G., & Banaji, M. R. (1995). Implicit social cognition: Attitudes, self-esteem, and stereotypes. *Psychological Review, 102*(1), 4−27. https://doi.org/10.1037/0033-295X.102.1.4.

hooks, b. (2014). *Teaching to transgress.* New York, NY: Routledge.

Jannetta, J., & Lynch, M. (2017). *Buying into procedural justice: An examination of training surveys from the national initiative for building community Trust and Justice. [A virtual presentation by the urban Institute for the national initiative for building community Trust and Justice.*

Kang, J. (2011). Bits of bias. In J. Levinson, & R. Smith (Eds.), *Implicit bias across the law* (pp. 11−40). Oxford, England, UK: Oxford University Press.

Kerrison, E. M., Goff, P. A., Burbank, C. & Hyatt, J. M. (in press). On creating ethical, productive, and durable action research partnerships with police officers and their departments: A case study of the national Justice database. Police Practice and Research: International Journal.

Lum, C., Telep, C. W., Koper, C. S., & Grieco, J. (2012). Receptivity to research in policing. *Justice Research and Policy, 14*(1), 61−95. https://doi.org/10.3818/JRP.14.1.2012.61.

Maxwell, K. E., Nagda, B. R., & Thompson, M. C. (2012). *Facilitating intergroup dialogues: Bridging differences, catalyzing change.* Sterling, VA: Stylus Publishing, LLC.

Mendes, W. B., Blascovich, J., Hunter, S. B., Lickel, B., & Jost, J. T. (2007). Threatened by the unexpected: Physiological responses during social interactions with expectancy-violating partners. *Journal of Personality and Social Psychology, 92*(4), 698−716.

Nutley, S. M., Walter, I., & Davies, H. T. (2007). *Using evidence: How research can inform public services.* Bristol, UK: Policy press.

Papazoglou, K., & Andersen, J. P. (2014). A guide to utilizing police training as a tool to promote resilience and improve health outcomes among police officers. *Traumatology: International Journal, 20*(2), 103−111. https://doi.org/10.1037/h0099394.

Payne, B. K. (2006). Weapon bias: Split-second decisions and unintended stereotyping. *Current Directions in Psychological Science, 15*(6), 287−291. https://doi.org/10.1111/j.1467-8721.2006.00454.x.

Payne, Y. A., & Bryant, A. (2018). Street participatory action research in prison: A methodology to challenge privilege and power in correctional facilities. *The Prison Journal, 98*(4), 449−469. https://doi.org/10.1177/0032885518776378.

Pew Research Center. (2017). *Behind the badge: Amid protests and calls for reform, how police view their jobs, key issues and recent fatal encounters between blacks and police.* https://www.pewresearch.org/.

Poggi, G. (1965). A main theme of contemporary sociological analysis: Its achievements and limitations. *British Journal of Sociology, 16*(4), 283−294. https://doi.org/10.2307/589157.

Richeson, J. A., & Shelton, J. N. (2007). Negotiating interracial interactions: Costs, consequences, and possibilities. *Current Directions in Psychological Science, 16*(6), 316−320.

Richeson, J. A., & Trawalter, S. (2005). Why do interracial interactions impair executive function? A resource depletion account. *Journal of Personality and Social Psychology, 88*(6), 934–947.

Smith, M. R., & Alpert, G. P. (2007). Explaining police bias: A theory of social conditioning and illusory correlation. *Criminal Justice and Behavior, 34*(10), 1262–1283. https://doi.org/10.1177/0093854807304484.

Spencer, K. B., Charbonneau, A. K., & Glaser, J. (2016). Implicit bias and policing. *Social and Personality Psychology Compass, 10*(1), 50–63. https://doi.org/10.1111/spc3.12210.

Steele, C. M. (1988). The psychology of self-affirmation: Sustaining the integrity of the self. *Advances in Experimental Social Psychology, 21*, 261–302. https://doi.org/10.1016/S0065-2601(08)60229-4.

Stephan, W. G., & Stephan, C. W. (1985). Intergroup anxiety. *Journal of Social Issues, 41*(3), 157–175.

Swencionis, J. K., & Goff, P. A. (2017). The psychological science of racial bias and policing. *Psychology, Public Policy, and Law, 23*(4), 398–409. https://doi.org/10.1037/law0000130.

Trawalter, S., Richeson, J. A., & Shelton, J. N. (2009). Predicting behavior during interracial interactions: A stress and coping approach. *Personality and Social Psychology Review, 13*(4), 243–268. https://doi.org/10.1177/1088868309345850.

Trinkner, R., Tyler, T. R., & Goff, P. A. (2016). Justice from within: The relations between a procedurally just organizational climate and police organizational efficiency, endorsement of democratic policing, and officer well-being. *Psychology, Public Policy, and Law, 22*(2), 158–172.

Tyler, T. R., & Fagan, J. (2008). Legitimacy and cooperation: Why do people help the police fight crime in their communities? *Ohio State Journal of Criminal Law, 6*(1), 231–276.

Psychic wounds: consequences of a lack of personal wellness

5

The moral risks of policing

Daniel M. Blumberg[a], Konstantinos Papazoglou[b],
Sarah Creighton[c]

[a]DEPARTMENT OF UNDERGRADUATE PSYCHOLOGY, CALIFORNIA SCHOOL OF PROFESSIONAL PSYCHOLOGY, ALLIANT INTERNATIONAL UNIVERSITY, SAN DIEGO, CA, UNITED STATES; [b]YALE SCHOOL OF MEDICINE, NEW HAVEN, CT, UNITED STATES; [c]ASSISTANT CHIEF (RETIRED), SAN DIEGO POLICE DEPARTMENT, SAN DIEGO, CA, UNITED STATES

Introduction

It is not hyperbolic to suggest that tensions between the police and the public in many communities is at an all-time high. Conflicts exist despite active efforts on the part of law enforcement agencies, community leaders, schools, and public, private, and non-profit organizations to improve relations. Although small steps of progress occur, there remains fairly intractable mistrust on both sides.[1]

To a large degree, police misconduct is responsible for eroding public trust. Such behavior is highlighted in frequent media reports of excessive or unnecessary force as well as in the now fairly routine cases of overturned convictions based on unethical investigative techniques. Many people are simply afraid of their local police officers (i.e., Kendall, 2015). Despite the efforts of police executives to develop benevolent and trustworthy relationships between their officers and the local community, tensions between the two sides still exist.

Aims of present chapter

The present chapter attempts to shine a different light on the issue of police misconduct. First, the authors emphasize personal integrity and discuss ways in which this characteristic may decline among law enforcement personnel because of routine police practices. Then, in an effort to understand this phenomenon and because a comprehensive police-specific theory does not yet exist, the authors explore, in great detail,

---

[1]Parts of current chapter have been published by same authors in: Blumberg, D.M., Papazoglou, K., & Creighton, S. (2018). Bruised Badges: The Moral Risks of Police Work and a Call for Officer Wellness. *International Journal of Emergency Mental Health & Human Resilience, 20*(2), 1−14. Permission for those parts' reprint in this chapter was provided by the International Journal of Emergency Mental Health and Human Resilience, OMICS International Publisher Editorial Officials.

existing theories of ethical decision-making, and directly relate them to current police practices. Taken together these various theories help to explain why working as a police officer can foster a reduction in one's commitment to ethical principles and actions.

In the end, the authors argue for changing the narrative about police misconduct. Instead of focusing primarily on the impossible task of eliminating all forms of misconduct, steps can be taken to destigmatize the majority of unethical behavior, to understand that it is fairly predictable, and to establish consistent and constructive disciplinary responses that would reverse or even prevent such phenomena from happening. These efforts will help to enable individuals and organizations to intervene at the earliest signs of misconduct when careers can be saved and the most serious harm may be able to be prevented.

Police misconduct: theoretical conceptualizations and practical dilemmas

The conversation about police misconduct typically centers on a rather dichotomous discussion between individuals (i.e., bad apples) and police organizations (e.g., Klockars, Ivkovic, & Haberfield, 2006, 2004; Caldero & Crank, 2011; Dean, Bell, & Lauchs, 2010; Heffernan, 1982; Klockars, Ivkovic, Harver, & Haberfeld, 2000, pp. 1—11; Miller & Braswell, 1992; Schafer & Martinelli, 2008). Of course, police misconduct should be viewed from both individual and organizational parameters, especially when it comes to developing intervention and prevention strategies. Nevertheless, scholars continue to discuss: how to label deviant behavior among police officers; what constitutes corruption; if corruption is or is not distinguishable from police misconduct, and so forth (see, for example, Stinson, Liederbach, & Brewer, 2016). This may serve an important role when seeking to achieve a greater understanding of behavioral outcomes, particularly in relation to developing policies to deal with these various problematic behaviors. At the same time, however, this conceptual debate, from a purely psychological perspective, is too abstruse, because it does not go far enough to examine personality and motivational factors.

Conversely, when one emphasizes individual dimensions, the dialogue shifts from one of organizational policy to the concept of police officers' personality and decision-making. From this perspective, it is not very helpful to reduce the argument to a dichotomy between keeping "good" cops and weeding out "bad" cops, especially because the vast majority of individuals who enter law enforcement have honorable intentions to maintain peace and order in the communities they serve. Rather, the more constructive approach examines police officers' ethical decision-making. One can argue that ethical decision-making generally leads to ethical behavior, and, conversely, unethical decision-making is likely to lead to unethical behavior. (For the present purposes, the term police misconduct is used to describe all types of unethical behaviors by police officers.)

A recent extensive analysis of the most serious cases of police misconduct (i.e., when a police officer is arrested for his/her behavior) found that "police crimes are not uncommon" (Stinson et al., 2016, p. 21). Certainly, there are far more less-serious incidents of misconduct, which result in outcomes less severe than an officer's arrest (e.g., termination, administrative discipline, etc.). Therefore, considering the ubiquitousness of police misconduct, a logical starting place is to examine if some police officers are more likely than others to make unethical decisions.

Police integrity and ethical decision-making

Integrity is a personality trait that is strongly associated with ethical decision-making. According to Schlenker (2008), "Integrity involves honesty, trustworthiness, fidelity in keeping one's word and obligations, and incorruptibility, or an unwillingness to violate principles regardless of the temptations, costs, and preferences of others" (p. 1081). In this model, the opposite of integrity is expediency, which involves "the ideas that principles can and should be tailored to fit the context, that it is important to take advantage of profitable opportunities and foolish to fail to do so, and that deviations from principles can usually be justified" (Schlenker, 2008, p. 1080). One can infer, then, that some unethical behavior will be committed by police officers who are capable of embracing expedient beliefs.

The Integrity Scale

The Integrity Scale (Schlenker, 2008), an 18-item self-report instrument, was developed and validated over a series of studies with college students. The scale also has been used with nursing students (Krueger, 2014) and with West Point cadets (Graves et al., 2010). Items measure one's unwillingness to rationalize unprincipled behavior, one's commitment to principles despite temptations, and one's belief in the inherent importance of principled conduct (Miller & Schlenker, 2011, p. 3). Validation studies confirmed that integrity, as measured by the scale, is a single latent dimension that is separate from other factors (e.g., moral disengagement, Machiavellianism), which are thought to be related to ethical or antisocial behavior: "Integrity thus provides a distinctive individual difference variable that is useful in *predicting the violation of moral rules*" (Schlenker, 2008, p. 1118, emphasis added); the higher one's score is on the scale, the greater the commitment to ethical principles. The scale includes many items that represent ethical decisions, which are routinely faced by police officers.

A recent study (Blumberg, Giromini, & Jacobson, 2016) administered the Integrity Scale to police recruits. This study found that police recruit participants scored higher on the Integrity Scale prior to police academy training than the college students who participated in the Scale's development studies (Blumberg et al., 2016, p. 74). This is a reassuring finding. First, it signifies that law enforcement agencies generally do not hire "bad apples," which can be attributed to comprehensive pre-hire background investigations and assessments, including thorough psychological evaluations. Moreover, these findings support the contention that most individuals who seek careers in law enforcement do so with noble intentions (e.g., Caldero & Crank, 2011) and confirm Ford's (2003) claim that police recruits enter the profession with high integrity. Indeed, research findings regarding individuals' motivations to join NYPD showed that a significant percentage of recruits entered law enforcement for the opportunity to serve their communities and to help people (Raganella & White, 2004; White, Cooper, Saunders, & Raganella, 2010). Together, these findings serve to disprove anecdotal contentions that the main reason individuals seek police jobs is a desire for power, authority, and control.

The role of police training on integrity

The next step is to explore the impact of police training on integrity. Some researchers (e.g., Chappell & Lanza-Kaduce, 2010; Ford, 2003; Garner, 2005) suggested that the nature of law enforcement training, beginning in the academy, plays a role (e.g., solely paramilitary training, low emphasis on interpersonal relations, inadequate communication training) in leading police officers toward unethical decision-making. This is a compelling position, which is consistent with several theories of ethical decision-making that will be presented later in this chapter, and remains a viable area of continued exploration. However, Blumberg et al. (2016) compared their participants' Integrity Scale scores from prior to academy training with scores obtained at the conclusion of academy training and found that, overall, police academy training had "minimal or no impact on the recruits' levels of self-reported integrity" (Blumberg et al., 2016, p. 77). Thus, at least while still in the confines of the training environment, there were no significant changes in recruits' integrity. This does not mean that the academy training—content and delivery—had no deleterious impact on recruits' integrity. It only demonstrates that any negative impact was not significantly apparent upon academy graduation.

After graduating from the police academy, the newly sworn officers begin training in the field, followed by a probationary period of employment. Research demonstrated that police recruits start and finish their academy training with higher than average levels of self-reported integrity (Blumberg et al., 2016). However, it is not particularly uncommon for police officers to engage in ethically questionable behaviors (e.g., Stinson et al., 2016). Although the Integrity Scale measures what is essentially a core feature of one's identity (Miller & Schlenker, 2011; Schlenker, 2008), could the police acculturation process of field training negatively impact these new officers' commitment to ethical principles? The answer is a discouraging (and potentially alarming) "yes."

Although the effect size was small ($d = 00.29$) and the response rate was low, Blumberg and Giromini (unpublished manuscript) found a statistically significant decline in self-reported integrity scores among recent academy graduates after they served as patrol officers for one year. Specifically, some officers were more willing to endorse items that rationalize unprincipled behavior after only one year in the field than they were before they started working as police officers. This finding indicates that police work during the first year after academy training may play a crucial role in lowering officers' commitment to ethical principles. Although that study did not assess actual unethical behavior, the increase in expedient beliefs can be viewed as, at least, a potential downward trend in which violations of ethical rules can be predicted (Schlenker, 2008). Further research is needed to assess the course of self-reported integrity throughout officers' careers, but the decline in these early career officers' integrity scores was noteworthy.

This last conclusion leads to an extremely important discussion about the reasons why, after a relatively short tenure in their jobs, police officers might experience personal integrity decline. The literature on ethical decision-making provides numerous answers and, toward this direction, there are many theories to explain why people act unethically. Each of these theories now will receive a detailed examination vis-à-vis typical police practices and the nature of police officers' routine daily duties. Such an analysis will help to guide intervention and preventative strategies. Moreover, when applied to police work, a thorough understanding of the combined impact of all of these theories of ethical decision-making leads to the inescapable conclusion that police misconduct is inevitable.

The remainder of this chapter examines the individual and organizational theoretical sources of unethical decision-making and offers a discussion of numerous prevention and intervention efforts. Although future research is encouraged to test some of these theories with a police sample, preventative and intervention strategies should not wait for such empirical validation; existing findings are robust, albeit on populations other than police officers. In addition to helping police executives and researchers/scholars to understand how these phenomena manifest in law enforcement, the following discussion relates these theories of unethical behavior to the routine practices of police officers in an effort to normalize and destigmatize the fact that misconduct will continue to occur.

Etlology of police officers' unethical behavior

In this section, the authors examine the literature on ethical decision-making through the lenses of law enforcement training, typical police practices, and police officers' routine on-duty experiences. A core assumption at this point is that a reduction in personal integrity may make it easier for a person to decide to commit an unethical act. However, as will become clear, a decline in personal integrity is not necessary for one to engage in ethically ambiguous behaviors. In fact, some of these behaviors are committed by police officers who maintain a morally superior attitude (e.g., Ashforth & Anand, 2003, p. 15). Nevertheless, a thorough discussion of this area of the literature is essential to demonstrate the extent to which police executives and policy makers actually can contribute to the very problem, which they intend to solve.

Organizational explanations for unethical behavior

It is not an outright indictment of all law enforcement agencies to assert that there are current practices associated with fostering unethical behavior by police officers. There are rather routine habits in local government and police administration, which are themselves of questionable ethicality and which serve as fairly poor models for the rank and file. For example, the awarding of some contracts or occasional requests for nepotism-related preferential treatment demonstrate a blurry ethical line. Most organizations have taken important steps to address all forms of police misconduct. Many of these efforts are working, but still more can be done. Specific prevention and intervention strategies will be discussed in the last section of the present chapter. At this point, however, the authors examine the organization's role in officers' unethical decision-making.

Organizations are responsible for setting the ethical tone at all levels of the workforce. Employees learn whether or not a particular behavior is ethically acceptable and, perhaps just as importantly, they are taught how deviations from ethically acceptable behavior are handled by the organization. It has been proposed that organizations often normalize unethical behavior (Ashforth & Anand, 2003). Specifically, through processes of acculturation and institutionalization, ethically questionable behaviors can be taught, fostered, condoned, and perpetuated "… to such an extent that individuals may be unable to see the inappropriateness of their behavior" (Ashforth & Anand, 2003, p. 4).

Police training indoctrinates new hires to become successful officers (e.g., Berg, 1990; Chappell & Lanza-Kaduce, 2010; Haarr, 2001). This is often accomplished through modeling as newer employees attempt to adopt the values of training officers (Bennett, 1984) and peers (e.g., Haarr, 2005). At the same time, however, part of the training overemphasizes the dangerousness of the job by constantly stressing physical survival on the streets at all costs (e.g., Ford, 2003). Although safety should never be compromised, training could present the job's dangerousness more accurately to avoid instilling new officers with an unrealistically threatening availability heuristic.

Training also highlights and promotes unethical and ethically ambiguous behaviors and attitudes of veteran officers (e.g., Chappell & Lanza-Kaduce, 2010; Garner, 2005). This creates organizational structures that reinforce officers' unconscious adoption of unethical behavior. Blumberg et al. (2016) summarized research in this area:

> *Specifically, byproducts of the training may be (a) to foster us versus them attitudes, (b) to instill strong bonds among (officers) in order to rely on each other to stay out of trouble or to avoid punishment, (c) to learn that there is a difference between the letter of the law and the spirit of the law (i.e., police officers often have to use discretion), and, (d) to understand that morality is sometimes situational or relative, for example, police officers are legally permitted to lie to or deceive a suspect (p. 65).*

In addition to training factors, various operational practices help to explain unethical police behavior. For example, Brown, Sautter, Littvay, Sautter, and Bearnes (2010) suggested that when organizations quantify a job, employees may find it impractical to be empathic toward others (p. 207). In this regard, law enforcement organizations that overemphasize the number of tickets, contacts and arrests, out of service time, calls responded to, response times, and crime statistics are perpetuating a dehumanizing narrative (e.g., Brown et al., 2010), which makes it more likely that officers will make unethical decisions. This is not to malign the effectiveness of the more obvious organizational attempts to prevent and/or confront misconduct (e.g., strong Professional Integrity Units and the availability of wellness, psychological services, and peer support services), which will be discussed in more detail in the last section of the present chapter. Instead, these dehumanizing practices serve as a catalyst for creating an organizational culture, which is conducive to changing police officers at an individual level in ways that help to explain their unethical decision-making.

A related concept that can help to explain unethical behavior by police officers is noble cause corruption. The noble cause is a moral commitment by most police officers to protect society and to maintain peace and order (Caldero & Crank, 2011). Law enforcement organizations foster corruption of the noble cause by condoning police work in which the ends (public safety and crime control) justify the means (use of deception, breaking rules to catch offenders, etc.) (e.g., Crank, Flaherty, & Giacomazzi, 2007). This parallels findings from the world of business where "cutting corners" may be viewed as acceptable; this can be particularly insidious in light of most police officers' primary reason for entering the field in the first place (see Baron, Zhao, & Miao, 2015, p. 114).

Therefore, it may be important for law enforcement organizations to tread carefully and recognize differences in officers' primary motives for becoming a police officer. Some may view their primary role as a crime fighter, while others joined the field to be of service to the community. The job requires both roles (Manzella & Papazoglou, 2014), which are often incompatible; protecting the public and serving the public are not always experienced as concordant responsibilities (e.g., Cooper, 2012; Crank et al., 2007). For many officers, much of their time is spent performing duties associated with the job of a social worker rather than actual crime fighting. This may lead some to experience role conflict, which can lead to noble cause corruption (Cooper, 2012).

Additionally, when law enforcement organizations promote the noble cause, they essentially invite officers to engage in behaviors that are known to be a violation of policy or law. This form of misconduct is often committed by groups of officers (e.g., excessive force on an already subdued suspect) because of implicit or explicit peer pressure (Porter & Warrender, 2009). Rather than being premeditated, though, this form of unethical behavior tends to be a situational response to circumstances (e.g., coercing a confession from a suspect in an attempt to secure a conviction) (Porter & Warrender, 2009, p. 94).

Individual explanations for unethical behavior

The organizational influences weigh heavily on officers and directly impact their decision-making capabilities. This section presents many theories that explain why individuals engage in ethically questionable behaviors, which can help elucidate how personal integrity can decline in police officers. Each of these theories offers an explanation for unethical behavior. They are not mutually exclusive; some overlap with each other, while others seem to build on each other to clarify this complex subject. In the end, no single explanation is possible or, frankly, should be sought. Instead, a multi-faceted analysis of sources of unethical decision-making by police officers can lead to a far more vigorous and comprehensive set of prevention and intervention strategies.

Moral Compromise. The regular use of discretion by police officers, a practice that should never be constrained, nevertheless, can be considered a precursor to ethically questionable behavior. Officers are taught and encouraged to use their judgment when applying the spirit of the law. Law enforcement agencies constantly receive input from community groups regarding enforcement priorities in those communities. This input is communicated to officers on the streets who are faced with a constant balancing act.[2] Crank et al. (2007) explained "… that serious crimes are more likely to result in arrest suggest that police are committed to a utilitarian ethic that weighs more importantly the greater good brought about by serious crime arrests than arrests simply based on legal criteria" (p. 104).

Nevertheless, this routinely exposes police officers to situations in which they are forced to make moral compromises, such as "when legality conflicts with other values, like effectiveness, efficiency, and possibly even the public interest" (Loyens, 2014, p. 62). Thus, officers learn that certain crimes may or should be ignored, while some behaviors, which previously led to arrest, are no longer to be treated as crimes. In some jurisdictions, officers are explicitly instructed that they are supposed to treat certain members of the community differently from others. For example, officers are told that some misdemeanors committed by homeless persons in one large metropolitan community are no longer to be considered crimes, while the same behaviors by others remain grounds for arrest.

These situations in which police officers are forced to make moral compromises may lead to a decline in personal integrity. Specifically, in order to competently perform the routine duties of their jobs, police officers' conduct is, at times, in conflict with their deeply held values, e.g., to serve and protect (e.g., Benjamin, 1990). Throughout their police career, officers' personal values can be pitted against their role as law enforcers, including situations when interacting with those involved in the adult entertainment industry, medical marijuana dispensaries, sex workers, drug addicts, and so forth. In such circumstances, research on cognitive dissonance (e.g., Festinger & Carlsmith, 1959) demonstrated that either officers change their behavior, which is not possible if they want to keep their jobs (see Haarr, 2005), or they will begin to experience shifts in their personal values.

Moral Injury. One consequence of moral compromise is moral injury. "Moral injury is a particular type of psychological trauma characterized by intense guilt, shame, and spiritual crisis, which can develop when one violates his or her moral beliefs, is betrayed, or witnesses trusted individuals committing atrocities" (Jinkerson, 2016, p. 122). Among its various sequelae, it has been posited that moral injury may lead to criminal behavior and domestic violence (Litz et al., 2009, p. 698). Certainly, the extent of trauma experienced by many police officers is well understood (e.g., Papazoglou, 2013), and there is increasing awareness of the extent to which those suffering from Post-traumatic Stress Disorder (PTSD) may resort to unethical behavior (e.g., LaMotte & Murphy, 2017). Furthermore, Papazoglou and Chopko (2017) suggested that police moral injury may

---

[2]For that matter, officers routinely have to adapt to decriminalization of various laws, which reflects the moral relativity of society, e.g., marijuana legalization.

lead to officers' susceptibility to PTSD and compassion fatigue, as well as to emotional and moral exhaustion. Therefore, moral injury may be another source of unethical decision-making among police officers.

Moral Distress. Moral distress has been defined as the psychological disequilibrium and inner conflict experienced by caregiving professionals when they are confronted with situations that prevent them from doing what is morally right (Jameton, 1984). In police work, many officers may experience distress when faced with the reality that they are not able to adequately attend or sufficiently help everyone who asks for police assistance. For that matter, they can begin to feel ineffective when racing from one call for service to the next, i.e., often not having enough time to thoroughly do what they think they could have done to help. In other cases, officers are required to enforce the law and to use force when necessary (e.g., crowd management during demonstrations), even in situations where they may not see the appropriateness. The dilemma occurs when officers are faced with a conflict between what they believe is morally right and what they are ordered by their supervisors to do or by what the organization's policies mandate them to do (Kälvemark, Höglund, Hansson, Westerholm, & Arnetz, 2004; Papazoglou & Chopko, 2017). Therefore, moral distress may lead officers to experience guilt, shame, and burnout, which jeopardize their foundational values of integrity, citizenship, justice, and pride (Laguna, Linn, Ward, & Ruplaukyte, 2010; Miller, 2000).

Moral Licensing. Another theory addresses a potential consequence of police officers' positive use of discretion. After giving a warning rather than a ticket or sending a pre-teen shoplifter home rather than to juvenile hall, police officers may feel as though they have earned a metaphorical pass on a future unethical decision. They essentially give themselves a license to be bad after "banking" credits for being good (e.g., Merritt, Effron, & Monin, 2010; Merritt et al., 2012). Results from numerous studies have demonstrated that people may feel entitled to act unethically after behaving in an ethically responsible way (e.g., Blanken, van de Ven, & Zeelenberg, 2015). From the police officers' perspective, the misconduct may be fairly minor, such as justifying leaving work early, conducting personal business (e.g., stopping at the bank or dry cleaners) on duty, or accepting a small gratuity after doing a good job. Research has shown, moreover, that this moral licensing "… is most likely to occur in situations where multiple goals conflict" (Mullen & Monin, 2016, p. 381).

More specifically, and quite germane to the discussion of the relations between the community and the police, research on moral licensing has shown that people may be more likely to express prejudiced attitudes after establishing some *bona fides* that they are not racist or sexist (Monin & Miller, 2001). By acting in a non-racist or sexist manner (e.g., comforting a female victim), police officers may believe that they have demonstrated moral credentials, which would mitigate negative reactions to future expressions of prejudiced attitudes.

In some rather astounding recent research, Cascio and Plant (2015) demonstrated a phenomenon they refer to as prospective moral licensing. They found that people will behave in "morally dubious ways by giving themselves credit for something they have not actually done," but "what they think they will do" at some point in the future (p. 115). It remains to be seen if similar findings would be observed with a sample of police officers, but there is no denying that police officers know with great confidence that their future behavior will include good deeds. As well, it is not uncommon to see officers acting in this way. For example, many officers (as well as police executives) ask for and expect admission and access to restricted areas of concerts and sporting events when they are in uniform, but not even working the event. The concept of moral licensing, based on the establishment of moral credits and moral credentials (and possibly future moral behavior), presents an additional challenge to police executives who seek effective strategies to curtail unethical behavior.

For example, commendation and discipline processes in police departments can encourage moral licensing when agencies are not careful about monitoring and demanding consistency from supervisors. Whether through written evaluations, written commendations, or even simple verbal appreciation and recognition, if one leader does it well for his/her team and another leader does not, it can create a sense of entitlement to "self reward" or pay oneself back for what a good leader should have noticed, commended, and rewarded. The same is true with the imposition of discipline. When those who comply with ethical rules see others not being held accountable it is easier to rationalize future indiscretions or take advantage because they have been performing as better officers by comparison.

Moral licensing also can take the form of a job performance slowdown when officers have had something taken away (pay or benefits), been asked to "do more with less," or, particularly, when departments are under public scrutiny for an incident that is being investigated. For example, it is not uncommon to hear an officer say, "If I'm not worth a 5% pay raise due to budget constraints, maybe I should reduce my activity by 5%."

Future-Self Orientation. Research has shown that short-term unethical behavior is likely to occur when people are disconnected from their future self (Bartels & Rip, 2010; Hershfield, Cohen, & Thompson, 2012). Specifically, "lies, bribes, false promises, and cheating" increased when participants did "not have a good sense of how my self will feel in the future" (Hershfield et al., 2012, pp. 299–300). It is believed that this may be due to a desire to "speed up rewards" in the present time (Bartels & Rip, 2010, p. 67).

One can argue that it would not be uncommon for police officers to lack continuity between their present and future self. This stems from present law enforcement training practices that accentuate dangerousness (e.g., Ford, 2003) as well as a prominent availability heuristic derived from near constant media reports of on-duty injuries to and deaths of police officers. Additionally, even if it is apocryphal, a common belief among police officers is that their post-retirement lifespan is rather short. Therefore, when police officers do not foresee a positive or healthy future self, they may feel less concerned about making unethical decisions in the present time.

Another form of a lack of future-self orientation stems from officers' looking unsuccessfully at their career opportunities. Officers usually carry a stigmatizing tail (spoken or unspoken) after being disciplined, even if only for a minor indiscretion.

Knowing that a promotion or a transfer to a specialized unit may no longer be an option or may be on hold for an inordinate length of time, officers' motivation may wane. This leaves them with a narrow career focus with few or dim future opportunities. Similarly, the same challenge to one's future-self orientation occurs among candidates who are unsuccessful in a promotional process. It becomes difficult to see beyond the "shame of their failure." They may resent the department for passing them over and may struggle to accept that they will not get the raise or the aspired promotion envisioned in their future plan. These feelings can contribute to the short-term reward mentally, which may lead to unethical behaviors (Bartels & Rip, 2010; Hershfield et al., 2012).

Slippery Slope. Research on the slippery slope helps to explain how unethical behavior can evolve. Welsh, Ordonez, Snyder, and Christian (2015) found that "small indiscretions may snowball into major violations over time if left unchecked" (p. 125). Additionally, Zhang, Cornwell, and Higgins (2014) determined that people are likely to repeat their ethical or unethical behavior in a manner that is consistent with their previous decision (p. 185). Thus, rather than recoiling from a transgression with a return to moral behavior, the slippery slope serves a disinhibiting effect, whereby one unethical decision makes it easier to repeat and, even to commit greater, unethical acts. These findings suggest that police officers who commit what would be considered a minor transgression through, for example, a sense of moral licensing, may be vulnerable to begin a trajectory of unethical decisions and behavior. For instance, many officers may consider certain behaviors too trivial, like leaving a little earlier and then a little earlier, veering out of their division or patrol beat, conducting a little personal business on duty, and so forth. Although it remains to be tested empirically how these "minor-wrongdoings" may lead to greater acts of misconduct, results from research on the slippery slope should alert police executives to develop early prevention strategies to combat police misconduct.

The Role of Emotions and Intuition. A compelling perspective in the literature on ethical decision-making focuses less on the cognitive processes associated with a moral decision and more on intuitive and emotional experiences (e.g., Dienstbier, Hillman, Lehnhoff, Hillman, & Valkenaar, 1975; Haidt, 2001). Zhong (2011) explained:

> *Thus, rather than viewing the formation of moral judgments as applying a set of neatly derived, universally applicable laws of logic, recent research on moral intuition and embodied morality proposes a messier picture in which morality is grounded in our flesh and bones and intertwined with emotions, tactile sensory input, and other concrete somatic experiences (p. 6).*

Specifically, his research showed that intuitive conditions led to better moral decision-making than strictly deliberative decision-making conditions (p. 16).

At the same time, there are potentially negative consequences of these intuitive decision-making conditions. Haidt, Rozin, McCauley, and Imada (1997) discussed the role that the emotion of disgust plays in individuals' judgments of what is morally reprehensible. Such a feeling is deeply ingrained in human physiological and tactile sensations associated with physical cleanliness, such that "moral intuitions may stem from socially adapted experiences of purity violations. Thus, it is no surprise that disgust, the signature emotional reaction to purity violations, plays an important role in determining moral judgment" (Zhong, 2011, p. 5). It appears, then, that ethical decision-making is impacted when individuals are physically disgusted, particularly to others' "lack of cleanliness."

The previous concern is extremely relevant when discussing unethical behavior among police officers. Police officers are trained to be vigilant, which tends to make them quite sensitive to sensory stimuli. On a daily basis, police officers encounter people and situations that are filthy and smelly, living conditions that seem uninhabitable, and circumstances that are, simply, to many people perceived as disgusting. Officers are frequently mandated to touch people covered with various bodily fluids. Also, officers have to remain alert so as not to be infected by others' contagious diseases or stuck by hypodermic needles left in people's pockets. The resulting level of disgust may contribute to dehumanizing those with whom they come in contact, which makes it less discordant to treat them unethically. This last issue will be discussed further in the next section on moral disengagement.

A different aspect of intuitive decision-making stems from the physiological state that most people experience when they contemplate acting immorally. Research consistently demonstrated that people tend to react to impending unethical behavior, such as lying and cheating, with negative somatic conditions (e.g., sweaty palms, elevated heart rate) (e.g., Zhong, 2011). This suggests that people who are desensitized to acting deceptively will feel less guilt which results in milder, if any, negative somatic states. Without the role of these physiological reactions, people may be more likely to make unethical decisions. Once again, although this is something to be explored empirically, it is possible to infer from the existing literature that police training, which includes considerable amounts of repetition, reduces police officers' physiological reactions to, for example, their legally approved acts of deception, which may in turn make them less intrinsically aversive to acting unethically.

Beyond the relationship between physiological and emotional states vis-à-vis ethical behavior, recent research demonstrated the important role that emotions play in ethical decision-making (Fida et al., 2015; Krishnakumar & Rymph, 2012). In very clear terms, Krishnakumar and Rymph (2012) wrote: "The more skilled a person is in dealing with his/her emotions, the more likely that person is to make more ethical decisions" (p. 321). Their research showed that less ethical decisions were made by people who experienced higher levels of negative emotions, but that individuals with high emotional intelligence made better decisions possibly because they were better able to cope with their negative emotions (p. 336–337). Furthermore, Fida et al. (2015) showed that negative emotions, which resulted from frustrating work situations, led to greater rationalization of unethical work behaviors. They posited that "the perception of organizational context as unsupportive may reduce empathy and therefore facilitate the activation of cognitive processes aimed at reducing guilt or shame that would deter resorting to harmful actions …" (p. 140).

Taken together, the literature on emotions and ethical decision-making is central to any discussion of police integrity. Police officers routinely find themselves in situations that evoke strong emotions. These situations include encountering every form of human suffering and depravity. However, they also involve frustrations associated with organizational practices, administrative bureaucracy, and the realities of the criminal justice system. Although high emotional intelligence may mitigate the impact that these intense emotions have on police officers' ethical decision-making, when it comes to reducing police misconduct, greater attention needs to be given to emotional regulation and emotion-centered prevention strategies.

Moral Disengagement. One of the most comprehensive theories to explain why people make unethical decisions is moral disengagement (Bandura, 1999). Essentially, to commit an unethical act, people have to "turn off" the processes that would typically inhibit them from behaving unethically (Detert, Trevino, & Sweitzer, 2008). The result is that people justify their unethical behavior through a variety of self-deceptive measures (Tenbrunsel & Messick, 2004). Bandura (1999) described eight mechanisms through which moral disengagement occurs. Each of these mechanisms serves to distance the person from feeling morally responsible for committing unethical behavior by: reducing the perceived seriousness of the act (Moral Justification, Advantageous Comparison, and Euphemistic Labeling); reducing the perceived negative ramifications of the act (Disregard or Distortion of Consequences); minimizing one's role in committing the act (Displacement of Responsibility and Diffusion of Responsibility); or, shifting the focus of the act onto the recipients of the act by seeing them as deserving (Dehumanization) or even responsible for the act (Attribution of Blame) (Bandura, 1999).

Research on moral disengagement has been informative. In a longitudinal study of adolescents, moral disengagement predicted levels of aggression and violence (Paciello, Fida, Tramontano, Lupinetti, & Caprara, 2008). In the workplace, moral disengagement has been shown to "initiate … facilitate … (and) perpetuate corruption" (Moore, 2008, p. 129). In a more recent series of studies, Moore, Detert, Trevino, Baker, and Mayer (2012) found that "the propensity to morally disengage correlates positively with Machiavellianism and relativism; negatively with moral identity, empathy, cognitive moral development, idealism, and dispositional guilt; and is not significantly correlated with dispositional shame" (p. 35). Furthermore, studying a sample of police detectives, Loyens (2014) demonstrated the extent to which "rule bending" was explained by moral justification and displacement of responsibility (p.72). Loyens (2014) stressed that these mechanisms are rooted in social contexts, which include job characteristics, such that "sometimes situational aspects or organizational patterns can even 'override' individual values and compel people to engage in actions they would otherwise not take part in" (p. 64).

Each of the following mechanisms, through which moral disengagement occurs, can be demonstrated through the lenses of routine police training, organizational priorities and policies, peer interaction, and officer wellness.

Moral Justification. Moral justification occurs when "detrimental conduct is made personally and socially acceptable by portraying it as serving socially worthy or moral purposes" (Bandura, 1999, p. 194). This appears to be the basic mechanism when considering noble cause corruption (e.g., Caldero & Crank, 2011; Crank et al., 2007; Loyens, 2014). For example, police officers may feel justified when breaking a rule to apprehend a criminal or when deceiving a witness to obtain cooperation.

Euphemistic Labeling. Euphemistic labeling occurs when "language is widely used to make harmful conduct respectable and to reduce personal responsibility for it" (Bandura, 1999, p. 195). This can be done at an organizational level through creative spin doctoring, which dilutes the significance of a morally ambiguous or unjust action. For example, relocating homeless people from their preferred location may be viewed as more acceptable or less disruptive by calling it a "homeless sweep." Similarly, on an individual level, language euphemisms facilitate the self-deception that may be necessary to make one's own unethical behavior less inconsistent with one's moral self-concept (e.g., Tenbrunsel & Messick, 2004). For example, the terms "deceptive devices" and "creative investigative techniques" can be used to describe numerous types of morally questionable law enforcement activities, which do not cause police officers to doubt whether or not they are behaving unethically in such situations.

Advantageous Comparison. In advantageous comparison, "How a behavior is viewed is colored by what it is compared against. By exploiting the contrast principle, reprehensible acts can be made righteous" (Bandura, 1999, p. 196). When the unethical behavior of officers from a particular law enforcement agency dominates a news cycle (e.g., the LAPD officers' treatment of Rodney King), it is easy for top executives from other agencies to minimize the severity of their own officers' behavior. This also may happen on a micro-level when officers learn of a colleague's termination for an egregious act and feel as though their moral indiscretions are quite innocuous.

Displacement of Responsibility. Displacement of responsibility occurs when people "view their actions as stemming from the dictates of authorities; they do not feel personally responsible for the actions" (Bandura, 1999, p. 196). History is filled with deplorable examples of people attempting to mitigate responsibility by claiming that they were just following orders (e.g., Nazi soldiers and doctors during the Holocaust). This is a particularly challenging concern for law enforcement agencies when officers assert during investigations into their ethically questionable behavior that they were only doing what they were taught (or shown) to do in the academy or by a Field Training Officer (e.g., Bennett, 1984; Chappell & Lanza-Kaduce, 2010; Ford, 2003; Haarr, 2001).

On a more frequent basis, officers may not feel ethically responsible when they are acting in ways that they believe are responsive to the community. For example, a direct consequence of community oriented policing after asking community members to describe their enforcement priorities is that officers view themselves as simply "oiling the squeaky wheel." When community members are encouraged to "say something when they see something," a radio call is generated, which then provides the officers with the opportunity to displace responsibility for these enforcement activities onto community priorities. Such a situation gives officers the permission and apparent probable cause to strictly monitor or even arrest people who community members argue are "the criminal element."

Diffusion of Responsibility. Diffusion of responsibility allows individuals to diminish accountability by sharing blame with others. "People act more cruelly under group responsibility than when they hold themselves personally responsible for their actions" (Bandura, 1999, p. 198). Police officers support each other during calls for service. There are times when a group of officers may engage in behavior that none of them would consider when alone. When confronted, they can "use the argument: 'I only played such a small part that I am not really responsible' or 'Everybody does it'" (Loyens, 2014, p. 65). Such situations may occur during officer involved shooting cases; as soon as one officer fires his/her weapon, other officers on the scene start shooting as well.

Disregard or Distortion of Consequences. This emotional disengagement mechanism occurs when people fail to recognize the actual consequences of their behavior. "As long as the harmful results of one's conduct are ignored, minimized, distorted, or disbelieved, there is little reason for self-censure to be activated" (Bandura, 1999, p. 199). Disregarding or distorting consequences occurs routinely during noble cause corruption, whereby officers ignore or minimize their actions by focusing on ends rather than means. Many police officers simply do not recognize the seriousness of their unethical behaviors (e.g., Lobnikar & Mesko, 2015). For example, an illegal search may result in an otherwise legitimate arrest being thrown out. At the same time, when officers observe a lack of organizational response to misconduct (i.e., inadequate and inconsistent disciplinary procedures), they are likely to believe that there will be few, if any, consequences for their unethical actions.

Dehumanization. Dehumanization allows perpetrators of unethical behavior to disengage from "self-censure for cruel conduct ... by stripping people of human qualities. Once dehumanized, they are no longer viewed as persons with feelings, hope, and concerns but as subhuman objects" (Bandura, 1999, p. 200). On a specific level, unethical acts may not result in any self-reprisal when officers refer to and, thus, perceive a crime suspect as less than human (e.g., "dirt bag," "animal,"). On a broader level, which may be fostered and perpetuated by overt or implicit organizational messages, dehumanization occurs when police officers maintain an *us* versus *them* attitude about the public they are sworn to serve and protect (e.g., Detert et al., 2008). Officers regularly believe that people bring despair onto themselves and that problems such as addiction, homelessness, and alcoholism are the result of personal weakness. Also, officers may use derogatory epithets to refer to those residing in low income or crime-ridden areas of a city. Such demeaning terms can serve to alleviate the emotional distress police officers may feel when seeing and interacting with people living in such despairing conditions. Simultaneously, though, the dehumanization contributes to moral disengagement, which makes the commission of unethical behaviors more tolerable and more acceptable emotionally, rationally, and behaviorally.

Current budgetary limitations, which result in a lack of staffing and, potentially, equipment, also perpetuate the dehumanizing process. As a result of the rush that is imposed by a constant barrage of radio calls and the necessity to "clear" them, officers can become resentful of the repetitive calls to handle the same drunk, drug addict, or other subjects who comprise the bulk of their directed activity. Furthermore, the ongoing use of police and fire personnel as transportation to hospitals gets exasperating. Unfortunately, most departments cannot decline to provide service to chronic abusers of police service. It also is rather common among some officers to dehumanize these repeat individuals according to their condition or complaint.

Attribution of Blame. *Attribution of blame occurs when:*

> *... people view themselves as faultless victims driven to injurious conduct by forcible provocation. Punitive conduct is, thus, seen as justifiable ... Victims then get blamed for bringing suffering on themselves ... By fixing blame on others or on circumstances, not only are one's own injurious actions excusable, but one even can feel self-righteous in the process (Bandura, 1999, p. 203).*

This is not a new concept or one that is unique to moral disengagement (e.g., Ryan, 1976). However, in conjunction with dehumanization, it helps to explain the attitude of many police officers who come to believe that people living in certain areas deserve whatever happens to them. Likewise, this construct explains why officers may adopt the notion that certain victims attract the victimization onto themselves. Such a perspective allows some police officers to feel faultless when committing unethical acts against certain groups of individuals.

Moral disengagement (and the specific mechanisms that comprise it) is a meaningful theory when attempting to understand police misconduct. The widespread extent of moral disengagement among police officers in general remains to be examined empirically (see Loyens, 2014), but a strong argument can be made that current police training and police practices tend to foster this phenomenon. For example, it is pervasive among many officers, from the time that they are hired, through training, and well into their careers to be congratulated and characterized as "elite," "the cream of the crop," "special," or being in the top 2% of those who applied. The mechanisms of moral disengagement may flourish when officers are reinforced and then continually propped up to believe that they are superior to members of the community.

When it comes to preventing misconduct, police executives would be wise to focus on efforts to significantly reduce not only moral disengagement among the workforce, but also to directly address and eliminate their role in its occurrence.

The discussion of theoretical explanations for police misconduct has a few limitations. Although conclusions from many of the cited studies were based on empirical evidence, few of them included a law enforcement sample. Considerably more research should be done to empirically determine if the relationship between a given theory and unethical decision-making would be applied and generalized to police populations. Additionally, there is considerable conceptual overlap among many of the theories presented. They should not be viewed as distinct causal explanations for police officers' unethical decision-making. Instead, these theories are presented to provide a broad view of possible explanations of the etiology and processes associated with police misconduct. It is quite likely that various factors lead police officers to make unethical decisions; also, there may be multiple factors involved in a single police officer's misconduct. Therefore, such a wide-angle perspective is necessary in order to develop the most efficacious prevention and intervention strategies to cope with this complex issue in policing.

Prevention and intervention strategies

The various theories to explain unethical decision-making provide specific guidance to those who are interested in developing and implementing efforts to obviate police misconduct. Moreover, there is considerable overlap among amelioration strategies that would reverse or prevent the occurrence of police misconduct. Although the ultimate goal is to improve police officers' ethical decision-making, the following sections focus on considerations from current literature. Police executives are encouraged to consider these best practices when developing and implementing policies and training curricula, so that they can achieve the greatest impact on their officers' performance.

Hiring efforts

As previously mentioned, recent research demonstrated that new law enforcement hires had higher than average self-reported integrity scores (Blumberg et al., 2016). Nevertheless, a more concerted effort to screen-out dishonest or unethical job applicants through direct integrity testing could be considered (e.g., Berry, Sackett, & Wiemann, 2007). It has been reported that there are over "40 published integrity tests, and at least 15–20 of these are in widespread use …" Murphy, 2000, p. 268). Interestingly, although these tests appear to be adequate in predicting job performance, at least in particular jobs, the mechanism for this has yet to be determined (Murphy & Dzieweczynski, 2005, p. 350).

Instead of focusing on integrity testing during the hiring process, and especially considering the results on the decline in integrity occurring one year post-academy training, hiring efforts should instead focus on other measurable traits. One approach is to take a screening-in orientation in which agencies only hire applicants whose background investigation can verify overtly practical examples of strong ethical decision-making and consistently high levels of integrity (Blumberg, Griffin, & Jones, 2014). Another approach is to focus on screening-out applicants who are prone to moral disengagement. Detert et al. (2008) specifically recommended to avoid hiring applicants who have been assessed "to be high on trait cynicism and chance locus of control orientation or low on moral identity and empathy …" (p. 386). Similarly, applicants who are determined through comprehensive background investigations to have displayed high levels of aggression during early adolescence may be more vulnerable to becoming morally disengaged (e.g., Paciello et al., 2008). Lastly, Moore et al. (2012) developed a brief instrument to assess applicants' level of moral disengagement, which looks somewhat promising in its ability to predict job misbehavior (p. 40).

The role of police training

Out of necessity, and because of the relatively limited duration of most police academies, police training disproportionately focuses on the use of force, defensive tactics, and worst-case scenario problem-solving where physical survival is the primary consideration. However, prioritizing physical survival in police training can have a deleterious impact on new officers coming into the profession with a once balanced and healthy outlook of the world. For most new officers, preparing to work in dangerous, toxic, and life-threatening situations through academy and field training, which predisposes them to expect the worst, is in stark contrast with how they will spend most of their time on-duty. Unfortunately, the overemphasis on worst-case scenarios may mentally predispose officers to excessive suspiciousness and leave them expecting the worst from each member of the community they serve, which is a prescribed trajectory toward moral disengagement.

Although previous research has discussed the potential negative impact of training on police integrity, training both at the academy and post-academy (i.e. Advanced Officer Training) levels can focus specifically on efforts to prevent police misconduct. Initially, these efforts should focus on having police recruits and officers identify and solve complex moral dilemmas (e.g., Kish-Gephart, Harrison, & Trevino, 2010; Sturm, 2015), which police officers will likely encounter on and off the job. To this end, it is imperative that training explicitly underscores the serious consequences that officers may face for violating ethical mandates (e.g., Lobnikar & Mesko, 2015). It is as essential for training to help officers mentally prepare for these on- and off-duty ethical dilemmas as it is to prepare them for any other job responsibility.

Police training should incorporate more case studies of officer misconduct and ethical breaches from within the officers' agency. It becomes easy to defensively dismiss misconduct by officers from other agencies as the result of differences in agency standards or values. Discipline imposed for misconduct may also vary, allowing officers to distance themselves from the possibility of similar consequences from their own agency. Although there may be some challenges with releasing specific information about employee misconduct and subsequent discipline, the ability to learn from others' behavior and consequences from within one's agency can be invaluable.

Another component of police training should address aspects of moral disengagement. It is less likely for officers to behave unethically when *us* versus *them* attitudes are eliminated. One approach to achieve this is through "priming participants to feel connected through the thread of common morality" (Young & Durwin, 2013, p. 305). This moral realism is seen as a mechanism to help people feel connected to even those who are quite dissimilar from oneself (Anderson & Papazoglou, 2014; Young & Durwin, 2013). Police officers can be trained to identify ways in which they may relate to others. For example, when interacting with a criminal suspect or a disrespectful community member, officers may find that they share an affinity for a sports team or listen to the same music. Likewise, when interacting with victims, training can help officers to "put a face to the pain" by humanizing them in an effort to maintain compassion. By emphasizing commonalities (e.g., "The same thing could have happened to my parents."), training can help officers to improve empathy and to reduce cynicism (e.g., Anderson & Papazoglou, 2014; Creighton & Blumberg, 2016).

Emotional Intelligence. The previous paragraph hints at the promising area of emotional intelligence. Although beyond the scope of the present chapter, research on emotional intelligence has consistently shown that individuals with higher emotional intelligence tend to make fewer unethical decisions (e.g., Krishnakumar & Rymph, 2012). Also, the good news is that it appears that emotional intelligence can be improved through specific training programs (e.g., Nelis et al., 2011; Schutte, Malouff, & Thorsteinsson, 2013), including police training programs (e.g., Ebrahim Al Ali, Garner, & Magadley, 2012). As Brunetto, Teo, Shacklock, and Farr-Wharton (2012) stated: "It may be just as important for a modern day police officer to be emotionally aware as it is for them to be physically fit and knowledgeable about the law" (p.436). There is strong evidence that emotional intelligence training could help police officers in many ways, including, ultimately, to maintain a commitment to ethical decision-making. Such emotional intelligence training should not be limited to theoretical discussions, but can be infused in traditional training formats where officers process ethical dilemmas and engage in ethical decision-making. The inclusion of emotional intelligence objectives also can be seamlessly incorporated into existing tactical and operational field training, so that officers receive direct support to strengthen these skills.

Wellness efforts

With increased empathy and lower cynicism, which are byproducts of less dehumanization, police officers run the risk of experiencing compassion fatigue (e.g., Battle, 2012; Papazoglou, 2017; Tehrani, 2010). Compassion fatigue can occur when helping professionals continually deal with traumatized people; the ongoing exposure to others' emotional pain can lead to a variety of distressing symptoms (Anderson & Papazoglou, 2015; Papazoglou, 2017). For police officers, routine contact with victims of crimes, accidents, and natural and manmade disasters can take a long-term toll on their physical, emotional, cognitive, and social functioning. This makes it even more important for law enforcement agencies to emphasize officers' wellness efforts.

With regard to ethical decision-making, in addition to supporting projects to improve and maintain high levels of emotional intelligence, wellness efforts should provide resources for officers to develop effective and well-rounded stress management skills. They also can focus directly on bolstering officers' future-self orientation (e.g., Hershfield et al., 2012). This can include retirement planning seminars, newsletters that contain a regular feature on retired officers' activities and updates, and ongoing initiatives to improve officers' health, fitness, and nutrition.

Wellness (and ethics, for that matter) needs to be treated as a perishable skill. Research on emotional intelligence (e.g., Caldwell & Hayes, 2016; Ebrahim Al Ali et al., 2012;

Nellis et al., 2011; Smith, Profetto-McGrath, & Cummings, 2009) has demonstrated the inter-relationships among high emotional intelligence, stress/trauma management, and ethical decision making. Therefore, wellness and efforts to increase and maintain emotional intelligence should be viewed as critical to police performance as other perishable skills, which receive ongoing mandated, in-service training and assessment at regular intervals throughout a law enforcement career, such as firearms, defensive tactics, and emergency vehicle operations. Police agencies should not wait until there is a problem in these areas to require "re-qualification." Similarly, when it comes to wellness, law enforcement agencies can no longer afford to remain reactive and respond only after a significant incident occurs. Proactive, ongoing efforts to maintain officer wellness should constitute a critical component of a comprehensive program to combat police misconduct.

Community relations & community-oriented policing

When police organizations take proactive steps to have their officers engage members of the community in non-enforcement activities (e.g., participation in local charity fund-raisers, attendance at various school functions, and involvement at street fairs and other community events), they show a commitment to eliminating the *us* versus *them* orientation among their officers as well as among community members. The impact of this from the moral disengagement literature is evident. In addition, these activities help to build mutual respect and trust between local police agencies and their communities. Through greater familiarity with all members of the community, police officers may begin to reduce their often unrealistically increased sense of dangerousness.

Likewise, a recommitment to community oriented policing may lead to greater ethical decision-making. Cooper (2012) believed that "police who regularly employ community or problem-oriented policing activities also engage less often in noble cause corruption" (p. 178). For many reasons, including creating a sense of accountability to the community, this approach has police officers emphasizing their connectedness with the community, which makes it more difficult for the mechanisms of moral disengagement to flourish.

Oversight and discipline

When one understands that numerous sources are responsible for police officers' un-ethical decision-making, a logical conclusion to draw is that misconduct can never be totally eliminated. In fact, one could argue that it is a mistake for law enforcement executives to consider police misconduct as an anomaly. The job of police officer is very difficult and some mistakes, including certain unethical decisions, may be quite challenging for certain officers to avoid making. It would be far more advantageous to reinterpret unethical decision-making on the part of police officers as a "normal" component of the job. This would help to destigmatize the behavior, bring it into the open, significantly reduce officers' tendencies to cover for each other, and address it in an organizationally healthy and constructive manner. Analogous to committing a foul during a football game, in this case, the offender is not shamed for the indiscretion. Yellow, and sometimes red, cards could occur as a predictable part of the job. Appropriate grievance processes would remain, and the offending officer would ultimately accept the discipline (assuming that he/she wants to remain employed).

Expecting misconduct to occur, however, does not mean that it will be ignored or tolerated. Quite the contrary, a crucial step toward preventing unethical behavior is to implement fair, consistent, and, even, strict intervention strategies. Porter and Warrender (2009) argued, "If punishment was harsher, or more likely, it may discourage officers to engage in deviant behavior" (p. 96). There are, of course, realistic obstacles to implementation of harsher punishments for police misconduct. Current practices include unnecessarily long bureaucratic time delays for administering discipline. Police unions will need to cooperate, and collective bargaining agreements will have to be modified under the premise of collaboration in the workplace. Nevertheless, addressing police misconduct should be the responsibility of all stakeholders.

Beyond disciplinary interventions, law enforcement executives who accept the likelihood of police misconduct will encourage their agencies to develop a variety of interventions and preventative measures. Punch (2000) argued that this occurs through "aggressive investigations and promoting integrity" (p. 317). Much of Punch's (2000) focus recognized the need for agencies to destigmatize the problem, so that they can address the issue more proactively. "Alongside an Internal Affairs Unit, there should be a department responsible for coordinating the efforts to enhance integrity through education, publications, codes, seminars, role-play and simulations, posters, guest speakers, surveys, and the generation of positive news" (Punch, 2000, pp. 320–321).

Moreover, law enforcement organizations (including leadership in police unions) should consider including (or strengthening) categories of objective, observable evidence of ethical behavior on officers' annual performance evaluations. Officers whose ratings fall short of these standards associated with positive incidents of ethical behavior would be targeted for early intervention efforts. It would be more efficient to address minor indiscretions before they reach the slippery slope where officers are at greater risk of committing more serious offenses. Law enforcement executives can do more to prevent a decline in police officers' commitment to ethical principles if their goal is to curtail, rather than to eliminate, police misconduct.

Regardless of the cause of police misconduct, theories that explain unethical decision-making guide preventative and intervention strategies. Rather than approaching it in an ephemeral fashion, the authors believe that law enforcement agencies should design and implement comprehensive programs and goal-oriented policies to combat police misconduct on an ongoing basis. Such programs and policies should incorporate the foundational theoretical framework of ethical decision-making in order to address and contain the various sources of misconduct in the police context. Finally, when one understands the myriad reasons why police officers make unethical decisions, a new narrative emerges in which police professionals will no longer focus on the "bad apples or bad barrels" ideology. Instead, police professionals will begin focusing on improving officer and organizational wellness and on finding ways to proactively maintain police officer integrity.

References

Anderson, J. P., & Papazoglou, K. (2014). Friends under fire: Cross-cultural relationships and trauma exposure among police officers. *Traumatology, 20*(3), 182–190. https://doi.org/10.1037/h0099403.

Anderson, J. P., & Papazoglou, K. (2015). Compassion fatigue and compassion satisfaction among police officers: An understudied topic. *International Journal of Emergency Mental Health and Human Resilience, 17*(3), 661–663. https://doi.org/10.4172/1522-4821.1000243.

Ashforth, B. E., & Anand, V. (2003). The normalization of corruption in organizations. *Research in Organizational Behavior, 25*, 1–52. https://doi.org/10.1016/S0191-3085(03)25001-2.

Bandura, A. (1999). Moral disengagement in the perpetration of inhumanities. *Personality and Social Psychology Review, 3*(3), 193–209. https://doi.org/10.1207/s15327957pspr0303_3.

Baron, R. A., Zhao, H., & Miao, Q. (2015). Personal motives, moral disengagement, and unethical decisions by entrepreneurs: Cognitive mechanisms on the 'slippery slope'. *Journal of Business Ethics, 128*(1), 107–118. https://doi.org/10.1007/s10551-014-2078-y.

Bartels, D. M., & Rip, L. J. (2010). Psychological connectedness and intertemporal choice. *Journal of Experimental Psychology: General, 139*, 49–69. https://doi.org/10.1037/a0018062.

Battle, L. (2012). Compassion fatigue, compassion satisfaction, and burnout among police officers who have experienced previous perceived traumas. *Dissertation Abstracts International Section A, 73*, 2296.

Benjamin, M. (1990). *Splitting the difference: Compromise and integrity in ethics and politics.* Lawrence, KS: University Press of Kansas.

Berg, B. L. (1990). First day at the police academy: Stress-reaction-training as a screening-out technique. *Journal of Contemporary Criminal Justice, 6*, 89–105.

Bennett, R. R. (1984). Becoming blue: A longitudinal study of police recruit occupational socialization. *Journal of Police Science and Administration, 12*(1), 47–58.

Berry, C. M., Sackett, P. R., & Wiemann, S. (2007). A review of recent developments in integrity test research. *Personnel Psychology, 60*(2), 271–301. https://doi.org/10.1111/j.1744-6570.2007.00074.x.

Blanken, I., van de Ven, N., & Zeelenberg, M. (2015). A meta-analytic review of moral licensing. *Personality and Social Psychology Bulletin, 41*(4), 540–558. https://doi.org/10.1177/0146167215572134.

Blumberg, D.M. & Giromini, L. (unpublished manuscript). Reexamining police integrity one year post-academy.

Blumberg, D. M., Giromini, L., & Jacobson, L. B. (2016). Impact of police academy training on recruits' integrity. *Police Quarterly, 19*(1), 63–86. https://doi.org/10.1177/1098611115608322.

Blumberg, D. M., Griffin, D. A., & Jones, O. (2014). Improving peace officer hiring decisions: An integrated organizational approach. *Organizational Cultures: An International Journal, 13*(3), 1–19. Retrieved from http://www.i-scholar.in/index.php/OCIJCG/article/view/57304.

Brown, T. A., Sautter, J. A., Littvay, L., Sautter, A. C., & Bearnes, B. (2010). Ethics and personality: Empathy and narcissism as moderators of ethical decision making in business. *The Journal of Education for Business, 85*(4), 203–208. https://doi.org/10.1080/08832320903449501.

Brunetto, Y., Teo, S. T. T., Shacklock, K., & Farr-Wharton, R. (2012). Emotional intelligence, job satisfaction, well-being, and engagement: Explaining organizational commitment and turnover intentions in policing. *Human Resource Management Journal, 22*(4), 428–441. https://doi.org/10.1111/j.1748-8583.2012.00198.x.

Caldero, M. A., & Crank, J. P. (2011). *Police ethics: The corruption of noble cause*. Burington, MA: Elsevier, Inc.

Caldwell, C., & Hayes, L. A. (2016). Self-efficacy and self-awareness: Moral insights to increased leader effectiveness. *The Journal of Management Development, 35*(9), 1163–1173. https://doi.org/10.1108/JMD-01-2016-0011.

Cascio, J., & Plant, E. A. (2015). Prospective moral licensing: Does anticipating doing good later allow you to be bad now? *Journal of Experimental Social Psychology, 56*, 110–116. https://doi.org/10.1016/j.jesp.2014.09.009.

Chappell, A. T., & Lanza-Kaduce, L. (2010). Police academy socialization: Understanding the lessons learned in a paramilitary—bureaucratic organization. *Journal of Contemporary Ethnography, 39*(2), 187–214. https://doi.org/10.1177/0891241609342230.

Cooper, J. A. (2012). Noble cause corruption as a consequence of role conflict in the police organization. *Policing and Society, 22*(2), 169–184. https://doi.org/10.1080/10439463.2011.605132.

Crank, J., Flaherty, D., & Giacomazzi, A. (2007). The noble cause: An empirical assessment. *Journal of Criminal Justice, 35*(1), 103–116. https://doi.org/10.1016/j.jcrimjus.2006.11.019.

Creighton, S., & Blumberg, D. M. (March, 2016). Officer wellness is fundamental to officer safety: The San Diego Model. In *Police executive research forum, critical issues in policing series: Guiding principles in use of force* (pp. 23–24). Washington, D.C.: Police Executive Research Forum.

Dean, G., Bell, P., & Lauchs, M. (2010). Conceptual framework for managing knowledge of police deviance. *Policing and Society, 20*(2), 204–222. https://doi.org/10.1080/10439461003668476.

Detert, J. R., Trevino, L. K., & Sweitzer, V. L. (2008). Moral disengagement in ethical decision-making: A study of antecedents and outcomes. *Journal of Applied Psychology, 93*(2), 374–391. https://doi.org/10.1037/0021-9010.93.2.374.

Dienstbier, R. A., Hillman, D., Lehnhoff, J., Hillman, J., & Valkenaar, M. C. (1975). An emotion-attribution approach to moral behavior: Interfacing cognitive and avoidance theories of moral development. *Psychological Review, 82*(4), 299–315.

Ebrahim Al Ali, O., Garner, I., & Magadley, W. (2012). An exploration of the relationship between emotional intelligence and job performance in police organizations. *Journal of Police and Criminal Psychology, 27*(1), 1–8. https://doi.org/10.1007/s11896-011-9088-9.

Festinger, L., & Carlsmith, J. M. (1959). Cognitive consequences of forced compliance. *Journal of Abnormal And Social Psychology, 58*, 203–210.

Fida, R., Paciello, M., Tramontano, C., Fontaine, R. G., Barbaranelli, C., & Farnese, M. L. (2015). An integrative approach to understanding counterproductive work behavior: The roles of stressors, negative emotions, and moral disengagement. *Journal of Business Ethics, 130*(1), 131–144. https://doi.org/10.1007/s10551-014-2209-5.

Ford, R. E. (2003). Saying one thing, meaning another: The role of parables in police training. *Police Quarterly, 6*(1), 84–100. https://doi.org/10.1177/1098611102250903.

Garner, R. (2005). Police attitudes: The impact of experience after training. *Applied Psychology in Criminal Justice, 1*(1), 56–70.

Graves, T. R., Pleban, R. J., Miller, M. L., Branciforte, J. V., Donigian, A. M., Johnson, V., et al. (2010). *Enhancing perception in ethical decision making: A method to address ill-defined training domains (research report No. ARI-RR-1932).* Fort Benning, GA: U.S. Army Research Institute for the Behavioral and Social Sciences.

Haarr, R. N. (2001). The making of a community policing officer: The impact of basic training and occupational socialization on police recruits. *Police Quarterly, 4*(4), 402–433. https://doi.org/10.1177/109861101129197923.

Haarr, R. N. (2005). Factors affecting the decision of police recruits to "drop out" of police work. *Police Quarterly, 8*(4), 431–453. https://doi.org/10.1177/1098611103261821.

Haidt, J. (2001). The emotional dog and its rational tail: A social intuitionist approach to moral judgment. *Psychological Review, 108*(4), 814–834. https://doi.org/10.1037/0033-295X.108.4.814.

Haidt, J., Rozin, P., McCauley, C., & Imada, S. (1997). Body, psyche, and culture: The relationship between disgust and morality. *Psychology & Developing Societies, 9*(1), 107–131. https://doi.org/10.1177/097133369700900105.

Heffernan, W. C. (1982). Two approaches to police ethics. *Criminal Justice Review, 7*(1), 28–35. https://doi.org/10.1177/073401688200700109.

Hershfield, H. E., Cohen, T. R., & Thompson, L. (2012). Short horizons and tempting situations: Lack of continuity to our future selves leads to unethical decision making and behavior. *Organizational Behavior and Human Decision Processes, 117*(2), 298–310. https://doi.org/10.1016/j.obhdp.2011.11.002.

Jameton, A. (1984). *Nursing practice: The ethical issues.* Englewood Cliffs, NJ: Prentice-Hall.

Jinkerson, J. D. (2016). Defining and assessing moral injury: A syndrome perspective. *Traumatology, 22*(2), 122–130. https://doi.org/10.1037/trm0000069.

Kalvemark, S., Hoglund, A. T., Hansson, M. G., Westerholm, P., & Arnetz, B. (2004). Living with conflict: Ethical dilemma and moral distress in the healthcare system. *Social Science & Medicine, 58,* 1075–1084. https://doi.org/10.1016/S0277-9536(03)00279-X.

Kendall, M. (April 10, 2015). *The police can't police themselves. And now the public is too scared to cooperate with them.* The Washington Post. Retrieved from https://www.washingtonpost.com.

Kish-Gephart, J. J., Harrison, D. A., & Trevino, L. K. (2010). Bad apples, bad cases, and bad barrels: Meta-analytic evidence about sources of unethical decisions at work. *Journal of Applied Psychology, 95*(1), 1–31. https://doi.org/10.1037/a0017103.

Klockars, C. B., Ivkovic, S. K., & Haberfeld, M. R. (2004). *The contours of police integrity.* Thousand Oaks, CA: Sage.

Klockars, C. B., Ivkovic, S. K., & Haberfeld, M. R. (2006). *Enhancing police integrity.* Dordrecht, The Netherlands: Springer.

Klockars, C. B., Ivkovic, S. K., Harver, W. E., & Haberfeld, M. R. (2000). *The measurement of police integrity.* US Department of Justice, Office of Justice Programs, National Institute of Justice.

Krishnakumar, S., & Rymph, D. (2012). Uncomfortable ethical decisions: The role of negative emotions and emotional intelligence in ethical decision-making. *Journal of Managerial Issues, 24*(3), 321–344.

Krueger, L. M. (2014). *Academic dishonesty among associate degree nursing students* (Vol. 74). Dissertation Abstracts International Section A.

Laguna, L., Lim, A., Ward, K., & Rupslaukyte, R. (2010). An examination of authoritarian personality traits among police officers: The role of experience. *Journal of Police and Criminal Psychology, 25*(2), 99–104. https://doi.org/10.1007/s11896-009-9060-0.

LaMotte, A. D., & Murphy, C. M. (2017). Trauma, posttraumatic stress disorder symptoms, and dissociative experiences during men's intimate partner violence perpetration. *Psychological Trauma: Theory, Research, Practice, and Policy, 9*(5), 567−574. https://doi.org/10.1037/tra0000205.

Litz, B. T., Stein, N., Delaney, E., Lebowitz, L., Nash, W. P., Silva, C., et al. (2009). Moral injury and moral repair in war veterans: A preliminary model and intervention strategy. *Clinical Psychology Review, 29*(8), 695−706. https://doi.org/10.1016/j.cpr.2009.07.003.

Lobnikar, B., & Mesko, G. (2015). Perception of police corruption and the level of integrity among Slovenian police officers. *Police Practice and Research, 16*(4), 341−353. https://doi.org/10.1080/15614263.2015.1038031.

Loyens, K. (2014). Rule bending by morally disengaged detectives: An ethnographic study. *Police Practice and Research, 15*(1), 62−74. https://doi.org/10.1080/15614263.2013.770941.

Manzella, C., & Papazoglou, K. (2014). Training police trainees about ways to manage trauma and loss. *International Journal of Mental Health Promotion, 16*(2), 103−116. https://doi.org/10.1080/14623730.2014.903609.

Merritt, A. C., Effron, D. A., Fein, S., Savitsky, K. K., Tuller, D. M., & Monin, B. (2012). The strategic pursuit of moral credentials. *Journal of Experimental Social Psychology, 48*(3), 774−777. https://doi.org/10.1016/j.jesp.2011.12.017.

Merritt, A. C., Effron, D. A., & Monin, B. (2010). Moral self-licensing: When being good frees us to be bad. *Social and Personality Psychology Compass, 4*(5), 344−357. https://doi.org/10.1111/j.1751-9004.2010.00263.x.

Miller, L. (2000). Law enforcement traumatic stress: Clinical syndromes and intervention strategies. *Trauma Response, 6*(1), 15−20.

Miller, L. S., & Braswell, M. C. (1992). Police perceptions of ethical decision-making: The ideal versus the real. *American Journal of Police, XI*(4), 27−45.

Miller, M. L., & Schlenker, B. R. (2011). Integrity and identity: Moral identity differences and preferred interpersonal reactions. *European Journal of Personality, 25*, 2−15. https://doi.org/10.1002/per.765.

Monin, B., & Miller, D. T. (2001). Moral credentials and the expression of prejudice. *Journal of Personality and Social Psychology, 81*(1), 33−43. https://doi.org/10.1037/0022-3514.81.1.33.

Moore, C. (2008). Moral disengagement in processes of organizational corruption. *Journal of Business Ethics, 80*(1), 129−139. https://doi.org/10.1007/s10551-007-9447-8.

Moore, C., Detert, J. R., Trevino, L. K., Baker, V. L., & Mayer, D. M. (2012). Why employees do bad things: Moral disengagement and unethical organizational behavior. *Personnel Psychology, 65*(1), 1−48. https://doi.org/10.1111/j.1744-6570.2011.01237.x.

Mullen, E., & Monin, B. (2016). Consistency versus licensing effects of past moral behavior. *Annual Review of Psychology, 67*, 363−385. https://doi.org/10.1146/annurev-psych-010213-115120.

Murphy, K. R. (2000). What constructs underlie measures of honesty or integrity? In R. D. Goffin, E. Helmes, R. D. Goffin, & E. Helmes (Eds.), *Problems and solutions in human assessment: Honoring Douglas N. Jackson at seventy* (pp. 265−283). New York, NY, US: Kluwer Academic/Plenum Publishers. https://doi.org/10.1007/978-1-4615-4397-8_12.

Murphy, K. R., & Dzieweczynski, J. L. (2005). Why don't measures of broad personality dimensions of personality perform better as predictors of job performance? *Human Performance, 18*(4), 343−357. https://doi.org/10.1207/s15327043hup1804_2.

Nelis, D., Kotsou, I., Quoidbach, J., Hansenne, M., Weytens, F., Dupuis, P., et al. (2011). Increasing emotional competence improves psychological and physical well-being, social relationships, and employability. *Emotion, 11*(2), 354−366. https://doi.org/10.1037/a0021554.

Paciello, M., Fida, R., Tramontano, C., Lupinetti, C., & Caprara, G. V. (2008). Stability and change of moral disengagement and its impact on aggression and violence in late adolescence. *Child Development, 79*(5), 1288–1309. https://doi.org/10.1111/j.1467-8624.2008.01189.x.

Papazoglou, K. (2013). Conceptualizing police complex spiral trauma and its applications in the police field. *Traumatology, 19*(3), 196–209. https://doi.org/10.1177/1534765612466151.

Papazoglou, K. (2017). The examination of different pathways leading towards police traumatization: Exploring the role of moral injury and personality in police compassion fatigue. *Dissertation Abstracts International, 77*.

Papazoglou, K., & Chopko, B. (2017). The role of moral suffering (moral injury and moral distress) in police compassion fatigue and PTSD: An unexplored topic. *Frontiers in Psychology, 8*, 1999. https://doi.org/10.3389/fpsyg.2017.01999.

Porter, L. E., & Warrender, C. (2009). A multivariate model of police deviance: Examining the nature of corruption, crime, and misconduct. *Policing and Society, 19*(1), 79–99. https://doi.org/10.1080/10439460802457719.

Punch, M. (2000). Police corruption and its prevention. *European Journal on Criminal Policy and Research, 8*(3), 301–324. https://doi.org/10.1023/A:1008777013115.

Raganella, A. J., & White, M. D. (2004). Race, gender, and motivation for becoming a police officer: Implications for building a representative police department. *Journal of Criminal Justice, 3*(6), 501–513. https://doi.org/10.1016/j.jcrimjus.2004.08.009.

Ryan, W. (1976). *Blaming the victim: Revised* (Updated Edition). NY: Vintage Books Edition.

Schafer, J. A., & Martinelli, T. J. (2008). First-line supervisors' perceptions of police integrity: The measurement of police integrity revisited. *Policing: An International Journal of Police Strategies & Management, 31*(2), 306–323. https://doi.org/10.1108/13639510810878749.

Schlenker, B. R. (2008). Integrity and character: Implications of principled and expedient ethical ideologies. *Journal of Social and Clinical Psychology, 27*(10), 1078–1125. https://doi.org/10.1521/jscp.2008.27.10.1078.

Schutte, N. S., Malouff, J. M., & Thorsteinsson, E. B. (2013). Increasing emotional intelligence through training: Current status and future directions. *The International Journal of Emotional Education, 5*(1), 56–72.

Smith, K. B., Profetto-McGrath, J., & Cummings, G. G. (2009). Emotional intelligence and nursing: An integrative literature review. *International Journal of Nursing Studies, 46*(12), 1624–1636. https://doi.org/10.1016/j.ijnurstu.2009.05.024.

Stinson, P. M., Liederbach, J., & Brewer, S. L., Jr. (2016). *Police integrity lost: A Study of law enforcement officers arrested. Final technical report, award number: 2011-IJ-CX-0024, national institute of justice, office of justice program*. U.S. Department of Justice.

Sturm, R. E. (2015). Decreasing unethical decisions: The role of morality-based individual differences. *Journal of Business Ethics*, 1–21. https://doi.org/10.1007/s10551-015-2787-x.

Tehrani, N. (2010). Compassion fatigue: Experiences in occupational health, human resources, counselling and police. *Occupational Medicine, 60*(2), 133–138. https://doi.org/10.1093/occmed/kqp174.

Tenbrunsel, A. E., & Messick, D. M. (2004). Ethical fading: The role of self-deception in unethical behavior. *Social Justice Research, 17*(2), 223–236. https://doi.org/10.1023/B:SORE.0000027411.35832.53.

Welsh, D. T., Ordonez, L. D., Snyder, D. G., & Christian, M. S. (2015). The slippery slope: How small ethical transgressions pave the way for larger future transgressions. *Journal of Applied Psychology, 100*(1), 114–127. https://doi.org/10.1037/a0036950.

White, M. D., Cooper, J. A., Saunders, J., & Raganella, A. J. (2010). Motivations for becoming a police officer: Re-assessing officer attitudes and job satisfaction after six years on the street. *Journal of Criminal Justice, 38*(4), 520–530. https://doi.org/10.1016/j.jcrimjus.2010.04.022.

Young, L., & Durwin, A. J. (2013). Moral realism as moral motivation: The impact of meta-ethics on everyday decision-making. *Journal of Experimental Social Psychology, 49*(2), 302–306. https://doi.org/10.1016/j.jesp.2012.11.013.

Zhang, S., Cornwell, J. F., & Higgins, E. T. (2014). Repeating the past: Prevention focus motivates repetition, even for unethical decisions. *Psychological Science, 25*(1), 179–187. https://doi.org/10.1177/0956797613502363.

Zhong, C. B. (2011). The ethical dangers of deliberative decision making. *Administrative Science Quarterly, 56*(1), 1–25. https://doi.org/10.2189/asqu.2011.56.1.001.

6

The neurobiology of police health, resilience, and wellness

Christine C. Kwiatkowski[a,b], Claire E. Manning[d],
Andrew L. Eagle[d], Alfred J. Robison[c]

[a]MICHIGAN STATE UNIVERSITY, NEUROSCIENCE PROGRAM, EAST LANSING,
MI, UNITED STATES; [b]MICHIGAN STATE UNIVERSITY, SCHOOL OF CRIMINAL JUSTICE,
EAST LANSING, MI, UNITED STATES; [c]MICHIGAN STATE UNIVERSITY, DEPARTMENT OF
PHYSIOLOGY, EAST LANSING, MI, UNITED STATES; [d]EAST LANSING, MI,
UNITED STATES

Introduction

Police officers are exposed to disturbing and life-threatening trauma when responding to critical incidents. Regardless of the peril to themselves, officers must engage in threatening situations as part of their jobs, which can be a tremendous source of stress that affects their physical and psychological health. This stress can come in the form of repeated (i.e., chronic) stress or an acute traumatic stress, the experience of a particularly shocking and/or dangerous event. Chronic exposure to work-related stress and trauma elevates officer risk for adverse health outcomes, such as cardiovascular disease, metabolic syndrome, poor sleep, post-traumatic stress disorder (PTSD), depression, and other psychiatric disorders (Hartley, Burchfiel, Fekedulegn, Andrew, & Violanti, 2011; Komarovskaya et al., 2011; McCaslin et al., 2006; Papazoglou, 2013; Stanley, Hom, & Joiner, 2016; Violanti et al., 2007). In one study, Santa Maria et al. (2018) found that job demand relative to both workload and the experience of citizen assault predicted symptoms of depression and anxiety among police officers. This was mediated by emotional exhaustion, suggesting that police work is personally as well as professionally demanding and can place significant strain on coping resources that counteract the effects of chronic stress (Santa Maria et al., 2018). The effects of the high job demand inherent to law enforcement are compounded by exposure to personal threat. For example, Chopko and Schwartz (2012) identified personal injury during assault as a significant correlate of PTSD symptoms among police. Similarly, McCaslin et al. (2006) found that trauma exposure accompanied by the perception of great personal threat is associated with symptoms of PTSD including disassociation, anxious arousal, and fear among police officers. Importantly, symptoms of hyperarousal can sensitize an officer's threat response such that s/he more readily ascribes danger and reacts to environmental stressors, even in circumstances during which this response is not beneficial. Taken together, the effects of work-related stress influence officer health and sensitivity to threat, which negatively impacts quality of life and job performance.

It is thus both troublesome yet unsurprising that law enforcement officers are at an increased risk for suicidal ideation and suicide deaths (Stanley et al., 2016). In 2017, more officers were identified as dying by suicide than in the line of duty (Heyman, Dill, & Douglas, 2018). Indeed, law enforcement has been identified as one of the most challenging professions, not only for on the job risks but further health disparities compared to other employed populations (Hartley et al., 2011). Though the elevated mortality and morbidity associated with policing is increasingly recognized, officers generally lack access to resources and training that could buffer the effects of work-related stressors (Manzella & Papazoglou, 2014). This is a problem that should not be ignored because officers are uniquely unable to limit their exposure to stress and trauma given the nature of the profession.

The deleterious consequences of stress, however, are not guaranteed: some officers, despite chronic stress or trauma exposure, have few or no symptoms (Peres et al., 2011) and are thus considered "resilient." Resilience of this nature is defined as successful adaptation to stress and adversity (Charney, 2004), and experimental models suggest that stress resilience may be driven by mechanisms in the brain. Depending on the model, the prevalence of resilience can be quite high; among mice exposed to chronic social and physical stress, approximately 30% are resilient to the effects of stress and show no observable deleterious symptoms (Krishnan et al., 2007). A great deal of cellular and molecular research from the rodent brain indicates that resilience is an active compensatory process and not simply the absence of a maladaptive stress response (Han & Nestler, 2017). Specifically, there are neurophysiological changes in response to stress that are associated with resilience and enhanced coping skills (Feder, Nestler, & Charney, 2009).

Resilience has also been examined in human populations. Among police, mental preparedness and resilience training that focuses on regulation of physiological arousal and enhancement of executive function and perceptual abilities improves both officer well-being and performance during highly realistic training scenarios (Andersen & Gustafsberg, 2016; Andersen, Papazoglou, Arnetz, & Collins, 2015; Arnetz, Nevedal, Lumley, Backman, & Lublin, 2009). This suggests a need within the law enforcement community to engage in evidence-based efforts to foster resilience in officers. However, in order for these efforts to be effective, it is necessary to have a fundamental under-standing of the biology of stress and resilience, especially in the central nervous system (CNS). The response to stress relies on a multitude of brain regions and peripheral systems, depending on emotional, executive, and memory centers of the brain, and autonomic responses in the periphery. At a broad level, these systems communicate together in a complex interplay of coordinated activity that enables our conscious understanding of our environment and ability to interact with it. Alterations in the function of these brain circuits play critical roles in the stress response of the healthy brain and the pathophysiology of stress vulnerability.

The acute, adaptive response to threats

Humans have evolved in an ever-changing world that requires adaptations to react to potential acute threats in order to survive. This rapid, complex response to a threat relies on a multitude of brain regions (see Fig. 6.1), and an understanding of this adaptive response is key to understanding a maladaptive response to chronic and/or traumatic stress. Detection of an external stressor begins with a sensory experience of an environmental stimulus, like seeing a person. This is first processed by the visual thalamus and is then concurrently and separately transmitted to regions of the brain for stimulus identification and the selection of an appropriate behavioral response, including processing centers of sensory cortices and subcortical structures in the brain like the amygdala, hypothalamus, and brain stem. The thalamus-to-amygdala pathway underlies the selection of the behavioral response which occurs rapidly and initiates the peripheral "fight-or-flight" stress response. This is largely conveyed through the autonomic nervous system (ANS) and the hypothalamus-pituitary-adrenal (HPA) axis (Fig. 6.2 and see below). Following sensory stimulus identification, emotional and cognitive evaluation can update the selection of response with reference to experience and context, either energizing the individual for action against a threat or dampening the response after evaluation has determined there is no threat. It is thus likely that the stress response would be engaged with identification of a person fitting a suspect's description and tempered with the appearance of a child. Cortical and subcortical structures, including the sensory cortex, prefrontal cortex (PFC) and hippocampus, are involved in the evaluative updating of the response.

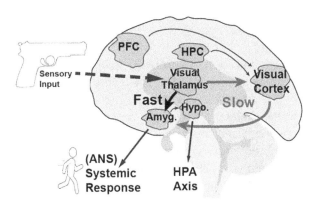

FIG. 6.1 Role of the cortico-amygdala loop in fear responses. Sensory input concerning a potential threat (i.e., a gun) arrives via the visual thalamus which activates the amygdala, the fast pathway (red [light gray in print version]). The amygdala immediately initiates a systemic threat response via the autonomic nervous system (ANS) and the hypothalamus/pituitary/adrenal (HPA) axis. The visual thalamus also sends information about the potential threat to the visual cortex which processes it in the context of experience via the hippocampus (HPC) and situation via the prefrontal cortex (PFC). If the cortex determines that the input does not constitute a threat (i.e., the gun is clearly a toy), it then exerts top-down control over the amygdala to shut off the threat response, a slower process (blue [dark gray in print version]).

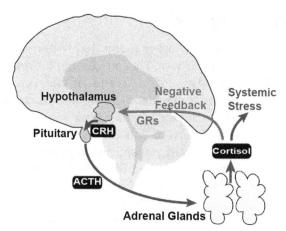

FIG. 6.2 The hypothalamus/pituitary/adrenal axis. The hypothalamus releases corticotropin-releasing hormone (CRH) which stimulates the pituitary gland to release adrenocorticotropic hormone (ACTH) which in turn activates the adrenal glands to secrete cortisol (glucocorticoid). Cortisol initiates systemic stress responses, and also feeds back to bind glucocorticoid receptors throughout the HPA axis and shut the process down, preventing excessive cortisol release.

The stress response, once initiated, is a two-step, interconnected system involving the ANS and HPA axis. The ANS is a subsystem of the peripheral nervous system (PNS), which comprises the ANS and the peripheral and cranial nerves of the somatic nervous system. The ANS is composed of sympathetic and parasympathetic components which act in physiological antagonism to escalate and de-escalate the immediate stress response (Wehrwein, Orer, & Barman, 2016). The sympathetic nervous system, in particular, prepares the body to respond to acute stressors by mobilizing peripheral systems to engage in the classic "fight or flight" response by increasing oxygen and blood flow throughout the body and concurrently suppressing functions less essential to immediate survival (e.g., digestion) (Chrousos, 2009). Sympathetic neurons exit the spinal cord to signal to postganglionic neurons which then innervate target glands, blood vessels, or smooth muscle (Wehrwein et al., 2016) to stimulate activity of the heart and increase blood flow to the skeletal muscles to prepare the body for "fight or flight". This is often experienced as increased heart rate and/or heavier breathing. When the acute stress response is over, the parasympathetic nervous system aids in the return to baseline function (Wehrwein et al., 2016), activating the systems important for long-term survival. Peripheral information is also communicated back to the CNS via sensory pathways that modulate ongoing sympathetic activity or parasympathetic outflow (Haines, 2013).

In tandem, the HPA axis also mobilizes to modulate the CNS and PNS response using widely circulating hormones to communicate across regions. The hypothalamus acts as the central integrator of autonomic function, engaging the sympathetic nervous system via the brainstem or the spinal cord (Haines, 2013). The hypothalamus is a small centralized region located at the base of the brain that also allows the CNS to regulate endocrine function through modulation of the pituitary gland. The hypothalamus releases corticotropin-releasing hormone (CRH, also known as corticotropin-releasing factor, CRF), a hormone that stimulates the pituitary gland to release corticotropin (also known as adrenocorticotropic hormone, ACTH). Corticotropin can diffuse through the blood and body to activate the adrenal glands on the kidneys. This stimulates the production of glucocorticoids (e.g., cortisol in humans), which can coordinate a number of brain and peripheral systems to mobilize a stress response, including increasing metabolism to provide energy through glucose production. Notably, the HPA axis responds over a slower time course than the ANS, with the duration of its acute effects progressing during the hour following the onset of an acute stressor (Droste et al., 2008; Ulrich-Lai & Herman, 2009). Thus, the stress response involves a dramatic shift in physiological function that extends well beyond the experience of the initial stressor.

Taken together, given a threat, the brain stress systems regulate the activation of the ANS and the HPA axis stress response. The function of the ANS is to mobilize innate defensive behaviors in response to threat and aid in the restoration of normal physiological function once the threat is neutralized, whereas the HPA axis modulates the coordination of this response. However, these brain and peripheral systems can become perturbed in response to traumatic and/or chronic stress.

Modulation of the acute threat response

Humans have adapted to varying levels of chronic and traumatic stress, with mixed outcomes. Successful adaptation hinges on the body's ability to maintain normal physiological function and stable internal conditions (i.e., homeostasis) to ensure optimal cognitive and physical performance, even when demand increases. Increased demand, or stress, on the body's systems can be divided into two broad categories: internal and external stressors (Ulrich-Lai & Herman, 2009). Internal, or systemic, stressors are disruptions in homeostasis from within the body, such as a sudden change in blood glucose or rapid blood loss (e.g., wounding). These stressors utilize ascending sensory signaling pathways involving the periphery that innervate the affected organ to signal the brain to initiate the stress response. External stressors are events or threats imposed on the individual from an external source (e.g., work, relationships, or life-threatening situations). These stressors are perceived or anticipated, initiating the stress response via descending CNS signaling pathways that prepare the body to neutralize the stressor. Though these two categories of stressors are certainly not mutually exclusive, and may both affect law enforcement officers, external stressors and threats are of primary relevance to law enforcement work exposures and performance.

Understanding the level of threat an external stressor poses is critical for self-preservation. This process involves the cortico-amygdala loop, a circuit involving the amygdala and PFC, to (1) detect emotional stimuli, and (2) properly interpret stimuli to select an appropriate behavioral response. The amygdala, a center for the learning of emotion associated with threat detection, fear, and anxiety, guides approach and avoidance behavior in response to emotional or otherwise "motivationally salient" stimuli, e.g. a stimulus that could potentially signal a threat to the individual or peer. During this threat response, sensory cortices (environmental information) combine with PFC and hippocampus (current plans and related experiences) to activate the amygdala, which in turn signals other regions of the brain, like the locus coeruleus (LC) and hypothalamus, that a potential threat is present. For example, activation of the amygdala increases vigilance through LC release of catecholamine neurotransmitter (e.g., epinephrine, norepinephrine) to the hypothalamus to engage the stress response for survival (Davis & Whalen, 2001; Haines, 2013; Rodrigues, LeDoux, & Sapolsky, 2009). Consider the experience of hearing an unexpected sound in a silent room and how its source engages attention and focus until the origin of the sound is evaluated. Conversely, the amygdala can modulate motor behavior through its communication to other brain regions, such as motor cortex and subcortical regions involved in fear. A great deal about these circuits and their potential dysfunction has been uncovered by studying rat and mouse responses to fear. In rodent models, the typical survival fear response is to "freeze", or stop all movement, to avoid detection by a potential predator. The amygdala swiftly and directly coordinates freezing. Given its role in governing the body's responses to fear and stress, pathophysiological changes in the amygdala are related to emotional dysregulation and a maladaptive stress response. In particular, aberrant amygdala reactivity corresponds to states of anxiety, hyperarousal, hypervigilance, and impairments in fear learning (Hayes, LaBar, Petty, McCarthy, & Morey, 2009). The amygdala is thus an integral component of the limbic system, shaping behavior, emotion, and overall psychiatric health.

One of the amygdala's many functions is to act as a threat detector, while the frontal cortex, including the PFC, is responsible for executive information, cognition, behavior inhibition, and emotion (Gospic et al., 2011). The PFC receives sensory and emotional information from a variety of brain regions, including the sensory cortices, hippocampus, and amygdala. This information is synthesized by the PFC to facilitate, inhibit, or update an appropriate response. This process involves recruitment of the hippocampus, an area important for learning and memory, which provides declarative knowledge (memory for facts and events) and contextual information, e.g. memory associated with an event or location (Eichenbaum & Cohen, 2014). If a threat is regarded as benign or is no longer present, PFC can attenuate the activity of the amygdala (Sapolsky, 2017) and inhibit the stress response (Ulrich-Lai & Herman, 2009). For example, an initial stimulus, such as a loud blast could initiate a threat response and amygdala activity. If the loud blast occurs in an expected context, e.g. fireworks display, the hippocampus can provide this "safe" information to the PFC, which inhibits any further stress response. However, if the loud blast occurs out-of-place or in a novel context, the PFC would likely facilitate a threat response. When behavioral action is required for an imminent threat, PFC projections to motor regions initiate action (Haines, 2013) and enhance the stress response (Ulrich-Lai & Herman, 2009). Taken together, the PFC is another critical component of the threat response, acting as seat of executive function and self-regulation. However, in cases of chronic stress and trauma, the PFC can undergo maladaptive changes and is thus no longer able to guide appropriate responses.

The maladaptive stress response

The dual stress response and glucocorticoid effects on the brain

Acute stress modulation involves a rapid evaluation of stimulus and context before influencing the interconnected systems of the ANS and HPA axis. This is not to say the ANS and HPA axis are static under normal conditions; even common events in the environment elicit responses. However, frequent and extreme disruptions in the normal function of stress coping mechanisms can cause prolonged dysregulation of these systems. It follows that dysregulation manifests in a reduced ability to correctly identify and contextualize potential threat stimuli. Of particular risk is the HPA axis due to the prolonged nature of its signaling cascades, as the HPA axis mobilizes to modulate protracted stress responses using stable and widely circulating hormones to communicate across the brain and body over a prolonged period of time (Droste et al., 2008; McEwen, 2007; McEwen et al., 2015; McEwen & Morrison, 2013; Ulrich-Lai & Herman, 2009). Thus, the HPA system both provides a platform where the stress response involves a dramatic shift in physiological function that extends well beyond the experience of the initial stressor and a nexus by which to alter stress modulation circuitry.

In view of the relationship between the ANS and HPA axis, mobilization of the HPA axis is centrally mediated by many of the same regions responsible for activating the autonomic stress response (Myers, Scheimann, Franco-Villanueva, & Herman, 2017). Specifically, the hypothalamus initiates a neuroendocrine signaling pathway that begins with CRH release into blood supply (i.e., portal system) of the anterior pituitary to stimulate ACTH release (Haines, 2013). Increased plasma ACTH causes the adrenal glands to increase glucocorticoid secretion into the bloodstream, circulating to targets all over the body to serve as a primary regulator of the stress response and prepare the body to better respond to future stress (Charmandari, Tsigos, & Chrousos, 2005; Sapolsky, Romero, & Munck, 2000). The role of glucocorticoids is not fully understood, but is generally dependent upon concentration of glucocorticoids and the location of the target organ (Sapolsky et al., 2000). Glucocorticoids potentiate the ANS response in some cases and inhibit the overall stress system in others (Ulrich-Lai & Herman, 2009). For example, glucocorticoids increase cardiac output in response to general stressors, but inhibit the stress response during hemorrhage in order to prevent vasoconstrictive stress hormones from overcompensating and stopping the heart (Sapolsky et al., 2000). Glucocorticoids are also critical for providing negative feedback to the hypothalamus and anterior pituitary to suppress any further secretion of stress hormones. As such, interruptions of glucocorticoid signaling can dramatically affect the entire process of the HPA axis.

Glucocorticoids primarily exert their actions through two receptors: the mineralocorticoid receptor (MR) and glucocorticoid receptor (GR). MRs will bind to several steroid hormones with regularity and are considered activated under baseline conditions; though, they are protected from excessive glucocorticoid stimulation through enzyme activity. In contrast, the GR is more selective for glucocorticoids and can be stimulated through elevated glucocorticoid concentrations as might be the case for an officer who is regularly exposed to threat (Grad & Picard, 2007). Both of these receptors canonically exert their effects through genomic mechanisms: binding to their ligands and translocating to the cell nucleus to alter gene expression (Charmandari et al., 2005; Zalachoras, Houtman, & Meijer, 2013). GR-induced gene expression can cause dramatic shifts in the activity of the cell, leading to short- or long-term alterations, representing one mechanism whereby an officer's physiology can change in response to stress. Given their wide circulation and broad effects on the brain and body, prolonged exposure to glucocorticoids can dramatically impact systemic health and contribute to the pathophysiology of stress vulnerability.

Individuals suffering from psychiatric disorders associated with stress have altered HPA activity, indicated by altered peripheral cortisol levels and GRs under baseline or acute stress conditions. For example, unmedicated depressed individuals have elevated baseline cortisol, and reduced numbers of peripheral GRs (Calfa et al., 2003; O'Keane, Frodl, & Dinan, 2012; Owens & Nemeroff, 1993), suggesting that there is reduced efficacy of glucocorticoids on their receptors, which is thought to be causal in at least some forms of depression. In contrast, individuals with PTSD have normal or lower baseline cortisol (Mason, Giller, Kosten, Ostroff, & Podd, 1986), and normal pituitary and adrenal function (Yehuda, Golier, Halligan, Meaney, & Bierer, 2004), but have higher numbers of peripheral GRs that are more reactive to cortisol (Yehuda, Boisoneau, Mason, & Giller, 1993; Yehuda, Golier, Yang, & Tischler, 2004), indicating heightened reactivity under normal conditions. Thus, the physiology of an officer with PTSD may differ from that of an unaffected officer driving different emotional and behavioral responses that could contribute to job performance. Furthermore, peripheral GR appears to be altered across generations in cases of extreme stress (e.g., Holocaust survivors and their children), and specific GR genetic haplotypes are predictive of PTSD symptoms (van Zuiden et al., 2012; Yehuda et al., 2016). In anxiety disorders, which are highly comorbid with both depression and PTSD, the relationship to the HPA axis activity is less clear. Recent structured reviews of the literature suggest anxious persons may have slightly elevated cortisol at baseline and that increased cortisol during exposure therapy sessions may facilitate a reduction in anxiety, such as in phobia extinction, but these results are not significant in meta-analyses (Elnazer & Baldwin, 2014; Fischer & Ehlert, 2018). Taken together, this suggests that common maladaptive HPA activity in humans can be ascribed to differences in GR reactivity to traumatic or prolonged stresses evidenced by changes in GRs in the periphery.

However, the principle mechanism by which cortisol exposure induces long-term maladaptive responses to stress is by changing the brain. Under normal conditions, glucocorticoids acting on GRs in the HPA axis regulate the return to normal function, i.e. negative feedback or the shutting off of the stress response. Other brain regions like the hippocampus and amygdala are also enriched for GR expression (Patel et al., 2000; Sousa, Tannery, & Lafer, 1989), and thus are also sites of glucocorticoid action. The hippocampus, amygdala, and PFC are brain regions poised in the corticolimbic circuitry of the brain to control emotional and cognitive processes. While acute stress exposure can render the body capable of more quickly responding to threat, chronic stress can have deleterious consequences at the cellular level in these regions. Research in animals indicates that chronic stress results in memory impairments and less regulatory control over the stress response, likely via changes in hippocampus, amygdala, and PFC function resulting from chronic activation of GRs in these areas (Rodrigues et al., 2009; Sapolsky, 2003; Sapolsky et al., 2000). Such changes are considered the biological underpinnings of stress vulnerability, and while there is an overall dearth of research in human populations, there is correlational evidence that chronic stress and cortisol exposure is related to stress vulnerability in police populations.

The effects of stress on the hippocampus, prefrontal cortex, and the amygdala

The hippocampus is a subcortical brain region important for memory formation, especially those memories for events and context. Interestingly, it is enriched with both MRs and GRs (Sapolsky et al., 2000), which is normally adaptive for acute stress, i.e. threats can modulate our memory of events for future preparedness. However, this also makes the hippocampus especially vulnerable to the adverse effects of stress (Finsterwald & Alberini, 2014; Sapolsky, 2003). In a healthy brain, stress-based activation of GRs leads to short-term reductions in neuronal excitability that are hypothesized to return the hippocampus to its baseline firing rate and protect information encoded during acute stress (Joëls & Karst, 2012; Joëls, Krugers, Lucassen, & Karst, 2009). This mechanism is critical for long-term memories in rodents and humans (Abercrombie, Kalin, Thurow, Rosenkranz, & Davidson, 2003; Akirav et al., 2004; Buchanan & Lovallo, 2001). In contrast, prolonged exposure to glucocorticoids results in impairments in hippocampal-dependent memory performance (Sapolsky, 2003), thereby weakening recall of important context information during threat appraisal, e.g. whether the remembered event occurred during safe or non-safe situations. Indeed, threat general-ization, or a failure to associate potential threats to specific situations (context), is a prominent feature of PTSD (Liberzon & Abelson, 2016). This leads to these individuals unconsciously or consciously perceiving all stimuli in their environment as potential threats which could explain, in part, why disordered neighborhoods put officers on high alert even though the majority of neighborhood occupants do not pose a threat. Underlying the memory impairment are glucocorticoid-related functional and morphological changes in hippocampal neurons. For example, reductions in hippo-campal activity associated with chronic, but not acute, stress result in impairments in the strengthening of connections between neurons (i.e. synaptic strengthening) based on experience, which is critical to new learning and memory consolidation (Pavlides, Nivón, & McEwen, 2002). During chronic stress, hippocampal cells also become more vulnerable to damage due to unsustainable demands on their cellular resources (Joëls & Karst, 2012), and, ultimately, memories can be weakened (Howland & Cazakoff, 2010). Consistent with these findings, elevated glucocorticoid levels stemming from chronic stress are associated with atrophy of hippocampal neurons, such as the retraction of dendrites (small branching structures on neurons that make connections to other neurons), and a general reduction in hippocampal volume in rodents (Rodrigues et al., 2009; Sapolsky, 2003). Importantly, structural differences in the hippocampus are observed in humans exposed to chronic stress as well. For example, reduced hippocampal volume is associated with PTSD symptoms among police officers exposed to work-related traumatic events (Lindauer, Vlieger, et al., 2004; Shucard et al., 2012), although some compelling twin studies suggest that lower hippocampal volume may precede stress exposure and even be a risk factor for PTSD (Gilbertson et al., 2002; Pitman et al., 2012). This suggests that trauma experienced during police work can create risk for memory impairments and threat generalization.

The consequences of chronic stress on the PFC are less well understood, though there is new evidence emerging that stress drastically reduces its function (Girotti et al., 2018). For example, prolonged glucocorticoid exposure is related to cell atrophy and decreased synaptic strength in the connections between neurons (Czéh, Perez-Cruz, Fuchs, & Flügge, 2008; McEwen & Morrison, 2013; Rodrigues et al., 2009). In addition to structural changes in PFC neurons, chronic stress is also associated with decreased PFC function (McKlveen, Myers, & Herman, 2015). Together, these changes compromise executive function (i.e., decision making) as well as connectivity with other brain regions (de Kloet, de Kloet, de Kloet, & de Kloet, 2018), resulting in deficits in cognition and regulatory control over the stress response. For example, impairments in PFC function, such as decreased PFC activity, disinhibits the amygdala and other emotional processing brain regions, facilitating states of hyperarousal and biasing toward rapid, automatic, and often erroneous behavior rather than informed decision making in humans (de Kloet et al., 2018; Girotti et al., 2018; Maren & Holmes, 2015; Rodrigues et al., 2009; Ulrich-Lai & Herman, 2009). In one study of executive function and PTSD, veterans with PTSD demonstrated significantly less PFC activity during exposure to unpleasant imagery compared to combat-exposed, non-PTSD controls, suggesting a loss of regulatory control over negative affective states which can maintain stress pathology for longer durations, i.e. extending PTSD symptoms for months or years (Rabinak et al., 2014). Taken together, these findings suggest that chronic stress and concomitant glucocorticoid exposure contribute to emotional dysregulation via compromised PFC and hippocampal function.

In contrast to the hippocampus and PFC, chronic stress and increased glucocorticoid exposure *enhances* structural and functional properties of the amygdala, a region known for its role in arousal, anxiety, fear, and emotional processing (Ekman, Levenson, & Friesen, 1983; Russell, 1980; Tye, 2018), and which makes direct synaptic connections to both the PFC and the hippocampus (McGaugh, McIntyre, & Power, 2002; McGaugh & Roozendaal, 2002; Roozendaal, Brunson, Holloway, McGaugh, & Baram, 2002; Schoenbaum, Setlow, Saddoris, & Gallagher, 2003). In particular, chronic stress causes cell hypertrophy with increases in dendritic spine formation and arborization as well as increased connectivity between neurons (Vyas, Mitra, Shankaranarayana Rao, &

Chattarji, 2002). This corresponds to increases in activity of amygdala neurons related to glucocorticoid-mediated reductions in inhibitory signaling in the amygdala. As a result, after chronic stress, activity in the amygdala is more easily strengthened, especially during the formation and recall of a fear memory (Rodrigues et al., 2009; Roozendaal, McEwen, & Chattarji, 2009). The enhanced amygdala activity also elicits hyperarousal, which is associated with increases in amygdala activity and is related to states of hypervigilance and enhanced threat sensitivity (Liberzon & Abelson, 2016).

Clinical imaging studies from PTSD support that the amygdala becomes overactive after trauma exposure. In military and law enforcement populations, however, imaging studies of PTSD and control groups among police and combat veterans have yielded mixed results regarding the relationship between stress and amygdala reactivity and volume (Lindauer, Booij, et al., 2004; Lindauer, Vlieger, et al., 2004; Rabinak et al., 2014; Shin et al., 2004; Shucard et al., 2012), which may be attributed to differences in experimental design. Yet evidence suggests that amygdala activity, as well as excessive activity across many stress-related brain regions, is correlated with symptom severity (Liberzon & Abelson, 2016). For example, Shucard et al. (2012) found a significant relationship between self-reported arousal to negative stimuli, symptoms of re-experiencing trauma, and decreases in amygdala volume among police with a history of exposure to work-related trauma, suggesting that structural changes in the amygdala are also related to stress vulnerability. In sum, the amygdala has a central role in the processing of emotional stimuli and the formation of fear memories, both of which are enhanced under conditions of chronic stress and increased glucocorticoid exposure. Furthermore, the enhanced fear and disrupted processing of emotions persists for long periods of time, often many years after the original stress exposure or event has passed.

The amygdala is also regulated by other steroids, such as CRH, that are independent of the typical HPA axis response (Carter, Pinnock, & Herbert, 2004). Supporting this, an overabundance of CRH in the brain produces higher reactivity and anxiety behaviors in rodents (File & Aranko, 1988; Lee, Schulkin, & Davis, 1994; Stenzel-Poore, Heinrichs, Rivest, Koob, & Vale, 1994; Swerdlow, Geyer, Vale, & Koob, 1986). Though CRH may interact with the HPA system, there are many neurons in the amygdala which contain CRH receptors or produce the hormone itself, indicating that CRH in the amygdala can directly modulate anxiety and hypervigilance behaviors, independent of CRH in the HPA axis (Matys et al., 2004; Reul & Holsboer, 2002). During acute stress, CRH is released into the amygdala (Koob & Heinrichs, 1999; Merlo Pich et al., 1995), and activation of CRH receptors can cause increases in amygdala neuron activity (Hillhouse & Grammatopoulos, 2006). Increases in CRH and subsequent increased amygdala excitability drive increased synaptic strength in the amygdala and cause behavioral responses such as hyperarousal, anxiety, and fear in rodents (discussed above) (Pelton, Lee, & Davis, 1997; Sajdyk, Schober, Gehlert, & Shekhar, 1999). In view of these findings, elevated glucocorticoid levels secondary to chronic, work-related stress exposure could act to sensitize an officer to threat and enhance threat responding behavior.

Collectively, the interactions of these brain systems suggest that chronic stress upregulates the activity of the amygdala while decreasing the function of regulatory regions, such as the PFC and hippocampus. This in turn leads to an enhancement in reactivity to potential threats (real or imagined) under baseline conditions at the expense of proper decision-making and appropriate memory formation and retrieval, and dysregulation of these interconnected systems is exacerbated by the lack a dedicated mechanism for a return to baseline conditions. Thus, the cortico-amygdala loop is a critical site of stress susceptibility as it responds strongly to glucocorticoids but lacks the streamlined feedback of the core HPA axis. This suggests that treatments aimed at restoring the function of the cortico-amygdala loop may ameliorate or prevent stress-related pathology in police officers. Moreover, changes in peripheral stress hormones could act as biomarkers which may be used in prior control settings to train officers and enhance their coping to prolonged or traumatic stressors.

Resilience

It has long been observed that not all who are exposed to chronic stress and trauma suffer adverse consequences, but the neurobiology of stress resilience has only become a mainstream field of study in the last two decades. Resilience can be characterized as successful adaptation to stress and adversity (Charney, 2004), but it is not simply a passive attribute that occurs in the absence of deleterious consequences of stress (Han & Nestler, 2017). Rather, resilience is an active process driven by physiological changes in brain circuitry responsible for regulating emotion and reward. Though many brain regions are involved in the manifestation of resilience, overall evidence suggests that a greater capacity for emotional regulation is associated with resilience, indicating the continued importance of the amygdala, PFC, and hippocampus, in addition to the mesolimbic reward circuitry (see below).

Maintenance of healthy emotional regulation and a well-controlled fear response following stress is a vital component of resilience. Specifically, normal threat perception, fear responses, and fear extinction are related to resilience (Wu et al., 2013). The BDNF-TrkB signaling pathway, a molecular process in neurons that is essential for neuron growth and plasticity (e.g. synaptic strengthening), has been implicated in sustaining normal function in the fear circuitry by preserving regulatory control of the amygdala by the PFC and hippocampus (Mahan & Ressler, 2012; Wu et al., 2013).

Optimal function of the reward circuitry is another critical feature of stress resilience (Wu et al., 2013). The reward circuitry conveys information about the rewarding properties of stimuli in our environment and guides adaptive behavioral responses to reward (Robinson & Berridge, 1993). The mesolimbic reward circuitry consists of dopamine-releasing neurons that extend from a deep subcortical structure called the ventral tegmental area (VTA) to the nucleus accumbens (NAc). The NAc is critical to reward and motivation toward obtaining pleasant stimuli, such as food, sex, or social interaction. Disruptions in function of the reward circuitry are related to a variety of psychiatric conditions, including addiction and depression. For example, a signature feature of depression and other mood disorders is anhedonia, the lack of pleasure in response to previously rewarding stimuli. It is thus unsurprising that patients with both PTSD and depression demonstrate attenuated responses in the NAc (Pizzagalli et al., 2009; Sailer et al., 2008), a center of reward and motivated behavior. Stress vulnerability is associated with increased neuronal excitability in the VTA, the primary source of dopamine input into the NAc (Krishnan et al., 2007). Additionally, there is a differential pattern of gene expression and regulation in the VTA associated with resilience. Interestingly, some of the highly expressed genes observed in resilience are associated with attenuation of neuronal excitability, countering patterns of activity associated with stress vulnerability (Krishnan et al., 2007).

Though research is limited, there is evidence describing reward function among resilient humans exposed to combat. Human imaging studies provide preliminary evidence that stable function of the reward circuitry is critical for resilience. For example, in an imaging study examining the relationship between resilience and reward circuitry function, resilient Special Forces soldiers demonstrated stable activation of the NAc and PFC during a reward appraisal task. In contrast, civilian controls showed significant increases in activity relative to reward value (Vythilingam et al., 2009). In another imaging study of stress vulnerability among combat exposed soldiers, significantly decreased activity in the NAc was observed after, but not before, combat exposure among subjects returning from military service with increased PTSD symptoms compared to controls. In view of the finding that vulnerable subjects also displayed increased amygdala activity alongside decreases in NAc activity, researchers concluded that imbalanced responsivity to risk and reward is associated with stress vulnerability (Admon et al., 2013). Taken together, these studies indicate that maintaining stable function of the reward circuitry is an important component of resilience among those exposed to work-related trauma.

Stable activity in the cortico-amygdala circuit and hippocampus may also underlie resilience to stress. For example, in an imaging study examining the effect of psychotherapy on subclinical PTSD in police officers compared to no-intervention subclinical PTSD and resilient (police) controls, a significant pattern of cortico-amygdala loop activity was associated with resilience. Specifically, resilient officers demonstrated increases in mPFC activity with concurrent decreases in amygdala activity when recalling traumatic memories (Peres et al., 2011), suggesting that a tightly controlled fear response and emotional self-regulation, likely via PFC control over amygdala activity, are associated with stress resilience. Moreover, trauma exposure in police led to significant reductions in activation in the hippocampus during a memory task (Hennig-Fast et al., 2009), which would predict the potential for serious memory impairments related to aberrant fear learning. However, the observed pattern may reflect changes induced by trauma because controls were trauma naïve rather than resilient officers (Hennig-Fast et al., 2009). In sum, preliminary research investigating the mechanisms of resilience among humans with work-related trauma exposure shows significant differences in emotional processing networks associated with threat and fear processing between resilient and stress vulnerable individuals, suggesting that balanced and well-controlled responses to emotional stimuli are hallmarks of resilience.

Conclusions

In this chapter, we have attempted to summarize preclinical and human literature describing the mechanisms of the acute stress response, maladaptive responses to chronic or traumatic stress, and the resilience of some individuals to these maladaptive responses. Although it is clear that we have good evidence for some of these mechanisms, we are only beginning to develop the tools and techniques that will allow us to take advantage of this knowledge to promote resilience and wellness in individuals exposed to chronic or traumatic stress through their jobs, such as police officers. Nevertheless, police training may include health information about stress vulnerability and potentially protective factors that improve officer quality of life. In addition, returning some semblance of control to officers under perpetual stress via evidence-based resilience training that focuses on officers' ability to regulate the stress response could be an invaluable component of officer education and may improve both health and performance.

References

Abercrombie, H. C., Kalin, N. H., Thurow, M. E., Rosenkranz, M. A., & Davidson, R. J. (2003). Cortisol variation in humans affects memory for emotionally laden and neutral information. *Behavioral Neuroscience, 117*(3), 505–516.

Admon, R., Lubin, G., Rosenblatt, J. D., Stern, O., Kahn, I., Assaf, M., et al. (2013). Imbalanced neural responsivity to risk and reward indicates stress vulnerability in humans. *Cerebral Cortex, 23*(1), 28–35. https://doi.org/10.1093/cercor/bhr369.

Akirav, I., Kozenicky, M., Tal, D., Sandi, C., Venero, C., & Richter-Levin, G. (2004). A facilitative role for corticosterone in the acquisition of a spatial task under moderate stress. *Learning & Memory, 11*(2), 188–195. https://doi.org/10.1101/lm.61704.

Andersen, J. P., & Gustafsberg, H. (2016). A training method to improve police use of force decision making:A randomized controlled trial. *SAGE Open, 6*(2). https://doi.org/10.1177/2158244016638708, 2158244016638708.

Andersen, J. P., Papazoglou, K., Arnetz, B. B., & Collins, P. (2015). Mental preparedness as a pathway to police resilience and optimal functioning in the line of duty. *International Journal of Emergency Mental Health and Human Resilience, 17*(3), 624–627.

Arnetz, B. B., Nevedal, D. C., Lumley, M. A., Backman, L., & Lublin, A. (2009). Trauma resilience training for police: Psychophysiological and performance effects. *Journal of Police and Criminal Psychology, 24*(1), 1–9. https://doi.org/10.1007/s11896-008-9030-y.

Buchanan, T. W., & Lovallo, W. R. (2001). Enhanced memory for emotional material following stress-level cortisol treatment in humans. *Psychoneuroendocrinology, 26*(3), 307–317.

Calfa, G., Kademian, S., Ceschin, D., Vega, G., Rabinovich, G. A., & Volosin, M. (2003). Characterization and functional significance of glucocorticoid receptors in patients with major depression: Modulation by antidepressant treatment. *Psychoneuroendocrinology, 28*(5), 687–701.

Carter, R. N., Pinnock, S. B., & Herbert, J. (2004). Does the amygdala modulate adaptation to repeated stress? *Neuroscience, 126*(1), 9−19. https://doi.org/10.1016/j.neuroscience.2004.01.018.

Charmandari, E., Tsigos, C., & Chrousos, G. (2005). Endocrinology of the stress response. *Annual Review of Physiology, 67*(1), 259−284. https://doi.org/10.1146/annurev.physiol.67.040403.120816.

Charney, D. S. (2004). Psychobiological mechanisms of resilience and vulnerability. *Focus, 2*(3), 368−391. https://doi.org/10.1176/foc.2.3.368.

Chopko, B. A., & Schwartz, R. C. (2012). Correlates of career traumatization and symptomatology among active-duty police officers AU - Chopko, Brian A. *Criminal Justice Studies, 25*(1), 83−95. https://doi.org/10.1080/1478601X.2012.657905.

Chrousos, G. P. (2009). Stress and disorders of the stress system. *Nature Reviews Endocrinology, 5*, 374. https://doi.org/10.1038/nrendo.2009.106.

Czéh, B., Perez-Cruz, C., Fuchs, E., & Flügge, G. (2008). Chronic stress-induced cellular changes in the medial prefrontal cortex and their potential clinical implications: Does hemisphere location matter? *Behavioural Brain Research, 190*(1), 1−13. https://doi.org/10.1016/j.bbr.2008.02.031.

Davis, M., & Whalen, P. J. (2001). The amygdala: Vigilance and emotion. *Molecular Psychiatry, 6*(1), 13−34.

Droste, S. K., de Groote, L., Atkinson, H. C., Lightman, S. L., Reul, J. M. H. M., & Linthorst, A. C. E. (2008). Corticosterone levels in the brain show a distinct ultradian rhythm but a delayed response to forced swim stress. *Endocrinology, 149*(7), 3244−3253. https://doi.org/10.1210/en.2008-0103.

Eichenbaum, H., & Cohen, N. J. (2014). Can we reconcile the declarative memory and spatial navigation views on hippocampal function? *Neuron, 83*(4), 764−770. https://doi.org/10.1016/j.neuron.2014.07.032.

Ekman, P., Levenson, R. W., & Friesen, W. V. (1983). Autonomic nervous system activity distinguishes among emotions. *Science, 221*(4616), 1208−1210.

Elnazer, H. Y., & Baldwin, D. S. (2014). Investigation of cortisol levels in patients with anxiety disorders: A structured review. *Curr Top Behav Neurosci, 18*, 191−216. https://doi.org/10.1007/7854_2014_299.

Feder, A., Nestler, E. J., & Charney, D. S. (2009). Psychobiology and molecular genetics of resilience. *Nature Reviews Neuroscience, 10*, 446. https://doi.org/10.1038/nrn2649. https://www.nature.com/articles/nrn2649#supplementary-information.

File, S. E., & Aranko, K. (1988). Sodium valproate and chlordiazepoxide in the elevated plus-maze test of anxiety in the rat. *Neuropsychobiology, 20*(2), 82−86. https://doi.org/10.1159/000118478.

Finsterwald, C., & Alberini, C. M. (2014). Stress and glucocorticoid receptor-dependent mechanisms in long-term memory: From adaptive responses to psychopathologies. *Neurobiology of Learning and Memory, 112*, 17−29. https://doi.org/10.1016/j.nlm.2013.09.017.

Fischer, S., & Ehlert, U. (2018). Hypothalamic-pituitary-thyroid (HPT) axis functioning in anxiety disorders. A systematic review. *Depression and Anxiety, 35*(1), 98−110. https://doi.org/10.1002/da.22692.

Gilbertson, M. W., Shenton, M. E., Ciszewski, A., Kasai, K., Lasko, N. B., Orr, S. P., et al. (2002). Smaller hippocampal volume predicts pathologic vulnerability to psychological trauma. *Nature Neuroscience, 5*(11), 1242−1247. https://doi.org/10.1038/nn958.

Girotti, M., Adler, S. M., Bulin, S. E., Fucich, E. A., Paredes, D., & Morilak, D. A. (2018). Prefrontal cortex executive processes affected by stress in health and disease. *Progress in Neuro-Psychopharmacology and Biological Psychiatry, 85*, 161−179. https://doi.org/10.1016/j.pnpbp.2017.07.004.

Gospic, K., Mohlin, E., Fransson, P., Petrovic, P., Johannesson, M., & Ingvar, M. (2011). Limbic justice—amygdala involvement in immediate rejection in the ultimatum game. *PLoS Biology, 9*(5), 1−8.

Grad, I., & Picard, D. (2007). The glucocorticoid responses are shaped by molecular chaperones. *Molecular and Cellular Endocrinology, 275*(1−2), 2−12. https://doi.org/10.1016/j.mce.2007.05.018.

Haines, D. E. (Ed.). (2013). *Fundamental neuroscience for basic and clinical applications* (4 ed.). Elsevier/ Saunders.

Han, M.-H., & Nestler, E. J. (2017). Neural substrates of depression and resilience. *Neurotherapeutics, 14*(3), 677−686. https://doi.org/10.1007/s13311-017-0527-x.

Hartley, T. A., Burchfiel, C. M., Fekedulegn, D., Andrew, M. E., & Violanti, J. M. (2011). Health disparities in police officers: Comparisons to the U.S. General population. *International Journal of Emergency Mental Health, 13*(4), 211−220.

Hayes, J. P., LaBar, K. S., Petty, C. M., McCarthy, G., & Morey, R. A. (2009). Alterations in the neural circuitry for emotion and attention associated with posttraumatic stress symptomatology. *Psychiatry Research: Neuroimaging, 172*(1), 7−15. https://doi.org/10.1016/j.pscychresns.2008.05.005.

Hennig-Fast, K., Werner, N. S., Lermer, R., Latscha, K., Meister, F., Reiser, M., … Meindl, T. (2009). After facing traumatic stress: Brain activation, cognition and stress coping in policemen. *Journal of Psychiatric Research, 43*(14), 1146−1155. https://doi.org/10.1016/j.jpsychires.2009.03.001.

Heyman, M., Dill, J., & Douglas, R. (2018). *The ruderman white paper on mental health and suicide of first responders.* Retrieved from https://rudermanfoundation.org/white_papers/police-officers-and-firefighters-are-more-likely-to-die-by-suicide-than-in-line-of-duty/.

Hillhouse, E. W., & Grammatopoulos, D. K. (2006). The molecular mechanisms underlying the regulation of the biological activity of corticotropin-releasing hormone receptors: Implications for physiology and pathophysiology. *Endocrine Reviews, 27*(3), 260−286. https://doi.org/10.1210/er.2005-0034.

Howland, J. G., & Cazakoff, B. N. (2010). Effects of acute stress and GluN2B-containing NMDA receptor antagonism on object and object-place recognition memory. *Neurobiology of Learning and Memory, 93*(2), 261−267. https://doi.org/10.1016/j.nlm.2009.10.006.

Joëls, M., & Karst, H. (2012). Corticosteroid effects on calcium signaling in limbic neurons. *Cell Calcium, 51*(3), 277−283. https://doi.org/10.1016/j.ceca.2011.11.002.

Joëls, M., Krugers, H. J., Lucassen, P. J., & Karst, H. (2009). Corticosteroid effects on cellular physiology of limbic cells. *Brain Research, 1293*, 91−100. https://doi.org/10.1016/j.brainres.2009.03.036.

de Kloet, E. R., de Kloet, S. F., de Kloet, C. S., & de Kloet, A. D. (2018). Top-down and bottom-up control of stress-coping. *Journal of Neuroendocrinology*, 1−16. https://doi.org/10.1111/jne.12675.

Komarovskaya, I., Maguen, S., McCaslin, S. E., Metzler, T. J., Madan, A., Brown, A. D., … Marmar, C. R. (2011). The impact of killing and injuring others on mental health symptoms among police officers. *Journal of Psychiatric Research, 45*(10), 1332−1336. https://doi.org/10.1016/j.jpsychires.2011.05.004.

Koob, G. F., & Heinrichs, S. C. (1999). A role for corticotropin releasing factor and urocortin in behavioral responses to stressors. *Brain Research, 848*(1−2), 141−152.

Krishnan, V., Han, M.-H., Graham, D. L., Berton, O., Renthal, W., Russo, S. J., … Nestler, E. J. (2007). Molecular adaptations underlying susceptibility and resistance to social defeat in brain reward regions. *Cell, 131*(2), 391−404. https://doi.org/10.1016/j.cell.2007.09.018.

Lee, Y., Schulkin, J., & Davis, M. (1994). Effect of corticosterone on the enhancement of the acoustic startle reflex by corticotropin releasing factor (CRF). *Brain Research, 666*(1), 93−98.

Liberzon, I., & Abelson, J. L. (2016). Context processing and the neurobiology of post-traumatic stress disorder. *Neuron, 92*(1), 14−30. https://doi.org/10.1016/j.neuron.2016.09.039.

Lindauer, R. J. L., Booij, J., Habraken, J. B. A., Uylings, H. B. M., Olff, M., Carlier, I. V. E., … Gersons, B. P. R. (2004). Cerebral blood flow changes during script-driven imagery in police officers with post-traumatic stress disorder. *Biological Psychiatry, 56*(11), 853−861. https://doi.org/10.1016/j.biopsych.2004.08.003.

Lindauer, R. J. L., Vlieger, E.-J., Jalink, M., Olff, M., Carlier, I. V. E., Majoie, C. B. L. M., … Gersons, B. P. R. (2004). Smaller hippocampal volume in Dutch police officers with posttraumatic stress disorder. *Biological Psychiatry, 56*(5), 356−363. https://doi.org/10.1016/j.biopsych.2004.05.021.

Mahan, A. L., & Ressler, K. J. (2012). Fear conditioning, synaptic plasticity and the amygdala: Implications for posttraumatic stress disorder. *Trends in Neurosciences, 35*(1), 24–35. https://doi.org/10.1016/j.tins.2011.06.007.

Manzella, C., & Papazoglou, K. (2014). Training police trainees about ways to manage trauma and loss. *International Journal of Mental Health Promotion, 16*(2), 103–116. https://doi.org/10.1080/14623730.2014.903609.

Maren, S., & Holmes, A. (2015). Stress and fear extinction. *Neuropsychopharmacology, 41*, 58. https://doi.org/10.1038/npp.2015.180.

Mason, J. W., Giller, E. L., Kosten, T. R., Ostroff, R. B., & Podd, L. (1986). Urinary free-cortisol levels in posttraumatic stress disorder patients. *The Journal of Nervous and Mental Disease, 174*(3), 145–149.

Matys, T., Pawlak, R., Matys, E., Pavlides, C., McEwen, B. S., & Strickland, S. (2004). Tissue plasminogen activator promotes the effects of corticotropin-releasing factor on the amygdala and anxiety-like behavior. *Proceedings of the National Academy of Sciences of the U S A, 101*(46), 16345–16350. https://doi.org/10.1073/pnas.0407355101.

McCaslin, S. E., Rogers, C. E., Metzler, T. J., Best, S. R., Weiss, D. S., Fagan, J. A., … Marmar, C. R. (2006). The impact of personal threat on police officers' responses to critical incident stressors. *The Journal of Nervous and Mental Disease, 194*(8), 591–597. https://doi.org/10.1097/01.nmd.0000230641.43013.68.

McEwen, B. S. (2007). Physiology and neurobiology of stress and adaptation: Central role of the brain. *Physiological Reviews, 87*(3), 873–904. https://doi.org/10.1152/physrev.00041.2006.

McEwen, B. S., Bowles, N. P., Gray, J. D., Hill, M. N., Hunter, R. G., Karatsoreos, I. N., et al. (2015). Mechanisms of stress in the brain. *Nature Neuroscience, 18*(10), 1353–1363. https://doi.org/10.1038/nn.4086.

McEwen, B. S., & Morrison, J. H. (2013). The brain on stress: Vulnerability and plasticity of the prefrontal cortex over the life course. *Neuron, 79*(1), 16–29. https://doi.org/10.1016/j.neuron.2013.06.028.

McGaugh, J. L., McIntyre, C. K., & Power, A. E. (2002). Amygdala modulation of memory consolidation: Interaction with other brain systems. *Neurobiology of Learning and Memory, 78*(3), 539–552.

McGaugh, J. L., & Roozendaal, B. (2002). Role of adrenal stress hormones in forming lasting memories in the brain. *Current Opinion in Neurobiology, 12*(2), 205–210.

McKlveen, J. M., Myers, B., & Herman, J. P. (2015). The medial prefrontal cortex: Coordinator of autonomic, neuroendocrine and behavioural responses to stress. *Journal of Neuroendocrinology, 27*(6), 446–456. https://doi.org/10.1111/jne.12272.

Merlo Pich, E., Lorang, M., Yeganeh, M., Rodriguez de Fonseca, F., Raber, J., Koob, G. F., et al. (1995). Increase of extracellular corticotropin-releasing factor-like immunoreactivity levels in the amygdala of awake rats during restraint stress and ethanol withdrawal as measured by microdialysis. *Journal of Neuroscience, 15*(8), 5439–5447.

Myers, B., Scheimann, J. R., Franco-Villanueva, A., & Herman, J. P. (2017). Ascending mechanisms of stress integration: Implications for brainstem regulation of neuroendocrine and behavioral stress responses. *Neuroscience & Biobehavioral Reviews, 74*, 366–375. https://doi.org/10.1016/j.neubiorev.2016.05.011.

O'Keane, V., Frodl, T., & Dinan, T. G. (2012). A review of Atypical depression in relation to the course of depression and changes in HPA axis organization. *Psychoneuroendocrinology, 37*(10), 1589–1599. https://doi.org/10.1016/j.psyneuen.2012.03.009.

Owens, M. J., & Nemeroff, C. B. (1993). The role of corticotropin-releasing factor in the pathophysiology of affective and anxiety disorders: Laboratory and clinical studies. *Ciba Foundation Symposia, 172*, 296–308. discussion 308-216.

Papazoglou, K. (2013). Conceptualizing police complex spiral trauma and its applications in the police field. *Traumatology, 19*(3), 196–209. https://doi.org/10.1177/1534765612466151.

Patel, P. D., Lopez, J. F., Lyons, D. M., Burke, S., Wallace, M., & Schatzberg, A. F. (2000). Glucocorticoid and mineralocorticoid receptor mRNA expression in squirrel monkey brain. *Journal of Psychiatric Research, 34*(6), 383–392. https://doi.org/10.1016/S0022-3956(00)00035-2.

Pavlides, C., Nivón, L. G., & McEwen, B. S. (2002). Effects of chronic stress on hippocampal long-term potentiation. *Hippocampus, 12*(2), 245–257. https://doi.org/10.1002/hipo.1116.

Pelton, G. H., Lee, Y., & Davis, M. (1997). Repeated stress, like vasopressin, sensitizes the excitatory effects of corticotropin releasing factor on the acoustic startle reflex. *Brain Research, 778*(2), 381–387.

Peres, J. F. P., Foerster, B., Santana, L. G., Fereira, M. D., Nasello, A. G., Savoia, M., … Lederman, H. (2011). Police officers under attack: Resilience implications of an fMRI study. *Journal of Psychiatric Research, 45*(6), 727–734. https://doi.org/10.1016/j.jpsychires.2010.11.004.

Pitman, R. K., Rasmusson, A. M., Koenen, K. C., Shin, L. M., Orr, S. P., Gilbertson, M. W., … Liberzon, I. (2012). Biological studies of post-traumatic stress disorder. *Nature Reviews Neuroscience, 13*(11), 769–787. https://doi.org/10.1038/nrn3339.

Pizzagalli, D. A., Holmes, A. J., Dillon, D. G., Goetz, E. L., Birk, J. L., Bogdan, R., … Fava, M. (2009). Reduced caudate and nucleus accumbens response to rewards in unmedicated individuals with major depressive disorder. *American Journal of Psychiatry, 166*(6), 702–710. https://doi.org/10.1176/appi.ajp.2008.08081201.

Rabinak, C. A., MacNamara, A., Kennedy, A. E., Angstadt, M., Stein, M. B., Liberzon, I., et al. (2014). Focal and aberrant prefrontal engagement during emotion regulation in veterans with posttraumatic stress disorder. *Depression and Anxiety, 31*(10), 851–861. https://doi.org/10.1002/da.22243.

Reul, J. M., & Holsboer, F. (2002). Corticotropin-releasing factor receptors 1 and 2 in anxiety and depression. *Current Opinion in Pharmacology, 2*(1), 23–33.

Robinson, T. E., & Berridge, K. C. (1993). The neural basis of drug craving: An incentive-sensitization theory of addiction. *Brain Research Reviews, 18*(3), 247–291. https://doi.org/10.1016/0165-0173(93)90013-P.

Rodrigues, S. M., LeDoux, J. E., & Sapolsky, R. M. (2009). The influence of stress hormones on fear circuitry. *Annual Review of Neuroscience, 32*(1), 289–313. https://doi.org/10.1146/annurev.neuro.051508.135620.

Roozendaal, B., Brunson, K. L., Holloway, B. L., McGaugh, J. L., & Baram, T. Z. (2002). Involvement of stress-released corticotropin-releasing hormone in the basolateral amygdala in regulating memory consolidation. *Proceedings of the National Academy of Sciences of the U S A, 99*(21), 13908–13913. https://doi.org/10.1073/pnas.212504599.

Roozendaal, B., McEwen, B. S., & Chattarji, S. (2009). Stress, memory and the amygdala. *Nature Reviews Neuroscience, 10*, 423. https://doi.org/10.1038/nrn2651.

Russell, J. A. (1980). A circumplex model of affect. *Journal of Personality and Social Psychology, 39*(6), 1161.

Sailer, U., Robinson, S., Fischmeister, F. P. S., König, D., Oppenauer, C., Lueger-Schuster, B., … Bauer, H. (2008). Altered reward processing in the nucleus accumbens and mesial prefrontal cortex of patients with posttraumatic stress disorder. *Neuropsychologia, 46*(11), 2836–2844. https://doi.org/10.1016/j.neuropsychologia.2008.05.022.

Sajdyk, T. J., Schober, D. A., Gehlert, D. R., & Shekhar, A. (1999). Role of corticotropin-releasing factor and urocortin within the basolateral amygdala of rats in anxiety and panic responses. *Behavioural Brain Research, 100*(1–2), 207–215.

Santa Maria, A., Wörfel, F., Wolter, C., Gusy, B., Rotter, M., Stark, S., … Renneberg, B. (2018). The role of job demands and job resources in the development of emotional exhaustion, depression, and anxiety among police officers. *Police Quarterly, 21*(1), 109–134. https://doi.org/10.1177/1098611117743957.

Sapolsky, R. M. (2003). Stress and plasticity in the limbic system. *Neurochemical Research, 28*(11), 1735–1742. https://doi.org/10.1023/a:1026021307833.

Sapolsky, R. M. (2017). *Behave: The biology of humans at our best and worst.* New York: Penguin Press.

Sapolsky, R. M., Romero, L. M., & Munck, A. U. (2000). How do glucocorticoids influence stress responses? Integrating permissive, suppressive, stimulatory, and preparative actions*. *Endocrine Reviews, 21*(1), 55–89. https://doi.org/10.1210/edrv.21.1.0389.

Schoenbaum, G., Setlow, B., Saddoris, M. P., & Gallagher, M. (2003). Encoding predicted outcome and acquired value in orbitofrontal cortex during cue sampling depends upon input from basolateral amygdala. *Neuron, 39*(5), 855–867.

Shin, L. M., Orr, S. P., Carson, M. A., Rauch, S. L., Macklin, M. L., Lasko, N. B., ... Pitman, R. K. (2004). Regional cerebral blood flow in the amygdala and medial PrefrontalCortex during traumatic imagery in male and female vietnam veterans with PTSD. *Archives of General Psychiatry, 61*(2), 168–176. https://doi.org/10.1001/archpsyc.61.2.168.

Shucard, J. L., Cox, J., Shucard, D. W., Fetter, H., Chung, C., Ramasamy, D., et al. (2012). Symptoms of posttraumatic stress disorder and exposure to traumatic stressors are related to brain structural volumes and behavioral measures of affective stimulus processing in police officers. *Psychiatry Research: Neuroimaging, 204*(1), 25–31. https://doi.org/10.1016/j.pscychresns.2012.04.006.

Sousa, R. J., Tannery, N. H., & Lafer, E. M. (1989). In situ hybridization mapping of glucocorticoid receptor messenger ribonucleic acid in rat brain. *Molecular Endocrinology, 3*(3), 481–494.

Stanley, I. H., Hom, M. A., & Joiner, T. E. (2016). A systematic review of suicidal thoughts and behaviors among police officers, firefighters, EMTs, and paramedics. *Clinical Psychology Review, 44*, 25–44. https://doi.org/10.1016/j.cpr.2015.12.002.

Stenzel-Poore, M. P., Heinrichs, S. C., Rivest, S., Koob, G. F., & Vale, W. W. (1994). Overproduction of corticotropin-releasing factor in transgenic mice: A genetic model of anxiogenic behavior. *Journal of Neuroscience, 14*(5 Pt 1), 2579–2584.

Swerdlow, N. R., Geyer, M. A., Vale, W. W., & Koob, G. F. (1986). Corticotropin-releasing factor potentiates acoustic startle in rats: Blockade by chlordiazepoxide. *Psychopharmacology, 88*(2), 147–152.

Tye, K. M. (2018). Neural circuit motifs in valence processing. *Neuron, 100*(2), 436–452. https://doi.org/10.1016/j.neuron.2018.10.001.

Ulrich-Lai, Y. M., & Herman, J. P. (2009). Neural regulation of endocrine and autonomic stress responses. *Nature Reviews Neuroscience, 10*, 397. https://doi.org/10.1038/nrn2647. https://www.nature.com/articles/nrn2647#supplementary-information.

Violanti, J. M., Andrew, M., Burchfiel, C. M., Hartley, T. A., Charles, L. E., & Miller, D. B. (2007). Post-traumatic stress symptoms and cortisol patterns among police officers. *Policing: An International Journal of Police Strategies & Management, 30*(2), 189–202. https://doi.org/10.1108/13639510710753207.

Vyas, A., Mitra, R., Shankaranarayana Rao, B. S., & Chattarji, S. (2002). Chronic stress induces contrasting patterns of dendritic remodeling in hippocampal and amygdaloid neurons. *Journal of Neuroscience, 22*(15), 6810–6818. doi:20026655.

Vythilingam, M., Nelson, E. E., Scaramozza, M., Waldeck, T., Hazlett, G., Southwick, S. M., ... Ernst, M. (2009). Reward circuitry in resilience to severe trauma: An fMRI investigation of resilient special forces soldiers. *Psychiatry Research: Neuroimaging, 172*(1), 75–77. https://doi.org/10.1016/j.pscychresns.2008.06.008.

Wehrwein, E. A., Orer, H. S., & Barman, S. M. (2016). Overview of the anatomy, physiology, and pharmacology of the autonomic nervous system. *Comprehensive Physiology, 6*(3), 1239–1278. https://doi.org/10.1002/cphy.c150037.

Wu, G., Feder, A., Cohen, H., Kim, J., Calderon, S., Charney, D., et al. (2013). Understanding resilience. *Frontiers in Behavioral Neuroscience, 7*(10). https://doi.org/10.3389/fnbeh.2013.00010.

Yehuda, R., Boisoneau, D., Mason, J. W., & Giller, E. L. (1993). Glucocorticoid receptor number and cortisol excretion in mood, anxiety, and psychotic disorders. *Biological Psychiatry, 34*(1–2), 18–25.

Yehuda, R., Daskalakis, N. P., Bierer, L. M., Bader, H. N., Klengel, T., Holsboer, F., et al. (2016). Holocaust exposure induced intergenerational effects on FKBP5 methylation. *Biological Psychiatry, 80*(5), 372−380. https://doi.org/10.1016/j.biopsych.2015.08.005.

Yehuda, R., Golier, J. A., Halligan, S. L., Meaney, M., & Bierer, L. M. (2004). The ACTH response to dexamethasone in PTSD. *American Journal of Psychiatry, 161*(8), 1397−1403. https://doi.org/10.1176/appi.ajp.161.8.1397.

Yehuda, R., Golier, J. A., Yang, R. K., & Tischler, L. (2004). Enhanced sensitivity to glucocorticoids in peripheral mononuclear leukocytes in posttraumatic stress disorder. *Biological Psychiatry, 55*(11), 1110−1116. https://doi.org/10.1016/j.biopsych.2004.02.010.

Zalachoras, I., Houtman, R., & Meijer, O. C. (2013). Understanding stress-effects in the brain via transcriptional signal transduction pathways. *Neuroscience, 242*, 97−109. https://doi.org/10.1016/j.neuroscience.2013.03.038.

van Zuiden, M., Geuze, E., Willemen, H. L., Vermetten, E., Maas, M., Amarouchi, K., … Heijnen, C. J. (2012). Glucocorticoid receptor pathway components predict posttraumatic stress disorder symptom development: A prospective study. *Biological Psychiatry, 71*(4), 309−316. https://doi.org/10.1016/j.biopsych.2011.10.026.

7

Compassion fatigue & burnout

Chuck Russo[a], Prashant Aukhojee[b], Brooke McQuerrey Tuttle[c],
Olivia Johnson[d], Mark Davies[e], Brian A. Chopko[f],
Konstantinos Papazoglou[g]

[a]AMERICAN MILITARY UNIVERSITY/AMERICAN PUBLIC UNIVERSITY, CHARLES TOWN, WV,
UNITED STATES; [b]UNIVERSITY OF TORONTO, TORONTO, ON, CANADA; [c]CENTER FOR FAMILY
RESILIENCE DEPARTMENT OF HUMAN DEVELOPMENT AND FAMILY SCIENCE, OKLAHOMA
STATE UNIVERSITY, TULSA, OK, UNITED STATES; [d]BLUE WALL INSTITUTE, BELLEVILLE, IL,
UNITED STATES; [e]BC COUNSELLING, SURREY, BC, CANADA; [f]CRIMINOLOGY AND JUSTICE
STUDIES PROGRAM, DEPARTMENT OF SOCIOLOGY, KENT STATE UNIVERSITY AT STARK,
NORTH CANTON, OH, UNITED STATES; [g]YALE SCHOOL OF MEDICINE, NEW HAVEN, CT,
UNITED STATES

Compassion fatigue: introduction and definition

Caregiving and public service occupations often expose working professionals to pain, trauma, sorrow, loss, and suffering. While such exposure has been widely documented, the effects on the professional's physical and emotional health have also become much clearer. Nearly three decades of research on the negative aspects of working in caregiving professions exists (e.g., Figley, 1995; McCann & Pearlman, 1990; Pearlman, 1998; Pearlman & Mac Ian, 1995; Sabo, 2011). During this same timeframe, a noted evolution was witnessed in the nomenclature used to identify and define the physical and emotional repercussions of exposure to trauma (Marchand, 2007). Terminology used to describe such exposure has included burnout, secondary traumatic stress, secondary victimization, and vicarious trauma. Maslach (1982) described the repercussions of such exposure as a "syndrome of emotional exhaustion, depersonalization, and reduced personal accomplishment ..." (p. 3), which can occur in occupations that deal with the negative aspects of the human component (Marchand, 2007).

Repercussions do not merely come from working with, interacting with, or communicating with people, but rather, consequences are associated with repeated and cumulative exposure to traumatized individuals and their experiences (Cocker & Joss, 2016; Rafferty, n.d.). Interactions with traumatized individuals can result in witnessing the true depths of human misery and suffering. This exposure to suffering is often chronic and repeated over time. The current terminology to describe this form of occupational stress is compassion fatigue.

Compassion fatigue is often associated with those in the formal caregiving-type occupations. Compassion fatigue results from exposure to or interaction with individuals who have been traumatized (Cocker & Joss, 2016). Individuals in service-oriented occupations (e.g., nurses, physicians, police officers, child protective service workers, etc.) are at increased risk of interacting and dealing with traumatized individuals, in-turn increasing the chances of exposure to compassion fatigue (Cocker & Joss, 2016). Research suggests that certain occupations dealing with or being exposed to certain types of trauma and trauma victims (i.e., sexual assault victims, crimes involving children) are at increased risk for developing compassion fatigue. Additional aspects of one's work can also influence the development of compassion fatigue. These include the lack of social support, prior trauma, and the inability to meet personal or professional caregiving responsibilities (Adams, Boscarino, & Figley, 2006). Compassion fatigue is in essence the "cost of caring for others" in distress (Figley, 1995). This cost of caring takes a toll both physically and emotionally.

The adverse effects of compassion fatigue manifest in numerous ways in a distinctive manner amongst individuals (Todaro-Franceschi, 2019, p. 5). This affects personal and professional functioning (Mason & Toner, 2012), where signs and symptoms may include outbursts of anger and/or rage, irritability, substance abuse, lack of compassion or understanding, diminished pleasure and decreased job satisfaction, increased sick time/absence from work, inability to make decisions, dissociation, and decreased intimacy (Mathieu, 2007). Compassion fatigue can be deceptive in that many people are drawn into service-oriented occupations to help others. This need to help is central to the fundamental beliefs and values that inspired such choices in the first place (Mathieu, 2007). Unfortunately, the occupations that draw one in or that one is passionate about, may ultimately bring about negative consequences to one's interpersonal relationships, as well as affecting their physical, emotional, and spiritual health and wellness (Mason & Toner, 2012).

Review of literature

The term compassion fatigue was first coined by Charles Figley in the 1980's. Since its inception, the concept of compassion fatigue has been widely embraced by the psychological community. Despite its acceptance, it has never merited its own diagnostic category by any edition of the Diagnostic and Statistical Manual of Mental Disorders (DSM 5). In fact, compassion fatigue is often erroneously equated with burnout (the intense ill-managed stressors that emanate within the workplace) (Boyle, 2015). Newell and MacNeil (2010) noted that burnout, though serious, is much easier to remedy than compassion fatigue, which they consider to be a more serious psychological condition.

Compassion fatigue refers to an identifiable set of negative psychological symptoms that caregivers experience as a result of providing care while being exposed to either primary trauma (experiencing the trauma first hand) or secondary trauma (rendering care to those experiencing trauma) (Figley, 1995). Compassion fatigue is typically conceptualized as psychological erosion. It is not normally attributed to a single exposure to trauma, but generally associated with ongoing, repeated exposure to traumatic situations. Over time the act of providing care in the context of human suffering and trauma wears down the individual's psychological resilience and results in a myriad of negative psychological symptoms. As described in Figley's (2002) Compassion Fatigue Process, the caregiver's concern and empathy for those they are trying to help exposes them emotionally to the negative side effects associated with both prolonged stress and trauma.

In their survey of the literature, Andersen and Papazoglou (2015), found that the majority of research done on compassion fatigue has been done with medical health care providers (e.g., doctors, nurses, therapists), social workers, and counselors. They noted that despite the fact that policing would put officers at high risk for compassion fatigue, little research has been done with this population. Our understanding of the nature of compassion fatigue is based on the experiences reported by those who work in medicine and social support services. The genesis and experience of compassion fatigue by an oncology doctor may be distinctly different than the compassion fatigue suffered by a traffic police officer who repeatedly responds to fatal accident scenes. These differences call for more empirical research within a police population. Additionally, Papazoglou and Chopko (2017) noted how important moral injury/distress is in studying compassion fatigue among police officers, but they also note how little research on moral injury and compassion fatigue pertains to police officers.

Much overlap exists between the symptoms associated with compassion fatigue and posttraumatic stress disorder symptoms (Figley, 1995, p. xv; Papazoglou, Koskelainen, & Stuewe, 2019), for instance, symptoms may include hyper arousal; anxiety; depression, avoidance and withdrawal; intrusive images and thoughts; sleeplessness; reduced concentration, among many others (Meadors, Lamson, Swanson, White, & Sira, 2010). The distinction that is often made between posttraumatic stress disorder (PTSD) and compassion fatigue is that the genesis of PTSD is primary trauma (Figley, 1995, p. 8), while compassion fatigue is due to secondary trauma (Cocker & Joss, 2016). However, the categories of primary trauma and secondary trauma have become less distinct in the DSM 5. In Part A of the diagnosis for PTSD, within the types of exposure, the DSM 5 includes "A1: Direct exposure; A4: Repeated or extreme indirect exposure to aversive details of the traumatic event(s), usually in the course of professional duties (e.g., first responders collecting human remains; police officers repeatedly exposed to details of child abuse)" (American Psychiatric Association, 2013, pp. 271–272). Perhaps what differentiates PTSD from compassion fatigue is not so much the genesis of the trauma (primary vs. secondary), but the intensity of the symptom cluster experienced by the individual. Based on an in-depth review of the literature, it may be reasonable to conclude that compassion fatigue, along with other traumatic phenomenologies (e.g., vicarious trauma) consists of subclinical symptoms that form PTSD (Sui & Padmanabhanunni, 2016). That is, compassion fatigue may be a less severe form of PTSD (IAFF Staff, 2018). More work to clearly define the diagnostic criteria is imperative to clarify the exact nature and underlying causes of compassion fatigue.

Police compassion fatigue

The occupational demands of police work often entail officers being exposed to individuals who have been hurt, abused, injured, or even killed. Police work is an occupation marked with dangerous and distressing incidents (Burke & Mikkelsen, 2007; Crank, 2004;

Cross & Ashley, 2004; Karlsson & Christianson, 2003; Kelley, 2005; Violanti, Castellano, ORourke, & Paton, 2006; Waters & Ussery, 2007). The foundation of police work includes serving and protecting with calls ranging from monotonous to life-threatening (Cross & Ashley, 2004; Henry, 2004; Papazoglou, Koskelainen, McQuerrey Tuttle, & Pitel, 2017; Slate, Johnson, & Colbert, 2007; Violanti et al., 2006; Waters & Ussery, 2007; Weiss et al., 2010). Officers are regularly exposed to critical incidents (e.g., vehicular accidents and fatalities, cases of abuse and mistreatment of vulnerable populations, dealing with violent subjects) that have long-lasting effects on their overall mental health (Cross & Ashley, 2004; Karlsson & Christianson, 2003). It is not a normal condition for the human brain to be exposed to human misery at the heightened levels experienced by many first re-sponders. In addition, sustained and continuous exposure to stress and critical incidents can contribute to declining mental function (Heim & Nemeroff, 2009). Mental functioning is a necessity in police work. Officers must enter a career with exceptional mental health and are expected to remain that way for the duration of their careers.

The cost of caring (Figley, 1995) in police work is seen in the form of compassion fatigue and can have adverse effects on the physical, emotional, and mental health of officers, which is directly and indirectly related to overall work performance (Andersen & Papazoglou, 2015). Seeing the worst parts of society, along with caring for victims, can negatively influence job performance. For example, officers may misplace aggression and anger in the form of excessive use of force issues and citizen complaints, both of which can lead to liability issues. In addition to job performance concerns, officers may struggle on a personal level both physically and mentally when combatting compassion fatigue. Officers are skilled at concealing their emotions such that others may be un-aware that something is going on in the officer's life until problematic behavior surfaces.

Officers are often reluctant to admit that they may be struggling, especially with mental health issues (Olson & Wasilewski, 2016). Issues that can affect one's mental and emotional health often carry a stigma, even more so within subcultures like law enforcement (Violanti, Owens, McCanlies, Fekedulegn, & Andrew, 2018; Workman-Stark, 2017). Police culture influences how incidents are framed and how they are perceived by officers (Waters & Ussery, 2007). Officers' feelings of reluctance toward mental health improvement programs exemplifies the dark side of police culture where seeking help is stigmatized as weakness (Hohner, 2017; Workman-Stark, 2017). Hohner (2017) adds that officers are worried about peer support programs backfiring, as they fear that their expression of concerns and negative experiences might be conveyed to management. Additionally, availability and accessibility to mental health resources within police agencies may prevent officers from receiving the help they need (Violanti, Mnatsakanova, Burchfiel, Hartley, & Andrew, 2012). Generally, officers that expressed job dissatisfaction due to organizational and departmental factors were more likely to experience symptoms of depression, anxiety and traumatic stress (Gershon, Barocas, Canton, Xianbin Li, & Vlahov, 2009).

Individual officers have varying reactions when exposed to traumatic or potentially traumatic incidents. Those who may have a negative reaction to an incident will often refuse to come forward, for fear of what their peers may think. This leaves many officers to actually suffer in silence. The repression of emotions among police officers has been associated with poor health holistically (Wastell, 2002), and those who suffer in silence may revert to maladaptive coping mechanisms like drugs and/or alcohol to try to deal with the stress and trauma (Cross & Ashley, 2004; Hackett & Violanti, 2003; Violanti & Samuels, 2007; Waters & Ussery, 2007). Asking for help in police work is difficult for many officers, because many believe that doing so could cost them their career, livelihood, and the respect of fellow officers. An occupation that operates at societal extremes reiterates the necessity to reinforce such cultural beliefs (Crank, 2004; Karlsson & Christianson, 2003; Kelley, 2005).

Current findings regarding police compassion fatigue

The amount of research examining compassion fatigue with workers in healthcare professions such as nurses and mental health professionals has grown considerably in recent years (e.g., Cocker & Joss, 2016; Czaja, Moss, & Mealer, 2012; Mason et al., 2014; Meadors et al., 2010; Sabo, 2006). Few studies, however, have investigated compassion fatigue with law enforcement officers where participant samples were critically reviewed to be unrepresentative and small (Andersen & Papazoglou, 2015). Furthermore, compassion fatigue in officers has been shown to increase, and compassion satisfaction (the pleasure derived from being able to do one's work) decrease, as the number of perceived traumas experienced grows (Battle, 2012). Regarding prevalence, approximately 15% of general duty officers across North America and Europe were found to be experiencing substantial levels of compassion fatigue, indicating this problem is not limited to geographic areas (Andersen, Papazoglou, & Collins, 2018). Furthermore, almost 40% of the participating officers in one study reported low levels of compassion satisfaction (Papazoglou et al., 2019).

Compassion fatigue has also been shown to be negatively associated with compassion satisfaction (Papazoglou, 2018). However, a positive relationship between compassion satisfaction and work engagement in officers has also been found in other studies (Audin, Burke, & Ivtzan, 2018; Mason et al., 2014). Work engagement refers to issues such as feeling proud of one's occupation as well as being dedicated to, and absorbed in, one's work. The recent rise of the Ferguson Effect, or officers disengaging from their work duties and communities due to negative media attention, is especially concerning as there may be substantial implications on the health of officers (Chiappo-West, 2018).

Prior research also suggests that the frequency and type of traumatic exposure in policing may be more likely to induce compassion fatigue compared to other trauma types (Violanti & Gehrke, 2004). For instance, dealing with the death of a fellow officer in the line of duty, as well as being involved in situations that poses a threat to survival, puts officers at a higher risk of developing compassion fatigue with symptoms akin to PTSD (Violanti & Gehrke, 2004). Officers working mainly with sexual assault and rape victims were more likely to develop compassion fatigue compared with officers performing more general police duties (Turgoose, Glover, Barker, & Maddox, 2017). Approximately 25% of law enforcement officers assigned to an Internet child exploitation task force experienced low compassion satisfaction (Bourke & Craun, 2014; Burns, Morley, Bradshaw, & Domene, 2008). Frequent indirect exposure to child exploitation material, low levels of support from the law enforcement organization, and heavy workloads have all been related to lower levels of compassion satisfaction (Brady, 2017).

Individual officer characteristics such as gender and personality traits have also been linked to compassion fatigue in extant research. For example, female officers dealing with abused children were at increased risk for developing compassion fatigue (Violanti & Gehrke, 2004). Another study found not only a strong relationship between post-traumatic stress symptoms and compassion fatigue, but also found gender differences between detectives investigating sexual offenses against children such that open communication with spouses was related to lower levels of compassion satisfaction with female, but not male detectives (Lane, Lating, Lowry, & Martino, 2010). One suggested reason for this finding was that female officers might perceive their caregiving in the line of duty to be inadequate compared to caregiving in their personal lives (Lane et al., 2010). Negative personality traits such as high levels of authoritarianism were also found to be a risk factor for lower compassion satisfaction, as this type of person may lack social support and feelings of connection with the community (Craigie et al., 2016; Papazoglou, 2018; Papazoglou et al., 2019).

Researchers have also identified protective factors in the relationship between work stress and compassion fatigue. Higher levels of social support from friends and family predicted greater compassion satisfaction in samples consisting of predominantly male officers (Brady, 2017). Another researcher found that (1) life balance including healthy eating, exercise, and engaging in leisure activities, (2) opportunities to reflect on occupational experiences through professional or peer counseling, and (3) supportive supervisors are all associated with lower levels of compassion fatigue (Tehrani, 2010).

Impact of compassion fatigue

The review of scholarly literature reveals that compassion fatigue can lead to numerous health symptoms and increase susceptibility to other conditions such as PTSD, depression, and anxiety disorders (Cocker & Joss, 2016). More specifically, research indicates that compassion fatigue may affect law enforcement professionals behaviorally (e.g., aloofness, hypervigilance, cynicism), cognitively (e.g., derealization, depersonalization, lack of concentration), as well as emotionally (e.g., irritability, agitation, apathy, negativity) (Bride, Radey, & Figley, 2007; Figley, 2002). The impact of compassion fatigue can be incapacitating for one's health and wellbeing when left unaddressed for an extended period of time; that is, the aforementioned negative impact on different areas (behaviors, cognitions, emotions) becomes more intense and deteriorating over time. A common misconception among officers is that mental health challenges can be remedied through maladaptive coping (e.g. alcohol use, smoking, self-blame) (Acquadro Maran, Varetto, Zedda, & Ieraci, 2015; Cross & Ashley, 2004; Gershon, 2000). Studies have reported that approximately 25% of police officers are dependent on alcohol as a result of workplace stressors (Cross & Ashley, 2004; Violanti, n.d.). Substance use may have started out as a means to socialize amongst colleagues, yet for some, what was initially occasional developed into a maladaptive coping mechanism to fade out the trauma and diminish the stress experienced on the job (Cross & Ashley, 2004). Acquadro Maran et al. (2015) noted that the risk of enduring distress and of developing PTSD increases when officers cope using maladaptive strategies. Unfortunately, despite an officer's best effort at self-therapy via passive and problematic personal coping practices, the issues affecting their mental wellbeing remains to be satisfactorily dealt with (Cross & Ashley, 2004).

The impact of compassion fatigue on officers' health and wellbeing is one side of the spectrum. Alternatively, it should be considered that compassion fatigue is very likely to affect officers' performance at work. Trauma scholars mentioned that caregiving professionals may even experience dissociation during their work with traumatized individuals (Danieli, 1996). Mathieu (2007) mentions that while each individual may express certain unique symptoms of compassion fatigue; those entering in the danger zone of compassion fatigue may show warning signs of "intrusive imagery or dissociation." Healthcare professionals experiencing compassion fatigue have often felt that they were "frequently dissociated [and] walked around in an altered state …" (Babbel, 2012). Similarly, police officers support numerous victims of crimes, accidents, or natural catastrophes over the course of their career. Therefore, compassion fatigue may create ripple effect of poor health and mental malfunctioning. Research has shown that those who suffer from previous mental health challenges are more likely to develop PTSD in the experience of a life-threatening situation (McFarlane, 2000; Sayed, Iacoviello, & Charney, 2015).

Officers' personal and family lives are also impacted by compassion fatigue (Sprang, Clark, & Whitt-Woosley, 2007). At the end of their shift, police officers return back to their families and they assume the role of a parent, spouse, son/daughter, and friend. Officers who suffer from police compassion fatigue may become cynical, apathetic, negative, and aloof which could negatively influence their interactions with family and friends (Cox, Marchionna, & Fitch, 2017; Fuller, 2003). As a result, a snowball phenomenon may occur and mundane or minor family or personal issues may remain unresolved and aggravate over time until they lead to family discord or potential divorce (Miller, 2007).

Burnout

Definition

Burnout is a common term used across various sectors of the workforce. The American Psychological Association defines burnout as "characterized by emotional exhaustion, and negative attitudes and feelings toward one's co-workers and job role." (Wilson, 2011, p. 17)

Burnout is a common psychological response to chronic occupational stress and is found across human services sectors where employees routinely interact with others (Magnusson, Theorell, Oxenstierna, Hyde, & Westerlund, 2008; Maslach, Jackson, & Leiter, 1996). Excessive work demands, met with inadequate coping and support resources, can lead to burnout. Historically, burnout is considered to have three major dimensions which include exhaustion, depersonalization or cynicism, and a decreased sense of personal accomplishment (Burke, 1994; Martinussen, Richardsen, & Burke, 2007; Maslach, 1982; Turgoose et al., 2017). Exhaustion is related to the feeling of emotional exhaustion from one's work and arises when situations call for emotional responses that are inauthentic and incongruent with one's felt emotions. Depersonalization is disengagement from work or enthusiasm about one's work. Depersonalization arises when workers are repeatedly exposed to negative social interactions and subsequently create distance between them-selves and others based on the interactions encountered on the job. A decreased sense of personal accomplishment is when one no longer feels as if they are making meaningful contributions in their work and this occurs when the population being served is regularly dissatisfied with one's actions (Maslach, 1982; Schaufeli & Janczur, 1994). Among these three dimensions, exhaustion is considered the core of burnout (Maslach, Schaufeli, & Leiter, 2001). A two-component model of burnout was proposed that focused more broadly on the element of exhaustion to include cognitive, physical, and emotional exhaustion as well as disengagement which encompassed cynicism as well as distancing (Demerouti, Bakker, Vardakou, & Kantas, 2003). Collectively, the experiences that lend themselves to causing burnout are not uncommon experiences in the field of policing.

Burnout in policing

Police work is widely recognized as a stressful and dangerous occupation that has been associated with burnout (Backteman-Erlanson, Padyab, & Brulin, 2013; Burke & Mikkelsen, 2006; Moon & Jonson, 2012; Shane, 2010; Vila, 2006; Violanti & Aron, 1993). The nature of police work, coupled with the emotional demands required of officers when oscillating between responding to the suffering of others and confronting potential danger in the line of duty, give rise to psychological burnout (Martinussen et al., 2007). Studies have shown that burnout is common among police. For example, a study rep-resenting police officers across four agencies which varied in size found that a majority of officers reported moderate to high levels of exhaustion, depersonalization, and low personal accomplishment (Hawkins, 2001). Similarly, a recent study investigating burnout among a large sample of over 2000 officers across the United States found that officers frequently felt "used up" at the end of their workdays which is central to the exhaustion component of burnout (McCarty & Skogan, 2013).

While burnout is an individual psychological response to stress, risk factors for burnout are categorized as individual factors, job-related factors, or organizational factors (Cooper, Dewe, & O'Driscoll, 2001; Maslach et al., 2001). Gender differences and length of time spent in police work are connected to burnout as well as negative organizational climate, lack of social support, and nature of job duties (McCarty & Skogan, 2013; Schaufeli & Enzmann, 1998). Burnout impacts the health of officers and also strains their work performance and police organizations (Conrad & Kellar-Guenther, 2006; Kohan & Mazmanian, 2003; Queirós, Kaiseler, & Silva, 2013).

Risk for burnout

Individual and interpersonal risk factors for burnout range from gender and race to length of service, prior work experience, and work-family conflict. Several studies have yielded inconsistent findings on gender differences in burnout among police officers. It is often assumed that females experience higher rates of burnout compared to males and several studies have confirmed that female officers do report greater levels of burnout (Johnson, 1991; Schaufeli & Enzmann, 1998). However, others have found no significant differences in burnout among male and female officers (Kop, Euwema, & Schaufeli, 1999; McCarty, Zhao, & Garland, 2007). Studies examining race have shown that African American officers experience less burnout than their white counterparts and are less likely to feel negative at work (Dowler, 2005; McCarty & Skogan, 2013). However, the interaction between race and gender shows that African American female officers report significantly higher levels of burnout than other officers (McCarty et al., 2007). Length of service as a police officer is also predictive of burnout with burnout increasing over time (Turgoose et al., 2017). Conversely, prior military experience among law enforcement officers has been protective against job-related burnout (Ivie & Garland, 2011). Interpersonal factors such as work-family conflict have also been connected to burnout dimensions, providing evidence that family pressures associated with police work lead to officer burnout (Martinussen et al., 2007; McCarty, 2013).

The dangerous nature of police work and operational aspects of the job also place officers at risk for experiencing burnout. The perception of danger is an important factor in predicting burnout such that officers' perceptions of greater danger are linked to higher levels of burnout (McCarty & Skogan, 2013). A possible interpretation of this finding may be related to the fact that exposure to trauma increases depersonalization and exhaustion; hence, officers are more susceptible to experiencing burnout. Similarly, exposure to negative events, like violent arrests or officer-involved shootings, have been associated with the experience of burnout among female officers (McCarty et al., 2007). On the other hand, Burke (1997) found that officers who were more frequently exposed to stressful events felt more accomplished in their work while officers who encountered fewer stressful events experienced decreased personal accomplishment. Moreover, police work is emotionally demanding and regularly requires officers to engage in emotional labor to manage and display emotions not actually felt when experiencing emotional incongruities in the line of duty (Van Gelderen, Konijn, & Bakker, 2017). For example, the police role regularly requires the display of emotions which are not actually felt (e.g. displaying empathy for a crime victim who is known to the officer for having ties to a supremacist group and has been the perpetrator of crime during previous contacts).

This disconnect between expressed emotion and felt emotion can lead to emotional exhaustion and cynicism (Bakker & Heuven, 2006; Hochschild, 1979, 1983; Rafaeli & Sutton, 1989; Turgoose et al., 2017). Added risk for burnout comes from the lack of reciprocity in the relationship between oneself and the population being served (Schaufeli & Janczur, 1994). Therefore, it is not surprising that public scrutiny of police, combined with unfavorable encounters with the public, give rise to cynicism and depersonalization among police.

In addition to job-related factors, organizational factors present risk for officer burnout and have been shown to have a stronger relationship with burnout than operational factors of police work (Kohan & Mazmanian, 2003). Research has demonstrated that negative organizational climate is associated with the emotional exhaustion aspect of burnout for police officers (Backteman-Erlanson et al., 2013). To this end, a sense of unfairness in the organization also predicts burnout among officers (McCarty & Skogan, 2013). Conversely, higher levels of social support from within the organization are associated with lower levels of burnout (McCarty & Skogan, 2013; Perez, Jones, Englert, & Sachau, 2010). The connection between perceived support from peers or supervisors and subsequent burnout has been established for officers in administrative roles as well (McCarty, 2013). Studies have shown that relations in police organizations are precursors to burnout across ranks and for both male and female police officers.

Consequences of burnout

Long-term exposure to work stress, excessive emotional demands, sense of little autonomy over work, and organizational stress, can lead to burnout among police officers (Hallsten, Bellaagh, & Gustafsson, 2002; Kohan & Mazmanian, 2003; McCarty & Skogan, 2013). Burnout carries consequences for police officers, their families, their job performance, and their organizations. Burnout can impact sleep, physical health, and make officers vulnerable to mental health conditions such as depression and PTSD. Maladaptive coping skills associated with burnout, like alcohol use, perpetuate issues that extend beyond the individual. Burnout also influences the way officers respond to their family members, thereby affecting the family system. Furthermore, burnout is related to aggressive behavior among officers, which has implications for their performance in the line of duty. Aspects of burnout that are strongly connected to police aggressive behavior include depersonalization and low personal accomplishment (Queirós et al., 2013). Finally, disengagement and cynicism in the line of duty can cause issues on the job and place strain on police organizations due to officer turnover and negative police-community relations (Kohan & Mazmanian, 2003; Kop et al., 1999; Maslach & Jackson, 1981).

Current findings on reducing burnout

While research has established numerous risk factors for burnout, factors that protect against police burnout have also been found. At the individual level, empathy has been associated lower levels of police burnout, which suggests that officers who are empathetic may be less likely to develop burnout. Researchers suggest that empathy may help officers find meaning in their work and thereby protect against the development of burnout (Turgoose et al., 2017). Similarly, officers who experience compassion satisfaction from their work, or positive feelings associated with helping others (Stamm, 2002), experience lower levels of burnout (Chiappo-West, 2018). High levels of professional efficacy, or the feeling that one's work makes a difference, are associated with lower burnout. The influence of spirituality on burnout among police indicates that higher spirituality is associated with lower levels of emotional exhaustion and depersonalization and higher levels of personal accomplishment.

At the organizational level, supportive relationships with peers and supervisors is helpful in preventing burnout as well (Perez et al., 2010). Organizational features such as leadership style within the police agency can minimize burnout. Recent research examined the moderating effects of police leadership on the relationship between stress and burnout. The perception of high levels of transformational leadership was associated with lower levels of burnout for officers. Transformational leadership was found to be most effective at reducing burnout under low stress conditions in the workplace (Russell, 2014). Stress management training and the presence of formal debriefing in law enforcement agencies has also been connected to reduced levels of police burnout (Miller, Unruh, Zhang, Liu, & Wharton, 2017). Currently, a mindfulness intervention program is being tested with a sample of police officers in Brazil to determine its effectiveness in reducing police burnout (Trombka et al., 2018). This aligns with the recommendations from recent research to utilize psychoeducation and resilience training programs to address police stress and related outcomes such as burnout (Papazoglou & Andersen, 2014).

The impacts of compassion fatigue versus burnout on police work

Research has shown that both compassion fatigue and burnout share common symptoms such as alcohol abuse, aloofness, and emotional exhaustion (Figley, 2002; Hooper, Craig, Janvrin, Wetsel, & Reimels, 2010; Jacobson, 2012). In addition, both burnout and compassion fatigue may affect caregiving professionals' decision-making at work as well as their job performance and job satisfaction (Salloum, Kondrat, Johnco, & Olson, 2015). Both conditions may increase an individual's tendency to quit job, increase absenteeism, and experience a loss of motivation for work (Salloum et al., 2015). However, there is compelling evidence that suggests that these conditions are distinct. The most prominent point that distinguishes the two is that compassion fatigue originates from exposure to traumatic situations. More specifically, research scholars contend that prolonged exposure to potentially traumatic situations is intertwined with caregiving professionals' inability to disengage themselves from (Figley, 1995, 2002) or inability to engage themselves with the victims' traumatic experiences (Papazoglou, Marans, Keesee, & Chopko, n.d.); thus, leading frontline professionals to experience compassion fatigue over time. On the other hand, professional burnout is the result of lack of professional efficacy due to high job demands (e.g., heavy workload, shift work), lack of resources at work (e.g., necessary equipment is not available), lack of social support from peers and supervisors, and excessive work-related stress (Burke & Mikkelsen, 2006; Martinussen et al., 2007).

Conclusions

The current chapter presented the definition and negative impact of compassion fatigue and burnout on police officers' health, wellbeing, and job performance. Stress and trauma are widespread in police work and it is highly likely that officers may experience burnout and compassion fatigue symptoms. Nevertheless, the impact of compassion fatigue and burnout is reversible and preventable as long as officers engage in healthy, adaptive coping strategies to deal with compassion fatigue and burnout. Maladaptive ways of coping are strategies that officers use order to avoid, procrastinate (or assumingly procrastinate), or deal with the experienced issue by jeopardizing their own health and wellbeing. That is, in their efforts to suppress any emotional reactions in response to a critical incident, officers may self-medicate by abusing alcohol or other types of substances. While maladaptive coping may suppress issues, they remain unresolved when dealt with in this way and can accumulate over time as officers are continuously exposed to traumatic, critical incidents throughout their careers.

On the other hand, adaptive ways of coping can armor officers with necessary strategies they need to effectively manage the challenges of police work. However, police leaders, police clinicians, police families, as well as officers themselves should synergistically support adaptive coping skills. Scholarly literature has documented numerous strategies for healthy coping to deal with compassion fatigue and burnout. While not the primary scope of present chapter, research with police and military personnel showed that self-help techniques could better help officers cope with burnout and compassion fatigue. Some self-help strategies include journaling, mindfulness, spirituality/religiosity, relaxation techniques, humor, physical exercise, social support network, and even eco-therapy.

As previously noted, a holistic approach is imperative in order to help officers prevent or handle the impact of burnout and compassion fatigue. That being said, police supervisors should openly discuss with their officers any issues or concerns they experience in the line of duty and collaborate with the peer support units to tangibly support officers who need help. It should be noted that any unaddressed "minor" issues might accumulate over time and increase risk for compassion fatigue and burnout symptoms. Open and honest dialogues between supervisors and officers may help to de-stigmatize issues such as compassion fatigue, burnout, and their psychological ramifications. Policies to minimize the risk for compassion fatigue and burnout within police organizations are recommended. Perhaps, in some cases (e.g., Internet Child Exploitation Units) police supervisors may recommend that officers who serve in their units have the option to rotate to different positions before they succumb to the negative effects of compassion fatigue or burnout. In addition, police leaders may advocate that evidence-based psychological strategies be incorporated in police training curricula so that mental health prevention and wellbeing are embedded in the culture.

Furthermore, the role of police clinicians is integral toward helping officers prevent or fight compassion fatigue and burnout. Clinicians may engage in the education or translation of knowledge on topics such as compassion fatigue and burnout as well as assist with the development or training curricula. If officers suffer from moderate to severe compassion fatigue or burnout, treatment should be carried out in ways that empower officers to address their issues and return to their positions to serve their communities.

References

Acquadro Maran, D., Varetto, A., Zedda, M., & Ieraci, V. (2015). Occupational stress, anxiety and coping strategies in police officers. *Occupational Medicine, 65*(6), 466−473. https://doi.org/10.1093/occmed/kqv060.

Adams, R. E., Boscarino, J. A., & Figley, C. R. (2006). Compassion fatigue and psychological distress among social workers: A validation study. *American Journal of Orthopsychiatry, 76*(1), 103−108. https://doi.org/10.1037/0002-9432.76.1.103.

American Psychiatric Association. (2013). *Diagnostic and statistical manual of mental disorders* (5th ed.). Arlington, VA: American Psychiatric Publishing, Inc. American Psychiatric Publishing Inc (5th editio) https://doi.org/10.1176/appi.books.9780890425596.893619.

Andersen, J. P., & Papazoglou, K. (2015). Compassion fatigue and compassion satisfaction among police officers: An understudied topic. *International Journal of Emergency Mental Health and Human Resilience, 17*(3), 661−663. https://doi.org/10.4172/1522-4821.1000259.

Andersen, J. P., Papazoglou, K., & Collins, P. (2018). Association of authoritarianism, compassion fatigue, and compassion satisfaction among police officers in North America: An exploration. *International Journal of Criminal Justice Sciences, 13*(2), 405−419. https://doi.org/110.5281/zenodo.2657663.

Audin, K., Burke, J., & Ivtzan, I. (2018). Compassion fatigue, compassion satisfaction and work engagement in residential child care Article history. *Scottish Journal of Residential Child Care, 17*. Retrieved from https://www.celcis.org/files/8715/3719/1694/2018_Vol_17_No_3_Audin_K_Compassion_fatigue_compassion_satisfaction_and_work_engagement_in_residential_childcare.pdf.

Babbel, S. (2012). *Compassion fatigue: Bodily symptoms of empathy*. Retrieved from https://www.psychologytoday.com/ca/blog/somatic-psychology/201207/compassion-fatigue.

Backteman-Erlanson, S., Padyab, M., & Brulin, C. (2013). Prevalence of burnout and associations with psychosocial work environment, physical strain, and stress of conscience among Swedish female and male police personnel. *Police Practice and Research, 14*(6), 491−505. https://doi.org/10.1080/15614263.2012.736719.

Bakker, A. B., & Heuven, E. (2006). Emotional dissonance, burnout, and in-role performance among nurses and police officers. *International Journal of Stress Management, 13*(4), 423−440. https://doi.org/10.1037/1072-5245.13.4.423.

Battle, L. (2012). Compassion fatigue, compassion satisfaction, and burnout among police officers who have experienced previous perceived traumas. *Dissertation Abstracts International Section A: Humanities and Social Sciences, 73*(6-A).

Bourke, M. L., & Craun, S. W. (2014). Secondary traumatic stress among internet crimes against children task force personnel. *Sexual Abuse: A Journal of Research and Treatment, 26*(6), 586–609. https://doi.org/10.1177/1079063213509411.

Boyle, D. A. (2015). Compassion fatigue. *Nursing, 45*(7), 48–51. https://doi.org/10.1097/01.NURSE.0000461857.48809.a1.

Brady, P. Q. (2017). Crimes against caring: Exploring the risk of secondary traumatic stress, burnout, and compassion satisfaction among child exploitation investigators. *Journal of Police and Criminal Psychology, 32*(4), 312. https://doi.org/10.1007/s11896-016-9223-8.

Bride, B. E., Radey, M., & Figley, C. R. (2007). Measuring compassion fatigue. *Clinical Social Work Journal, 35*(3), 155–163. https://doi.org/10.1007/s10615-007-0091-7.

Burke, R. J. (1994). Stressful events, work-family conflict, coping, psychological burnout, and well-being among police officers. *Psychological Reports, 75*(2), 787–800. https://doi.org/10.2466/pr0.1994.75.2.787.

Burke, R. J. (1997). Toward an understanding of psychological burnout among police officers. *International Journal of Stress Management, 4*(1), 13–27. https://doi.org/10.1007/BF02766070.

Burke, R. J., & Mikkelsen, A. (2006). Burnout among Norwegian police officers: Potential antecedents and consequences. *International Journal of Stress Management, 13*(1), 64–83. https://doi.org/10.1037/1072-5245.13.1.64.

Burke, R. J., & Mikkelsen, A. (2007). Suicidal ideation among police officers in Norway. *Policing: An International Journal of Police Strategies & Management, 30*(2), 228–236. https://doi.org/10.1108/13639510710753234.

Burns, C. M., Morley, J., Bradshaw, R., & Domene, J. (2008). The emotional impact on and coping strategies employed by police teams investigating internet child exploitation. *Traumatology, 14*(2), 20–31. https://doi.org/10.1177/1534765608319082.

Chiappo-West, G. (2018). Compassion satisfaction, burnout, secondary traumatic stress, and work engagement in police officers in Arizona. *Dissertation Abstracts International: Section B: The Sciences and Engineering, 79*(1-B) ((E)).

Cocker, F., & Joss, N. (2016). Compassion fatigue among healthcare, emergency and community service workers: A systematic review. *International Journal of Environmental Research and Public Health, 13*(6), 618. https://doi.org/10.3390/ijerph13060618.

Conrad, D., & Kellar-Guenther, Y. (2006). Compassion fatigue, burnout, and compassion satisfaction among Colorado child protection workers. *Child Abuse & Neglect, 30*(10), 1071–1080. https://doi.org/10.1016/j.chiabu.2006.03.009.

Cooper, C. L., Dewe, P. J., & O'Driscoll, M. P. (2001). A special form of strain: Job-related burnout. In *Organizational stress: A review and critique of theory, research, and applications* (pp. 79–116). London, UK: SAGE Publications, Inc. https://doi.org/10.4135/9781452231235.n4.

Cox, S. M., Marchionna, S., & Fitch, B. D. (2017). The police culture and work stress. In *Introduction to policing* (3rd ed., p. 177).

Craigie, M., Osseiran-Moisson, R., Hemsworth, D., Aoun, S., Francis, K., Brown, J., et al. (2016). The influence of trait-negative affect and compassion satisfaction on compassion fatigue in Australian nurses. *Psychological Trauma: Theory, Research, Practice, and Policy, 8*(1), 88–97. https://doi.org/10.1037/tra0000050.

Crank, J. P. (2004). *Understanding police culture* (2nd ed.). Cincinnati, OH: Anderson Publishing Co.

Cross, C. L., & Ashley, L. (2004). Police trauma and addiction. Coping with the dangers of the job. *FBI Law Enforcement Bulletin, 73*(10), 24–32. Retrieved from http://www.fbi.gov/stats-services/publications/law-enforcement-bulletin/2013/june/archive.

Czaja, A. S., Moss, M., & Mealer, M. (2012). Symptoms of posttraumatic stress disorder among pediatric acute care nurses. *Journal of Pediatric Nursing, 27*(4), 357–365. https://doi.org/10.1016/j.pedn.2011.04.024.

Danieli, Y. (1996). Who takes care of the caregiver? In R. J. Apfel, & B. Simon (Eds.), *Minefields in their hearts: The mental health of children in war and communal violence* (pp. 189−205). New Haven, CT: Yale University Press.

Demerouti, E., Bakker, A. B., Vardakou, I., & Kantas, A. (2003). The convergent validity of two burnout instruments: A multitrait-multimethod analysis. *European Journal of Psychological Assessment, 19*(1), 12−23. https://doi.org/https://doi.org/10.1027//1015-5759.19.1.12.

Dowler, K. (2005). Job satisfaction, burnout, and perception of unfair treatment: The relationship between race and police work. *Police Quarterly, 8*(4), 476−489. https://doi.org/10.1177/1098611104269787.

Figley, C. R. (1995). *Compassion fatigue: Coping with secondary traumatic stress disorder in those who treat the traumatized. BrunnerMazel psychosocial stress series.* New York, NY: Bruner/Mazel.

Figley, C. R. (2002). *Coping with secondary traumatic stress disorder in those who treat the traumatized.* London, UK: Brunner-Routledge.

Fuller, M. E. (2003). *Living with a cop: A handbook for police officers and their families.* Alberta: Lethbridge. Retrieved from https://opus.uleth.ca/bitstream/handle/10133/1150/Fuller_Merle_E.pdf.

Gershon, R. (2000). *National institute of justice final report "project shields.* Retrieved from https://www.ncjrs.gov/pdffiles1/nij/grants/185892.pdf.

Gershon, R. R. M., Barocas, B., Canton, A. N., Xianbin Li, L., & Vlahov, D. (2009). Mental, physical, and behavioral outcomes associated with perceived work stress in police officers. *Criminal Justice and Behavior, 36*(3), 275−289. https://doi.org/10.1177/0093854808330015.

Hackett, D. P., & Violanti, J. M. (2003). *Police suicide: Tactics for prevention and intervention.* Springfield, IL: Charles C. Thomas.

Hallsten, L., Bellaagh, K., & Gustafsson, K. (2002). *Burnout in Sweden−a population study* (Stockholm).

Hawkins, H. C. (2001). Police officer burnout: A partial replication of maslach's burnout inventory. *Police Quarterly, 4*(3), 343−360. https://doi.org/10.1177/109861101129197888.

Heim, C., & Nemeroff, C. B. (2009). Neurobiology of posttraumatic stress disorder. *CNS Spectrums, 14*(1 Suppl. 1), 13−24.

Henry, V. E. (2004). *Death work: Police, trauma, and the psychology of survival.* New York, NY: Oxford University Press.

Hochschild, A. (1979). Emotion work, feeling rules, and social structure. *American Journal of Sociology, 85*(3), 551−575. https://doi.org/10.1086/227049.

Hochschild, A. (1983). *The managed heart: Commercialization of human feeling.* Berkeley, CA: University of California Press.

Hohner, C. (2017). *"The environment says it" s okay': The tension between peer support and police culture Recommended Citation.* Retrieved from https://ir.lib.uwo.ca/etd.

Hooper, C., Craig, J., Janvrin, D. R., Wetsel, M. A., & Reimels, E. (2010). Compassion satisfaction, burnout, and compassion fatigue among emergency nurses compared with nurses in other selected inpatient specialties. *Journal of Emergency Nursing, 36*(5), 420−427. https://doi.org/10.1016/j.jen.2009.11.027.

IAFF Staff. (2018). *Compassion fatigue: When caring hurts.* Retrieved from https://www.iaffrecoverycenter.com/blog/compassion-fatigue-caring-hurts/.

Ivie, D., & Garland, B. (2011). Stress and burnout in policing: Does military experience matter? *Policing. An International Journal of Police Strategies & Management, 34*(1), 49−66. https://doi.org/10.1108/13639511111106605.

Jacobson, J. M. (2012). Risk of compassion fatigue and burnout and potential for compassion satisfaction among employee assistance professionals: Protecting the workforce. *Traumatology, 18*(3), 64−72. https://doi.org/10.1177/1534765611431833.

Johnson, L. B. (1991). Job strain among police officers: Gender comparisons. *Police Studies, 14*(1), 12–16.

Karlsson, I., & Christianson, S. (2003). The phenomenology of traumatic experiences in police work. *Policing: An International Journal of Police Strategies & Management, 26*(3), 419–438. https://doi.org/10.1108/13639510310489476.

Kelley, T. M. (2005). Mental health and prospective police professionals. *Policing: An International Journal of Police Strategies & Management, 28*(1), 6–29. https://doi.org/10.1108/13639510510580959.

Kohan, A., & Mazmanian, D. (2003). Police work, burnout, and pro-organizational behavior. *Criminal Justice and Behavior, 30*(5), 559–583. https://doi.org/10.1177/0093854803254432.

Kop, N., Euwema, M., & Schaufeli, W. (1999). Burnout, job stress and violent behaviour among Dutch police officers. *Work & Stress, 13*(4), 326–340. https://doi.org/10.1080/02678379950019789.

Lane, E. J., Lating, J. M., Lowry, J. L., & Martino, T. P. (2010). Differences in compassion fatigue, symptoms of posttraumatic stress disorder and relationship satisfaction, including sexual desire and functioning, between male and female detectives who investigate sexual offenses against children: A pilot study. *International Journal of Emergency Mental Health, 12*, 257–266.

Magnusson, H.,L. L., Theorell, T., Oxenstierna, G., Hyde, M., & Westerlund, H. (2008). Demand, control and social climate as predictors of emotional exhaustion symptoms in working Swedish men and women. *Scandinavian Journal of Public Health, 36*(7), 737–743. https://doi.org/10.1177/1403494808090164.

Marchand, C. (2007). *An investigation of the influence of compassion fatigue due to secondary traumatic stress on the Canadian youth worker.* Retrieved from http://marchandchris.tripod.com/PDF/CompassionFatiguehistoryconcept.pdf.

Martinussen, M., Richardsen, A. M., & Burke, R. J. (2007). Job demands, job resources, and burnout among police officers. *Journal of Criminal Justice, 35*(3), 239–249. https://doi.org/10.1016/j.jcrimjus.2007.03.001.

Maslach, C. (1982). *Burnout - the cost of caring: How to recognize, prevent, and cure the burnout syndrome for nurses, teachers, counsellors, doctors, therapists, police, social workers, and anyone else who cares about people.* Englewood Cliffs, NJ: Prentice Hall.

Maslach, C., & Jackson, S. E. (1981). *MBI: Maslach burnout inventory - manual.* Palo Alto, CA: Consulting Psychologists Press.

Maslach, C., Jackson, S. E., & Leiter, M. (1996). *The Maslach burnout inventory - manual* (3rd ed.). Mountain View, CA: Consulting Psychologists Press.

Maslach, C., Schaufeli, W. B., & Leiter, M. P. (2001). Job burnout. *Annual Review of Psychology, 52*(1), 397–422. https://doi.org/10.1146/annurev.psych.52.1.397.

Mason, V. M., Leslie, G., Clark, K., Lyons, P., Walke, E., Butler, C., et al. (2014). Compassion fatigue, moral distress, and work engagement in surgical intensive care unit trauma nurses. *Dimensions of Critical Care Nursing, 33*(4), 215–225. https://doi.org/10.1097/DCC.0000000000000056.

Mason, R., & Toner, B. (2012). *When domestic violence, mental health and substance use problems Co-occur* (Toronto, ON).

Mathieu, F. (2007). Running on empty: Compassion fatigue in health professionals. *Rehab & Community Care Medicine, 4*, 1–7.

McCann, I. L., & Pearlman, L. A. (1990). Vicarious traumatization: A framework for understanding the psychological effects of working with victims. *Journal of Traumatic Stress, 3*(1), 131–149. https://doi.org/10.1007/BF00975140.

McCarty, W. (2013). Gender differences in burnout among municipal police sergeants. *Policing: An International Journal of Police Strategies & Management, 36*(4), 803–818. https://doi.org/10.1108/PIJPSM-03-2013-0026.

McCarty, W. P., & Skogan, W. G. (2013). Job-related burnout among civilian and sworn police personnel. *Police Quarterly, 16*(1), 66−84. https://doi.org/10.1177/1098611112457357.

McCarty, W. P., Zhao, J., & Garland, B. E. (2007). Occupational stress and burnout between male and female police officers. *Policing: An International Journal of Police Strategies & Management, 30*(4), 672−691. https://doi.org/10.1108/13639510710833938.

McFarlane, A. C. (2000). Posttraumatic stress disorder: A model of the longitudinal course and the role of risk factors. *Journal of Clinical Psychiatry, 61*(5), 15−23.

Meadors, P., Lamson, A., Swanson, M., White, M., & Sira, N. (2010). Secondary traumatization in pediatric healthcare providers: Compassion fatigue, burnout, and secondary traumatic stress. *Omega: The Journal of Death and Dying, 60*(2), 103−128. https://doi.org/10.2190/OM.60.2.a.

Miller, L. (2007). Police families: Stresses, syndromes, and solutions. *American Journal of Family Therapy, 35*(1), 21−40. https://doi.org/10.1080/01926180600698541.

Miller, A., Unruh, L., Zhang, N., Liu, X., & Wharton, T. (2017). Professional quality of life of Florida emergency dispatchers. *International Journal of Emergency Services, 6*(1), 29−39. https://doi.org/10.1108/IJES-01-2017-0001.

Moon, M. M., & Jonson, C. L. (2012). The influence of occupational strain on organizational commitment among police: A general strain theory approach. *Journal of Criminal Justice, 40*(3), 249−258. https://doi.org/10.1016/j.jcrimjus.2012.02.004.

Newell, J. M., & MacNeil, G. A. (2010). Professional burnout, vicarious trauma, secondary traumatic stress, and compassion fatigue: A review of theoretical terms, risk factors, and preventive methods for clinicians and researchers. *Best Practices in Mental Health: An International Journal, 6*(2), 57−68.

Olson, A., & Wasilewski, M. (2016). *Suffering in silence: Mental health and stigma in policing.* Retrieved from https://www.policeone.com/police-products/human-resources/articles/218917006-Suffering-in-silence-Mental-health-and-stigma-in-policing/.

Papazoglou, K. (2018). The examination of different pathways leading towards police traumatization: Exploring the role of moral injury and personality in police compassion fatigue. *Dissertation Abstracts International: Section B: The Sciences and Engineering, 79*(3-B).

Papazoglou, K., & Andersen, J. P. (2014). *Exploring compassion fatigue and compassion satisfaction among police.* https://doi.org/10.1037/e559062014-001.

Papazoglou, K., & Chopko, B. (2017). The role of moral suffering (moral distress and moral injury) in police compassion fatigue and PTSD: An unexplored topic. *Frontiers in Psychology, 8.* https://doi.org/10.3389/fpsyg.2017.01999.

Papazoglou, K., Koskelainen, M., McQuerrey Tuttle, B., & Pitel, M. (2017). Examining the role of police compassion fatigue and negative personality traits in impeding the promotion of police compassion satisfaction: A brief report. *Journal of Law Enforcement, 6*(3), 1−14.

Papazoglou, K., Koskelainen, M., & Stuewe, N. (2019). Examining the relationship between personality traits, compassion satisfaction, and compassion fatigue among police officers. *SAGE Open, 9*(1), 215824401882519 https://doi.org/10.1177/2158244018825190.

Papazoglou, K., Marans, S., Keesee, T., & Chopko, B. (2019). Police compassion fatigue, FBI Bulletin.

Pearlman, L. A. (1998). Trauma and the self: A theoretical and clinical perspective. *Journal of Emotional Abuse, 1*, 7−25.

Pearlman, L. A., & Mac Ian, P. S. (1995). Vicarious traumatization: An empirical study of the effects of trauma work on trauma therapists. *Professional Psychology: Research and Practice, 26*(6), 558−565. https://doi.org/10.1037/0735-7028.26.6.558.

Perez, L. M., Jones, J., Englert, D. R., & Sachau, D. (2010). Secondary traumatic stress and burnout among law enforcement investigators exposed to disturbing media images. *Journal of Police and Criminal Psychology, 25*(2), 113−124. https://doi.org/10.1007/s11896-010-9066-7.

Queirós, C., Kaiseler, M., & Silva, A. (2013). Burnout as predictor of aggressivity among police officers. *European Journal of Policing Studies, 1*(2), 110–135.

Rafaeli, A., & Sutton, R. I. (1989). The expression of emotion in organizational life. *Research in Organizational Behavior, 11*, 1–42.

Rafferty, R. (2016). Compassion fatigue & resiliency. Alaska, Retrieved from http://www.ashnha.com/wp-content/uploads/2016/11/Compassion-fatigue-and-Resiliency.pdf

Russell, L. (2014). An empirical investigation of high-risk occupations. *Management Research Review, 37*(4), 367–384. https://doi.org/10.1108/MRR-10-2012-0227.

Sabo, B. M. (2006). Compassion fatigue and nursing work: Can we accurately capture the consequences of caring work? *International Journal of Nursing Practice, 12*(3), 136–142. https://doi.org/10.1111/j.1440-172X.2006.00562.x.

Sabo, B. (2011). Reflecting on the concept of compassion gatigue. *Online Journal of Issues in Nursing, 16*(1). https://doi.org/10.3912.OJIN.Vol16NoQ1Man01.

Salloum, A., Kondrat, D. C., Johnco, C., & Olson, K. R. (2015). The role of self-care on compassion satisfaction, burnout and secondary trauma among child welfare workers. *Children and Youth Services Review, 49*, 54–61. https://doi.org/10.1016/j.childyouth.2014.12.023.

Sayed, S., Iacoviello, B. M., & Charney, D. S. (2015). Risk factors for the development of psychopathology following trauma. *Current Psychiatry Reports, 17*(8), 70. https://doi.org/10.1007/s11920-015-0612-y.

Schaufeli, W., & Enzmann, D. (1998). The burnout companion to study and practice: A critical analysis. In *Issues in occupational health*. Philadelphia, PA: Taylor & Francis.

Schaufeli, W., & Janczur, B. (1994). Burnout among nurses. *Journal of Cross-Cultural Psychology, 25*(1), 95–113. https://doi.org/10.1177/0022022194251006.

Shane, J. M. (2010). Organizational stressors and police performance. *Journal of Criminal Justice, 38*(4), 807–818. https://doi.org/10.1016/j.jcrimjus.2010.05.008.

Slate, R. N., Johnson, W. W., & Colbert, S. S. (2007). Police stress: A structural model. *Journal of Police and Criminal Psychology, 22*(2), 102–112. https://doi.org/10.1007/s11896-007-9012-5.

Sprang, G., Clark, J. J., & Whitt-Woosley, A. (2007). Compassion fatigue, compassion satisfaction, and burnout: Factors impacting a professional's quality of life. *Journal of Loss & Trauma, 12*(3), 259–280. https://doi.org/10.1080/15325020701238093.

Stamm, B. H. (2002). Measuring compassion satisfaction as well as fatigue: Developmental history of the compassion satisfaction and fatigue test. Figley, C. In *Treating compassion fatigue* (p. 108).

Sui, X.-C., & Padmanabhanunni, A. (2016). Vicarious trauma: The psychological impact of working with survivors of trauma for South African psychologists. *Journal of Psychology in Africa, 26*(2), 127–133. https://doi.org/10.1080/14330237.2016.1163894.

Tehrani, N. (2010). Compassion fatigue: Experiences in occupational health, human resources, counselling and police. *Occupational Medicine, 60*, 133–138.

Todaro-Franceschi, V. (2019). *Compassion fatigue and burnout in nursing*. New York, NY: Springer Publishing Company. https://doi.org/10.1891/9780826155214.

Trombka, M., Demarzo, M., Bacas, D. C., Antonio, S. B., Cicuto, K., Salvo, V., et al. (2018). Study protocol of a multicenter randomized controlled trial of mindfulness training to reduce burnout and promote quality of life in police officers: The POLICE study. *BMC Psychiatry, 18*(1), 151. https://doi.org/10.1186/s12888-018-1726-7.

Turgoose, D., Glover, N., Barker, C., & Maddox, L. (2017). Empathy, compassion fatigue, and burnout in police officers working with rape victims. *Traumatology, 23*(2), 205–213. https://doi.org/10.1037/trm0000118.

Van Gelderen, B. R., Konijn, E. A., & Bakker, A. B. (2017). Emotional labor among police officers: A diary study relating strain, emotional labor, and service performance. *International Journal of Human Resource Management, 28*(6), 852−879. https://doi.org/10.1080/09585192.2016.1138500.

Vila, B. (2006). Impact of long work hours on police officers and the communities they serve. *American Journal of Industrial Medicine, 49*(11), 972−980. https://doi.org/10.1002/ajim.20333.

Violanti, J.M. (2014). Dying from the job: The mortality risk for police officers, Retrieved from https://eticosolutions.com/index.php?option=com_phocadownload&view=category&download=11:student-data-files&id=4:circadian-articles&lang=en

Violanti, J. M., & Aron, F. (1993). Sources of police stressors, job attitudes, and psychological distress. *Psychological Reports, 72*(3), 899−904. https://doi.org/10.2466/pr0.1993.72.3.899.

Violanti, J. M., Castellano, C., O'Rourke, J., & Paton, D. (2006). Proximity to the 9/11 terrorist attack and suicide ideation in police officers. *Traumatology, 12*(3), 248−254. https://doi.org/10.1177/1534765606296533.

Violanti, J. M., & Gehrke, A. (2004). Police trauma encounters: Precursors of compassion fatigue. *International Journal of Emergency Mental Health, 6*(2), 75−80.

Violanti, J. M., Mnatsakanova, A., Burchfiel, C. M., Hartley, T. A., & Andrew, M. E. (2012). Police suicide in small departments: A comparative analysis. *International Journal of Emergency Mental Health, 14*(3), 157−162.

Violanti, J. M., Owens, S. L., McCanlies, E., Fekedulegn, D., & Andrew, M. E. (2018). Law enforcement suicide: A review. *Policing: International Journal, 42*(2), 141−164. https://doi.org/10.1108/PIJPSM-05-2017-0061.

Violanti, J. M., & Samuels, S. (2007). Trauma and police suicide ideation. In *From under the blue shadow: Clinical and behavioral perspectives on police suicide* (pp. 89−118). Springfield, IL: Charles C. Thomas.

Wastell, C. A. (2002). Exposure to trauma: The long-term effects of suppressing emotional reactions. *The Journal of Nervous and Mental Disease, 190*(12), 839−845. https://doi.org/10.1097/01.NMD.0000042454.90472.4F.

Waters, J. A., & Ussery, W. (2007). Police stress: History, contributing factors, symptoms, and interventions. *Policing: An International Journal of Police Strategies & Management, 30*(2), 169−188. https://doi.org/10.1108/13639510710753199.

Weiss, D. S., Brunet, A., Best, S. R., Metzler, T. J., Liberman, A., Pole, N., et al. (2010). Frequency and severity approaches to indexing exposure to trauma: The Critical Incident History Questionnaire for police officers. *Journal of Traumatic Stress, 23*(6), 734−743. https://doi.org/10.1002/jts.20576.

Wilson, S. M. (2011). Avoid the burn. *GradPSYCH Magazine, 9*(2), 17. Retrieved from https://www.apa.org/gradpsych/2011/03/corner.

Workman-Stark, A. L. (2017). Understanding police culture. In *Inclusive policing from the inside out* (pp. 19−35). Cham: Springer. https://doi.org/10.1007/978-3-319-53309-4_2.

8

Moral injury in law enforcement

Katy Kamkar[a], Chuck Russo[b], Brian A. Chopko[c], Brooke McQuerrey Tuttle[d], Daniel M. Blumberg[e], Konstantinos Papazoglou[f]

[a]CENTRE FOR ADDICTION AND MENTAL HEALTH, UNIVERSITY OF TORONTO, DEPARTMENT OF PSYCHIATRY, TORONTO, ON, CANADA; [b]AMERICAN MILITARY UNIVERSITY/AMERICAN PUBLIC UNIVERSITY, CHARLES TOWN, WV, UNITED STATES; [c]CRIMINOLOGY AND JUSTICE STUDIES PROGRAM, DEPARTMENT OF SOCIOLOGY, KENT STATE UNIVERSITY AT STARK, NORTH CANTON, OH, UNITED STATES; [d]CENTER FOR FAMILY RESILIENCE DEPARTMENT OF HUMAN DEVELOPMENT AND FAMILY SCIENCE, OKLAHOMA STATE UNIVERSITY, TULSA, OK, UNITED STATES; [e]DEPARTMENT OF UNDERGRADUATE PSYCHOLOGY, CALIFORNIA SCHOOL OF PROFESSIONAL PSYCHOLOGY, ALLIANT INTERNATIONAL UNIVERSITY, SAN DIEGO, CA, UNITED STATES; [f]YALE SCHOOL OF MEDICINE, NEW HAVEN, CT, UNITED STATES

Definition

The idea of moral injury has been pervasive in human societies for thousands of years, and perhaps since the existence of humankind. In the Greco-Roman tradition, warrior narratives reference the experience of moral conflicts on the battlefield (called miasma or "μίασμα" — moral pollution and purification), defining it as a situation wherein someone with legitimate and recognized authority betrays what is right in a critical situation (Shay, 2014). In the modern era, conceptualization of moral injury is derived from research and clinical work with United States military personnel and veterans. It became apparent through both research and clinical practice that veterans who served in combat zones were exposed to traumas that altered their moral beliefs and values systems; that is, some veterans experienced a violation of their morals or beliefs during their service and became skeptical about whether or not the world is a just, benevolent, and safe place. Thereby, a formal definition refers to moral injury as exposure to unprecedented traumatic life events wherein one perpetrates, fails to prevent, or witnesses actions that "transgress deeply held moral beliefs and expectations" (Litz et al., 2009, p. 1). Similarly, the US Marine Corps uses the term "inner conflict" when referring to experiences involving moral injury (Nash & Litz, 2013). Inner conflict may occur not only when a Marine experiences extraordinary violence (e.g., terrorists use children as "shields") but also in moments when they are ordered to leave a wounded comrade behind in order to save their own lives.

Events that may lead to moral injury include handling/uncovering human remains, the inability to render help to severely wounded victims, involvement in friendly fire

Power. https://doi.org/10.1016/B978-0-12-817872-0.00008-2

incidents, being present when noncombatants are harmed or killed by accident, witnessing others injure or kill unnecessarily without intervening to stop their actions, or observing war-related destruction of property, and killing enemy soldiers (Drescher et al., 2011; Frankfurt & Frazier, 2016; Litz et al., 2009). These experiences violate individuals' moral belief systems and share core features of guilt and shame for having been involved in these events.

Contrasting military and police moral injury

While extant literature provides insight into the range of moral injury experiences associated with military service and combat, a void in the literature exists regarding moral injury and police work (Papazoglou, 2018). One of the few studies examining this issue found that medically discharged police officers with posttraumatic stress disorder (PTSD) diagnoses experienced moral injury in the form of shame. Their experiences were characterized by feelings of embarrassment for not being strong enough to continue working as officers due to emotional distress (McCormack & Riley, 2016).

Common experiences in policing which mirror military experiences associated with moral injury are abundant. For instance, some studies have shown that between 17% and 25% of police officers report killing or seriously injuring a suspect in the line of duty (Chopko, Palmieri, & Adams, 2015; Weiss et al., 2010). The act of killing someone in the line of duty is ranked as one of the most stressful experiences officers encounter at work (Violanti & Aron, 1995). Examples of situations that may lead to moral injury in both military members and police officers include a noncombatant/civilian being killed without being able to save them despite heroic efforts (e.g., not being able to extricate a civilian from a burning structure in time to save their life), accidently killing a noncombatant/civilian (e.g., misidentifying the noncombatant as the enemy/suspect), knowing a fellow soldier/officer who was killed, accidently killing a fellow soldier/officer, being ordered by a superior to commit a morally injurious act, and failing to stop immoral acts committed by other soldiers/officers (Currier, Holland, Drescher, & Foy, 2015; Drescher et al., 2011; Hoge et al., 2004; Vargas, Hanson, Kraus, Drescher, & Foy, 2013). While similarities in trauma exposure exist between military and police occupations, their dosage of exposure to traumatic, morally injurious experiences differs. Many people serve in the military for a limited number of years (e.g., 4 year enlistment), and even when assigned to combat units, they are typically not exposed to warfare for this entire period. Conversely, officers are repeatedly exposed to various types of traumatic experiences over the course of their careers, often lasting dozens of years.

Police officers also experience traumatic events which are unique to police work and not shared by military personnel. For instance, officers have commonly reported that the physical safety of their families has been threatened by suspects they encounter at work (Chopko et al., 2015; Weiss et al., 2010). Considering that police officers typically serve areas in closeness, proximity to where they reside and military members engage in combat in different countries, the immediate threat not only to the officers but also their loved ones may compound the trauma experienced on the job. Another difference between the police and military is that the two main job duties of a typical police officer involve vastly different roles of being both a crime fighter and like a social service worker (Manzella & Papazoglou, 2014).

Common psychological effects in the aftermath of moral injury are seen across military and police populations. A common factor linking both the military and police is the development of guilt and shame surrounding traumatic experiences. Ruminating about the traumatic event is a frequent experience for both police officers and military members. Even when the use of lethal force is determined to be justified, police officers commonly question their actions. Officers typically have mere seconds to react, yet they often replay the event in their mind repeatedly in an attempt to determine if another course of action could have resulted in a different outcome (Chopko, 2010; Kureczka, 2002). Counterfactual rumination, a common experience for trauma survivors, involves self-blame for the trauma that occurred, even in the face of clear evidence that others were solely responsible for what occurred (Davis & Lehman, 1995). Factors related to police use of force incidents that may compound the frequency of rumination and intensity of traumatic stress experienced include: court cases regarding the incident that may go on for years, fear of being convicted of a crime (until it is determined that the use of force was justified), being sued in civil court, intense and often misleading media coverage of the incident, and racial tensions in the community (Bohrer, 2005; Kureczka, 2002). In addition to use of force incidents, officers commonly experience rumination and guilt for not saving victims from serious harm or death. This is a common occurrence even when it was not possible for anyone to have saved the victim (i.e., counterfactual rumination). Many people become police officers to help and save others, and feelings of failure are common with this population when victims are harmed or die (Kirschman, Kamena, & Fay, 2014).

Police officers may experience similar levels of traumatic stress symptoms compared to combat soldiers. For example, one study found that PTSD symptom levels for police officers from US small to mid-size police agencies were almost identical to US infantry soldiers at the end of active combat tours in Iraq and Afghanistan (Chopko, Palmieri, & Adams, 2018b). A distinction between events involving threat to self and the witnessing of harm to others in both the police and military populations has garnered increased attention in the professional literature (Chopko, Palmieri, & Adams, 2018a; Marotta-Walters, Choi, & Shaine, 2015; Stein et al., 2012). A consistent finding of these studies is that events involving threat of harm to self are more strongly related to PTSD symptoms compared to the witnessing of harm to others.

Violations of deeply held values, central to moral injury, are strongly influenced by one's religious and/or spiritual beliefs (Evans et al., 2018). Research with military personnel and veterans has found that greater religiosity and spirituality is associated with lower PTSD symptoms (Currier, Holland, & Drescher, 2015; Hourani et al., 2012). In contrast, research examining police officers has found that the amount of effort put forth toward religious and/or spiritual practice was not related to reduced psychological distress (e.g., PTSD symptoms, depression, suicidal ideation; Chopko, Facemire, Palmieri, & Schwartz, 2016). Additionally, a greater amount of perceived religious and/or spiritual growth was related to more, not less, psychological distress. The authors of this research contend that guilt and shame surrounding the traumatic experiences initiates a spiritual quest to deal with the distress, accounting for the positive relationship between psychological distress and spiritual growth. Further research is needed to better understand this issue, as well as all aspects of moral injury, in the police population.

Translating knowledge from military to police

There are prevalent commonalities as well as distinct differences between military and police moral injury. Knowledge gained from the study of moral injury in the military can be applied, translated, and refined to better understand the experience of police officers. Moral injury research and clinical work with the military population have provided a strong foundation for the pursuit of understanding moral injury in similar subcultures, such as police. Conceptualization of moral injury in police work requires researchers and clinicians to consider whether the definition of moral injury developed by Litz et al. (2009) sufficiently explains this phenomenon as it unfolds in police work. However, translating knowledge from military to police should be made with caution considering that police moral injury differs in nature from that of the military moral injury. That is, police moral injury is rendered chronic in nature since exposure to morally injurious events can be omnipresent over the course of an officer's career. In addition, police officers' identities are versatile between that of a crime fighter and a social service worker and frequently oscillate between that of a police officer during their shifts and that of a parent, spouse, child, friend during their personal lives during even a single day. That is, the aforementioned unique nature of police officers' lives renders police moral injury complex in nature considering that police officers more likely suppress or surreptitiously ruminate about their morally injurious experiences in their personal and family contexts. Let alone, police officers are expected to perform well and do "what is right" even though they have been suffering from exposure to morally injurious incidents over the course of their career. The aforementioned issues render police moral injury chronic and complex in nature as opposed to the military moral injury which can be more acute in nature; for instance, military personnel while deployed in a combat zone may be exposed to a plethora of unprecedented violence and trauma during a short period of time.

Theoretical contributions to police moral injury would be well served if the voices of officers were included in the development and refinement of conceptualization and operationalization of police moral injury. Focus groups and case studies would provide meaningful insight into the lived experiences of officers who have had their morals, beliefs, or values system shattered by moral injury experiences. Such work will shed light on the unique nature of police moral injury and, perhaps, inform revisions to the Litz et al. (2009) definition of moral injury as it applies to policing. Another challenge for translating knowledge developed in the military context is the measurement of moral injury. Existing moral injury measurements (e.g., Moral Injury Events Scale - MIES developed by Nash et al. (2013)) have been developed by military scholars. For instance, the MIES scale (Nash et al., 2013) predominantly refers to fellow service members and military leaders. Nevertheless, police officers quite often interact with civilians and not solely police peers and supervisors; that is, the measurement of police moral injury may differ compared to the measurement of military moral injury. Public scrutiny and criticism of police decision-making, which is easily accessible due to advancements in social media and technology, may have negative repercussions in the experience of moral injury among police. Therefore, items regarding contact with civilians and coverage by media may be considered in the measurement of police moral injury.

Undeniably, clinical work and research with veterans and active duty military personnel have established the foundation of conceptualization and measurement for moral injury in the modern era. In addition, military scholars have raised awareness that moral injury should be addressed in psychological treatment (Farnsworth, Drescher, Nieuwsma, Walser, & Currier, 2014; Litz et al., 2009). To this end, police scholars are encouraged to translate elements of military moral injury to police work or, alternatively, adapt military moral injury knowledge toward police moral injury in order to better support police officers as well as their families and the communities they serve.

The impact of moral injury in police officers' health and work

The experience of moral injury carries negative physical and psychological effects for officers. Moral injury, although not recognized as a mental health disorder within the Diagnostic and Statistical Manual of Mental Disorders, Fifth Edition (DSM-5) (American Psychiatric Association, 2013), can lead to lasting emotional and psychological impact. It is, therefore, a significant mental health issue that needs to be recognized during mental health assessment for a more comprehensive case conceptualization; be targeted throughout treatment interventions; and be part of evidence-based education around mental health prevention and promotion. Moral injury has been associated with intrusion, avoidance and arousal symptoms of PTSD (Feinstein, Pavisian, & Storm, 2018); depression, suicidal ideation, and anger (Bryan, Bryan, Morrow, Etienne, & Ray-Sannerud, 2014; Gaudet, Sowers, Nugent, & Boriskin, 2016); and as discussed earlier with guilt and shame (Nazarov et al., 2015). Taking a broader perspective approach also helps to further understand the impact of moral injury and related diagnoses such as posttraumatic stress disorder (PTSD) or Depression, which are all part of Operational Stress Injuries (OSI).

Initially conceptualized within the Canadian Armed Forces (Standing Senate Committee on National Security and Defense, 2015), OSI include any persistent psychological difficulties resulting from operational or service-related duties. Common mental health problems at the core of OSI include PTSD, anxiety disorders, depression, substance use disorders, suicidal ideation or any other conditions that may interfere with a person's level of functioning, personal, social or occupational. Stressors related to employment, finances, family, relationships as well as pain and physical health issues and changes within role or identity can all be part of OSI which, in turn, cause further pain, suffering and impaired functioning.

OSI, and in particular trauma, can shatter an individual's core belief system whereby one's views of self, others, the future and the world can fundamentally change. How events, circumstances or situations are perceived, interpreted or viewed can drastically change following traumatic events and, as well, often reflect elements of moral injury. This can lead to potential difficulty regulating emotions, experiencing intense mixed and negative emotions, difficulty making healthy decisions and taking proactive strategies, difficulty resuming regular work duties, decreased work productivity, reduced self-efficacy at work and feeling incompetent. As well, over time, any future events or situations tend to be filtered through the lens that has been altered, thus, further compounding suffering and impaired functioning.

Individual differences vary between officers as well, depending on how each person processes events or circumstances. What may set in motion a fundamental change in one individual may have an entirely different effect on another individual, or possibly even no impact. This makes understanding, recognizing, and treating OSI far more difficult compared to physical injuries experienced by officers.

While most attention has been given to emotions such as anxiety and fear resulting from traumatic incidents that police officers have often faced in line of duty, other emotions such as guilt and shame have received less attention despite their contributions to health and work outcomes (e.g., Cohen, Wolf, Panter, & Insko, 2011; Wright & Gudjonsson, 2007). Mixed emotions related to guilt and shame often result in internal conflict within the self where actions of self or others are not in harmony with one's moral values, standard, beliefs or conscience. Guilt and shame are related to maintaining and exacerbating psychopathology, interpersonal conflict, self-isolation and avoidance, disruption in work activities, prolonged recovery, and present a significant barrier to personal, social and occupational functioning. Officers often report difficulty with resuming their regular work activities or with the return to process after a period of absence as a result of feeling ashamed, or not wanting to go out to public places or attending social events out of fear of seeing people or colleagues due to guilt or shame. Those emotions can lead at times to more self-isolation and prominent avoidance than other emotions such as fear or anxiety.

Other types of moral distress in police work

In addition to the risk for moral injury presented by operational stressors already discussed (e.g. shooting someone after believing the person had a gun and realizing afterward the person did not possess a weapon; witnessing horrific crime scenes), organizational stressors can also present risk for moral distress.

Common organizational stressors related to job stress and burnout (Cooper & Marshall, 1976; Finney, Stergiopoulos, Hensel, Bonato, & Dewa, 2013) include stressors intrinsic to the job; role in organization and rewards; supervisory relationships and organizational structure and climate. Organization stressors can lead to officers' feeling they have little/no control over their work. For example, just being "along for the ride" may be a common sentiment among those experiencing organizational stressors.

In policing, risk for moral injury related to organization stressors can occur and be compounded by excessive work demands that are difficult to manage; limited opportunities for training and limited resources; heavy workloads; lack of support; dissatisfaction around one's role in the organization (e.g., role ambiguity or the role not fitting one's interest, skills or training); unclear responsibilities; strained relationships with supervisors; unresolved interpersonal conflicts; harassment and bullying in the workplace; or lack of perceived organizational support following high-profile police incidents. When officers are unable to pursue what they believe or perceive to be the right plan of action or decision or fail to meet their own expectations due to, for instance, work related obstacles, interpersonal conflicts, limited resources or circumstances beyond their control, they may subsequently feel guilty, demoralized and/or helpless. Any of the stressors named above can lead to internal conflict or transgression of one's moral values and belief system and, in turn, set the stage for moral injury.

Moral distress is also related to variety of other emotional, psychological, and physiological reactions such as sleep disturbance, bad dreams, appetite changes, feelings of worthlessness, reduced sense of self-confidence, and headaches (Fry, Harvey, Hurley, & Foley, 2002). The emotional and psychological impact of moral distress can also over time increase the risk for burnout (Fumis; Amarante; Nascimento, & Junior, 2017).

Traumatic incidents noted above, including operational and organizational stressors can lead to not only trauma reactions that are fear-based or trauma reactions that are loss-based, but also to moral injury-based trauma reactions (Gray et al., 2012; Held, Klassen, Brennan, & Zalta, 2018; Litz, Lebowitz, Gray, & Nash, 2016). Trauma reactions that are fear-based can include for instance, fear for safety of self or others following increased violence, assaults, gang related incidents, or as a result of limited staffing in smaller communities. They can also include fear of impending doom; fear of something bad happening to self or others; and anxiety being in social situations or in public places and witnessing interpersonal conflicts or arguments. Trauma reactions that are loss-based can include, for instance, losing a colleague to suicide; death of a colleague following a shooting incident; or a death scene that resembled an officer's personal life (e.g., having a child of same age; a house looking the same as the officer's house). For moral injury-based trauma reactions, the symptoms can be similar to OSI symptoms and may include mixed emotions such as feelings of shame, guilt, remorse, or anger; irritability, negative beliefs about oneself; self-blame; avoidance and self-isolation; withdrawal from social situations; distressing intrusive memories of traumatic incidents and related nightmares; difficulties with sleep; and difficulties with concentration and making decisions. The symptoms related to moral injury can also contribute to maintenance and/or exacerbation of psychological disorders related to OSI.

Taken together, building awareness of the harmful impact of moral injury, providing education around moral injury, and recognizing the signs and symptoms of moral injury can inform prevention initiatives and contribute to resilience building among officers and help optimize treatment interventions to improve quality of life and well-being, and personal and occupational functioning. At the organizational level, creating healthy culture, providing a people-oriented culture and people focused leadership, building organizational capacities and resources, and implementing psychological health and safety strategies to alleviate organizational stressors could help reduce the risk of moral injury.

Conclusion

Morally injurious experiences are prevalent in police work. Current scholarly literature shows that moral injury violates the moral belief system of the individual, leading to negative and distressing views of self, others, and the world. It also results in a host of negative emotional reactions with guilt and shame as predominant emotions experienced. Taken together, moral injury can have a virulent impact on police officers' health, wellbeing and overall functioning. Nevertheless, emphasis should be placed on the fact that moral injury is not an inevitable condition. When addressed early, or through prevention, the negative impact of moral injury on officers can be reduced. It is possible that officers may be inclined to employ unhealthy ways of coping (e.g., alcohol, isolation, cynicism) to battle moral injury symptoms as a desperate way to prevent the negative impact of moral injury in their lives. In many occasions, officers may not be familiar with healthy ways of coping or preventative strategies to protect them against the incapacitating impact of moral injury.

Research on police moral injury is in its infancy. However, as discussed in current chapter, police professionals and scholars can translate military moral injury knowledge into police work. That way, police officers will become cognizant of moral injury in their work. The successful application of moral injury research findings in police work requires a synergistic effort emanated from police leaders, police clinicians, police families, and officers themselves. It is essential that the possibility of moral conflicts is addressed at the organizational level within police departments. When moral injury is openly addressed in an unapologetic and de-stigmatizing way, officers will feel more comfortable to share about moral distress experienced on the job. Such dialogue should take place during department meetings because they are facilitated in a collective context in which officers have the opportunity to get feedback from their colleagues and supervisors. This would allow for early signs of moral injury or any inner conflict to be verbalized and processed within a supportive context.

Analogously, police moral dilemmas and conflicts should be addressed during police training and, hence, incorporated into police training curricula. The authors of the present chapter suggest that police training should encompass the different nuances of critical incidents (e.g., moral dilemmas, stress levels, decision making, use of force) and such incidents should not solely be approached from an operational perspective. Moral injury can potentially affect officers' capacity for decision making during critical moments (e.g., shoot or no shoot) and affect their clarity of judgment in the line of duty. Police trainers should encourage officers to share any moral dilemmas they experience during training so that they are best prepared for real life situations of police work where moral dilemmas and conflicts are omnipresent.

The role of police clinicians in preventing and treating moral injury is vital. Police clinicians may collaborate with officers who are part of peer support units and help them identify peers who struggle with moral injury, moral conflicts, and moral dilemmas. In addition, clinical treatment, especially in regards to stress and trauma, should explore any morally injurious symptoms experienced by police officers who participate in treatment. Assessing for moral injury allows treatment to address the holistic needs of officers. Often, issues experienced by police officers in the past have remained unaddressed or ignored because the severity of such issues was undervalued or understudied. In addition, clinicians may guide and encourage officers to practice strategies that can help them prevent the impact of moral injury in their lives. For instance, prior research with veterans has shown that volunteerism, journaling, mindfulness, and gratitude letters are some ways that can help officers express their moral conflicts while engaging in activities where they can realize that the world has potential for kindness and fairness and not just violence and unfairness.

Psychological health and safety in the workplace should include education around moral injury in policing as well as increased efforts to reduce likelihood of moral injury or moral distress resulting from operational or organizational stressors. Further research, education, and training are needed to better identify all aspects of moral injury in the police population and to inform prevention and intervention around moral injury in policing.

References

American Psychiatric Association. (2013). *Diagnostic and statistical manual of mental disorders* (5th ed.). New York American Psychiatric Press Inc. American Psychiatric Publishing, Inc https://doi.org/10. 1176/appi.books.9780890425596.893619.

Bohrer, S. (2005). After firing the shots, what happens? *FBI Law Enforcement Bulletin, 74*, 8−13.

Bryan, A. O., Bryan, C. J., Morrow, C. E., Etienne, N., & Ray-Sannerud, B. (2014). Moral injury, suicidal ideation, and suicide attempts in a military sample. *Traumatology, 20*(3), 154−160. https://doi.org/10.1037/h0099852.

Chopko, B. A. (2010). Posttraumatic distress and growth: An empirical study of police officers. *American Journal of Psychotherapy, 64*(1), 55−72. https://doi.org/10.1176/appi.psychotherapy.2010.64.1.55.

Chopko, B. A., Facemire, V. C., Palmieri, P. A., & Schwartz, R. C. (2016). Spirituality and health outcomes among police officers: Empirical evidence supporting a paradigm shift. *Criminal Justice Studies, 29*(4), 363−377. https://doi.org/10.1080/1478601X.2016.1216412.

Chopko, B. A., Palmieri, P. A., & Adams, R. E. (2015). Critical incident history questionnaire replication: Frequency and severity of trauma exposure among officers from small and midsize police agencies. *Journal of Traumatic Stress, 28*(2), 157−161. https://doi.org/10.1002/jts.21996.

Chopko, B. A., Palmieri, P. A., & Adams, R. E. (2018a). Relationships among traumatic experiences, PTSD, and posttraumatic growth for police officers: A path analysis. *Psychological Trauma: Theory, Research, Practice, and Policy, 10*(2), 183–189. https://doi.org/10.1037/tra0000261.

Chopko, B. A., Palmieri, P. A., & Adams, R. E. (2018b). Trauma-related sleep problems and associated health outcomes in police officers: A path analysis. *Journal of Interpersonal Violence, 1–24*. https://doi.org/10.1177/0886260518767912.

Cohen, T. R., Wolf, S. T., Panter, A. T., & Insko, C. A. (2011). Introducing the GASP scale: A new measure of guilt and shame proneness. *Journal of Personality and Social Psychology, 100*(5), 947–966. https://doi.org/10.1037/a0022641.

Cooper, C. L., & Marshall, J. (1976). Occupational sources of stress: A review of the literature relating to coronary heart disease and mental ill health. *Journal of Occupational Psychology, 49*(1), 11–28. https://doi.org/10.1111/j.2044-8325.1976.tb00325.x.

Currier, J. M., Holland, J. M., & Drescher, K. D. (2015). Spirituality factors in the prediction of outcomes of PTSD treatment for U.S. Military veterans. *Journal of Traumatic Stress, 28*(1), 57–64. https://doi.org/10.1002/jts.21978.

Currier, J. M., Holland, J. M., Drescher, K., & Foy, D. (2015). Initial psychometric evaluation of the moral injury questionnaire-military version. *Clinical Psychology & Psychotherapy, 22*(1), 54–63. https://doi.org/10.1002/cpp.1866.

Davis, C. G., & Lehman, D. R. (1995). Counterfactual thinking and coping with traumatic life events. In N. J. Roes (Ed.), *What might have been: The social psychology of counterfactual thinking* (pp. 353–374). Hillsdale, NJ: Lawrence Erlbaum Associates, Inc.

Drescher, K. D., Foy, D. W., Kelly, C., Leshner, A., Schutz, K., & Litz, B. (2011). An exploration of the viability and usefulness of the construct of moral injury in war veterans. *Traumatology, 17*(1), 8–13. https://doi.org/10.1177/1534765610395615.

Evans, W. R., Stanley, M. A., Barrera, T. L., Exline, J. J., Pargament, K. I., & Teng, E. J. (2018). Morally injurious events and psychological distress among veterans: Examining the mediating role of religious and spiritual struggles. *Psychological Trauma: Theory, Research, Practice, and Policy, 10*(3), 360–367. https://doi.org/10.1037/tra0000347.

Farnsworth, J. K., Drescher, K. D., Nieuwsma, J. A., Walser, R. B., & Currier, J. M. (2014). The role of moral emotions in military trauma: Implications for the study and treatment of moral injury. *Review of General Psychology, 18*(4), 249–262. https://doi.org/10.1037/gpr0000018.

Feinstein, A., Pavisian, B., & Storm, H. (2018). Journalists covering the refugee and migration crisis are affected by moral injury not PTSD. *JRSM Open, 9*(3), 1–7. https://doi.org/10.1177/2054270418759010.

Finney, C., Stergiopoulos, E., Hensel, J., Bonato, S., & Dewa, C. S. (2013). Organizational stressors associated with job stress and burnout in correctional officers: A systematic review. *BMC Public Health, 13*(1), 82. https://doi.org/10.1186/1471-2458-13-82.

Frankfurt, S., & Frazier, P. (2016). A review of research on moral injury in combat veterans. *Military Psychology, 28*(5), 318–330. https://doi.org/10.1037/mil0000132.

Fry, S., Harvey, R., Hurley, A., & Foley, B. (2002). Development of a model of moral distress in military nursing. *Nursing Ethics, 9*(4), 373–387. https://doi.org/10.1191/0969733002ne522oa.

Fumis, R. R. L., Amarante, G. A. J., Nascimento, A. F., & Junior, J. M. V. (2017). Moral distress and its contribution to the development of burnout syndrome among critical care providers. *Annals of Intensive Care, 71*(7), 1–8. https://doi.org/10.1186/s13613-017-0293-2.

Gaudet, C. M., Sowers, K. M., Nugent, W. R., & Boriskin, J. A. (2016). A review of PTSD and shame in military veterans. *Journal of Human Behavior in the Social Environment, 26*(1), 56–68. https://doi.org/10.1080/10911359.2015.1059168.

Gray, M. J., Schorr, Y., Nash, W., Lebowitz, L., Amidon, A., Lansing, A., et al. (2012). Adaptive disclosure: An open trial of a novel exposure-based intervention for service members with combat-related psychological stress injuries. *Behavior Therapy, 43*(2), 407–415. https://doi.org/10.1016/j.beth.2011.09.001.

Held, P., Klassen, B. J., Brennan, M. B., & Zalta, A. K. (2018). Using prolonged exposure and cognitive processing therapy to treat veterans with moral injury-based PTSD: Two case examples. *Cognitive and Behavioral Practice, 25*(3), 377–390. https://doi.org/10.1016/j.cbpra.2017.09.003.

Hoge, C. W., Castro, C. A., Messer, S. C., McGurk, D., Cotting, D. I., & Koffman, R. L. (2004). Combat duty in Iraq and Afghanistan and mental health problems. *New England Journal of Medicine, 351*(17), 1798–1800. https://doi.org/10.1056/NEJM200410213511722.

Hourani, L. L., Williams, J., Forman-Hoffman, V., Lane, M. E., Weimer, B., & Bray, R. M. (2012). Influence of spirituality on depression, posttraumatic stress disorder, and suicidality in active duty military personnel. *Depression Research and Treatment*, 425–463. https://doi.org/10.1155/2012/425463.

Kirschman, E., Kamena, M., & Fay, J. (2014). *Counseling cops: What clinicians need to know. Counseling cops: What clinicians need to know.* New York, NY: The Guilford Press.

Kureczka, A. W. (2002). Surviving Assaults after the Physical battle ends, the Psychological battle begins. *FBI Law Enforcement Bulletin, 71*, 18–21.

Litz, B. T., Lebowitz, L., Gray, M. J., & Nash, W. P. (2016). *Adaptive disclosure: A new treatment for military trauma, loss, and moral injury.* New York, NY: The Guilford Press.

Litz, B. T., Stein, N., Delaney, E., Lebowitz, L., Nash, W. P., Silva, C., et al. (2009). Moral injury and moral repair in war veterans: A preliminary model and intervention strategy. *Clinical Psychology Review, 29*(8), 695–706. https://doi.org/10.1016/j.cpr.2009.07.003.

Manzella, C., & Papazoglou, K. (2014). Training police trainees about ways to manage trauma and loss. *International Journal of Mental Health Promotion, 16*(2), 103–116. https://doi.org/10.1080/14623730.2014.903609.

Marotta-Walters, S., Choi, J., & Shaine, M. D. (2015). Posttraumatic growth among combat veterans: A proposed developmental pathway. *Psychological Trauma: Theory, Research, Practice, and Policy, 7*(4), 356–363. https://doi.org/10.1037/tra0000030.

McCormack, L., & Riley, L. (2016). Medical discharge from the "family," moral injury, and a diagnosis of PTSD: Is psychological growth possible in the aftermath of policing trauma? *Traumatology, 22*(1), 19–28. https://doi.org/10.1037/trm0000059.

Nash, W. P., & Litz, B. T. (2013). Moral injury: A mechanism for war-related psychological trauma in military family members. *Clinical Child and Family Psychology Review, 16*(4), 365–375. https://doi.org/10.1007/s10567-013-0146-y.

Nash, W. P., Marino Carper, T. L., Mills, M. A., Au, T., Goldsmith, A., & Litz, B. T. (2013). Psychometric evaluation of the moral injury events scale. *Military Medicine, 178*(6), 646–652. https://doi.org/10.7205/MILMED-D-13-00017.

Nazarov, A., Jetly, R., McNeely, H., Kiang, M., Lanius, R., & McKinnon, M. C. (2015). Role of morality in the experience of guilt and shame within the armed forces. *Acta Psychiatrica Scandinavica, 132*(1), 4–19. https://doi.org/10.1111/acps.12406.

Papazoglou, K. (2018). The examination of different pathways leading towards police traumatization: Exploring the role of moral injury and personality in police compassion fatigue. *Dissertation Abstracts International: Section B: The Sciences and Engineering, 79*(3-B).

Shay, J. (2014). Moral injury. *Psychoanalytic Psychology, 31*(2), 182–191. https://doi.org/10.1037/a0036090.

Standing Senate Committee on National Security and Defence. (2015). *2015 interim report on the operational stress injuries of Canada's veterans.* Retrieved from https://sencanada.ca/content/sen/Committee/412/secd/rep/rep17jun15-e.pdf.

Stein, N. R., Mills, M. A., Arditte, K., Mendoza, C., Borah, A. M., Resick, P. A., et al. (2012). A scheme for categorizing traumatic military events. *Behavior Modification, 36*(6), 787–807. https://doi.org/10.1177/0145445512446945.

Vargas, A. F., Hanson, T., Kraus, D., Drescher, K., & Foy, D. (2013). Moral injury themes in combat veterans' narrative responses from the National Vietnam Veterans' Readjustment Study. *Traumatology, 19*(3), 243–250. https://doi.org/10.1177/1534765613476099.

Violanti, J. M., & Aron, F. (1995). Police stressors: Variations in perception among police personnel. *Journal of Criminal Justice, 23*(3), 287–294. https://doi.org/10.1016/0047-2352(95)00012-F.

Weiss, D. S., Brunet, A., Best, S. R., Metzler, T. J., Liberman, A., Pole, N., et al. (2010). Frequency and severity approaches to indexing exposure to trauma: The Critical Incident History Questionnaire for police officers. *Journal of Traumatic Stress, 23*(6), 734–743. https://doi.org/10.1002/jts.20576.

Wright, K., & Gudjonsson, G. H. (2007). The development of a scale for measuring offence- related feelings of shame and guilt. *Journal of Forensic Psychiatry and Psychology, 18*(3), 307–316. https://doi.org/10.1080/14789940701292810.

9

PTSD and other operational stress injuries among police officers: empirical findings and reflections from clinical practice

Breanne Faulkner[a, 1], Samantha Fuss[a, b], Lisa M.Z. Couperthwaite[c]

[a]*CENTRE FOR ADDICTION AND MENTAL HEALTH, TORONTO, ONTARIO, CANADA;*
[b]*DEPARTMENT OF PSYCHOLOGICAL SCIENCE, UNIVERSITY OF TORONTO – SCARBOROUGH CAMPUS, SCARBOROUGH, ONTARIO, CANADA;* [c]*DEPARTMENT OF PSYCHIATRY, UNIVERSITY OF TORONTO – ST. GEORGE CAMPUS, TORONTO, ONTARIO, CANADA*

> *People are not weak or strong, they are weak and strong.*
> Norman *Conti, Weak Links and Warrior Hearts (2011).*

Operational stress injury (OSI) is a broad term used to describe persistent psychological difficulties resulting from activities performed in the course of or related to one's job. This non-diagnostic term was originally coined in 2001 by Canadian Forces Lieutenant Colonel Stéphane Grenier in an effort to help reduce stigma about mental health issues that arise in response to occupational trauma, emphasizing their legitimacy as similar to physical injuries. By 2016, the term had also been widely used to recognize OSIs as issues faced by military and paramilitary organizations, including police[2]. Although the term OSI is often used to refer to Posttraumatic Stress Disorder (PTSD), it is an umbrella term used to describe any mental health issues that occur as a result of work-related operations, and can include Major Depressive Disorder, Generalized Anxiety Disorder, Panic Disorder, or Substance Use Disorders resulting from maladaptive coping via drugs or alcohol. Sources of operational stress injuries in first responder populations can include trauma exposure, cumulative stress and fatigue, grief, and moral injury, in addition to stressors associated with daily organizational demands. The existing empirical literature provides no clear consensus on the rates of OSI in policing, as rates of psychological injury and particularly

---

[1]Portions of this chapter originally appeared in the first author's doctoral dissertation, "Things are Changing:" Police Mental Health and Psychotherapeutic Help-Seeking in an Evolving Police Culture (Faulkner, 2018).

[2]Committee Report No. 5 - SECU (42–1) - House of Commons of Canada. (n.d.). Retrieved from http://www.ourcommons.ca/DocumentViewer/en/42-1/SECU/report-5.

Power. https://doi.org/10.1016/B978-0-12-817872-0.00009-4

suicide are rarely recorded by police agencies. Where statistics are available, they vary widely between studies and within agencies, roles, and regions (Ombudsman of Ontario, 2012; Violanti, 2008). Both the research and clinical experience, however, suggest cause for concern.

The literature suggests that compared to other occupational groups, police have higher rates of mortality due to stress-related conditions such as coronary disease and cancer, as well as higher rates of marital discord, alcoholism, suicide, performance anxiety, overachievement, absenteeism, emotional detachment, and posttraumatic stress (Carlier, Lamberts, & Gersons, 2000; Morley, 2011; Toch, 2002; Violanti, 2004, 2010). High rates of burnout, including symptoms of emotional exhaustion, irritability, cynicism, diminished compassion, and interpersonal withdrawal have been found in both Canadian and American samples of police officers (Kurtz, 2008; Padyab, Backteman-Erlanson, & Brulin, 2016; Turgoose, Glover, Barker, & Maddox, 2017). Importantly, when left unaddressed, burnout has been linked to the development of depression and anxiety disorders (Hakanen & Schaufeli, 2013), including among police officers (Golembiewski, Lloyd, Scherb, & Munzenrider, 1992; Stearns & Moore, 1993). Collins and Gibbs (2003) found that 41% of their sample of police met cutoffs for clinical levels of psychological distress. In a study by Gershon et al. (Gershon, Barocas, Canton, Li, & Vlahov, 2009), police officers who reported high levels of occupational stress were at an increased risk for a number of adverse health outcomes, especially depression, anxiety, burnout, somatization, and posttraumatic stress symptoms. This is despite the fact that, given the rigor of physical and psychological testing required of police recruits, law enforcement officers begin their careers as generally healthy and hardy individuals relative to the general population (Anshel, 2000; Violanti, 2004).

Several OSIs associated specifically with the unique stressors experienced by police officers have received empirical attention and support. Among others, these include posttraumatic stress, depression, alcohol use disorders, and relatedly, increased risk for suicide. The current chapter will draw on both empirical evidence and clinical experience to explicate the potential for posttraumatic stress in policing, as well as the prevalence, etiology, and trajectory of this condition in the context of the police role. We will provide an overview of evidence-based treatment for posttraumatic stress and its application with police populations. Next, we will outline other types of OSI commonly experienced among police. Finally, we will present a discussion of posttraumatic growth as it relates to police officers and the implications of this concept for clinical practice.

Posttraumatic stress and PTSD — an occupational hazard

Throughout their careers, police officers encounter numerous "critical" or traumatic incidents, which involve experiencing, witnessing, or being confronted with a situation involving actual or threatened death or serious injury, or a threat to the physical integrity of self. For example, most officers begin their careers in a uniformed patrol position, which may involve regular response to calls for severe car accidents, domestic violence, child abuse, sexual assault, homicide or suicide, active pursuits, violent disputes, or arrests. Police officers in investigative roles may have intimate and prolonged contact with victims and physical evidence at the scene of a violent crime or in its aftermath via photographs and interviews, putting them at risk for both direct and vicarious trauma. Those in more specialized police roles such as traffic accident reconstruction, prevention of child pornography and sex trafficking, or tactical emergency response may be at particular risk for significant trauma exposure. Research has suggested that police work is among the most "trauma sensitive" occupations, meaning that police officers are at high risk of experiencing traumatic events on the job (Carlier, Lamberts, et al., 2000; Carlier, Voerman, & Gersons, 2000). As a result of this exposure, police officers are vulnerable to the development of posttraumatic stress disorder and other trauma-related psychological conditions.

Given that exposure to trauma is a nearly inevitable aspect of the job of policing, most police officers will necessarily meet Criterion A for a diagnosis of Posttraumatic Stress Disorder (PTSD) as defined in the most recent edition of the Diagnostic and Statistical Manual (APA, 2013; see Table 9.1 for DSM-5 criteria for PTSD). This essential criterion states that an individual being diagnosed with PTSD must have been either directly or indirectly exposed to actual or threatened death, serious injury, or sexual violence (APA, 2013). Indirect exposure meeting this criterion includes witnessing another individual and/or learning of a close relative or friend experiencing such a traumatic incident. In addition, exposure criteria for PSTD include repetitive or cumulative exposure to the details of the traumatic event or events. When undertaken as a component of one's work, this can include repeated exposure to photos, videos, or detailed incident reports, as is common in the work of police investigators.

In a randomly-selected sample of 100 urban police officers, Hartley and colleagues (Hartley, Violanti, Fekedulegn, Andrew, & Burchfield, 2007) found that officers estimated having experienced an average of four traumatic events in the past year. In a sample of over 700 urban US police officers Weiss et al. (2001, as cited in Liberman et al., 2002) found that, on average, exposure to trauma over the course of a career included encounters with 25 recently dead bodies, 14 decaying corpses, 10 sexually assaulted children, colleagues badly injured twice accidently and once intentionally, and being shot at themselves once and injured more than once. Police officers are often the first responders to domestic violence and child welfare calls, as well as to the scenes of completed suicides (Horowitz et al., 2011; Koch, 2010). In one qualitative study, for example, officers estimated that they had been first responders to an average of 20 completed suicides throughout their careers (Koch, 2010). As a result of the routine and repetitive nature of trauma exposure over the course of a police officer's career, the effects of posttraumatic stress they experience tend to present somewhat differently than for individuals who have experienced a single traumatic event resulting in a diagnosis of PTSD.

In our experience working with police officers in an outpatient clinic for individuals with work-related psychological injuries, symptoms often onset slowly and initially without awareness, accumulating with increasing intensity in response to a series of

Table 9.1 DSM-5 criteria for posttraumatic stress disorder in adults (APA, 2013).

Criterion A			
Exposure to trauma, i.e., actual or threatened death, serious injury, or sexual violence (in *one or more* of the following ways)			
Direct experience of a traumatic event or events	Witnessing another person experience trauma(s)	Learning of trauma(s) experienced by a close other	Repeated or extreme exposure to details of trauma(s)

Criterion B				
Intrusion symptoms associated with the traumatic event(s) (*one or more* of the following)				
Recurrent, involuntary, and intrusive distressing memories of the traumatic event(s)	Recurrent distressing dreams, related in content and/or affect to the traumatic event(s)	Dissociative reactions experienced as if the traumatic event(s) were recurring	Intense or prolonged distress at exposure to trauma-related cues	Marked physiological reactions to internal or external trauma-related cues

Criterion C	
Avoidance of stimuli associated with the traumatic event(s) (*one or both* of the following)	
Avoidance of or efforts to avoid distressing memories, thoughts, or feelings about or closely associated with the traumatic event(s)	Avoidance of or efforts to avoid external reminders (people, places, objects) about or closely associated with the traumatic event(s)

Criterion D						
Negative alterations in cognitions and mood associated with the traumatic event(s), (*two or more* of the following)						
Inability to remember important aspects of the traumatic event(s)	Persistent, exaggerated negative beliefs about oneself, others, or the world	Persistent, distorted cognitions about the cause or consequences of the traumatic event(s)	Persistent negative emotional state (e.g., fear, horror, anger, guilt, or shame)	Markedly diminished interest or participation in significant activities	Feelings of detachment/ estrangement from others.	Persistent inability to experience positive emotions (e.g., love happiness, satisfaction)

Criterion E				
Marked alterations in arousal and reactivity associated with the traumatic event(s) (*two or more* of the following)				
Irritable behavior and angry outbursts	Reckless or self-destructive behavior	Hypervigilance	Exaggerated startle response	Problems with Sleep concentration disturbance

Criterion F
Criteria B, C, D, and E last more than 1 month

Criterion G
Clinically significant distress or impairment in social, occupational, or other areas of functioning

Criterion H
Symptoms are not attributable to the physiological effects of a substance or another medical condition

traumatic incidents, which may or may not be related. Often, though not always, they will experience an acute and impairing traumatic response triggered by a single event which prompts them to take a leave from work and/or seek out help. By the time we see these officers, they may have been suffering with a variety of difficulties they reasoned as simply "a part of the job" for years: difficulty sleeping, heightened irritability and anger outbursts, chronic vigilance to potential threats, fatigue, relationship problems, or emotional numbness. They may have been functioning on the job, but struggling significantly in their personal lives. Our clients sometimes seem perplexed by the intensity of their reaction to the particular call or calls that trigger their eventual decision to reach out, characterizing them as mundane, routine incidents indistinguishable from any number of those they've encountered in the past. This can result in confusion and shame, the perception that one is weak or different from his or her peers. In reality, years of trauma exposure, often combined with other significant personal and professional stressors, have resulted in accumulating strain to the officers capacity to cope. When this is the case, the addition of a single, seemingly minor incident can be like placing the final brick on top of a teetering Jenga tower, contributing enough weight and imbalance to collapse the entire structure. Given the amorphous and perpetual nature of precipitating events in this line of work, treatment and recovery from PTSD for police officers can also be especially complex and prolonged, especially if it begins after decades of exposure.

In addition to trauma exposure, there are four clusters of symptoms which must be present for one month or longer for a diagnosis of PTSD to be provided: Criterion B) intrusion, Criterion C) avoidance, Criterion D) alterations in mood or cognition, and Criterion E) alterations in physiological arousal (APA, 2013; see Table 9.1). These symptoms must be judged to be trauma-related, as well as being repetitive or persistent in nature. The classic presentation the media and lay public often associates with posttraumatic stress is one characterized by trauma-related intrusion symptoms, which include flashbacks, nightmares, triggered psychological and physiological responses to reminders of a traumatic event, and intensely distressing, vivid memories of the traumatic event (Criterion B; see Table 9.1). The image that comes to mind is of the combat veteran ducking for cover and shouting for help when a car backfires in the parking lot — reliving the IED blast that killed a fellow soldier while puzzled onlookers at the local market load their groceries into their SUVs. Certainly, flashbacks do occur among police officers suffering from PTSD, but intrusion symptoms characteristic of the condition are experienced in a variety of ways. The dissociative processes underlying the experience of flashbacks (Frewen & Lanius, 2014), for example, exist on a spectrum, ranging from having episodes of lost time during which one cannot recall completing tasks or having conversations, to a feeling of persistent mental fog as if a plate of glass separates oneself from the outside world, to full-blown flashbacks involving such intense recollection of a traumatic event that it is experienced as if it as happening in the here and now, along with the sounds, smells, and sensations experienced during the actual event, as in the example described above.

We have heard clients describe intrusion symptoms such as a sudden onset of deep sadness and tearfulness when the plot of a television show turns to child abuse, or a racing heart, extreme muscle tension, and a desire to escape when a family member brings up a murder case recently in the news. Triggers for these psychological and physiological responses can be directly related to a specific traumatic incident experienced on the job, or they can be more broad or thematic, the result of a tendency for posttraumatic symptoms to become generalized, particularly in clients with entrenched symptoms and in response to cumulative trauma over a prolonged period. This is similarly the case when it comes to trauma-related nightmares, which may take the form of a moment-by-moment replaying of the traumatic incident in real time, or alternatively, as bizarre, distressing dreams with emotional themes consistent with the traumatic event, such as being chased, targeted, or attacked.

Avoidance symptoms are the counterpart to intrusion and re-experiencing in PTSD (Criterion C; see Table 9.1). They are also an important factor in the development and maintenance of the condition, as is discussed in the next sections. Naturally, the intense distress associated with recollections of a traumatic event encourages individuals experiencing PTSD to engage in various behaviors aimed at avoiding reminders, thoughts, feelings, memories, or conversations related to it. Avoidance efforts can be both internal and external. In an example of external avoidance, an off-duty police officer may explicitly avoid a particular area of the city in which a traumatic incident occurred, taking alternative routes despite that it interferes with their regular routine or adds time to their commute. Many police officers we see in our clinic refuse to watch or read the news, aware that they are likely to be exposed to depictions of violence and suffering if not actual coverage of incidents to which they have responded or cases they are involved in investigating. Similarly, officers experiencing trauma-related symptoms often avoid crowded, busy, or unpredictable environments in their off-duty time, for example, by doing their grocery shopping at 6 a.m. after a night shift. Some of our clients significantly limit their exposure to the community in which they police because of intense and impairing anxiety they experience as they navigate it.

Internal avoidance involves efforts to reduce or block difficult thoughts and feelings associated with distressing or traumatic events by avoiding thinking about the events themselves, or working to minimize the experience of anxiety, shame, anger, sadness, or other emotions associated with them. Internal avoidance can take many forms, including self-medication or numbing, such as via substance abuse. Coping in this way puts officers suffering with PTSD at additional risk for developing a substance use disorder (Schaumberg et al., 2015), as discussed further in the section on other OSIs below. Individuals may also engage in internal avoidance by engaging in chronic distraction, for example through excessive use of video games or television during off-duty time, or by staying extremely busy, perhaps even taking on more work. Unfortunately, avoidance is not only counterproductive to recovery from traumatic stress as we will discuss, it is also often ineffective. Worse, chronic avoidance becomes a vicious cycle as it generally has the paradoxical effect of increasing the frequency and intensity of difficult trauma-related intrusive thoughts and feelings. Police officers experiencing a posttraumatic reaction will note that no matter how hard they work to minimize their exposure to trauma-related triggers or distance themselves from their internal world, they continue to experience repetitive, disturbing intrusions – and over time, symptoms worsen. The immediate relief avoidance provides in the short term comes at a very high cost in the long term. Lives become smaller, isolation increases, and relationships and wellbeing suffer. As discussed above, due to the cumulative nature of trauma exposure experienced by most police officers, many who go on to develop PTSD experience a delayed onset of full-blown symptomatology. They may have seemingly coped for many years with subthreshold symptoms using a variety of adaptive or mal-adaptive strategies such as avoidance. They may not recognize the impact of the trau-matic event or events until symptoms become extreme, sometimes years after the actual exposure.

Changes in indices of physiological arousal are also required for a diagnosis of PTSD (Criterion E; see Table 9.1). A byproduct of the involvement of the sympathetic nervous system in the response to a traumatic event, individuals experiencing a posttraumatic reaction show chronically heightened physiological reactivity (Lieberman, Gorka, Funkhouser, Shankman, & Phan, 2017). This can result in difficulties with sleep, anger management, and concentration, as well as an excessive startle response and, classically, chronic hypervigilance. In our clinical work with first responders, the concept of hypervigilance can be a contentious one. As many of our clients point out, in order to be successful and survive a career as a police officer, it is necessary to maintain a high level of situational awareness or alertness in the field – the ability to pick up and go, to make a split-second life or death decision at any moment. The real threat of danger and the uncertainty surrounding even seemingly-benign scenarios require officers to remain alert in order to ensure their own and others' safety. Gilmartin (2002) notes that most police officers develop a chronically high level of alertness on the job. He suggests that especially among young officers, this heightened state of alertness may be enjoyable, as it is often accompanied by quick and practical thinking, high energy, engagement in the work, and a strong sense of camaraderie with fellow officers. This high adrenaline state is often a necessary condition of police work, but it is unsustainable in the long term and likely to have negative health-related effects over time (Koch, 2010; Paton, Violanti, & Schmukler, 1999). Although vigilance is an important aspect of effective police perfor-mance, there are indications when it passes the clinical threshold into hypervigilance and becomes a constituent symptom of PTSD. In contrast with healthy situational awareness, hypervigilance results in persistent guardedness, reactivity, or fear in the absence of a reasonable, immediate threat of danger, and interferes with the ability to engage pro-ductively in workplace or personal life activities. In our clinical practice, we aim to treat hypervigilance, rather than problematizing or minimizing the adaptive vigilance that is required for survival in the field; indeed, this is delicate and nuanced work.

Finally, posttraumatic reactions meeting diagnostic criteria for PTSD involve a sig-nificant change in the individual's mood or emotional state, as well as their thinking styles or systems of belief (Criterion D; see Table 9.1). This includes: rigid and mal-adaptive shifts in perceptions of the world, oneself, or others; self-blame or inappropriate blame of others for the cause or consequences of the traumatic event; inability to recall important aspects of the event; persistent negative mood states, such as fear, shame, anger, sadness, or shock; an inability to experience positive emotions; a loss of interest or participation in previously valued activities; and/or feelings of disconnection from others or active isolation from important relationships. Research suggests that as a result of regular contact with anger, violence, cruelty, suffering, and dishonesty over the course of their careers, many officers experience a drastic change in their perceptions of the world, the citizens they serve, as well as in the value and impact of their work (Chan, 2001; Dick, 2000; Gilmartin, 2002; Koch, 2010; Miller, 2007). As William Westley (1970), preeminent researcher in police psychology aptly noted, "there is little opportunity in police work to celebrate humanity" (p. 10). For example, in her qualitative study of the social construction of acute stressors among police Dick (2000) found that several officers expressed the belief that the world is beyond help and intervention is pointless. In the absence of similarly routine exposure to resilience, kindness, compassion, or joy, it is likely to become increasingly difficult for officers to maintain balance in their view the world given their overrepresented experiences with hostility and unfixable human suffering. Police may begin to see the world as being fundamentally dangerous, cruel, or unjust and may see their own efforts to make a positive impact as essentially futile. Over time, such beliefs may erode resilience and put officers at increased risk for post-traumatic stress or other OSIs.

Along with shifting perceptions of the world and lifestyle changes associated with police work (e.g., shift work), clinical accounts suggests that police officers often experience a process of isolation from interpersonal relationships with non-police peers, with whom they may share less and less in common throughout the course of their careers (Gilmartin, 2002; Kirschman, 2007; Koch, 2010). Koch (2010) opined that a growing sense of suspiciousness and cynicism resulting from police work contributes to officers' difficulty delineating between those they can and cannot trust, including individuals who are a part of their personal lives, such as spouses, friends, or neighbors. An "us versus them" mentality may further contribute to challenges in relationships with non-police peers (Koch, 2010; Waters & Ussery, 2007; Woody, 2005). Stressors associated with the police occupational role are likely to exert particularly negative effects on family relationships when they result in work attitude carryover (e.g., hypervigilant, authoritative, cynical, or protective stances), excessive demands on family time, negative moods, and the development problematic behaviors such as displacement of aggression, alcohol abuse, or marital infidelity (Brodie & Eppler, 2012; Dowling, Moynihan, Genet, & Lewis, 2006; Kirschman, 2007). Officers experiencing PSTD often feel alienated or disconnected from their important relationships. They may begin to feel misunderstood or simply "different" from others. They may also purposely distance themselves from others as a way of minimizing potential exposure to trauma-related reminders or as a result of shame and sadness. Particularly when officers are struggling with anger management or intense hyperreactivity to possible threats, they may purposely isolate themselves as a way of shielding their loved ones from uncontrollable behaviors that could further damage relationships.

Etiology of PTSD

Memory, Information Processing, and Neurobiological Factors. Contemporary understandings of the development of PTSD emphasize the role of memory and information processing systems (Brewin, 2014; Brewin, Gregory, Lipton, & Burgess, 2010; Ehlers & Clark, 2000; van der Kolk, 1994). The dual representation theory of PTSD (Brewin, 2014; Brewin et al., 2010) provides a model for understanding the vivid, intrusive thoughts and imagery that haunt individuals experiencing posttraumatic stress. This model suggests that intrusive symptoms are the result of the particular way that trauma memories are processed and stored in the brain.

The dual representation theory (Brewin, 2014; Brewin et al., 2010) posits that two distinct types of memory representation are encoded at the time of an episodic event – a personal event experienced by an individual, such as meeting their new rescue dog for the first time or hearing a song on the radio last week. We can think of these types of memory representation as methods of organization – like two aspects of a filing system such as colour-coding and date/time stamps. One memory filing system processes and stores *sensory* (e.g., physical sensations, visual and auditory cues) and *affective* (e.g., was the experience neutral, happy, sad, frightening?) information associated with the experience – the aspects that "color" the memory. The other memory filing system places that sensory and affective input into *context*, with spatial, temporal, and personal data abstracted into a narrative or descriptive representation of the event – that is, when, where, and why did it happen, what meaning did it have, and what else was going on? Together, these methods of organizing episodic memories help us to make sense of them, understand their importance in our lives, and to recall them as events that happened in the past, even if we experience strong emotions associated with the memories in the present.

Normal episodic memories are encoded (stored) with sensory-affective and contextual representations of the event tightly connected in order to facilitate this awareness. In the dog adoption example, for instance, sensory-affective information (memories of the smell of the animal shelter, the sound of our new dog happily greeting us, and how happy and nervous we felt) would be stored in our brains together with personal and contextual data (an understanding of ourselves as a dog lover, an awareness of the challenges involved in dog ownership, the time of day and year, where we were standing spatially in the shelter as we made our decision to take him home). In contrast, as a result of their extreme emotional salience, trauma memories are encoded with robust sensory and affective representation, while relevant contextual information tends to be less fully articulated and also more loosely connected to the sensory-affective data. To use our earlier metaphor, trauma memories are primarily stored with vivid and evocative colour-coding, but very little other information with which to organize them.

This discrepancy in storage systems between normal and trauma memories subsequently affects the way that these memories are recalled. With healthy memorics, retrieval of stored sensory or affective information is typically accessed with contextualization easily available and intact, and they can be called upon voluntarily or involuntarily. For example, when you hear that song on the radio for a second time, you may think back to the first time you heard it and remember where you were headed and what you were doing that day. You experience this memory as just that: a memory. In contrast, the highly evocative trauma memory is typically triggered *involuntarily* in response to cognitive or sensory stimuli reminiscent of the initial event, such as the smell of gasoline or a thought about returning to work. Without the initial integration of contextual and temporal data with these sensory and affective cues, the trauma memory, once triggered, feels undifferentiated from the present and is absent of adaptive systems of meaning or order. The memory is typically not recalled in a coherent order, but rather as disjointed mess of unconnected and distressing thoughts or imagery. Trauma memories are experienced as if they are occurring in the here and now, and there is very little voluntary control over when and where and for how long this intense experiencing occurs. It is as if a file cabinet has been stuffed haphazardly full of documents and photographs, all labeled red for "danger," and each time there is a reminder of the traumatic event, a drawer bursts open and the papers fly out into the room. The dual representation theory (Brewin, 2014; Brewin et al., 2010) suggests that this is the mechanism responsible for intrusive symptoms of PTSD.

Intrusive symptoms are furthermore thought to be maintained by avoidance, which in effect perpetuates the lack of integration between sensory-affective information and the context of time, place, and meaning. Research has demonstrated, and we have observed in our clinical practice, that traumatized individuals with and without PTSD do not necessarily differ in the number of intrusive trauma memories they experience with associated sensory cues; rather, what differentiates those with a diagnosis of PTSD from those without is the severity of distress experienced in response to trauma memories, the lack of context or coherence they contain, and the experience of memories as if they are being relived in the present (Michael, Ehlers, Halligan, & Clark, 2005). Consistent with this understanding, the PTSD treatment protocols boasting the strongest empirical evidence generally focus on assisting the traumatized individual to challenge their avoidance of trauma-related memories via exposure and develop a coherent narrative of their experience, integrating sensory information and affective reactions with an adaptive, contextual understanding of what occurred and why (Foa & Rothbaum, 2001; Resick, Monson, & Chard, 2007).

Neurobological evidence also provides us with an understanding of the mechanisms of trauma. The amygdala is the brain's threat detector and the hub of affective responses to incoming stimuli. Brain neuroimaging research has consistently identified hyperreactivity in the amygdala of individuals with PTSD during exposure to threatening stimuli. Functional imaging studies suggest that heightened amygdala activity is coupled with inadequate inhibitory responses by the nucleus accumbens and medial prefrontal cortex, which play central roles in the brain's reward system, decision making, and long-term memory retrieval (Garfinkel & Liberzon, 2009). This pattern of neurobiological response helps to explain hyperarousal and hypervigilance to perceived dangers characteristic of individuals with PTSD. The traumatized brain has become highly sensitive to any indication of threat, and "false alarms" are endemic. Meanwhile, the hippocampus, which is responsible for organizing incoming information into long term memory and situating it in time and place, has been consistently shown in structural imaging studies to be smaller in PTSD samples than health controls, and research suggests that it does not function optimally in conditions of extreme stress (Garfinkel & Liberzon, 2009). Some have suggested that hippocampal dysfunction is the mechanism underlying the intrusive nature of trauma memories, decontextualized and without the necessary temporal and situational data to differentiate them from current events as described above (Brewin et al., 2010; van der Kolk, 1994); however, research also highlights the complexity of this proposed mechanism (Bergado, Lucas, & Richter-Levin, 2011; Garfinkel & Liberzon, 2009).

Other Factors. A number of conditions existing or occurring prior to, during, or following exposure to a traumatic event may help to explain why some traumatized individuals will go on to develop PTSD while others will not. Marchand and colleagues (Marchand, Nadeau, Beaulieu-Prévost, Boyer, & Martin, 2015) examined predictors of the development of PTSD in 83 police officers over the course of one year following a traumatic event. The results of linear regression were consistent with much of the existing research, and demonstrated that development of PTSD symptomatology was modulated by pre-traumatic (i.e., emotional coping strategies and number of children), peri-traumatic (i.e., physical and emotional reactions and dissociation), and post-traumatic factors (i.e., acute stress disorder, depression symptoms, and seeking of psychological help early on), all of which were positively associated with development of PTSD. These findings suggest that some of these factors, individually or in combination, may be used to predict the likelihood that an individual will go on to develop PTSD symptomatology following a traumatic incident.

A number of idiographic risk factors for PTSD have been identified by the literature, including family psychiatric history, female gender, younger age at the time of the trauma, previous trauma history, childhood adversity, lower socioeconomic status, lower education, and pre-existing psychopathology (Keane, Marshall, & Taft, 2006). Given how common childhood experiences of trauma or adversity are in the general population, this factor is especially relevant. Epidemiological research suggests that American youth experience sexual assault at a rate of 8%–12%, 9%–19% have experienced physical assault or abuse, 38%–70% have witnessed serious community violence, approximately 10% have witnessed violence between caregivers, and 1 in 5 have experienced the death of a loved one by suicide (Saunders & Adams, 2014). Many of our police officers will thus enter their careers with a significant existing vulnerability to the development of PTSD. Otte et al. (2005) showed that police cadets with a pre-existing history of childhood trauma found videos of actual duty-related critical incidents more distressing than those who did not have a previous trauma history. In another study (Pole et al., 2007), researchers found that cadets with a history of childhood trauma showed higher reactivity to a startling sound on psychophysiological indicators of distress (i.e., skin conductance), as well as higher negative affect and lower positive affect compared to cadets without previous trauma. They noted that the differences in psychophysiological measures resulted from chronic hyperactivity of the sympathetic nervous system among cadets with childhood trauma.

In addition to increased vulnerability to PTSD on the job, in our clinical work, we have certainly observed the complexity that a prior history of childhood trauma or adversity can contribute to the presentation, symptomatology, and treatment response of a police officer. Negative cognitions about the self and others tend to be more extreme and rigid to change, the officer may be more reliant on maladaptive or potentially dangerous behaviors to cope, and the origins and meaning of intrusive experiences and problematic beliefs can be difficult to disentangle and address as they may have roots throughout the life course.

Peri-traumatic factors increasing the risk for development of PTSD include those related to the individual experience as well as related to the event itself. A strong body of research has supported the role of peri-traumatic dissociation, for example, in the development of intrusion symptomatology and the likelihood of PTSD following a traumatic event (Keane et al., 2006), including among police officers (McCanlies, Sarkisian, Andrew, Burchfiel, & Violanti, 2017). Proposed mechanisms underlying this association include a perceived loss of control or fear of death due to dissociative symptoms (Gershuny, Cloitre, & Otto, 2003) and increased disorganization of trauma memories resulting in negative appraisals of the event and one's memories of it (Halligan, Michael, Clark, & Ehlers, 2003).

Another peri-traumatic factor that may increase the risk of the development of PTSD is personal injury or perceived threat to one's life. Research has elucidated significant connections between the presence of a physical injury following trauma and the development of PTSD. A study of soldiers comparing those with and without physical injuries involved in the same combat situations found that those with physical injuries were significantly more likely to have symptoms meeting diagnostic criteria for PTSD (at a rate of 16.7% vs. 2.5%) (Koren, Norman, Cohen, Berman, & Klein, 2005). Interestingly, this study found that the severity of the physical injury did not distinguish those with and without a diagnosis of PTSD (Koren et al., 2005). Approximately 28% of individuals hospitalized following physical trauma were found to develop PTSD 12 months after their initial injuries (Shih, Schell, Hambarsoomian, Marshall, & Belzberg, 2010). Specific types of physical injuries have been associated with increased risk of mental health problems including falls, burns, injuries to the spinal cord and those involving acquired brain injury (Sareen et al., 2013). In particular, mild traumatic brain injury (mTBI) appears to be a significant risk factor for the development of PTSD following physical injury (Roitman, Gilad, Ankri, & Shalev, 2013; Vasterling et al., 2018). Moreover, mTBI is associated with more severe PTSD symptoms among combat veterans than those with PTSD alone (Barnes, Walter, & Chard, 2012). Individuals with both mTBI and PTSD have been shown to perform more poorly on neuropsychological testing and exhibit higher levels of distress overall compared to those with either condition alone (Combs et al., 2015). Finally, another study of combat veterans found that those with a history of mTBI and PTSD also had more severe pain symptoms (Stojanovic et al., 2016). The risk of physical injury, such as via falls, transportation accident, violent acts, and physical exertion, are as plentiful as risks of psychological injury in the job of policing (Bureau of Labor Statistics, 2016; Cohen & Garis, 2018), making the potential for development of PTSD twofold.

After a traumatic event has been experienced, there are a number of factors that may modulate risk for development of PTSD. These include access to social support; subsequent stressors, traumas, or losses; the development of comorbid psychological conditions, such as depression, panic disorder, or a substance use disorder; and the use of maladaptive coping (APA, 2013; Keane et al., 2006).

Prevalence of PTSD among police. There is a significant literature supporting high rates of PTSD and posttraumatic stress symptoms (PTSS; i.e., diagnostically subthreshold symptoms of PTSD) among police officers, although rates have varied greatly from study to study, ranging from as low as 5% to as high as 50% (e.g., Brown, Fielding, & Grover, 1999; Huddleston, Stephens, & Paton, 2007; McCafferty, McCafferty, & McCafferty, 1992; Ménard & Arter, 2013; Thornton & Herndon, 2016). Rates of PTSD within the general population of the US and Canada are comparatively low, with lifetime rates estimated at approximately 6—8% and past year rates estimated at approximately 3.5% (Kessler, Berglund, et al., 2005; Kessler, Chiu, Demler, & Walters, 2005; Statistics Canada, 2013). Ménard and Arter (2013) reported that 18.5% of the 750 American police officers responding to an online survey met criteria for PTSD based on their responses to the PTSD Checklist – Civilian Version (PCL-C; Weathers, Huska, & Keane, 1991, p. 02130). In an online survey of almost 6000 public safety personnel in Canada, Carleton et al. (2017) found that 19.5% of provincial and municipal police officers and 30% of federal police officers screened positively for PTSD on the Posttraumatic Stress Disorder Checklist for DSM-5 (PCL-5; Weathers et al., 2013). Thornton and Herndon (2016) showed that of 76 front-line police officers, 11.8% were at clinical risk for PTSD, and 14.5% were experiencing a frequency and severity of hyperarousal, intrusion, and avoidance symptomology consistent with a diagnosis of PTSD. With regard to specific symptom clusters associated with PTSD, research examining the effects of perceived work stress in 1072 officers from a large urban police department (Gershon et al., 2009) found that 33% of respondents reported intrusive or recurrent thoughts, memories, or dreams about distressing work events, 24% felt detached from people and activities related to stressful events, and 23% avoided triggers or reminders related to a stressful event. Research with clinical samples of police (i.e., those seeking out psychotherapeutic treatment) has founds rates of PTSD over 60% (van der Meer et al., 2017). Ménard and Arter (2013) concluded from their study findings that 1 out of every 7 officers may be in need of a referral for therapeutic intervention, and that PTSD is likely underdiagnosed in law enforcement populations.

Impact of PTSD on health, wellbeing, and performance. Empirical inquiry has revealed significant connections between PTSS and PTSD in police officers and a number of consequences to their overall health, well-being, and functioning. A study of police officers in Brazil found that those with PTSD were more likely to be divorced, express the belief that their physical health was poor, utilize increased medical consultations, and report higher levels of suicidal ideation (Maia et al., 2007). Research examining correlates of PTSD among police officers involved in providing emergency response to the 9/11/2001 World Trade Center attacks also found that those officers whose symptoms met full criteria for a diagnosis of PTSD (as compared to subsyndromal PTSS) had higher rates of depressive and panic symptoms, alcohol use problems, and suicidal ideation (Pietrzak et al., 2012). Similarly, another study of police officers involved in the events of 9/11/2001 revealed higher levels of comorbid depressive and anxiety symptoms among those with PTSD compared to those whose symptoms did not meet criteria for PTSD (Bowler et al., 2016). Higher levels of PTSD symptoms were associated with lower social support at follow-up among 9/11 police officer responders (Schwarzer, Cone, Li, & Bowler, 2016). A study of police officers who had provided emergency response for an air disaster in Amsterdam in 1992 in which 43 people were killed found that officers involved in the incident reported significantly lower health-related quality of life compared to officers who had not been exposed to this traumatic incident (Slottje et al., 2007). Thus, symptoms and/or a diagnosis of PTSD have meaningful implications for a number of domains related to the health of officers including increased likelihood of additional psychological comorbidities such as depression and alcohol use problems, suicidal ideation, and negative associations with interpersonal functioning and relationship satisfaction.

Meta-analyses have demonstrated significant associations between PTSS and PSTD and numerous health-related conditions and/or physical symptoms. Specifically, PTSD has been associated with greater general health symptoms as well as increased medical conditions including gastrointestinal, pain-related, and cardiovascular symptoms (Pacella, Hruska, & Delahanty, 2013). Trauma exposure and the development of PTSD symptoms was found to predict cardiac events in women in a longitudinal study (Sumner et al., 2015). Increased rates of metabolic syndrome (including hypertension, elevated levels of insulin, triglycerides, and fasting glucose and decreased levels of high-density lipoprotein cholesterol; Rosenbaum et al., 2015) and obesity (Bartoli et al., 2015) have been found among individuals with PTSD, which may significantly increase the likelihood of developing cardiovascular disease in these individuals. Higher levels of C-Reactive protein, which contributes to inflammatory processes in the body, has been proposed as a mechanism through which PTSD impacts physical health trajectories (Solomon et al., 2017). Furthermore, PTSD has been associated with poorer health-related quality of life among combat veterans (Schry et al., 2015). In an effort to mitigate the effects of these increased health-related risks, a treatment focus on promoting healthy and adaptive behaviors and providing support for the process of behavioral change may prove useful for improving health outcomes.

Neurobiological impact of PTSD

Research has attempted to elucidate the impact of trauma exposure and the development of PTSS within law enforcement populations, acknowledging the inherent differences between adaptive neurobiological responses to trauma in the short-term and the physical impact of chronic trauma exposure in the long-term. The hypothalamic-pituitary-adrenal (HPA) axis is the body's main stress response system, involving both the central nervous system and hormonal or endocrine responses. Research has demonstrated that PTSD may be associated with significant changes to the overall functioning and reactivity patterns of the HPA axis, which suggests ongoing changes to the ways in which individuals react and respond to stress in the long-term from a biological perspective (Kinlein, Wilson, & Karatsoreos, 2015). Research has also shown that posttraumatic stress symptoms were related to lower awakening levels of salivary cortisol within a sample of police officers (Neylan et al., 2005), suggesting a significant relationship between posttraumatic stress symptoms and a negative feedback effect on the HPA axis. Conversely, another study of police officers with PTSD found higher early morning salivary cortisol levels (R. J. Lindauer, Olff, van Meijel, Carlier, & Gersons, 2006).

Such variability in findings related to cortisol patterns may reflect PTSD symptom chronicity, with higher salivary cortisol levels in the relative short-term in response to traumatic stress and lower levels of cortisol in the long-term, a sign of overall dysregulation of the HPA system (Bremner, 2001; Finsterwald & Alberini, 2014). A prospective study examined the impact of salivary cortisol patterns on the development of Acute Stress Disorder (ASD; trauma-related symptoms in the immediate aftermath of a traumatic event) following the first three years of police service (Inslicht et al., 2011). Interestingly, these authors found that a greater increase in salivary cortisol level from zero to 30 min after awakening was prospectively associated with increased dissociation and ASD symptoms within the first three years of policing, suggesting that increased reactivity of the HPA may serve as predisposing vulnerability factor for the development of trauma symptoms (Inslicht et al., 2011). Thus, the overall functioning of the HPA system may have important implications for the etiology of PTSD and its ongoing biological effects.

Studies have examined the correlates of PTSD symptoms on brain structural volumes among police officers (Lindauer et al., 2004; Lindauer et al., 2006; Shucard et al., 2012). Higher levels of intrusive symptoms of PTSD were found to be correlated with reduced brain volumes in a number of key structures including the amygdala, thalamus, and globus pallidus among police officers (Shucard et al., 2012). Similarly, reduced hippocampal volume was found to be associated with PTSD in a study of Dutch police officers (Lindauer et al., 2004). Such findings point to the possible impact of PTSD on a number of significant brain functions including learning, memory and attention. Indeed, police officers with PTSD were found to exhibit poorer performance on a delayed visual memory task and greater levels of incorrect intrusion responses on a verbal memory task (Lindauer et al., 2006). Specific neurobiological predisposing factors along with the continued physical impact of PTSD symptoms may have deleterious effects for numerous cognitive processes including memory and concentration, resulting in significant implications for performance in a field in which cognitive demands are extremely high, ever-changing, and complex.

Psychoeducation regarding the impact of traumatic experiences and posttraumatic stress on the brain and cognitive functioning can serve to validate and normalize the memory and attentional complaints that are so frequently reported among police officers seeking treatment. Furthermore, basic strategies to enhance cognitive functioning may improve quality of life and ability to complete tasks effectively, generating a greater sense of mastery and confidence as well as promoting engagement throughout the treatment process. Strategies may include simple techniques to enhance organizational, attentional, memory and problem-solving strategies or approaches (for a detailed review of cognitive strategies that may be useful for individuals with PTSD, see Huckans et al., 2010).

Pain and PTSD

Chronic pain symptoms frequently co-occur with PTSD (Asmundson, Coons, Taylor, & Katz, 2002). For those whom the triggering traumatic event resulted in physical injury, ongoing pain sensations may also act as physical reminders of the trauma, maintaining or exacerbating PTSD symptoms including intrusive experiencing, hypervigilance, and other arousal symptoms (Asmundson et al., 2002). It has thus been suggested that specific pharmacotherapy interventions targeting pain symptoms following significant trauma exposure and physical injury may result in reduced rates of PTSD (Holbrook, Galarneau, Dye, Quinn, & Dougherty, 2010). In a sample of military personnel who had incurred physical injuries in the course of combat, those who were provided with morphine in the acute stage of medical treatment were less likely to develop PTSD symptoms, even after adjusting for the severity of physical injuries (Holbrook et al., 2010). In another study of combat veterans, intrusion symptoms of PTSD were found to predict poorer physical health and greater levels of physical pain (Asnaani, Reddy, & Shea, 2014). Individuals with PTSD demonstrate an altered pain processing profile in quantitative testing, with a reduced perception of painful stimuli demonstrated by higher pain thresholds, and hyper-reactivity to suprathreshold pain stimulation, as suggested by increased intensity ratings of painful stimuli (Defrin et al., 2008). Thus, the presence of pain and symptoms associated with physical injuries may have important implications for the development and treatment of PTSD. Unfortunately, there appears to be a paucity of research examining treatment approaches that address both physical and psychological symptoms concurrently.

Ensuring that individuals receiving psychological treatment for PTSD have received appropriate clinical evaluation of pain symptoms and the promotion of active pain management strategies concurrent with trauma treatment may prove beneficial for treatment outcomes. Furthermore, examination of the cognitive components of pain experience (e.g., understanding the meaning or interpretation of pain symptoms) can be effectively integrated into cognitive-behavioural approaches for trauma treatment. For example, a police officer presenting with PTSD subsequent to a physical assault that resulted in a mild traumatic brain injury reported ongoing re-experiencing symptoms and emotional reactivity triggered by pain symptoms. Psychoeducation regarding chronic pain and the ways in which symptoms may be maintained and/or exacerbated by fear and avoidance can be an extremely useful intervention. In this case, information about pain chronicity and differences between acute and chronic pain served to decrease the perceived threat of the pain symptoms themselves by challenging the notion that these symptoms reflect an ongoing source or sign of danger for the body. An active pain management approach with a focus on the development of useful strategies to cope with and mitigate the effects of pain symptoms allowed for improvements in day-to-day functioning, task completion and quality of life. Ultimately, a treatment approach that focuses on pain and trauma symptoms concurrently is essential for adequately addressing these two intractable symptom dimensions following a trauma involving significant physical injury.

Evidence-based treatment for PTSD

What is evidence-based treatment? The American Psychological Association (APA) policy on evidence-based practice as defined by the APA Council of Representatives during its August 2005 meeting states the following:

> *Evidence-based practice in psychology (EBPP) is the integration of the best available research with clinical expertise in the context of patient characteristics, culture, and preferences. . . . The purpose of EBPP is to promote effective psychological practice and enhance public health by applying empirically supported principles of psychological assessment, case formulation, therapeutic relationship, and intervention (p. 5).*

The clinical and practical implications of this policy is that empirical support is not enough – consideration must also be given by trained person, such as a psychologist, who weighs this knowledge of empirically supported psychotherapies with the probable costs and benefits to the person receiving care, variations in presenting primary symptoms or comorbidities, patient demographics such as age or sex, sociocultural and familial factors (e.g., gender, gender identity, family culture, race, class, sexual orientation, religion, family composition), environmental context (e.g., police culture, major life events), personal preferences and values (e.g., preferred treatment modality, beliefs, goals), available resources (e.g., treatment funding) and other options for care (Sackett, Straus, Richardson, Rosenberg, & Haynes, 2000). In addition, there must be ongoing monitoring of progress by the treatment provider, along with an ability to be flexible and adjust the treatment plan as needed. Most importantly, the APA policy highlights the importance of the person receiving treatment being an active and informed participant.

The flexibility that this policy promotes allows treatment to be tailored to the specific individual receiving care. Having options can be valuable. If one approach is not good fit or the outcomes are suboptimal, another treatment can be trialed. With the large number of empirically supported treatments available, however, this may leave the individual receiving care and the clinician working with them wondering where to start.

Psychological treatments for PTSD, for example, can differ in the number of sessions a standardized protocol may dictate, the duration of sessions, strategies for approaching the trauma memory itself, the directness with which the trauma memory and other trauma-related cues are addressed, and the level of skill development the treatment incorporates. As such, treatment should always begin with a comprehensive psychological assessment. In addition to confirming diagnoses and assessing for comorbidities, such as depression or substance abuse, the purpose of the initial assessment is to begin to explore the unique elements of the client's personality, life experiences, values, and the context in which their difficulties occur in order to guide treatment planning.

Knowing the common elements of empirically supported treatments can also provide direction. At the 2014 annual meeting of the International Society of Traumatic Stress Studies, two psychologists organized a panel of pioneers in the treatment of PTSD and proposed that the group identify and discuss commonalities among evidence-based treatments and identify the most important interventions for successful therapy. Together, the panelists compiled a list of the most crucial components of available evidence-based treatments in successfully treating PTSD (Schnyder et al., 2015). They concluded that the six commonalities of empirically-supported treatment for PTSD are as follows:

1. Psychoeducation – for example, information on the nature and course of post-traumatic stress reactions, an introduction to treatment options and risks/benefits of those options;
2. Emotional regulation and adaptive coping skills – for example, teaching skills to cope with trauma reminders and soothe distress;
3. Some form of exposure to memories of traumatic experiences – for example, this may involve talking about, writing about, or intentionally thinking about the trauma memory; or, approaching avoided situations in a systematic and pre-planned manner with the support of the therapist;
4. Cognitive processing, restructuring, and/or meaning making – for example, examining ways that beliefs about oneself, others, or the world has changed as a result of the trauma; connecting or re-connecting with one's values and identifying what thoughts or emotions tend to interfere with acting in accordance with these values;
5. Working with emotions – for example, interventions targeting the processing of unresolved feelings in response to the trauma, such as fear, anger, guilt or shame;
6. Altering memory processes – the authors assert that central to all trauma-focused treatments is the creation of a coherent trauma narrative (a reorganization of the trauma memory in a way that helps the individual make sense of what they have experienced).

Most effective treatments for posttraumatic stress involve each of these elements in greater or lesser degrees. We now summarize empirical support for the three PTSD treatments that are arguably the most commonly implemented with first responder and other populations: Eye Movement Desensitization and Reprocessing (EMDR), Cognitive Processing Therapy (CPT), and Prolonged Exposure (PE).

Eye Movement Desensitization and Reprocessing. EMDR is one of three therapies and four medications that are conditionally recommended by the APA (2019). A conditional recommendation conveys that APA has determined the research evidence indicates good treatment outcomes; however, this evidence may not be as strong as for other interventions, there is a greater likelihood that potential risks may outweigh benefits, or the intervention may not be as beneficial for certain subgroups of people with PTSD or in certain treatment settings. Despite these caveats, EMDR is a quite well-known and widely implemented treatment for anxiety disorders and PTSD. The therapy also tends to be familiar, at least by name, among police officers in comparison to other conditionally recommended treatments. One reason for its appeal may be that in contrast with methods of trauma-focused cognitive behavior therapy that involve describing the trauma memory in great detail, the emphasis in EMDR is more indirect, and involves assisting the information processing system of the brain to make connections required to resolve psychological symptoms (Shapiro, 1989). A goal is for clients to maintain a sense of control during memory work, and they are asked to only briefly focus on the trauma memory while engaged in bilateral stimulation of the brain – usually involving eye movements, taps, or tones administered on each side of the body. The theory underlying these techniques is that bilateral stimulation allows the brain to make new connections in order to process the traumatic memory. In its traditional format, EMDR involves little homework between sessions, and the focus of treatment is broad, rather than specifically focusing on the traumatic incident or incidents themselves.

EMDR is an eight-phase treatment approach that has been used to treat a variety of psychological disorders, including PTSD and anxiety disorders, such as specific phobias (Barlow, 2014; Shapiro, 1989). In the first phase of treatment, the clinician takes a detailed history to identify the client's readiness and suitable targets for intervention. Following this is the preparation phase, in which the goal is formation of a therapeutic relationship. During the third phase of treatment, called the target assessment phase, clients identify and focus on a traumatic image or memory. The client is also asked to elicit negative cognitions or beliefs about the memory, rated on an 11-point scale of distress, and identify the physical location of distress in the body (e.g., physiological signals of anxiety such as a "pit" in the stomach). The therapist assists the client in generating positive cognitions that would be preferable to associate with the memory, which are rated on a 7-point scale of believability (i.e., how much the client believes the statement). During the fourth phase, or the desensitization phase, the client is asked to visualize the memory, rehearse the negative cognitions, concentrate on the physical sensations, and visually track the therapist who guides bilateral stimulation using taps, tones, or eye movement. For example, the therapist might tap the client gently on alternating sides of their body, administer a tone in alternating ears of the client's headphones, or use their finger to elicit side-to-side eye movements (called saccades) in the client. All of this occurs simultaneously and at specific intervals. The client is then asked to blank out the memory and take a breath, following which they are prompted to bring back the memory and cognitions again and rate their distress. Sets of bilateral stimulation are repeated until the distress rating is 0 or 1 out of 11. During the fifth phase, the installation phase, the client is asked how they feel about the positive cognition and give it a new rating of believability. The sixth, seventh and eighth phases involve a body scan, closure, and re-evaluation of treatment effects.

In terms of efficacy, randomized control trials have shown EMDR to be superior to waitlist controls in outcomes for PTSD (e.g., Rothbaum, Astin, & Marsteller, 2005). A study of 62 police officers randomly assigned to either EMDR or a standard stress management program of the same duration showed that the officers in the EMDR condition provided lower ratings on measures of PTSD symptoms, subjective distress, job stress, and anger, which were maintained at the 6-month follow-up (Wilson, Tinker, Becker, & Logan, 2001). A 2004 study that examined high-resolution brain SPECT imaging and EMDR in 6 police officers with PTSD who were involved in on-duty shootings found that all officers showed clinical improvement and brain imaging changes after participating in EMDR treatment. While some studies have reported no differences in the efficacy of EMDR versus trauma-focused CBT (e.g., Ironson, Freund, Strauss, & Williams, 2002; Rothbaum et al., 2005), several studies have shown CBT and other more traditional exposure-based therapies to be more effective than EMDR (e.g., Devilly & Spence, 1999; Muris, Merckelbach, Holdrinet, & Sijesnaar, 1998; Muris Merckelbach, van Haaften, & Mayer, 1997; Taylor et al., 2003). Dr. Francine Shapiro, the creator of EMDR, maintains that the lateral eye movements (or saccades) are an essential change agent in EMDR for attenuation of clinical symptoms; however, some dismantling studies have yielded mixed results (e.g., Pitman, Orr, Altman, Longpre, Poire, & Macklin, 1996), and others studies have found that eye movements do not improve outcome, nor do alternating stimuli such as finger taps (Leahy, Holland & McGinn, 2012). Some have argued that EMDR represents nothing more than an elaborated form of imaginal exposure (e.g., Barlow, 2002; Benish, Imel, & Wampold, 2008; Lohr, Tolin, & Lilienfeld, 1998).

Prolonged Exposure. PE (Foa, Hembree, & Rothbaum, 2007) is one of four treatment approaches for PTSD that has been strongly recommended by the APA (2019), meaning that there is a significant research base to support its efficacy with a variety of populations. PE has its theoretical basis in emotional processing theory (Foa & Kozak, 1986) and it evolved from a longstanding tradition of exposure-based treatment for anxiety disorders. Exposure-based interventions are intended to address the avoidance of stimuli that cause intense and excessive fear or anxiety by supporting the individual to confront those stimuli in safe but anxiety-inducing scenarios. The basic premise of emotional processing theory as it is applied to trauma is that processing of the traumatic memory is an essential component of effective treatment for PTSS. Edna Foa and her colleagues developed this approach to treat PTSD in the mid-eighties, initially applying the technique with populations of female rape survivors (Foa, Rothbaum, Riggs, & Murdock, 1991). Since then, numerous randomized controlled trials have been conducted comparing PE with other methods of treatment for PTSD in a variety of traumatized populations. Finding have consistently supported the efficacy of PE in the amelioration of PTSD symptoms and the maintenance of improvements over time. Specifically, PE has been found to result in superior PTSD outcomes than stress inoculation training (Foa et al., 1999) and cognitive restructuring (Foa et al., 2005), and comparable outcomes to those of CPT (Resick, Nishith, Weaver, Astin, & Feuer, 2002) and EMDR (Rothbaum et al., 2005), although level of overall functioning at a six-month follow-up was superior for PE in comparison to EMDR.

The PE protocol consists of 10–15 90-min treatment sessions. Each session is audiotaped so that the client can review the tape between sessions. This is necessary for the imaginal exposure intervention, and is also thought to assist clients in making valuable connections and modification in their beliefs as they listen back. Clients are first provided psychoeducation on the various impacts trauma can have on an individual, including a discussion of the factors that maintain symptoms of PTSD: avoidance and problematic beliefs about the trauma. At the outset of treatment, clients are introduced to a method of modulating their distress by intentionally slowing their breathing. Breathing retraining is deployed at the beginning of treatment in order to help the client develop a sense of competence and experience some relief, but it is made clear throughout the rest of treatment that breathing should not be used as a method of avoiding distress during exposure-based interventions, as this is thought to limit the effectiveness of the intervention.

The two exposure-based interventions comprising PE are called imaginal exposure and in vivo exposure. In vivo exposure refers to confrontation of distressing situations in real life, and addresses the avoidance of trauma-related sounds, smells, people, places, or objects among individuals experiencing PTSD. Imaginal exposure involves confrontation of the trauma memory vividly in one's imagination. This intervention also addresses avoidance, for example, of distressing aspects of the memory or the feelings that emerge in relation to it. The rationale underlying exposure is not just about challenging avoidance, however. Classically, exposure is aimed at helping individuals reach a state of habituation to the distressing memory or stimulus, meaning that it loses its power or becomes less distressing with repeated or prolonged exposures. Furthermore, repeated and prolonged exposures to feared stimuli, such as the trauma memory itself or a specific sound or smell associated with it, helps the client learn over time that these stimuli are actually quite safe. As upsetting as the memories of a traumatic event are, they cannot in fact hurt us. Exposure is aimed at fostering a sense of safety even in moments of distress, an experience that is compromised in individuals with PTSD. Many individuals with PTSD harbor the belief that if they confront these feared scenarios, they will feel anxious or sad forever. Exposure also allows clients to observe that this is not actually the case; eventually, distress will reduce, and the client will have had the experience of tolerating the distress until it did. This contributes to an understanding that one can expect the same process when confronting other feared situations, and also promotes a sense of enhanced competency and efficacy, self-states that are often challenged by a traumatic event.

The process of in vivo exposure involves first establishing a hierarchy of avoided or distressing situations, rating them from 0 to 100, least to most distressing. A disabled police officer's in vivo exposure hierarchy might include, for example, going to the mall food court during busy hours, visiting a location where a traumatic event occurred, or listening to sounds of tires screeching on the pavement. Exposure exercises begin with an item that ranges from a 40 to 60 on subjective ratings of distress, and the client is supported in confronting those situations without the use of avoidance or anxiety-modulation techniques (including slowed breathing). They are encouraged to stay in the situation or expose themselves to the stimulus for as long or as many times as it takes for the subjective experience of distress to reduce significantly, ideally by at least 50%. The client then graduates to the next item on the hierarchy. Clients are expected to engage in in vivo exposures several times per week between sessions as a part of their homework.

In imaginal exposure, the client is asked to retell the story of the most intrusive trauma memory from beginning to end, in the present tense, while vividly imagining it with eyes closed. The therapist prompts the clients for as many details as possible, including the sensory details, thoughts, and emotions they experienced at the time, and they are occasionally asked to rate their level of distress as they retell the trauma narrative. This is done during each session for several sessions, and repeated, for 45 min at a time. The client is encouraged to feel all their feelings and not to avoid their distress. After the imaginal exposure is complete, the client and therapist further process the memory and the therapist uses Socratic questions to help identify problematic beliefs or assumptions associated with the event – such as that they are to blame or should have done something differently to prevent it – and guide the client to more accurate or adaptive understandings. The client then listens to the audio tape of this session, including the imaginal exposure, once every day between sessions. In addition to the rationale for exposure-based treatments outlined above, imaginal exposure is aimed at helping the client to create a coherent narrative of their trauma experience, integrate that experience more fully into their normal episodic memory, and to help the client learn and experience the difference between the memory and the trauma itself. The goal is that the client begins to experience the trauma memory as something that has happened in the past and is over, rather than something that is constantly being replayed and re-experienced in the present.

There is a robust body of research support for PE with other populations who experience repeated or cumulative trauma, most notably, veterans. A large-scale study evaluating the effectiveness of national implementation of PE within Veteran's affairs found a significant reduction in both PTSD and depression scores among male and female veterans (Eftekhari et al., 2013). Positive screens for PTSD reduced from 87.6% to 46.2% in the sample. This finding is consistent with those in other similar studies, and has been demonstrated in both RCTs and normative healthcare contexts, with veterans having combat experience from both modern and historic era war zones (e.g., Goodson, Lefkowitz, Helstrom, & Gawrysiak, 2013; Rauch et al., 2009; Tuerk et al., 2011; Yoder et al., 2012). Unfortunately the literature on PTSD treatment among first responders has lagged behind those focusing on veterans; however, clinical experience tells us that PE is among the gold standards of treatment with this population. Of note, Tolin and Foa (1999) presented a case study of PE with a police officer diagnosed with chronic PTSD following a work-related incident. Using a time-series design, they demonstrated that there was significant symptom relief associated with the onset of PE which persisted at a 6-month follow-up period.

Cognitive Processing Therapy

CPT (Resick, Monson, & Chard, 2016) is another treatment approach that has received a strong recommendation by the APA (2019). CPT is a structured, 12-session therapy for PTSD and other trauma-related symptoms. It was initially developed to treat survivors or rape, and has since been implemented with a variety of populations and has been adapted specifically for military veterans and to address traumatic bereavement. Both individual, group, and combined versions of CPT have been protocolled. The underlying premise of CPT is that trauma can have a profound impact on basic belief systems, which then result in barriers to natural recovery. Based on the integration of social cognitive, information processing (Lang, 1977) and emotional processing (Foa, Steketee, & Rothbaum, 1989) theories of PTSD, the developers of CPT suggest that in order to reconcile information about the traumatic event with pre-existing cognitive schemas or beliefs, individuals tend to either assimilate, accommodate, or over-accommodate the new information. Each cognitive response is thought to occur rapidly and largely outside of awareness, leading to a strongly held and often significantly divergent view of self, others, or the world than existed prior to the traumatic event. *Assimilation* is a maladaptive response, and refers to altering incoming trauma-related information to match prior beliefs, promoting problematic conclusions about oneself or the world. For example, if an individual previously held the belief, as many of our police clients do, that they should be able to control or prevent bad things from happening, the experience of a trauma may result in a shift to the belief that they must have been incompetent or reckless in some way. *Accommodation*, in contrast, refers to the adaptive altering of beliefs to incorporate the new information (e.g., "I cannot prevent all bad things from happening, but I am still a competent person and a good cop"). *Over-accommodation* is also a maladaptive response to trauma, in which unhelpful beliefs about oneself and the world become overgeneralized or extreme order to facilitate safety and a sense of control (e.g., "all people have bad intentions or wish to harm me"). The goal of CPT is to help the client challenge beliefs that have been assimilated or over-accommodated as a result of a traumatic experience, in order to move closer to accommodation — that is, accepting the realities of what they have experienced and integrating new information into their systems of belief in a way that is adaptive and appropriate and will assist with the recovery process.

Treatment following the CPT protocol begins with psychoeducation regarding PTSD, including its symptoms and the proposed etiological mechanisms of the disorder. During this initial phase of treatment, there is emphasis on the ways in which ongoing trauma symptoms are often a reflection of an inability to fully process and integrate the experience of trauma, which maintains high levels of physiological and emotional reactivity after exposure to a traumatic event. Following basic psychoeducation, treatment begins to focus on the identification of specific feelings and beliefs associated with the trauma. In particular, there is an emphasis on ascertaining an individual's particular "stuck points" or the maladaptive beliefs that stem from or have become associated with the traumatic event. A significant emphasis is placed in CPT on areas of life and systems of belief commonly impacted by trauma, including safety, trust, power, control, esteem and intimacy (Resick et al., 2016). Throughout treatment, the therapist assists the client to disentangle and modify unhelpful and distressing beliefs and thought patterns about the traumatic event or events through the use of Socratic questioning and worksheets. The client is expected to practice identifying and challenging stuck points both within and outside of session, and homework is an integral component of this model of treatment as it is thought to directly challenge the avoidance that may be maintaining symptoms.

A second component of CPT involves exposure to the trauma memory via a written trauma narrative. Clients are asked to write an account of the most traumatic event from start to finish, in as much detail as possible, with the goal of facilitating the complete emotional processing of the experience. They are instructed to re-read the account each day, and to elaborate sensory details, thoughts, feelings, and physiological sensations into the narrative. The trauma account is shared in session and used to identify and target additional stuck points related to the event, specifically those involving self-blame. Subsequent research comparing the efficacy of a version of CPT without the addition of a written trauma account (CPT-C; i.e., cognitive only) has found that it is as effective as the original protocol (Walter, Dickstein, Barnes, & Chard, 2014). As such, treatment providers can make a clinical decision, along with their clients, about which protocol to employ.

Research has established the efficacy of CPT (including CPT-C) for the treatment of PTSD among various clinical samples and contexts including military personnel (Forbes et al., 2012; Monson et al., 2006; Rosen, Chard, Resick, & Frueh, 2014), survivors of sexual assault (Resick & Schnicke, 1992), and individuals affected by interpersonal violence (Resick et al., 2008). The mechanisms of change related to CPT have also been examined. Studies suggest that changes in trauma-related cognitions (including negative beliefs about the self) precede reductions in PTSD symptoms, which supports the theoretical underpinnings of the treatment approach and model (Schumm, Dickstein, Walter, Owens, & Chard, 2015). Furthermore, research has demonstrated reduced rates of treatment drop-out among veterans undergoing CPT as compared to those receiving Prolonged Exposure-based treatment (Kehle-Forbes, Meis, Spoont, & Polusny, 2016). While there is a limited research examining the efficacy of CPT to treat PTSD among police officers specifically, robust empirical evidence for its effectiveness in other populations with similar trauma-related elements, including exposure to violence, is supports a strong potential utility within law enforcement populations.

Other operational stress injuries

While PTSD is the psychological injury most commonly associated with policing, as has already been noted, there are a variety of negative psychological outcomes that can result from the unique stressors police officers experience on and off the job. The next section explores the risks for and prevalence of other types of OSIs that have received empirical support, including depression and problems with alcohol. We also discuss suicide and suicidal ideation, which are common sequelae of difficulties related to OSI, and a troubling outcome experienced by far too many of our first responders.

Depression

Given repeated exposure to suffering and hostility and in combination with the common perception of a lack of external supports, the police role may put officers at risk for depressed mood and other symptoms of Major Depressive Disorder. Black, McCabe, and McConnell (2013) found that 50% of officers surveyed in their study reported symptoms consistent with mild to severe depression, and 41% reached clinically significant levels of depression on the General Health Questionnaire (Goldberg & Williams, 1988), a measure of general psychopathology. In their study of effects of perceived work stress, Gershon et al. (2009) found that high perceived stress levels were related to depression among police officers. A large portion of their sample described often experiencing mood-related symptoms including low energy (81%), feeling blue (64%), or feeling physically, emotionally, and spiritually depleted (54%). Fox et al. (2012) found that 9% of their sample of American police officers met diagnostic criteria for depression. In a study by Darensburg et al. (2006), 16% of 100 officers surveyed met diagnostic cutoffs for depression (12.1% of male officers; 22% of female officers). Interestingly, rates of depression differed by age; no officers younger than 40 years of age met clinical cutoffs for depression, while 24.4% of officers aged 40–49 years and 20.0% of those aged 50 years and older did (Darensberg et al., 2006).

In addition to risk factors related specifically to their work, police officers experience stressors off the job which may contribute to mood-related pathology in combination with these risk factors. In their study of 100 randomly selected urban police officers, for example, Hartley et al. (2007) found that exposure to multiple negative life events outside of work was associated with elevated levels of depression. Given the negative effects of job-related stressors on the personal lives of some officers, discussed in previous sections, the work may exert risk for depression from both directions. Wang et al. (2010) demonstrated that a combination of individual and work-related factors predicted depressive symptomatology in a group of police recruits after one year on the job. Specifically, greater childhood trauma exposure, lower perceived self-worth during recruitment training, and greater perceived work stress during the first year of police work predicted higher levels of depression symptoms at 12-month follow-up, controlling for depression symptoms during training as well as comorbid PTSD symptoms at the 12-month follow-up.

Alcohol use disorders

The extant literature has also highlighted substance abuse – particularly alcohol abuse – as a mental health concern relevant to police officers. Colloquial accounts from police officers, as well as from mental health professionals working with police and their families highlight alcohol use as a common and culturally-sanctioned method of socialization and coping within this population (Gershon et al., 2009; Kirschman, 2007; Waters & Ussery, 2007). Violanti and colleagues have linked alcohol consumption to the stress associated with police work and police training (Violanti, 2001; Violanti et al., 2011; Violanti, Marshall, & Howe, 1985). Furthermore, he reported significant correlations between alcohol consumption and PTSD, particularly among young officers (Violanti, 2004). A survey of 1106 police officers conducted by the National Institute of Justice found that 21% of officers reported problem alcohol use meeting diagnostic cutoffs for Alcohol Use Disorder, and those suffering from high perceived stress were five times more likely to also report having an Alcohol Use Disorder (Gershon, 2000). Another study demonstrated that 34% of officers recruited from a large urban police department reported that they sometimes drank more than they had planned, 14% felt worried or guilty about their alcohol consumption, and 14% stated that they sometimes did not remember what happened when they were drinking (Gershon et al., 2009). Ménard and Arter (2013) found a rate of 16.7% of problem drinking among officers in their study, and Chopko, Palmieri, and Adams (2013) found that 18.4% of officers reported a moderate number of problems associated with drinking, 3.5% indicated high-risk drinking problems, and 0.6% reported a drinking pattern associated with severe risk.

Davey, Obst, and Sheehan (2001) surveyed 749 Australian police officers to assess factors contributing to their alcohol consumption and harmful drinking. They found that 37% of officers were at risk for harmful drinking on the basis of their scores on the Alcohol Use Disorders Identification Test (AUDIT; Babor, Higgins-Biddle, Saunders, & Monteiro, 2001) and 3.5% of officers scored within the alcohol dependent range. Although officers in this study self-reported that social factors were the most common contributors to their alcohol consumption, analyses demonstrated that self-reported stress levels were the factor most predictive of drinking. The authors noted that despite identifying social factors as the primary determinant of their drinking habits, officers appeared to in fact be drinking (or perhaps socializing while drinking) to cope.

Lindsay and Shelley (2009) similarly found that 3.9% of their sample reported drinking seven days a week, and that stress, social influence, and social conformity accounted for significant variance in alcohol consumption. Although stress was an important factor in this study, the use of alcohol to fit in was the most predictive of problem drinking. In Davey et al.'s (2001) study, 31% of officers saw nondrinkers as being unsociable and worthy of suspiciousness. This suggests that perceived norms around drinking within the workplace culture, especially as a social activity contributing to a sense of conformity or as a way to decompress after work, may result in higher rates of alcohol use and the potential for drinking problems among police officers.

Rates of alcohol abuse or dependence in the population at large are similar to or somewhat lower than those reported in the above studies. Results from the 2015 National Survey on Drug Use and Health (NSDUH) found the 6.2% of surveyed adults in the United States screened positive for an Alcohol Use Disorder (Center for Behavioral Health Statistics and Quality, 2015). The lifetime prevalence of Alcohol Use Disorder among Canadians in the general population is 18.1%, and past year prevalence is 3.2%

(Pearson, Janz, & Ali, 2013, pp. 82−624). Researchers have pointed out, however, that officers may be motivated to underreport their alcohol consumption for fear of departmental discipline, as having a substance use disorder would because for significant job consequences (Austin-Ketch et al., 2011; Violanti, 2003). In any case, an assessment of alcohol use should be a component of any comprehensive treatment planning endeavor with police officers.

Suicide

Finally, officers suffering from an OSI may also be at risk for suicide, and risk is further exacerbated by ready access to lethal means via firearms. Police suicide has been the subject of significant inquiry as well as some controversy in the study of police stress. Several researchers have argued that the rates of suicide among police are higher than those within the general population, while others have argued the opposite. Hackett and Violanti (2003) estimated that the rate of police suicide is about 1.5 times higher than the rate of suicide in population-wide statistics. In a study of Canadian police officers, Charbonneau (2000) found police suicide rates to be almost twice that of the general population. Rates were elevated primarily among young officers ranging from 20 to 39 years of age. In contrast, Aamodt and Stalnaker (2001) argued that although the suicide rate of 18.1 per 100,000 found among police personnel is higher than the 11.4 per 100,000 seen in the general population, it is not higher than would be expected for people of similar age, race, and gender. Hem, Berg, and Ekeberg (2001) reviewed 41 original studies from North America, Europe, and Australia on the topic of police suicide. They found that rates varied widely between studies, and were inconsistent and inconclusive: some studies found elevated suicide rates among police officers whereas others showed an average or low rate of suicide compared to the general population.

Comparisons between police and the general population may not be equivalent, however, as the general population includes a wide spectrum of vulnerable persons, while police officers are subjected to extensive screening for psychological fitness or wellbeing at the stage of recruitment (Ombudsman of Ontario, 2012). Violanti (2008) outlined several issues contributing to inconsistent findings in this area of research. These included challenges linking suicidal behavior or psychological distress to workplace issues, a motivated or incidental underreporting or misclassification of police suicides by police organizations or family members, a lack of nationwide comprehensive data, and difficulties conducting research with or collecting data from police officers and police organizations. As a result of these challenges, reliable and consistent statistics on police suicide are difficult to obtain. Berg, Hem, Lau, Loeb, and Ekeberg (2003) found that 24% of Norwegian police officers felt that life was not worth living, 6.4% had seriously considered suicide, and had 0.7% attempted suicide. A study of 1400 American police officers found that 13.4% admitted to giving suicide serious consideration since beginning their careers (Bishopp & Boots, 2014) and another found that 8.8% of officers surveyed reported past week suicidal ideation (Chopko, Palmieri, & Facemire, 2014). Violanti (2004; 2008) has linked traumatic exposure and PTSD symptomatology as well as depressive symptoms to suicide ideation among police officers. Violanti (2008) concluded that although we cannot determine a causal link between police work and suicide on the basis of past research, the existing data support with a degree of certainty that police work exacerbates the conditions for suicide, and that "the contextual nature of police work is a probabilistic link in the causal chain of suicide" (p. 305).

Posttraumatic growth — becoming strong in the broken places

> The world breaks everyone and afterward many are strong in the broken places.
>
> Ernest Hemmingway, A Farewell to Arms (1929).

The potential for growth through adversity has been espoused in philosophic teaching and religions throughout history, and scientific research has long suggested that individuals can experience positive outcomes from stressful life events (e.g., Taylor, 1983). Despite this, there is a disproportionately large volume of psychological research examining the negative psychological and physical consequences of these types of events, some of which has been reviewed in this chapter. Only in the past 20–30 years has the phenomenon of personal growth in the face of adversity been seriously examined by scientists and clinicians. Even more recent is the idea that "positive personal transformation" can occur in one or more areas of a person's life in the aftermath of trauma (Tedeschi & Moore, 2016, p. 4). In the 1990's, Richard G. Tedeschi, one of the preeminent researchers in this area, coined the term *posttraumatic growth*, or PTG, and has since been gathering data on how and why it occurs.

PTG refers to positive psychological and psychosocial changes associated with highly challenging life events or crises, and may include shifting priorities, strengthened interpersonal relationships, an increased sense of personal strength, a greater appreciation for life, or a deeper connection to spiritual, religious, or existential beliefs (Tedeschi & Calhoun, 1996; 2004). On average, research studies show that about 60% of people who experience trauma also report PTG (Calhoun and Tedeschi, 2006), which is notably greater than the rates of PTSD and other mental health issues following trauma, even among police officers who experience higher than average rates of PTSD (Thornton & Herndon, 2016).

From a theoretical standpoint, PTG differs from the related concept of resilience. Historically, the term resilience refers to "positive adaptation in the context of risk and adversity" (Masten & Powell, 2003, p. 4). The term comes from the Latin word *risilire*, meaning "to leap back" (Skovholt & Trotter-Mathison, 2016, p. 125) and resilience has often been understood as the ability to bounce back from life's challenges. PTG, on the other hand, reflects personal transformation and improved functioning in comparison to before a traumatic event, as a result of having experienced it (Ogińska-Bulik & Kobylarczyk, 2016). In fact, some researchers have suggested that individuals with higher levels of resilience may experience *lower levels* of PTG because the degree to which their core beliefs or assumptive world are challenged as a result of a traumatic event is less significant (e.g., see Ogińska-Bulik & Kobylarczyk, 2016 for a study related to firefighters). This is not to say that lower resilience is desirable in order to increase one's opportunities for PTG. Particularly for police officers who experience frequent exposure to trauma endemic to their work, promoting resilience is an essential effort in the pre-vention of OSIs and promotion of recovery following a workplace psychological injury. There is no amount of personal growth can undo or erase an officer's exposure to trauma. However, for those officers who are traumatized by events they inevitably directly or indirectly experience, the research on PTG offers hope and possibility that the natural responses to extraordinary events are not necessarily entirely negative. It is important for clinicians, organizations, and individual officers and their loved ones to know that PTG can, and often does, occur.

Tedeschi and Moore (2016) argue that people can use their struggles with terrible life events to develop in ways that might not otherwise have been possible. The model of PTG by Calhoun and Tedeschi (1998; 2006; Tedeschi & Calhoun, 2004) posits that PTG develops from the cognitive processing that occurs as people come to terms with the impact of a traumatic event. It suggests that the more a person's beliefs and assumptions about themselves, others, the world and future (e.g., beliefs about predictability, safety, identity) are challenged, and the more distress the individual experiences, and the greater their potential for PTG. In other words, those who are able to accommodate new, adaptive information resulting from a traumatic experience into their existing belief systems are poised to also internalize valuable psychological or psychosocial growth. People high in resilience, while they may suffer less significantly or persistently in the aftermath or a trauma, may also have less potential to experience PTG because the distress they experience more quickly returns to baseline and their underlying belief systems may remain largely unshaken. Resilient individual are less likely to experience the deep sense of "brokenness" that, albeit painful, propels growth when the conditions are fertile — even among those who meet criteria for PTSD.

The research suggests that individuals can both grow and experience difficult mental and emotional impacts of trauma simultaneously. A 2014 meta-analysis of forty-two studies published in the Journal of Anxiety Disorders found that the severity of posttraumatic distress positively predicts the degree of PTG (Shakespeare-Finch & Lurie-Beck, 2014). Although PTG does not put an end to suffering, it can make it easier to bear as it provides a sense of meaning for the trauma event and the emotional and mental pain experienced in response to it. Tedeschi and Calhoun (2004) explain that experiencing a trauma can result in a re-evaluation of an individual's view of their world, or the mental representations that have been formed over the course of the person's life about how the world works. For example, the person may experience a challenging or shattering of the assumptions they have made about how capable or vulnerable they are, how benevolent other people are, or how controllable the world is. This re-evaluation process can produce a variety of psychological symptoms, such as intense sadness or anxiety in response to questioning one's judgment, distrust in relationships, intrusive anxiety in response to reminders of the trauma, or nightmares resembling the trauma with themes of danger or injustice. Such symptoms are thought to represent a natural, self-protective reaction wherein the person's mind is attempting to process trauma-related thoughts, emotions and memories and make sense of an extraordinary situation. This process of re-evaluation can also be a catalyst for finding new meaning and purpose through a re-examination of past and present assumptions.

Although police officers' work regularly entails close encounters with danger, chaos, and unfixable human suffering that can, at times, negatively impact mental health, the potential for PTG is also great. Research with police has linked traumatic experiences on the job to PTG, particularly those involving a direct threat to officer's physical wellbeing, such as officer-involved shootings (Chopko, 2010; Chopko, Palmieri, & Adams, 2017). Given the frequency with which officers experience potentially traumatic events, there is utility in bolstering ones understanding of, and capacity for, both resilience and PTG. Although the strategies for achieving resilience and PTG can be different and researchers studying these processes make a distinction between the two, they are not mutually exclusive. Bolstering resilience provides officers with psychological inoculation to withstand negative impacts of frequent stressful and potentially traumatic events. It is also important for officers and organizations to be aware that when such events exceed the threshold of one's resilience or capacity to bounce back, with time and the proper supports, people often do bounce forward and grow.

Clinicians are uniquely positioned to facilitate PTG in police officers, although the process of achieving PTG is unique to the individual and follows no specific set of rules or timelines. Many authors encourage use of metaphorical terms used by the client to describe adversity, trauma and growth (Calhoun & Tedeschi, 2013; Zoellner & Maercker, 2006), and suggest that practitioners should be more willing to act as supportive, empathic "expert companions" rather than imposing their expertise (Calhoun & Tedeschi, 2012, p. 1) in order to facilitate the natural tendency toward growth. According to Calhoun and Tedeschi (2013), elements of interventions that are aimed at fostering PTG may include psychoeducation, development of emotion regulation and distress tolerance skills, the ability to trust and constructively self-disclose, and the development of a coherent and revised narrative of the traumatic event (Calhoun & Tedeschi, 2012, 2013; Tedeschi, Shakespeare-Finch, Taku, & Calhoun, 2018). In the final stages of treatment and PTG development, the client articulates new beliefs that are more robust to future challenges. For example, "I have been through hell and back and I know how strong and capable I am to face pain and suffering in the future," or, "my pain makes me human and also allows me to be a compassionate witness to other peoples' pain — I am an asset to my community." PTG subsequently increases resilience to future traumas and has thus been described as "a pathway to resilience" (Tedeschi & Moore, 2016).

The reduction of psychological symptoms such as nightmares, flashbacks, hyper-vigilance, depression and the like are important in our work, but we must not neglect the potential that lies in finding purpose in tragedy and achieving growth where possible. Most of all, it is important that police officers know that their life after trauma is not fixed or static. As therapists, our goal is to assist our clients to acknowledge their pain and show themselves compassion and kindness so that they might learn and grow from the experience at their own pace. Although it takes time, courage, hard work, and reaching out to others for help, "the greatest paradox of trauma is that out of loss, there can be growth — a new story of meaning and integrity and of a life that rewards you" (Tedeschi & Moore, 2016, p. 67).

References

Aamodt, M. G., & Stalnaker, N. A. (2001). Police officer suicide: Frequency and officer profiles. In D. C. Sheehan, & J. I. Warren (Eds.), *Suicide and Law Enforcement* (pp. 383–398). Washington, DC: US Government Printing Office.

American Psychiatric Association. (2013). In *Diagnostic and statistical manual of mental disorders* (5th ed.). Arlington, VA: American Psychiatric Publishing.

American Psychological Association. (2005). *Report of the 2005 presidential task force on evidence-based practice.* https://www.apa.org/practice/resources/evidence/evidence-based-report.pdf.

American Psychological Association. (2019). *PTSD Treatments* [Online article]. Retrieved from https://www.apa.org/ptsd-guideline/treatments/.

Anshel, M. H. (2000). A conceptual model and implications for coping with stressful events in police work. *Criminal Justice and Behavior, 27*, 375–400.

Asmundson, G. J., Coons, M. J., Taylor, S., & Katz, J. (2002). PTSD and the experience of pain: Research and clinical implications of shared vulnerability and mutual maintenance models. *Canadian Journal of Psychiatry, 47*(10), 930–937.

Asnaani, A., Reddy, M. K., & Shea, M. T. (2014). The impact of PTSD symptoms on physical and mental health functioning in returning veterans. *Journal of Anxiety Disorders, 28*(3), 310–317.

Austin-Ketch, T. L., Violanti, J. M., Fekedulegn, D., Andew, M. E., Burchfield, C. M., & Hartley, T. A. (2011). Addictions and the criminal justice system, what happens on the other side? Post-traumatic stress symptoms and cortisol measures in a police cohort. *Journal of Addictions Nursing, 23*, 22–39.

Babor, T. F., Higgins-Biddle, J. C., Saunders, J. B., & Monteiro, M. G. (2001). *AUDIT the alcohol use disorders identification test: Guideline for use in primary care* (2nd ed.). Geneva: World Health Organization.

Barlow, D. H. (2002). *Anxiety and its disorders: The nature and treatment of anxiety and panic* (2nd ed.). New York, NY: Guilford.

Barlow, D. H. (2014). *Clinical handbook of psychological disorders: A step-by-step treatment manual* (5th ed.). New York, NY: Guilford.

Barnes, S. M., Walter, K. H., & Chard, K. M. (2012). Does a history of mild traumatic brain injury increase suicide risk in veterans with PTSD? *Rehabilitation Psychology, 57*(1), 18.

Bartoli, F., Crocamo, C., Alamia, A., Amidani, F., Paggi, E., Pini, E., et al. (2015). *Posttraumatic stress disorder and risk of obesity: Systematic review and meta-analysis.*

Benish, S. G., Imel, Z. E., & Wampold, B. E. (2008). The relative efficacy of bona fide psychotherapies for treating post-traumatic stress disorder: A meta-analysis of direct comparisons. *Clinical Psychology Review, 28*, 746–758.

Berg, A. M., Hem, E., Lau, B., Loeb, M., & Ekeberg, Ø. (2003). Suicidal ideation and attempts in Norwegian police. *Suicide and Life-Threatening Behavior, 33*(3), 302–312.

Bergado, J. A., Lucas, M., & Richter-Levin, G. (2011). Emotional tagging—a simple hypothesis in a complex reality. *Progress in Neurobiology, 94*(1), 64–76.

Bishopp, S. A., & Boots, D. P. (2014). General strain theory, exposure to violence, and suicide ideation among police officers: A gendered approach. *Journal of Criminal Justice, 42*, 538–548.

Black, A., McCabe, D., & McConnell, N. (2013). Ten years on, living with the 'psychological troubles': Retired police officers in Northern Ireland. *Irish Journal of Psychology, 34*, 93–108.

Bowler, R. M., Kornblith, E. S., Li, J., Adams, S. W., Gocheva, V. V., Schwarzer, R., et al. (2016). Police officers who responded to 9/11: Comorbidity of PTSD, depression, and anxiety 10−11 years later. *American Journal of Industrial Medicine, 59*(6), 425−436.

Bremner, J. D. (2001). Hypotheses and controversies related to effects of stress on the hippocampus: An argument for stress-induced damage to the hippocampus in patients with posttraumatic stress disorder. *Hippocampus, 11*(2), 75−81.

Brewin, C. R. (2014). Episodic memory, perceptual memory, and their interaction: Foundations for a theory of posttraumatic stress disorder. *Psychological Bulletin, 140*(1), 69−97.

Brewin, C. R., Gregory, J. D., Lipton, M., & Burgess, N. (2010). Intrusive images in psychological disorders. *Psychological Review, 117*(1), 210−232.

Brodie, P. J., & Eppler, C. (2012). Exploration of perceived stressors, communication, and resilience in law-enforcement couples. *Journal of Family Psychotherapy, 23*, 20−41.

Brown, J., Fielding, J., & Grover, J. (1999). Distinguishing traumatic, vicarious and routine operational stressor exposure and attendant adverse consequences in a sample of police officers. *Work & Stress, 13*, 312−325.

Bureau of Labour Statistics. (2016). *Injuries, illnesses, and fatalities. Fact sheet: Police officers: August 2016.* Retrieved from https://www.bls.gov/iif/oshwc/cfoi/police-officers-2014.htm.

Calhoun, L. G., & Tedeschi, R. G. (1998). Posttraumatic growth: Future directions. In R. G. Tedeschi, C. L. Park, & L. G. Calhoun (Eds.), *Posttraumatic growth: Positive change in the aftermath of crisis* (pp. 215−238). Mahwah, NJ: Erlbaum.

Calhoun, L. G., & Tedeschi, R. G. (Eds.). (2006). *Handbook of posttraumatic growth: Research and practice.* Mahwah, NJ: Lawrence Erlbaum.

Calhoun, L., & Tedeschi, R. (2012). *Posttraumatic growth in clinical practice.* New York, NY: Routledge.

Calhoun, L. G., & Tedeschi, R. G. (2013). *Posttraumatic growth in clinical practice.* New York, NY, US: Routledge/Taylor & Francis Group.

Carleton, R. N., Afifi, T. O., Turner, S., Taillieu, T., Duranceau, S., LeBouthillier, D. M., et al. (2018). Mental disorder symptoms among public safety personnel in Canada. *Canadian Journal of psychiatry. Revue Canadienne de Psychiatrie, 63*(1), 54−64.

Carlier, I. V. E., Lamberts, R. D., & Gersons, B. P. R. (2000). The dimensionality of trauma: A multidimensional scaling comparison of police officers with posttraumatic stress disorder. *Psychiatry Research, 97*, 29−39.

Carlier, I. V., Voerman, A. E., & Gersons, B. P. (2000). The influence of occupational debriefing on posttraumatic stress symptomatology in traumatized police officers. *British Journal of Medical Psychology, 73*, 87−98.

Center for Behavioral Health Statistics and Quality. (2016). *2015 national survey on drug use and health: Detailed tables.* Rockville, MD: Substance Abuse and Mental Health Services Administration.

Chan, J. (2001). Negotiating the field: New observations on the making of police officers. *Australian and New Zealand Journal of Criminology, 34*, 114−133.

Charbonneau, F. (2000). Suicide among the police in Quebec. *Population, 55*, 367−378.

Chopko, B. A. (2010). Posttraumatic distress and growth: An empirical study of police officers. *American Journal of Psychotherapy, 64*, 55−72.

Chopko, B. A., Palmieri, P. A., & Adams, R. E. (2013). Associations between police stress and alcohol use: Implications for practice. *Journal of Loss & Trauma, 18*, 482−497.

Chopko, B. A., Palmieri, P. A., & Adams, R. E. (2018). Relationships among traumatic experiences, PTSD, and posttraumatic growth for police officers: A path analysis. *Psychological Trauma: Theory, Research, Practice, and Policy, 10*, 183−189.

Chopko, B. A., Palmieri, P. A., & Facemire, V. C. (2014). Prevalence and predictors of suicidal ideation among U.S. law enforcement officers. *Journal of Police and Criminal Psychology, 29*, 1−9.

Cohen, D. I. M., & Garis, L. (2018). *Determinants of injury and death in Canadian police officers.* University of the Fraser Valley Centre for Public Safety and Criminal Justice Research.

Collins, P., & Gibbs, C. (2003). Stress in police officers: A study of the origins, prevalence and severity of stress related symptoms within a county police force. *Occupational Medicine, 53,* 256—264.

Combs, H. L., Berry, D. T., Pape, T. L., Babcock-Parziale, J., Smith, B., Schleenbaker, R., et al. (2015). The effects of mild TBI, PTSD, and combined mild TBI/PTSD on returning veterans. *Journal of Neurotrauma, 32*(13), 956—966.

Darensburg, T., Andrew, M. E., Hartley, T. A., Burchfiel, C. M., Fekedulegn, D., & Violanti, J. M. (2006). Gender and age differences in posttraumatic stress disorder and depression among Buffalo police officers. *Traumatology, 12,* 220—228.

Davey, J. D., Obst, P. L., & Sheehan, M. C. (2001). Demographic and workplace characteristics which add to the prediction of stress and job satisfaction within the police workplace. *Journal of Police and Criminal Psychology, 16,* 29—39.

Defrin, R., Ginzburg, K., Solomon, Z., Polad, E., Bloch, M., Govezensky, M., et al. (2008). Quantitative testing of pain perception in subjects with PTSD—implications for the mechanism of the coexistence between PTSD and chronic pain. *Pain, 138*(2), 450—459.

Devilly, G. J., & Spence, S. H. (1999). The relative efficacy and treatment distress of EMDR and a cognitive-behavior trauma treatment protocol in the amelioration of posttraumatic stress disorder. *Journal of Anxiety Disorders, 13*(1—2), 131—157.

Dick, P. (2000). The social construction of the meaning of acute stressors: A qualitative study of the personal accounts of police officers using a stress counselling service. *Work & Stress, 14,* 226—244.

Dowling, F. G., Moynihan, G., Genet, B., & Lewis, J. (2006). A peer-based assistance program for officers with the New York City Police Department: Report of the effects of Sept. 11, 2001. *American Journal of Psychiatry, 163,* 151—152.

Eftekhari, A., Ruzek, J. I., Crowley, J. J., Rosen, C. S., Greenbaum, M. A., & Karlin, B. E. (2013). Effectiveness of national implementation of prolonged exposure therapy in veterans affairs care. *JAMA Psychiatry, 70*(9), 949—955.

Ehlers, A., & Clark, D. M. (2000). A cognitive model of posttraumatic stress disorder. *Behaviour Research and Therapy, 38*(4), 319—345.

Faulkner, B. (2018). *"'Things are changing:' Police Mental Health and Psychotherapeutic Help-Seeking in an Evolving Police Culture" Ph.D. Dissertation.* Toronto, Ontario, Canada: University of Toronto.

Finsterwald, C., & Alberini, C. M. (2014). Stress and glucocorticoid receptor-dependent mechanisms in long-term memory: From adaptive responses to psychopathologies. *Neurobiology of Learning and Memory, 0,* 17—29.

Foa, E. B., & Kozak, M. J. (1986). Emotional processing of fear: Exposure to corrective information. *Psychological Bulletin, 99*(1), 20—35.

Foa, E. B., Rothbaum, B. O., Riggs, D. S., & Murdock, T. B. (1991). Treatment of posttraumatic stress disorder in rape victims: A comparison between cognitive-behavioral procedures and counseling. *Journal of Consulting and Clinical Psychology, 59*(5), 715—723.

Foa, E. B., Dancu, C. V., Hembree, E. A., Jaycox, L. H., Meadows, E. A., & Street, G. P. (1999). A comparison of exposure, stress inoculation training, and their combination for reducing posttraumatic stress disorder in female assault victims. *Journal of Consulting and Clinical Psychology, 67*(2), 194—200.

Foa, E. B., & Rothbaum, B. O. (2001). *Treating the trauma of rape: Cognitive-behavioral therapy for PTSD.* Guilford Press.

Foa, E. B., Hembree, E. A., Cahill, S. P., Rauch, S. A. M., Riggs, D. S., Feeny, N. C., & Yadin, E. (2005). Randomized trial of prolonged exposure for posttraumatic stress disorder with and without cognitive restructuring: Outcome at academic and community clinics. *Journal of Consulting and Clinical Psychology, 73*(5), 953—964.

Foa, E. B., Hembree, E. A., & Rothbaum, B. O. (2007). Treatments that work. *Prolonged exposure therapy for PTSD: Emotional processing of traumatic experiences: Therapist guide.* New York, NY, US: Oxford University Press.

Forbes, D., Lloyd, D., Nixon, R. D. V., Elliott, P., Varker, T., Perry, D., et al. (2012). A multisite randomized controlled effectiveness trial of cognitive processing therapy for military-related posttraumatic stress disorder. *Journal of Anxiety Disorders, 26*(3), 442–452.

Fox, J., Desai, M. M., Britten, K., Lucas, G., Luneau, R., & Rosenthal, M. S. (2012). Mental-health conditions, barriers to care, and productivity loss among officers in an urban police department. *Connecticut Medicine, 76,* 525–531.

Frewen, P. A., & Lanius, R. A. (2014). Trauma-related altered states of consciousness: Exploring the 4-D model. *Journal of Trauma & Dissociation: The Official Journal of the International Society for the Study of Dissociation (ISSD), 15*(4), 436–456.

Gershon, R. (2000). *Project shields: Final Report (NCJ 185892).* Washington, DC: U.S. Department of Justice, Office of Justice Programs, National Institute of Justice. Retrieved from https://www.ncjrs.gov/pdffiles1/nij/grants/185892.pdf.

Garfinkel, S. N., & Liberzon, I. (2009). Neurobiology of PTSD: A review of neuroimaging findings. *Psychiatric Annals, 39*(6).

Gershon, R., Barocas, B., Canton, A., Li, X., & Vlahov, D. (2009). Mental, physical, and behavioral outcomes associated with perceived stress in police officers. *Criminal Justice and Behavior, 39,* 275–289.

Gershuny, B. S., Cloitre, M., & Otto, M. W. (2003). Peritraumatic dissociation and PTSD severity: Do event-related fears about death and control mediate their relation? *Behaviour Research and Therapy, 41*(2), 157–166.

Gilmartin, K. M. (2002). *Emotional survival for law enforcement: A guide for police officers and their families.* Tucson, AZ: E-S Press.

Goldberg, D., & Williams, P. (1988). *A user's guide to the general health questionnaire.* Windsor: NFER-Nelson.

Golembiewski, R. T., Lloyd, M., Scherb, K., & Munzenrider, R. F. (1992). Burnout and mental health among police officers. *Journal of Public Administration Research and Theory, 4,* 424–439.

Goodson, J. T., Lefkowitz, C. M., Helstrom, A. W., & Gawrysiak, M. J. (2013). Outcomes of prolonged exposure therapy for veterans with posttraumatic stress disorder. *Journal of Traumatic Stress, 26*(4), 419–425.

Hackett, D. P., & Violanti, J. M. (2003). *Police suicide: Tactics for prevention.* Springfield, IL: Charles C. Thomas.

Hakanen, J. J., & Schaufeli, W. B. (2012). Do burnout and work engagement predict depressive symptoms and life satisfaction? A three-wave seven-year prospective study. *Journal of Affective Disorders, 141,* 415–424.

Halligan, S. L., Michael, T., Clark, D. M., & Ehlers, A. (2003). Posttraumatic stress disorder following assault: The role of cognitive processing, trauma memory, and appraisals. *Journal of Consulting and Clinical Psychology, 71*(3), 419–431.

Hartley, T. A., Violanti, J. A., Fekedulegn, D., Andrew, M. E., & Burchfield, C. M. (2007). Associations between major life events, traumatic incidents, and depression among Buffalo police officers. *International Journal of Emergency Mental Health, 9,* 25–35.

Hem, E., Berg, A. M., & Ekeberg, O. (2001). Suicide in police: A critical review. *Suicide and Life-Threatening Behavior, 31,* 224–233.

Holbrook, T. L., Galarneau, M. R., Dye, J. L., Quinn, K., & Dougherty, A. L. (2010). Morphine use after combat injury in Iraq and post-traumatic stress disorder. *New England Journal of Medicine, 362*(2), 110–117.

Horowitz, S. H., Mitchell, D., LaRussa-Trott, M., Santiago, L., Pearson, J., Skiff, D. M., et al. (2011). An inside view of police officers' experience with domestic violence. *Journal of Family Violence, 26,* 617–625.

Huckans, M., Pavawalla, S., Demadura, T., Kolessar, M., Seelye, A., Roost, N., et al. (2010). A pilot study examining effects of group-based Cognitive Strategy Training treatment on self-reported cognitive problems, psychiatric symptoms, functioning, and compensatory strategy use in OIF/OEF combat veterans with persistent mild cognitive disorder and history of traumatic brain injury. *Journal of Rehabilitation Research and Development, 47*(1), 43–60.

Huddleston, L., Stephens, C., & Paton, D. (2007). An evaluation of traumatic and organizational experiences on the psychological health of New Zealand police recruits. *Work, 28,* 199–207.

Inslicht, S. S., Otte, C., McCaslin, S. E., Apfel, B. A., Henn-Haase, C., Metzler, T., et al. (2011). Cortisol awakening response prospectively predicts peritraumatic and acute stress reactions in police officers. *Biological Psychiatry, 70*(11), 1055–1062.

Ironson, G., Freund, B., Strauss, J. L., & Williams, J. (2002). Comparison of two treatments for traumatic stress: A community-based study of EMDR and prolonged exposure. *Journal of Clinical Psychology, 58*(1), 113–128.

Keane, T. M., Marshall, A. D., & Taft, C. T. (2006). Posttraumatic stress disorder: Etiology, epidemiology, and treatment outcome. *Annual Review of Clinical Psychology, 2,* 161–197.

Kehle-Forbes, S. M., Meis, L. A., Spoont, M. R., & Polusny, M. A. (2016). Treatment initiation and dropout from prolonged exposure and cognitive processing therapy in a VA outpatient clinic. *Psychological Trauma: Theory, Research, Practice, and Policy, 8*(1), 107.

Kessler, R. C., Berglund, P., Demler, O., Jin, R., Merikangas, K. R., & Walters, E. E. (2005). Lifetime prevalence and age-of-onset distributions of DSM-IV disorders in the national comorbidity survey replication. *Archives of General Psychiatry, 62*(6), 593–602.

Kessler, R. C., Chiu, W. T., Demler, O., & Walters, E. E. (2005). Prevalence, severity, and comorbidity of 12-month DSM-IV disorders in the national comorbidity survey replication. *Archives of General Psychiatry, 62*(6), 617–627.

Kinlein, S. A., Wilson, C. D., & Karatsoreos, I. N. (2015). Dysregulated hypothalamic–pituitary–adrenal Axis function contributes to altered endocrine and neurobehavioral responses to acute stress. *Frontiers in Psychiatry, 6.*

Kirschman, E. (2007). *I love a cop: What police families need to know* (2nd ed.). New York, NY: The Guilford Press.

Koch, B. J. (2010). The psychological impact on police officers of being first responders to completed suicides. *Journal of Police and Criminal Psychology, 25,* 90–98.

van der Kolk, B. A. (1994). The body keeps the score: Memory and the evolving psychobiology of posttraumatic stress. *Harvard Review of Psychiatry, 1*(5), 253–265.

Koren, D., Norman, D., Cohen, A., Berman, J., & Klein, E. M. (2005). Increased PTSD risk with combat-related injury: A matched comparison study of injured and uninjured soldiers experiencing the same combat events. *American Journal of Psychiatry, 162*(2), 276, 28.

Kurtz, D. L. (2008). Controlled burn: The gendering of stress and burnout in modern policing. *Feminist Criminology, 3,* 216–238.

Lang, P. J. (1977). Imagery in therapy: An information processing analysis of fear. *Behavior Therapy, 8*(5), 862–886.

Leahy, R. L., Holland, S. J. F., & McGinn, L. K. (2011). *Treatment plans and interventions for depression and anxiety disorders* (2nd ed.). New York, NY: Guildford Press.

Liberman, A. M., Best, S. R., Metzler, T. J., Fagan, J. A., Weiss, D. S., & Marmar, C. R. (2002). Routine occupational stress and psychological distress in police. *Policing: An International Journal of Police Strategies & Management, 25,* 421–439.

Lieberman, L., Gorka, S. M., Funkhouser, C. J., Shankman, S. A., & Phan, K. L. (2017). Impact of post-traumatic stress symptom dimensions on psychophysiological reactivity to threat and reward. *Journal of Psychiatric Research, 92,* 55–63.

Lindauer, R. J., Olff, M., van Meijel, E. P., Carlier, I. V., & Gersons, B. P. (2006). Cortisol, learning, memory, and attention in relation to smaller hippocampal volume in police officers with posttraumatic stress disorder. *Biological Psychiatry, 59*(2), 171–177.

Lindauer, R. J. L., Vlieger, E.-J., Jalink, M., Olff, M., Carlier, I. V. E., Majoie, C. B. L. M., et al. (2004). Smaller hippocampal volume in Dutch police officers with posttraumatic stress disorder. *Biological Psychiatry, 56*(5), 356–363.

Lindsay, V., & Shelley, K. (2009). Social and stress-related influences of police officers' alcohol consumption. *Journal of Police and Criminal Psychology, 24,* 87–92.

Lohr, J. M., Tolin, D. F., & Lilienfeld, S. O. (1998). Efficacy of eye movement desensitization and reprocessing: Implications for behavior therapy. *Behavior Therapy, 29*(1), 123–156.

Maia, D. B., Marmar, C. R., Metzler, T., Nóbrega, A., Berger, W., Mendlowicz, M. V., et al. (2007). Post-traumatic stress symptoms in an elite unit of Brazilian police officers: Prevalence and impact on psychosocial functioning and on physical and mental health. *Journal of Affective Disorders, 97*(1–3), 241–245.

Marchand, A., Nadeau, C., Beaulieu-Prévost, D., Boyer, R., & Martin, M. (2015). Predictors of post-traumatic stress disorder among police officers: A prospective study. *Psychological Trauma: Theory, Research, Practice and Policy, 7*(3), 212–221.

Masten, A. S., & Powell, J. L. (2003). A resilience framework for research, policy, and practice. In S. S. Luthar (Ed.), *Resilience and vulnerability: Adaptation in the context of childhood adversities* (pp. 1–25). New York, NY: Cambridge University Press.

McCafferty, F. L., McCafferty, E., & McCafferty, M. A. (1992). Stress and suicide in police officers. *Southern Medical Journal, 85,* 233–243.

McCanlies, E. C., Sarkisian, K., Andrew, M. E., Burchfiel, C. M., & Violanti, J. M. (2017). Association of peritraumatic dissociation with symptoms of depression and posttraumatic stress disorder. *Psychological Trauma: Theory, Research, Practice and Policy, 9*(4), 479–484.

van der Meer, C. A. I., Bakker, A., Smit, A. S., van Buschbach, S., den Dekker, M., Westerveld, G. J., et al. (2017). Gender and age differences in trauma and PTSD among Dutch treatment-seeking police officers. *The Journal of Nervous and Mental Disease, 205,* 87–92.

Ménard, K. S., & Arter, M. L. (2013). Police officer alcohol use and trauma symptoms: Associations with critical incidents, coping, and social stressors. *International Journal of Stress Management, 20,* 37–56.

Michael, T., Ehlers, A., Halligan, S. L., & Clark, D. M. (2005). Unwanted memories of assault: What intrusion characteristics are associated with PTSD? *Behaviour Research and Therapy, 43*(5), 613–628.

Miller, L. (2007). Line-of-duty death: Psychological treatment of traumatic bereavement in law enforcement. *International Journal of Emergency Mental Health, 9,* 13–23.

Monson, C. M., Schnurr, P. P., Resick, P. A., Friedman, M. J., Young-Xu, Y., & Stevens, S. P. (2006). Cognitive processing therapy for veterans with military-related posttraumatic stress disorder. *Journal of Consulting and Clinical Psychology, 74*(5), 898–907.

Morley, J. (September 25-27, 2011). Resilient employees, resilient organizations. In *Paper presented at at the breaking point, psychological injuries in the police workplace: Why "suck it up" doesn't cut it.* Ottawa, ON: Canadian Association of Chiefs of Police Conference.

Muris, P., Merckelbach, H., Holdrinet, I., & Sijsenaar, M. (1998). Treating phobic children: Effects of EMDR versus exposure. *Journal of Consulting and Clinical Psychology, 66*(1), 193–198.

Muris, P., Merckelbach, H., Van Haaften, H., & Mayer, B. (1997). Eye movement desensitisation and reprocessing versus exposure in vivo: A single-session crossover study of spider-phobic children. *British Journal of Psychiatry, 171*(1), 82−86.

Neylan, T. C., Brunet, A., Pole, N., Best, S. R., Metzler, T. J., Yehuda, R., et al. (2005). PTSD symptoms predict waking salivary cortisol levels in police officers. *Psychoneuroendocrinology, 30*(4), 373−381.

Ogińska-Bulik, N., & Kobylarczyk, M. (2016). Association between resiliency and posttraumatic growth in firefighters: The role of stress appraisal. *International Journal of Occupational Safety and Ergonomics, 22*(1), 40−48.

Ombudsman of Ontario. (2012). In *In tHe line of duty: Investigation into how the Ontario Provincial Police and the Ministry of Community Safety and Correctional Services have addressed operational stress injuries affecting police officers*. Ontario: Marin, A.

Otte, C., Neylan, T. C., Pole, N., Metzler, T., Best, S., Henn-Haase, C., et al. (2005). Association between childhood trauma and catecholamine response to psychological stress in police academy recruits. *Biological Psychiatry, 57*(1), 27−32.

Pacella, M. L., Hruska, B., & Delahanty, D. L. (2013). The physical health consequences of PTSD and PTSD symptoms: A meta-analytic review. *Journal of Anxiety Disorders, 27*(1), 33−46.

Padyab, M., Backteman-Erlanson, S., & Brulin, C. (2016). Burnout, coping, stress of conscience and psychosocial work environment among patrolling police officers. *Journal of Police and Criminal Psychology, 31*, 229−237.

Paton, D., Violanti, J. M., & Schmuckler, E. (1999). Chronic exposure to risk and trauma: Addiction and separation issues in police officers. In J. M. Violanti, & D. Paton (Eds.), *Police trauma: Psychological aftermath of civilian combat* (pp. 78−87). Springfield, IL: Charles C. Thomas Publisher Ltd.

Pearson, C., Janz, T., & Ali, J. (2013). *Health at a glance: Mental and substance use disorders in Canada. Statistics Canada Catalogue no* (X).

Pietrzak, R. H., Schecter, C. B., Bromet, E. J., Katz, C. L., Reissman, D. B., Ozbay, F., et al. (2012). The burden of full and subsyndromal posttraumatic stress disorder among police involved in the World Trade Center rescue and recovery effort. *Journal of Psychiatric Research, 46*(7), 835−842.

Pitman, R. K., Orr, S. P., Altman, B., Longpre, R. E., Poiré, R. E., & Macklin, M. L. (1996). Emotional processing during eye movement desensitization and reprocessing therapy of Vietnam veterans with chronic posttraumatic stress disorder. *Comprehensive Psychiatry, 37*(6), 419−429.

Pole, N., Neylan, T. C., Otte, C., Metzler, T. J., Best, S. R., Henn-Haase, C., et al. (2007). Associations between childhood trauma and emotion-modulated psychophysiological responses to startling sounds: A study of police cadets. *Journal of Abnormal Psychology, 116*(2), 352−361.

Rauch, S. A. M., Defever, E., Favorite, T., Duroe, A., Garrity, C., Martis, B., et al. (2009). Prolonged exposure for PTSD in a veterans health administration PTSD clinic. *Journal of Traumatic Stress, 22*(1), 60−64.

Resick, P. A., Nishith, P., Weaver, T. L., Astin, M. C., & Feuer, C. A. (2002). A comparison of cognitive-processing therapy with prolonged exposure and a waiting condition for the treatment of chronic posttraumatic stress disorder in femal rape victims. *Journal of Consulting and Clinical Psychology, 70*(4), 867−879.

Resick, P. A., Galovski, T. E., Uhlmansiek, M. O., Scher, C. D., Clum, G. A., & Young-Xu, Y. (2008). A randomized clinical trial to dismantle components of cognitive processing therapy for post-traumatic stress disorder in female victims of interpersonal violence. *Journal of Consulting and Clinical Psychology, 76*(2), 243.

Resick, P. A., Monson, C. M., & Chard, K. M. (2007). *Cognitive processing therapy: Veteran/military version*. Retrieved from http://alrest.org/pdf/CPT_Manual_-_Modified_for_PRRP%282%29.pdf.

Resick, P. A., Monson, C. M., & Chard, K. M. (2016). *Cognitive processing therapy for PTSD: A comprehensive manual*. Guilford Publications.

Resick, P. A., & Schnicke, M. K. (1992). Cognitive processing therapy for sexual assault victims. *Journal of Consulting and Clinical Psychology, 60*(5), 748.

Roitman, P., Gilad, M., Ankri, Y. L., & Shalev, A. Y. (2013). Head injury and loss of consciousness raise the likelihood of developing and maintaining PTSD symptoms. *Journal of Traumatic Stress, 26*(6), 727–734.

Rosenbaum, S., Stubbs, B., Ward, P. B., Steel, Z., Lederman, O., & Vancampfort, D. (2015). The prevalence and risk of metabolic syndrome and its components among people with posttraumatic stress disorder: A systematic review and meta-analysis. *Metabolism, 64*(8), 926–933.

Rosen, C. S., Chard, K. M., Resick, P., & Frueh, B. C. (2014). Cognitive processing therapy for posttraumatic stress disorder delivered to rural veterans via telemental health: A randomized noninferiority clinical trial. *Journal of Clinical Psychiatry, 75*(5), 470–476.

Rothbaum, B. M., Astin, M. C., & Marsteller, F. (2005). Prolonged Exposure versus Eye Movement Desensitization and Reprocessing (EMDR) for PTSD rape victims. *Journal of Traumatic Stress, 18*(6), 607–616.

Sackett, D., Straus, S. E., Richardson, S. W., Rosenberg, W., & Haynes, R. B. (2000). *Evidence-based medicine: How to practice and teach EBM* (2nd ed.). UK: Churchill Livingstone.

Sareen, J., Erickson, J., Medved, M. I., Asmundson, G. J., Enns, M. W., Stein, M., et al. (2013). Risk factors for post-injury mental health problems. *Depression and Anxiety, 30*(4), 321–327.

Saunders, B. E., & Adams, Z. W. (2014). Epidemiology of traumatic experiences in childhood. *Child and Adolescent Psychiatric Clinics of North America, 23*(2), 167–184.

Schaumberg, K., Vinci, C., Raiker, J. S., Mota, N., Jackson, M., Whalen, D., et al. (2015). PTSD-related alcohol expectancies and impulsivity interact to predict alcohol use severity in a substance dependent sample with PTSD. *Addictive Behaviors, 41*, 41–45.

Schnyder, U., Ehlers, A., Elbert, T., Foa, E. B., Gersons, B. P., Resick, P. A., et al. (2015). Psychotherapies for PTSD: What do they have in common? *European Journal of Psychotraumatology, 6*.

Schry, A. R., Rissling, M. B., Gentes, E. L., Beckham, J. C., Kudler, H. S., Straits-Tröster, K., et al. (2015). The relationship between posttraumatic stress symptoms and physical health in a survey of US veterans of the Iraq and Afghanistan era. *Psychosomatics, 56*(6), 674–684.

Schumm, J. A., Dickstein, B. D., Walter, K. H., Owens, G. P., & Chard, K. M. (2015). Changes in posttraumatic cognitions predict changes in posttraumatic stress disorder symptoms during cognitive processing therapy. *Journal of Consulting and Clinical Psychology, 83*(6), 1161.

Schwarzer, R., Cone, J. E., Li, J., & Bowler, R. M. (2016). A PTSD symptoms trajectory mediates between exposure levels and emotional support in police responders to 9/11: A growth curve analysis. *BMC Psychiatry, 16*(1), 201.

Shakespeare-Finch, J., & Lurie-Beck, J. (2014). A meta-analytic clarification of the relationship between posttraumatic growth and symptoms of posttraumatic distress disorder. *Journal of Anxiety Disorders, 28*(2), 223–229.

Shapiro, F. (1989). Efficacy of the Eye Movement Desensitization procedure in the treatment of traumatic memories. *Journal of Traumatic Stress, 2*(2), 199–223.

Shih, R. A., Schell, T. L., Hambarsoomian, K., Marshall, G. N., & Belzberg, H. (2010). Prevalence of PTSD and major depression following trauma-center hospitalization. *The Journal of Trauma, 69*(6), 1560.

Shucard, J. L., Cox, J., Shucard, D. W., Fetter, H., Chung, C., Ramasamy, D., et al. (2012). Symptoms of posttraumatic stress disorder and exposure to traumatic stressors are related to brain structural volumes and behavioral measures of affective stimulus processing in police officers. *Psychiatry Research: Neuroimaging, 204*(1), 25–31.

Skovholt, T. M., & Trotter-Mathison, M. (2016). *The resilient practitioner: Burnout and compassion fatigue prevention and self-care strategies for the helping professions* (3rd ed.). New York, NY: Routledge.

Slottje, P., Twisk, J. W., Smidt, N., Huizink, A. C., Witteveen, A. B., Van Mechelen, W., et al. (2007). Health-related quality of life of firefighters and police officers 8.5 years after the air disaster in Amsterdam. *Quality of Life Research, 16*(2), 239−252.

Solomon, Z., Levin, Y., Assayag, E. B., Furman, O., Shenhar-Tsarfaty, S., Berliner, S., et al. (2017). The implication of combat stress and PTSD trajectories in metabolic syndrome and elevated C-reactive protein levels: A longitudinal study. *Journal of Clinical Psychiatry, 78*(9), e1180−e1186.

Statistics Canada. (2013). *Section B − anxiety disorders.* Retrieved from http://www.statcan.gc.ca/pub/82-619-m/2012004/sections/sectionb-eng.htm.

Stearns, G. M., & Moore, R. J. (1993). The physical and psychological correlates of job burnout in the Royal Canadian Mounted Police. *Canadian Journal of Criminology, 35*, 127−148.

Stojanovic, M. P., Fonda, J., Fortier, C. B., Higgins, D. M., Rudolph, J. L., Milberg, W. P., et al. (2016). Influence of mild traumatic brain injury (TBI) and posttraumatic stress disorder (PTSD) on pain intensity levels in OEF/OIF/OND veterans. *Pain Medicine, 17*(11), 2017−2025.

Sumner, J. A., Kubzansky, L. D., Elkind, M. S., Roberts, A. L., Agnew-Blais, J., Chen, Q., et al. (2015). Trauma exposure and posttraumatic stress disorder symptoms predict onset of cardiovascular events in women. *Circulation, 132*(4), 251−259.

Taylor, S. E. (1983). Adjustment to threatening events: A theory of cognitive adaptation. *American Psychologist, 38*(11), 1161−1173.

Taylor, S., Thordarson, D. S., Maxfield, L., Fedoroff, I. C., Lovell, K., & Ogrodniczuk, J. (2003). Comparative efficacy, speed, and adverse effects of three PTSD treatments: Exposure therapy, EMDR, and relaxation training. *Journal of Consulting and Clinical Psychology, 71*(2), 330−338.

Tedeschi, R. G., & Calhoun, L. G. (1996). The posttraumatic growth inventory: Measuring the positive legacy of trauma. *Journal of Traumatic Stress, 9*, 455−471.

Tedeschi, R. G., & Calhoun, L. G. (2004). A clinical approach to posttraumatic growth. In P. A. Linley, & S. Joseph (Eds.), *Positive psychology in practice* (pp. 405−419). Hoboken, NJ: John Wiley & Sons.

Tedeschi, R. G., & Moore, B. A. (2016). *The posttraumatic growth workbook: Coming through trauma wiser, stronger and more resilient.* Oakland, CA: New Harbinger.

Tedeschi, R. G., Shakespeare-Finch, J., Taku, K., & Calhoun, L. G. (2018). *Posttraumatic growth: Theory, research, and applications.* New York: Routledge.

Thornton, M. A., & Herndon, J. (2016). Emotion regulation in police officers following distress: Effects of tenure and critical incidents. *Journal of Police and Criminal Psychology, 31*, 304−309.

Toch, H. (2002). *Stress in policing.* Washington, DC: American Psychological Association.

Tolin, D. F., & Foa, E. B. (1999). Treatment of a polie officer with PTSD using prolonged exposure. *Behavior Therapy, 10*(3), 527−538.

Tuerk, P. W., Yoder, M., Grubaugh, A., Myrick, H., Hamner, M., & Acierno, R. (2011). Prolonged exposure therapy for combat-related posttraumatic stress disorder: An examination of treatment effectiveness for veterans of the wars in Afghanistan and Iraq. *Journal of Anxiety Disorders, 25*(3), 397−403.

Turgoose, D., Glover, N., Barker, C., & Maddox, L. (2017). Empathy, compassion fatigue, and burnout in police officers working with rape victims. *Traumatology, 23*, 205−213.

Vasterling, J. J., Aslan, M., Lee, L. O., Proctor, S. P., Ko, J., Jacob, S., et al. (2018). Longitudinal associations among posttraumatic stress disorder symptoms, traumatic brain injury, and neurocognitive functioning in Army soldiers deployed to the Iraq war. *Journal of the International Neuropsychological Society, 24*(4), 311−323.

Violanti, J. M. (2001). Coping strategies among police recruits in a high-stress training environment. *The Journal of Social Psychology, 132*, 717−729.

Violanti, J. M. (2003). *Dying from the job: The mortality risk for police officers* [Online article]. Retrieved from http://www.stevedavis.org/spiritofthelaw/sol1art11.html.

Violanti, J. M. (2004). Predictors of police suicide. *Suicide and Life-Threatening Behavior, 34,* 277–283.

Violanti, J. M. (2008). Police suicide research: Conflict and consensus. *International Journal of Emergency Mental Health, 10,* 299–308.

Violanti, J. M. (2010). Police suicide: A national comparison with fire-fighter and military personnel. *Policing: An International Journal of Police Strategies & Management, 33,* 270–286.

Violanti, J. M., Marshall, J. R., & Howe, B. (1985). Stress coping and alcohol use: The police connection. *Journal of Police Science and Administration, 12,* 106–110.

Violanti, J. M., Slaven, J. E., Charles, L. E., Burchfield, C. M., Andrew, M. E., & Homish, G. G. (2011). Police and alcohol use: A descriptive analysis and associations with stress outcomes. *American Journal of Criminal Justice, 36,* 344–356.

Walter, K. H., Dickstein, B. D., Barnes, S. M., & Chard, K. M. (2014). Comparing effectiveness of CPT to CPT-C among U.S. Veterans in an interdisciplinary residential PTSD/TBI treatment program. *Journal of Traumatic Stress, 27*(4), 438–445.

Wang, Z., Inslicht, S. S., Metzler, T. J., Henn-Haase, C., McCaslin, S. E., Tong, H., et al. (2010). A prospective study of predictors of depression symptoms in police. *Psychiatry Research, 175,* 211–216.

Waters, J., & Ussery, W. (2007). Police stress: History, contributing factors, symptoms, and interventions. *Policing: An International Journal of Police Strategies & Management, 30,* 169–188.

Weathers, E. W., Huska, J. A., & Keane, T. M. (1991). *The PTSD check-list – civilian version (PCL-C). Available from E W. Weathers, national center for PTSD, boston veterans affairs medical center, 150 S. Huntington avenue, boston, MA.*

Weathers, F. W., Litz, B. T., Keane, T. M., Palmieri, P. A., Marx, B. P., & Schnurr, P. P. (2013). *The PTSD checklist for DSM-5 (PCL-5). Scale available from the national Center for PTSD.* www.ptsd.va.gov.

Weiss, D. S., Brunet, A., Best, S. R., Metzler, T. J., Liberman, A., Rogers, C., et al. (2001). *The critical incident history Questionnaire: A method for measuring total cumulative exposure to critical incidents* (Unpublished manuscript).

Westley, W. (1970). *Violence and the police: A sociological study of law, custom and morality.* Massachusetts, USA: MIT.

Wilson, S. A., Tinker, R. H., Becker, L. A., Logan, C. R., & July. (2001). Stress management with law enforcement personnel: A controlled outcome study of EMDR versus a traditional stress management program. *International Journal of Stress Management, 8*(3), 179–200.

Woody, R. H. (2005). The police culture: Research implications for psychological services. *Professional Psychology: Research and Practice, 36,* 525–529.

Yoder, M., Tuerk, P. W., Price, M., Grubaugh, A. L., Strachan, M., Myrick, H., et al. (2012). Prolonged exposure therapy for combat-related posttraumatic stress disorder: Comparing outcomes for veterans of different wars. *Psychological Services, 9*(1), 16–25.

Zoellner, T., & Maercker, A. (2006). Posttraumatic growth in clinical psychology — a critical review and introduction of a two component model. *Clinical Psychology Review, 26*(5), 626–653.

Intervention & prevention

10

Creating a culture of wellness

Felipe Rubim[a], Lucas Rubim[b], Alex R. Thornton[c]

[a]MUNICH CENTER FOR MATHEMATICAL PHILOSOPHY, LMU MUNICH, MUNICH, GERMANY;
[b]DEPARTMENT OF PSYCHOLOGY, UNIVERSITY OF TORONTO, TORONTO, ONTARIO, CANADA;
[c]KELLEY SCHOOL OF BUSINESS, INDIANA UNIVERSITY, BLOOMINGTON, INDIANA,
UNITED STATES

Introduction

The idea of creating a wellness culture can seem daunting, impossible even. Culture change, after all, is something that takes place over decades and sometimes, even centuries. However, when an entire profession is standing at the precipice of change, aware that it must happen and amiable to making positive improvements, culture change is not only possible, it is essential. Law enforcement is just one such profession and the opportunity to positively influence change on a global scale has never been better. Influencing the culture to make wellness a priority is not only a step in the right direction, it can be the catalyst that anchors a new generation of behavior choices bringing renewed vigor to the individual officer, the organization, and the profession.

Definitions of organizational culture abound (Morris, 2014), but most share a common respect for the seminal work of Edgar Schein (1985) who views the culture of an organization as a pattern of behaviors expressed by a group of professionals as they learn to cope with internal and external problems and mentor new members to learn the correct way to perceive, think, and feel while facing similar problems. In simpler terms, an organization's culture is represented by a shared value system that guides the thoughts and actions of its members (Cooke & Rousseau, 1988). The very definition of organizational culture demands that there be a defined value system, stemming from a shared mission, guiding the decisions and behaviors of group members.

The title of the chapter assumes something that is not necessarily accurate. Creating a culture of wellness implies the starting point of a well culture. For many organizations, that is not the case. In fact, a cursory review of the literature reveals nearly 200,000 articles pertaining to toxic cultures or the toxic workplace. Toxicity in the workplace is evidenced by employee negative health implications, either emotional or physical, driven by the way employees are treated on the job (Millage, 2016). Law enforcement officers, due to their repeated exposure to traumatic experiences over the life of their careers, are already at increased risk for negative physical and psychological health implications. Eradicating organizational practices that promote toxicity, such as the use

Power. https://doi.org/10.1016/B978-0-12-817872-0.00010-0

of fear and intimidation to manage staff, is necessary in prioritizing wellness. Healthy organizations are much easier to engage in culture change than their toxic counterparts.

Building a culture of wellness requires three major components: transformational leadership, employee engagement, and organizational justice. Transformational leadership, the most well-researched and highest regarded type of leadership within a policing context, consists of four distinct behaviors: idealized influence, inspirational motivation, individualized consideration, and intellectual stimulation (Bass & Avolio, 1993). Engaged employees express a fulfilling and active work-related state of mind inclusive of strong organizational identification and self-expression (Bakker, Albrecht, & Leiter, 2011; Rothbard & Patil, 2010). Organizational justice begins and ends with the policies and procedures intended to manage employee behaviors and the leader attitudes expressed throughout the administrative decision-making process (Borry et al., 2018). Individually, each component inspires a healthy organization and, when applied to the priority of building a culture of wellness, the constructs that support transformational leadership, employee engagement, and organizational justice can be refined to focus on wellness.

Transformational leadership

Transformational Leadership was created by James MacGregor Buns, a well-known and influential figure in political circles. An avid scholar and presidential biographer, Burns wrote numerous presidential biographies and books discussing all three branches of American federal government (Thompson, Gills, Denemark, & Chase-Dunn, 2015). Buns also innovated the study of leadership, with his 1978 book *Leadership*, which initiated transformational leadership theory, stressing the relationship between the leader and follower, and emphasizing the transformational role a leader possess. Through their role, leaders can (and should) inspire followers toward the development and enhancement of human behavior, leading to greater wellbeing for all workers (Burns, 1978).

While transactional leadership relies on the exchange between rewards or valued outcomes (i.e. work for pay, vacation, etc.) and hard work, transformational leadership goes further by taking emotions into account (Vito, Higgins, & Denney, 2014). Relying on charisma, inspiration, individual consideration and intellectual stimulation, a transformational leader drives followers to achieve their full potential, while also developing the goals driving employees as well as their higher needs, such as self-actualization and purpose-driven behavior (Burns, 1978; Mulla & Krishnan, 2011). Also important for this construct is the idea of *vision*, which followers use to tie their choices directly to the organization's mission in order to build a stronger future for both (Bush, 2018). It is through the connection of mission, charisma, and vision that the transformational leader optimizes influence amongst followers, while mentoring followers to achieve their potential (Bass, 1985).

Of all leadership theories — authentic, servant, values-based, transactional, transformational, and charismatic — transformational leadership has the strongest support in police organizations. In fact, in a meta-analysis of research conducted on police leadership published between 1990 and 2012, Pearson-Goff and Herrington (2014) found 57 studies of quality and relevance, highlighting 12 characteristics of highly effective police transformational leaders: trustworthy, ethical, role model, legitimate, decision making, clear communication, engendering organizational commitment, creating a shared vision, driving and managing change, caring for subordinates, and problem solving. Of the 12, four characteristics rose to the top: clear communication, ethical behavior, driving and managing change, and creating a shared vision (Pearson-Goff & Herrington, 2014). Transformational leadership is broken down into four constructs: Idealized Influence, Inspirational Motivation, Individualized Consideration, and Intellectual Stimulation, together reinforcing the 12 characteristics of highly effective police transformational leaders.

Idealized influence

Idealized influence is centered in a leader's ability to translate the organization's mission into a clear call-to-action while serving as a role model with impeachable ethical standards (Bass & Avolio, 1994; Gooty, Gavin, Johnson, Frazier, & Snow, 2009). When employees believe that their purpose aligns with the department's mission, they are inspired to live in a way that honors that mission. Transformational leaders use their charisma to regularly communicate inspirational messages, honoring those who successfully further that mission regularly. Doing so motivates positive behavior in all staff members, while further solidifying the value of the work being done and the organizational growth that occurs as a result (Vito et al., 2014). Through charisma, a sense of reverence for the leader is built in employees, who then look to the leader for guidance and direction. The leader, in turn, promotes strong moral and ethical principles which inspires followers to adhere to the value system of the organization while furthering employee respect and trust (Thomson, Rawson, Slade, & Bledsoe, 2016).

Inspirational motivation

The characteristic of motivation is highly important for the transformational leader, since it provides the energy needed to fuel followers to perform at their fullest potentials (Vito et al., 2014). In order to properly motivate followers, it is essential to know each team member on an individual level (see Individualized Consideration). The transformational leader is the connecting force between what each team member brings to the group and the over-arching mission of the team. Their responsibility is to engage entire teams into a larger strategy, motivating them to accomplish goals that will advance not only the mission-at-large but the individual's desire to achieve as well

(Thomson et al., 2016). This also promotes a sense of purpose while building individual confidence in the vision that the group shares. Compassion for followers is imperative for this characteristic, since it allows the transformational leader to see followers' needs and attend to them while accomplishing the organizational mission (Vito et al., 2014).

Individualized consideration

Leaders must build relationships with employees who report to them. Skills such as mentorship, support, transparency, respect and acknowledgment of follower contributions to the department have the power to transform units, teams, and entire division (Valero, Jung, & Andrew, 2015). The strongest leaders take an interest in the skills and talents each person brings to the team. Understanding what makes an individual uniquely qualified to fulfill specific requirements in a mission is essential to choosing the right person for the task at hand. As team members share values, needs, and preferences, the transformational leader integrates this information into the decision-making strategic process and creates a plan of action that engenders organizational commitment and shared vision. In so doing, there develops an emotional connection between leader and follower, which demonstrates that the organization − through leader behavior − cares.

Intellectual stimulation

Instrumental to transformational leadership is the willingness of the leader to open conversations of strategy and creative problem-solving, allowing followers to engage in the planning process. Leaders who are humble enough to desire the ideas of others lead the way toward innovation (Chen, Tang, Jin, Xie, & Li, 2014). The more willing a leader is to consider suggestions and ideas about innovative projects, the greater the likelihood that followers will think of alternatives to common knowledge and question basic assumptions as they build innovative solutions. This approach to stimulating knowledge and innovation drives and manages change while fostering follower creativity and independent thinking (Thomson et al., 2016).

Applying transformational leadership to the wellness culture

The first step in establishing a culture of wellness is to make the health, safety, and wellbeing of every officer − sworn and nonsworn − an organizational priority. As transformational leadership clearly states, organizational priorities belong in the mission of the department. Presently, few department mission statements speak directly to officer wellness. Making that slight adjustment inspires personnel to consider individual choices through the lens of organizational purpose and leader expectation. An additional benefit of including wellness in the department's mission statement is the subtle shift in attitudes. If wellness is a high enough priority to be included in a highly visible organizational tool like a mission statement, then the unspoken stigma surrounding it loses some of its strength.

The second strategic advantage of transformational leadership in creating a culture of wellness is the focus on tying individual talents, goals, and needs to a larger vision. Individual officers must be retrained to consider their own lifestyle choices through the lens of the organization's purpose. Leaders, through the development of individual relationships with their followers, become accountability partners on the wellness journey. With regularity, leaders at all levels of the organization should be asking questions pertaining to officer wellness plans. In a wellness culture, for example, it would not be surprising to hear a police captain ask a police sergeant, "What have you done this week to improve your mental, emotional, physical or social health?" Indeed, adding such questions into semi-annual reviews would go a long way toward shifting the conversation away from outdated cultural stigmas and toward wellness.

Finally, involving officers in a regular and open conversation about wellness is a vital part of stimulating innovative solutions. In fact, because police organizations mirror the men and women who form the department, there is no one-size-fits-all solution for ensuring wellness. Opening the floor to suggestions, whether through anonymous submission or open discussion, engages employees into the process of problem-solving which further engenders organizational commitment. Wellness resources are plentiful and varied, so rather than directing the command staff to choose which to offer, police departments are much better served creating a wellness toolkit — consisting of a mixture of evidence-based resources along with those proffered by employees — and requiring use of some, but not all. Officers may then choose what they are most comfortable with, recognizing that the choice has now shifted away from one of use to one of accountability. Where before, officers might say, "I'm fine. I don't need help," they will begin to acknowledge the organizational accountability requirement and say, "I am fine, but since I have to show what I'm doing to take better care of myself, I'll use this tool."

No conversation about police wellness would be complete without addressing the subcultures that exist in police organizations. Agencies are frequently separated, perhaps naturally, into groups based on position and/or authority level. For instance, street cops and management cops are distinctly different based on a combination of position and authority. To some, patrol officers are separate from community police officers due to the nature of the style of policing practiced. Regardless of position, authority, time-in-service, or special skills, building a wellness culture requires the buy-in and engagement of employees at all levels of the organization, sworn and nonsworn alike. Only the most inspirational, transparent leadership style can effectively overcome the inherited attitudes that divide officers. Indeed, uniting them under one singular mission with a shared vision of what defines success provides the best chance for policing organizations to transform from the daily grind to a thriving, supportive culture of wellness.

Employee engagement

Motivation, contribution, emotional, and even spiritual commitment are the many defining values of employee engagement. Common to these commitment principles, Macey and Schneider (2008) state that employee engagement has enormous influence on the efficacy of an organization, and as such, must be a top priority. In addition, employee commitment ties directly into the organization's purpose, leading to several organizational benefits including increased involvement, commitment, passion, enthusiasm, focused effort, and energy on the job.

The term *employee engagement* first surfaced in the 1990s, described in Kahn's (1990) pivotal work, *Psychological Conditions of Personal Engagement and Disengagement at Work*. According to Kahn, employee engagement is personal buy-in with the organization's purpose as evidenced by an employee's decision to fully undertake their assigned duties and roles on the basis of their experiences within the working environment (Bailey, Madden, Alfes, & Fletcher, 2015). More explicitly, Kahn (1990) concentrated on depicting the psychological conditions under which individuals involve themselves at work. Evidenced by attitude and behavior, these psychological states are viewed as mental encounters with the rational and oblivious elements of the work setting, and mediated by the person's perception of leadership, personal value, and connection to organizational purpose.

After nearly three decades of research into employee engagement, it is still recognized largely as an attitude evidenced by employee behaviors, but is now quantified by the following sub-categories: (1) personal role engagement; (2) work task or job engagement; (3) multidimensional engagement; (4) engagement as a composite attitudinal and behavioral construct; (5) engagement as management practice; and (6) self-engagement with performance (Bailey et al., 2015).

To be clear, employee engagement hinges on transformational leadership: purpose-driven innovation with open communication. When police leaders intentionally encourage their subordinates to be part of the solution, they improve the nature of employee engagement beyond the immediate network of influence. Giving employees a voice in any change process or, better yet, a continuous feedback loop for organizational policies (engagement as management practice) strengthens personal ownership and encourages multidimensional engagement for leaders and followers alike. Engagement need not be treated as a requirement of organizational overhaul; rather, engagement improves through the expansion of communication and an organizational attitude of collective excellence.

Burnout, a term frequently used in first-response circles, was originally defined by a lack of engagement. As a descriptor on the opposite end of the spectrum to engagement, much of the early research in first-responder job satisfaction focused on employee engagement and burnout. Maslach, an originator of engagement research, defined engagement as a continuous positive psychological state characterized by vigor, dedication, and absorption (Maslach & Leiter, 1997). That same body of research resulted in the dimensions of burnout to include exhaustion, cynicism, and ineffectiveness. Employee engagement, as the antithesis of burnout, indicates a work mindset that reflects a positive attitude of professional fulfillment toward the organization and its values (Robinson, Perryman, & Hayday, 2004).

Broken down, the attitudes of employee engagement can be evidenced in positive organizational behaviors. Vigor is demonstrated by high energy and the willingness to invest effort in one's work. Dedication indicates a deep involvement in the work being done, resulting in positive emotions about the significance of the job as well as professional enthusiasm, pride, and inspiration. Being absorbed with the work involves complete concentration to the point of experiencing time passing quickly and trouble detaching from tasks to end the workday. The root of our understanding of engagement is firmly grounded in positive psychology, which is a shift in the focus of traditional psychological study away from a preoccupation with repairing what is wrong in life and toward the creation of positive qualities (Seligman & Csikszentmihalyi, 2000).

This advance in understanding individual workplace attitudes led to a positive shift in organizational psychology research. Rather than focusing on employee deficits, researchers began quantifying what it took for employees to thrive. Since the early 2000's, studies have consistently shown that a positive relationship between job resources (such as role fit, skills variety, autonomy, task significance, supervisor feedback and support) and employee engagement. Indeed, employee engagement is crucial to both employees' wellness and organizational performance. To date, research has linked quality service, competitive edge, organizational and leader loyalty, employee satisfaction and retention, and performance to high levels of employee engagement (Albrecht, 2010; Halbesleben & Wheeler, 2008; Rich, Lepine, & Crawford, 2010).

Individual psychological capital

In *Positive Psychology: An Introduction,* Seligman and Csikszentmihalyi (2000) challenged organizational psychologists to change perspective when approaching organizational behavior. Rather than focusing on what was dysfunctional and wrong with people, Seligman and Csikszentmihalyi encouraged a method that highlighted what was good and right about them. The shift in focus uncovered the notion of engagement or a person's involvement in organizational goal attainment, resulting in individual goal alignment with that of the greater good.

As an individual becomes more engaged with organizational outcomes and begins to gauge personal success as it pertains to a company's performance, levels of psychological capital increase. Initially, psychological capital encompassed such characteristics as hope, wisdom, future-mindedness, creativity, spirituality, courage, responsibility, and perseverance. In 2004, researchers Fred Luthans, Kyle Luthans, and Bret Luthans dove into Seligman and Csikszentmihalyi's challenge with gusto and used Stajkovic and Luthans's (2003); Luthans et al., 2004 study of organizational motivation to determine what four core constructs of positive psychological capital and organizational behavior are most essential to uncovering a person's best self.

Positive Psychological Capital, or PsyCap, is represented by an individual's *state of development* combined with their positive psychological resources of hope, efficacy, resilience, and optimism. As a continuous state, PsyCap naturally lends itself to becoming the standard by which wellness initiatives are integrated into performance-management resources. Since its establishment, numerous studies have demonstrated that the core construct of PsyCap has a stronger impact than any one or more of the components that make it up (Newman, Ucbasaran, Zhu, & Hirst, 2014), and is related to desired work attitudes, behaviors, and performance over and above widely-recognized demographic characteristics and positive traits such as personality and self-evaluations (Luthans, Youssef-Morgan, & Avolio, 2015) across western and non-western cultures. In 2017, research revealed that the development of PsyCap also mediated high levels of depression, anxiety, stress, and post-traumatic stress in police and firefighters (Kosor, 2017). In short, the development of PsyCap in individuals has the support of hundreds of research studies and is instrumental to the establishment of a wellness culture. Its aptitude is both individual and organizational, and the resulting performance characteristics enhance mental wellness in tandem with employee engagement and resilience.

Employee citizenship behaviors

Organizational citizenship behavior, or OCB for short, is an individual's voluntary and optional commitment within an organization that is not explicitly outlined in the contractual agreement and/or in job requirements (Podsakoff, MacKenzie, & Podsakoff, 2018). Historically speaking, OCB is a relatively young theoretical concept, but as Organ wrote, "Beyond the call of duty harks back at least to the 18th century" (Organ, 2018, p. 7). The idea that people would go above and beyond what their expected job tasks required of them can be traced to military contexts, which eventually filtered down into the civilian sector. It is no surprise, then, that law enforcement personnel are perfectly suited to working the extra mile to complete the mission.

Daniel Katz and Robert Kahn (1966) asserted that spontaneous cooperation, or performing beyond formal role requirements, is motivated by a sense that one has full citizenship in the system. Moreover, Organ (1977) explained how organizational citizenship behavior is evident in voluntary gestures that help sustain a system of cooperation. These gestures are the sum of behaviors that enhance the mission, yet are not systematically tied to the formal structure of the organization or any type of reward associated with the behavior. For example, officers who spend unpaid time working cases or consoling family members of crime victims – not because they must, but because they care – are exhibiting employee engagement.

According to Organ (2018), one of the factors associated with OCB is conscientiousness. Some examples of consciousness include time management, punctuality, participating in off-hours organizational programs, maintaining a clean and organized environment, and other similar, positive performance behaviors. Indeed, there are also *don't-do* items, including not fussing about loss of privilege, not using negative words and comments, and not sharing dissatisfaction with peers. Tied directly to leadership and organizational justice are courtesy (gestures to prevent future problems in the organization) and voice (i.e. spontaneous cooperation).

Connecting the self to the organizational system

Over 50% of Americans are dissatisfied with their occupations (Gibbons, 2010). This number represents the highest level of dissatisfaction on record in more than 20 years (Anik, Aknin, Norton, Dunn, & Quoidbach, 2013). More alarming still is that, over this same time span, Americans have also increased their time at work, spending more time working than engaged in any other activity. Even without considering the recent challenge to police hiring and retention, leaders of organizations should be asking themselves what can be done in order to rescue employees' interest in department goals and values, ensure their engagement levels, and provide them opportunities to use their skills and abilities to the fullest. At least then, even though they are being asked to do more with less, they are experiencing fulfillment on the job.

It is widely accepted that the fit between the organization and the employee is fundamental for both success and employee gratification (Farooqui & Nagendra, 2014). Police organizations for decades have maintained a strict hiring process, doing an excellent job of managing the quality of officer hired because of the multifunctional role that a police officer fills. Not unlike work in the civilian sector, the law enforcement profession can begin to feel tedious and stressful over time. Techniques to overcome the weight of tedium and stress should focus on re-energizing the positive psychological attributes officers were hired with, which will trigger a re-emergence of positive organizational behaviors.

Many techniques have been suggested by scholars to address dissatisfaction while encouraging employees to give their best at work. For instance, Business Process Reengineering (BPR) is an approach wherein an organization radically redesigns its own business processes, rethinking the internal construction of employee communication and engagement methods, and innovating from scratch (Markos & Sridevi, 2010). Organizations embarking upon the culture shift toward wellness are well-served to approach the idea through BPR. Research reveals that not only is BPR successful in increasing employee performance, it enlivens staff through the inclusion of their voices in creating new working habits within a new working environment (Huang, Lee, & Chiu, 2014).

Another organizational-redesign technique that has aided police departments in overcoming employee dissatisfaction is the Perceived Organizational Support (POS) model. The success of this model hinges on leadership attitudes and behaviors exhibited by supervisors and the command staff (Tucker, 2015). In organizations where leaders embrace change first, officers perceive that their well-being is a priority of the organization, and believe that their contributions and efforts are valued by their leaders. In addition to being effective in promoting job satisfaction (Howard, Howard-Donofrio, & Boles, 2004), POS leads to higher productivity (Shanock & Eisenberger, 2006) and mediates occupational stress (Maguen et al., 2009).

Providing employees with organizational development tools that exist to connect their purpose to their fit within the department enhances employee engagement. Professional development and communication resources which encourage sworn and nonsworn officers to share their opinions, clarify career development plans (where employees can grow and see themselves growing with the department), and reach for performance bonuses and rewards contribute to employee retention and organizational citizenship (Sandhya & Kumar, 2011). Creating an environment where employees voluntarily apply their full effort is instrumental to the successful wellness culture because such an environment promotes the well-being of its members while encouraging engagement with the organization they are part of (Manguen et al., 2009).

Applying employee engagement to the wellness culture

Employee engagement reaffirms employees' needs to have a voice in the change process. The most prevalent tool used to gather employee feedback is a survey. As the wellness initiative takes hold, provide officers with a survey they can complete wherein they are asked to anonymously offer suggestions for practical solutions that will encourage employees to take action steps in their own wellness journeys. While research into wellness is plentiful, begin by asking employees what wellness looks like to them. As the conversation continues, through team meetings, internal communication, and the receipt of surveys, the administration can craft a wellness standard. Employees, as the primary drivers of what constitutes wellness, will embrace the new standard with less resistance.

Because wellness begins at the individual level and then expands outward, seek feedback from employees about how the organization can further support a wellness culture. Use their responses to develop a kit of resources or to structure performance evaluations that enhance their accountability to the new wellness standard. Leaders should be encouraged to speak frequently and openly about what they are doing to maintain wellness, engaging followers into similar conversations.

As with all culture-changing endeavors, leader behavior is pivotal. Prioritizing wellness begins with a change in verbiage, attitude, and behavior at the uppermost level of the police organization and extends both outward to the command staff and down into the rank-and-file. Employee engagement hinges on whether leaders are *all in* on the creation of a wellness culture. The more frequently staff hears about the changes that leaders are making to enhance their wellness, the more engaged employees become into the ownership of the concept. As the new reality of wellness spreads throughout the organization, the culture shift takes a stronghold and begins to permeate the very fabric of law enforcement as a professional, purpose-filled career.

Organizational justice

Since 1987, the term *organizational justice* has been used to collectivize concepts found in organizational and social psychology (Greenberg, 2011). Even older is one of the three key elements of organizational justice: procedural justice. Procedural justice has its roots in the legal profession (Colquitt, 2008) but has since been adopted to apply to the management practices inside organizations. Along with procedural justice, organizational justice is comprised of distributive justice and interactional justice. Distributive justice is grounded in equity theory, which is the belief that people tend to compare the consequences of their actions (good or bad) with those of their peer group. Interactional justice focuses not on the outcomes, but on the process by which those outcomes were determined to be fair (Colquitt, 2008). Research into the efficacy of organizational justice connect its constructs directly to organizational commitment and trust, increased work performance, positive evaluations of authority, and organizational citizenship behaviors (Cohen-Charash & Mueller, 2007; Tyler, 2011). However, in order for employees to perceive their organization to be fair and just, adherence to all three of its core constructs is essential.

Distributive justice

Administrative decisions pertaining to such things as pay, promotion, and disciplinary measures have far-reaching organizational implications. Distributive justice, simply put, is employee perceptions of whether administrative decisions are fair. Employees who believe that their leaders are distributing outcomes fairly have been shown to increase the amount of effort put into workplace tasks (Cohen-Charash & Spector, 2001). The inverse is also true. When employees believe supervisor decisions are unfair, their cognitions, emotions, and behaviors are negatively affected. In fact, research reveals that when an imbalance between the ratio of effort-to-reward exists, employees exhibit counterproductive behavior such as stealing from the company or reducing the amount of effort they put in during a regular shift of work (Colquitt, 2008).

Procedural justice

Grounded in dispute resolution practices, procedural justice focuses less on administrative decisions or outcomes and more on the process used to reach those decisions. One instrumental and necessary element in ensuring procedural justice is providing the impacted employees with a voice in the proceedings (Myhill & Bradford, 2013). Even if theirs is not the defining factor in the decision-making process, employees must feel as if they have some degree of control over the procedures at play in decisions affecting things such as pay, promotion, discipline, etc. (Brebels, De Cremer, Van Dijke, & Van Hiel, 2011). Additional elements essential to procedural justice in the larger context of organizational justice include bias suppression, accuracy of information, the willingness of leaders to overturn incorrect decisions, adhering to the accepted ethical codes of the profession, and organizational consistency practices (Colquitt, 2008).

Organizational consistency is the perception of the employees that policies and procedures are created with purpose and consistently applied to all personnel, without preferential treatment granted based on position, authority level, or social capital. Managing employee perceptions is not an easy undertaking, but it can be done through the strategic application of transparent communication practices that begins at the point of policy creation and extends through policy application. In the policing profession, organizational consistency is particularly important because officers are expected to frequently adjust to new policies as they are created from political and legislative changes (Wolfe, Nix, & Campbell, 2018). As politics change so do laws, and officers tasked with applying those laws are often excluded from the process until it is time to enforce them (O'Toole, 2004; Werts & Brewer, 2014). Living inside that reality only serves to reinforce officers' needs for organizational consistency, which is directly connected with organizational justice.

Interactional justice

While distributive and procedural justice focus on the decision and the process respectively, interactional justice is viewed through the behavioral lenses of the leaders involved – directly and indirectly – in the decision-making process (Myhill & Bradford, 2013). The emphasis of supervisor behavior in mediating employee perceptions cannot be underscored. Characteristics such as supervisor honesty, politeness, and respect throughout the process is a primary indicator of leader attitudes. When employees believe that there exists mistreatment on an individual level or that there was limited communication about the decisions made, there exists a gap in perceived justice. To maintain a trusting relationships with all employees, even when only one employee is under consideration pertaining to an administrative policy, leaders must uphold a level of consistent quality and fairness, communicating clear and truthful explanations throughout the process, while treating the individual respectfully no matter the outcome (Greenberg, 2011).

Applying organizational justice to the wellness culture

A fundamental truth about law enforcement is that officers seek justice. To expect them to accept internal injustices undercuts the very fabric of their strongly-held beliefs.

When building a wellness culture, the development of performance evaluations and consistent disciplinary procedures affirms an organizational commitment to justice as well.

The modification of performance evaluations to include measurable wellness components drives individual accountability to the organization's renewed prioritization of officer wellness. The addition of a wellness category can be supported by multiple dimensions of healthy behavior based on employee feedback. For example, of the wellness dimensions including physical, mental, emotional, cognitive, financial, spiritual, and financial, officer feedback should be solicited to determine not only which they deem instrumental to their wellness, but suggestions for how to quantify wellness inside each dimension should also be sought. After receiving the feedback, administrators must openly communicate the results and any decisions made pertaining to the performance evaluation changes. Doing so supports procedural and interactional justice, resulting in a stronger individual/organizational bond.

Developing a consistent disciplinary matrix is a resource that could easily be credited with eliminating pervasive organizational toxicity. Justice implies fairness, yet few police departments have standard procedures for handling disciplinary situations which opens the door to shifting perceptions of fairness (Shane, 2012). Standardizing disciplinary decisions not only simplifies the procedural process involved in meting out repercussions, it clearly defines organizational expectations. Employees who know in advance the likely outcome of their actions, based on a disciplinary standard, have no excuse for their choices after the fact. This level of transparency eases stress on leaders, who are frequently faced with providing limited information to followers while an investigation is underway. With a standardized disciplinary matrix in use, leaders would not force ambiguity onto the officers in their charge. Instead, everyone shares a general expectation of the outcome without such arguments as favoritism or chance entering the picture.

Conclusion

It is an honorable endeavor to lead the charge for culture change. Leaders at the highest levels of police organizations have a duty to provide healthy, supportive work environments. This responsibility is not without its challenges, but the rewards to officer wellness and community satisfaction are well worth the time and effort it takes to implement these positive changes. Whether your organization prefers taking small steps toward the development of a culture of wellness, or decides to completely overhaul the internal attitude about wellness through major policy changes, the best thing you can do for officer wellness is to lead transformationally, engage personnel in a process of transparency, and prioritize organizational justice. Officers will be inspired to own their personal wellness and will begin to view the concept as instrumental to their purpose on and off the job.

References

Albrecht, S. L. (2010). Employee engagement: 10 key questions for research and practice. In S. L. Albrecht (Ed.), *Handbook of employee engagement: Perspectives, issues, research and practice* (pp. 3–19). Edward Elgar.

Anik, L., Aknin, L. B., Norton, M. I., Dunn, E. W., & Quoidbach, J. (2013). Prosocial bonuses increase employee satisfaction and team performance. *PLSO One, 8*(9), 1–8.

Bailey, C., Madden, A., Alfes, K., & Fletcher, L. (2015). The meaning, antecedents and outcomes of employee engagement: A narrative synthesis. *International Journal of Management Reviews, 19*(1), 31–53. https://doi.org/10.1111/ijmr.12077.

Bakker, A. B., Albrecht, S. L., & Leiter, M. P. (2011). Key questions regarding work engagement. *European Journal of Work & Organizational Psychology, 20*, 4–28.

Bass, B. M. (1985). *Leadership and performance beyond expectation.* New York: Free Press.

Bass, B. M., & Avolio, B. J. (1993). Transformational leadership and organizational culture. *Public Administration Quarterly, 17*(1), 112. Retrieved from https://libcatalog.atu.edu:443/login?url=https://search.proquest.com/docview/226966626 ?accountid=8364.

Bass, B. M., & Avolio, B. J. (1994). *Improving organizational effectiveness through transformational leadership.* Thousand Oaks, CA: Sage Publications.

Borry, E., DeHart-Davis, L., Kaufmann, W., Merritt, C. C., Mohr, Z., & Tummers, L. G. (2018). Formalization and consistency heighten organizational rule following: Experimental and survey evidence. *Public Administration, 96*, 368–385.

Brebels, L., De Cremer, D., Van Dijke, M., & Van Hiel, A. (2011). Fairness as social responsibility: A moral self-regulation account of procedural justice enactment.(report). *British Journal of Management, 22,* S47.

Burns, J. M. (1978). *Leadership.* New York, NY: Harper & Row.

Bush, T. (2018). Transformational leadership: Exploring common conceptions. *Educational Management Administration & Leadership, 46*(6), 883–887. https://doi.org/10.1177/1741143218795731.

Chen, Y., Tang, G., Jin, J., Xie, Q., & Li, J. (2014). CEOs' transformational leadership and product innovation performance: The roles of corporate entrepreneurship and technology orientation. *Journal of Product Innovation Management, 31*, 2–17.

Cohen-Charash, Y., & Mueller, J. S. (2007). Does perceived unfairness exacerbate or mitigate interpersonal counterproductive work behaviors related to envy? *Journal of Applied Psychology, 92*(3), 666–680. https://doi.org/10.1037/0021-9010.92.3.666.

Cohen-Charash, Y., & Spector, P. E. (2001). The role of justice in organizations: A meta-analysis. *Organizational Behavior and human decision processes. 86*, 278–321.

Colquitt, J. (2008). Two decades of organizational justice: Findings, controversies, and future directions. In C. Cooper, & J. Barling (Eds.), *The sage handbook of organizational behavior* (pp. 73–78). Newbury Park, CA).

Cooke, R. A., & Rousseau, D. M. (1988). Behavioral norms and expectations: A quantitative approach to the assessment of organizational culture. *Group & Organization Studies, 13*, 245–273. https://doi.org/10.1177/105960118801300302.

Farooqui, S., & Nagendra, A. (2014). The impact of person organization fit on job satisfaction and performance of the employees. *Procedia Economics and Finance*, 122–129.

Gibbons, J. (2010). I can't get no...job satisfaction, that is: America's unhappy workers. *The Conference Board.* Report No. 1459-09-RR.

Gooty, J., Gavin, M., Johnson, P. D., Frazier, M. L., & Snow, D. B. (2009). In the eyes of the beholder: Transformational leadership, positive psychological capital, and performance. *Journal of Leadership & Organizational Studies, 15*(4), 353−367.

Greenberg, J. (2011). Organizational justice: The dynamics of fairness in the workplace. In Z. Sheldon (Ed.), *APA handbook of industrial and organizational psychology, vol. 3: Maintaining, expanding, and contracting the organization* (pp. 271−327). Washington, DC: American Psychological Association.

Halbesleben, J. R. B., & Wheeler, A. (2008). The relative roles of engagement and embeddedness in predicting job performance and intention to leave. *Work & Stress, 22*(3), 242−256. https://doi.org/10.1080/02678370802383962.

Howard, W. G., Howard-Donofrio, H., & Boles, J. S. (2004). Inter- domain work-family, family-work conflict and police work satisfaction. *Policing: An International Journal of Police Strategies & Management, 27,* 380−395.

Huang, S. Y., Lee, C., & Chiu, A. (2014). *How business process reengineering affects information technology investment and employee performance under different performance measurement* (Vol. 17, pp. 1133−1144). Springer Science Business Media.

Kahn, W. (1990). Psychological conditions of personal engagement and disengagement at work. *Academy of Management Journal, 33,* 692−724.

Katz, D., & Kahn, R. L. (1966). *The social psychology of organizations.* New York, NY: Wiley.

Kosor, R. (2017). *Testing a psychological readiness training intervention on depression, anxiety, stress, and PTSD in first responders.* ScholarWorks. Retrieved from https://scholarworks.waldenu.edu/dissertations/3303/.

Luthans, F., Luthans, K., & Luthans, B. (2004). Positive psychological capital: Beyond human and social capital. *Business Horizons, 47*(1), 45−50. https://doi.org/10.1016/j.bushor.2003.11.007.

Luthans, F., Youssef-Morgan, C., & Avolio, B. (2015). *Psychological capital and beyond.* New York, NY: Oxford University Press.

Macev, W. H., & Schneider, B. (2008). The meaning of employee engagement. *Industrial and Organizational Psychology, 1,* 3−30.

Maguen, S., Metzler, T. J., McCaslin, S. E., Inslicht, S. S., Henn- Haase, C., Neylan, T. C., et al. (2009). Routine work environment stress and PTSD symptoms in police officers. *The Journal of Nervous and Mental Disease, 197*(10), 754−760.

Markos, S., & Sridevi, M. S. (2010). Employee engagement: The key to improving performance. *International Journal of Business and Management, 5*(12), 89−96.

Maslach, & Leiter. (1997). *The truth about burnout.* San Francisco: Jossey-Bass.

Millage, A. (June 2016). *When toxic culture hits home* (Vol. 7). Academic OneFile. http://link.galegroup.com/apps/doc/A456275337/AONE?u=aktechuniv&sid=AONE&xid=3c49802c. (Accessed 31 May 2019).

Morris, J. P. (2014). Method in the madness: Towards developing a matrix for comparison of conceptual models of organizational culture. *Strategic Management Review, 8,* 1−16.

Mulla, Z., & Krishnan, V. (2011). Transformational leadership: Do the leader's morals matter and do the follower's morals change? *Journal of Human Values, 17,* 129−143. https://doi.org/10.1177/097168581101700203.

Myhill, A., & Bradford, B. (2013). Overcoming cop culture? Organizational justice and police officers' attitudes toward the public. *Policing, 36*(2), 338−356. https://doi.org/10.1108/13639511311329732.

Newman, A., Ucbasaran, D., Zhu, F., & Hirst, G. (2014). Psychological capital: A review and synthesis. *Journal of Organizational Behavior, 35*(1), S120−S138.

Organ, D. W. (1977). A reappraisal and reinterpretation of the satisfaction-causes-performance hypothesis. *Academy of Management Review, 2,* 46–53.

Organ, D. W. (2018). The roots of organizational citizenship behavior. In P. Podsakoff, S. Mackenzie, & N. Podsakoff (Eds.), *The Oxford handbook of organizational citizenship behavior.* New York, NY: Oxford University Press. https://doi.org/10.1093/oxfordhb/9780190219000.013.2.

O'Toole, L. J. (2004). The theory-practice issue in policy implementation research. *Public Administration, 82*(2), 309–329. https://doi.org/10.1111/j.0033-3298.2004.00396.x.

Pearson-Goff, M., & Herrington, V. (2014). Police leadership: A systematic review of the literature. *Policing: Journal of Policy Practice, 8*(1), 14–26. https://doi.org/10.1093/police/pat027.

Podsakoff, P. M., MacKenzie, S. B., & Podsakoff, N. P. (2018). *The oxford handbook of organizational citizenship behavior.* New York, NY: Oxford University Press.

Rich, B. L., Lepine, J. A., & Crawford, E. R. (2010). Job engagement: Antecedents and effects on job performance. *Academy of Management Journal, 53*(3). https://doi.org/10.5465/amj.2010.51468988.

Robinson, D., Perryman, S., & Hayday, S. (2004). *The drivers of employee engagement.* UK: Brighton. Institute for Employment Studies. report 408.

Rothbard, N. P., & Patil, S. V. (2010). Being there: Work engagement and positive organizational scholarship. In G. Spreitzer, & K. Cameroon (Eds.), *The Oxford handbook of positive organizational scholarship* (pp. 59–69). Oxford: Oxford University Press.

Sandhya, K., & Kumar, D. P. (2011). Employee retention by motivation. *Indian Journal of Science and Technology, 4*(12), 1778–1782.

Schein, E. H. (1985). *Organizational culture and leadership.* San Francisco, CA: Jossey-Bass.

Seligman, M. E. P., & Csikszentmihalyi, M. (2000). Positive psychology: An introduction. *American Psychologist, 55,* 5–14. https://doi.org/10.1037/0003-066X.55.1.5.

Shane, S. (2012). Reflections on the 2010 AMR decade award: Delivering on the promise of entrepreneurship as a field of research. *Academy of Management Review, 37*(1), 10–20. https://doi.org/10.5465/amr.2011.0078.

Shanock, S., & Eisenberger, R. (2006). When supervisors feel supported: Relationships with subordinates' perceived supervisor support, perceived organizational support and performance. *Journal of Applied Psychology, 91,* 689–695.

Stajkovic, A. D., & Luthans, F. (2003). Behavioral management and task performance in organizations: Conceptual background, meta-analysis, and test of alternative models. *Personnel Psychology, 56*(1), 155–194. https://doi.org/10.1111/j.1744-6570.2003.tb00147.x.

Thompson, W. R., Gills, B. K., Denemark, R. A., & Chase-Dunn, C. K. (2015). *Memoriam.* American Political Science Association.

Thomson, N. B., Rawson, J. V., Slade, C. P., & Bledsoe, M. (2016). Transformation and transformational leadership. *Academic Radiology, 23*(5), 592–599. https://doi.org/10.1016/j.acra.2016.01.010.

Tucker, J. M. (2015). Police officer willingness to use stress intervention services: The role of perceived organizational support (POS), confidentiality and stigma. *International Journal of Emergency Mental Health and Human Resilience, 17*(1), 304–314. Retrieved from http://digitalcommons.wcupa.edu/crimjust_facpub/4.

Tyler, T. (2011). *Why people cooperate: The role of social motivations.* Princeton, NJ: Princeton University Press.

Valero, J. N., Jung, K., & Andrew, S. A. (2015). Does transformational leadership build resilient public and nonprofit organizations? *Disaster Prevention and Management, 24*(1), 4–20. https://doi.org/10.1108/DPM-04-2014-0060.

Vito, G. F., Higgins, G. E., & Denney, A. S. (2014). Transactional and transformational leadership. *Policing: An International Journal of Police Strategies & Management, 37*(4), 809−822.

Werts, A. B., & Brewer, C. A. (2014). Reframing the study of policy implementation. *Educational Policy, 29*(1), 206−229. https://doi.org/10.1177/0895904814559247.

Wolfe, S. E., Nix, J., & Campbell, B. A. (2018). Police managers' self-control and support for organizational justice. *Law and Human Behavior, 42*(1), 71−82. https://doi.org/10.1037/lhb0000273.

11

Promoting wellness

Sarah Creighton[a], Chuck Kaye[b]

[a]ASSISTANT CHIEF (RETIRED), SAN DIEGO POLICE DEPARTMENT, SAN DIEGO, CA, UNITED STATES; [b]CHIEF OF POLICE, CITY OF CORONADO POLICE DEPARTMENT, CORONADO, CA, UNITED STATES

Structure and support

Police departments across the country are today, more than ever, focusing on officer wellness, looking to develop programs that encourage self-care, and increasing help resources for their employees. The impetus for many leaders is to manage risk, decrease police suicides, and decrease ineffective coping behaviors that often result in significant discipline and public notoriety. Progressive and compassionate leaders recognize the value of proactively designing programs in recognition of the inherently stressful nature of the occupation and in recognition that police officers are not immune to the cumulative impact of traumatic and chronic stress. They also realize that what happens at home likely has a direct impact on what happens at work, and vice versa. Regardless of their motivation, leaders must ensure that their organization is set up to support whatever they put in place with an emphasis on creating a culture that values and supports the whole employee through an entire career.

First steps in creating or augmenting existing wellness programming include creating or adapting the department's vision to include an internal focus inclusive of employee care. A consistent and common language reinforced through values, training, and supportive policies is also necessary to ensure that what is expected of leaders in the organization is understood, held accountable for, and rewarded. When employees know their wellbeing is important and supported by leadership, they are more likely to take advantage of services offered, ask their supervisors for help when they need it, and trust that asking for help will not be held against them. Officers working for agencies that support employee wellbeing also will encourage their peers to take advantage of and proactively refer them to department sanctioned resources.

Functionally, a department's wellness programming, whether formal or not, should be included on the organizational chart. Ideally, this is attached to a ranking department member who has direct and active involvement in or, at least, strong oversight of this agenda. When executive leadership designates a high-ranking member with oversight of their wellness programming, including help resources and training providers, it insures

Power. https://doi.org/10.1016/B978-0-12-817872-0.00011-2

mission consistency and strong messaging to the rank and file about the importance the department places on employee wellness. Developing a wellness culture requires a top-down commitment to understanding about why, and a willingness to impact how, the job effects today's officer. Depending on the size of the agency, the chief will likely take a more hands-on role to insure wellness is part of the fabric of the organization. Regardless of how things were done in the past or stigma that existed when the leader's career started, a continuing high rate of suicide and PTSD in law enforcement today shows there is a need for elevating the priority and the points of accessibility to medical and behavioral health care for officers.

There is no "one size fits all" solution or specific programming that works for all departments. Building a tailored program requires an overall vision of what a healthy organization looks like, and a mission that drives wellness efforts and programming that all personnel within the department believe is employee-centered and conducive for the culture. Needs assessment surveys of department personnel, sworn and civilian, glean important data for building a program that incorporates the ideas of employees and adds a level of ownership, making them more inclined to utilize services and to refer others.

Leadership in law enforcement requires a proactive, holistic approach. Today's leaders recognize that their role requires the development and maintenance of a work environment that promotes healthy and open discussions about the human side of policing. Never in history has there been a greater need. The necessity for an enhanced and more comprehensive role of leadership, including employee care, is evident. Executive leaders are obligated to develop and hold subordinates accountable to department values that include employee care, as well as ensuring that their leadership team understands the capability of available resources when problems are beyond their ability to assist. It is also important that they demonstrate a healthy philosophy about using resources and create healthy forums for expressing feelings and sharing how to cope with work induced stress; the time has passed when police executives can express any personal negative opinions or sentiments that contribute to the stigma of asking for help. To the greatest extent possible, supervisors and command staff should be represented at all wellness training, events, and briefings/team discussions about employee wellness. They even should be encouraged to share their own experiences about times when they struggled, resources they used, and how they built resilience skills. This is the only way for a culture of wellness to take root and begin to grow.

Succession planning offers executive leadership an opportunity to develop future leaders who are compassionate, empathetic, and understanding of today's workforce. Promotional candidates should be required to demonstrate their capacity to show empathy and compassion and should possess the flexibility and willingness to work with employees on an array of issues. Examples of when candidates demonstrated these skills can be sought during promotional interviews and should be incorporated in all interviews where employees are seeking the opportunity to lead. Candidates for promotion should be required to convey a solid understanding of Dr. Gilmartin's *Emotional Survival for Law Enforcement* (Gilmartin, 2002) and of basic stress management skills. Objective tests commonly used to demonstrate knowledge about the leadership role should include content from health and wellness publications, which promotional candidates are required to read and on which they are told they will be tested. The benefit of including wellness reading into promotional opportunities allows the organization an opportunity to expose all candidates, whether or not successful in the process, to timely and important information that can assist in the cultivation of a healthy organization. Attending to officer wellbeing can no longer be seen solely as a specialized competency provided by mental health professionals, chaplains, and trained peer supporters. Instead, leaders should view themselves as the "primary care giver" for their employees, sourcing out only when the employee cannot be served by them or when the support needed falls outside of their ability and expertise.

Many leaders say the right things to their employees, bring in or create excellent training and programs, and provide help resources that encourage officers to come forward when they are struggling. Problems occur and efforts are undermined when department or city policies do not support what the leader promises or offers, even with the best of intentions. It only takes one mishandled intervention to derail or destroy wellness programming. Leaders need to ensure that when they encourage officers to get help, particularly with alcohol and drug abuse or mental health conditions involving hospitalization or medication, the employee can and will be protected. This is a complex issue that needs to be researched extensively before making promises, taking into consideration applicable Federal and State law and statutes, as well as local government policies. Many departments offer their officers help with these issues when they come forward asking before such problems interfere with work performance, and with assurance that the officer will follow through with treatment. Smaller agencies with much fewer instances of employee drug, alcohol, or mental health issues must work out the intervention strategies with their city's centralized Human Resources (HR) department and Employee Assistance Program (EAP) well before a situation arises. It is much more difficult to intervene after an impairment leads to behavior that necessitates a fitness for duty evaluation or requires a disciplinary action. Although there is still hope for recovery after issues are exposed, overcoming them then is more challenging than when a preventative, proactive approach is taken.

Resources

Police departments across the country have offered a variety of help resources to their officers for decades. In large agencies, the most common and traditionally utilized resources include psychologists, chaplains, and peer counselors. Most commonly these resources are deployed immediately following a significant critical incident, and these professionals usually play some role in managing critical incident stress management debriefings. Smaller agencies must consider available resources and get creative when providing support to employees during these incidents. For example, many smaller agencies establish collaborative relationships with neighboring jurisdictions or other entities, such as local psychologists' associations, to provide the needed resources during times of crisis.

Psychological counseling is sometimes provided by the department to officers and, in rare cases, to their family members as well. Generally, there are a limited number of visits allowed. Accessibility to these services ranges from having therapists as department employees to mental health providers working under contact. Less progressive agencies make psychological counseling accessible only through the employees' medical insurance plan.

Police executives who seek to foster a culture of wellness have begun to provide a variety of more modern resources designed to help maintain employee health. These range from mindfulness coaches to emotional support animals, and other specialists (e.g., massage therapists, chiropractors, and yoga instructors) brought in on an occasional basis. The unique culture of the department and ease of resource accessibility will most significantly determine how widely resources will be utilized.

Whatever a department can and does provide regarding resource type requires each provider to have a strong understanding about their specific capabilities and limitations, an enhanced understanding about other available resources, and an understanding about the level of confidentiality afforded them by department policy and statute. It also is crucially important for police executives to ensure that: all resource providers know the vision; understand the department's mission and values related to employee care; and, fully understand the organization's culture in order to speak the same wellness language. Constant reinforcement of the mission and assurance that all providers understand the capacity and limitations of the others reduces the necessity for officers to seek out multiple resources and reinforces the synergy of all services. Most importantly it reduces the necessity for an officer to tell his or her story multiple times and affords officers the highest level of confidentiality. This can easily be accomplished by mandating consistent and ongoing training, which all providers attend, delivered by qualified trainers who understand the culture and the limitations that varying levels of confidentiality among resources options pose. This cohesion greatly reinforces the collective mission.

There is no shortage of "practitioners" who promise to develop and deliver programs or training to police departments. Some of these may have proven effective with military personnel or other crisis workers. Some of these programs have not been applied to law enforcement, and some of these providers have little, if any, experience working with police officers. It is essential for the success of any training to be delivered by facilitators with whom the officers can relate and who offer content that is directly relevant. Many well-intended resource providers are seen as outsiders who do not understand the nuances of the occupation, the culture of the department, or how what they are delivering fits in with existing programming. It is extremely difficult to overcome initial negative opinions formed by officers about un-relatable training. Criticism spreads like wildfire making it more challenging when future deliveries are attempted. Significant deliberation about content and the vetting of credible providers are essential when selecting programs either intended to serve as the foundation of, or as an augmentation to, any existing programming. Ideally, trusted and credible resources who have worked with and understand law enforcement and the specific organizational culture should be used. Minimally, if they do not have the experience working with the department, they should be teamed up with department members to assist in the development, marketing, and delivery of their training program.

Psychologists

The most significant stigma that still exists for officers today is the utilization of mental health professionals. Leaders should consider encouraging officers' use of psychologists by highlighting their ability to assist with performance enhancement. The use of sports psychology and the benefits to professional athletes can serve as an effective and positive comparison for police officers. The analogy highlights the necessity for proactive and ongoing use throughout a career and into retirement. The necessity for a similar mindset, seeing the opportunity to stay ahead of potential performance hindrances, can encourage the use of psychological services toward work and personal excellence, rather than as a result of weakness or only in response to problems. Addressing academy recruits early and often in their academy experience is particularly helpful to develop this mindset in today's officers. Introducing the psychologist and the notion of their use before recruits start training can go a long way in normalizing the use of their services. Making them available to recruits and their families while in the academy can also assist the recruits in the challenging adjustments required during their transition into law enforcement, adding the additional value to the department of increasing retention.

When possible, psychologists should be incorporated as instructors and co-facilitators for in-service training. Serving in this role can assist in normalizing the utilization of psychological services by officers. Psychologists can be particularly effective in facilitating important discussions about stress management, resilience building, police suicide, and ineffective coping (e.g., self-medication). Consideration should also be given to include them in less traditional human behavior topics like, noble cause, cognitive distortions, cynicism, ethics, emotional intelligence, implicit bias, and motivation. The incorporation of psychologists in the training environment assists in normalizing their role and presence and increases officers' willingness to seek out their services on an individual basis.

Psychologists should also be considered to provide wellness and resilience training to command and executive officers. They should participate in management meetings where they can learn more about the impact of traumatic and administratively induced stress on officers. This exposure allows the psychologists to understand management's perspective on commonly unaddressed and sometimes unavoidable administratively induced stressors. These stressors may include mandatory overtime, burnout, lengthy and sterile discipline processes where command staff is often perceived as evasive or non-communicative, and a perceived lack of consideration for officers' work and home balance, among many others. The participation of psychologists may result in problem solving ideas and stress reduction recommendations from a perspective not otherwise considered.

Psychologists selected to work with police officers should minimally be required to ride along with officers to learn about their job before they start counseling. An in-depth understanding of the occupation, including tendencies toward cynicism, the impact of shift work, sleep disruption, paramilitary management, and other dynamics unique to the occupation must be understood. Ideally, therapists should attain police psychology certification or possess a practical equivalency showing their knowledge and experience working with law enforcement. Having worked with law enforcement in another capacity or being certified by the State regulatory Police Training Commission is also beneficial. If that is not possible, it is a must for the psychologists to invest some time to understanding the work and its impact on officers and their loved ones.

Many departments provide psychological services through their city or county Employee Assistance Program (EAP). If this is the only option available to officers for psychological services, it is recommended that a knowledgeable, ranking member of the department meet with EAP counselors to provide a greater understanding of stress inducing conditions in the department and the occupation. These providers should be encouraged to gain exposure to the department in order to improve their relatability to officers who contact them. Many smaller agencies are required to form collaborative arrangements with other departments to be able to afford such psychological services for their employees.

Psychological services that are provided should be made easily accessible to officers and their family. Visits should be unlimited and at no cost to them. Moreover, immediate access is also important for whenever an officer requests it. This is vital to maintaining a culture of wellness, which is compromised if officers cannot get an appointment to a department psychologist or EAP counselor without a significant delay. If departments cannot provide this level of care, either by contract, having therapists as department employees, or through EAP, consideration should be given to developing a streamlined employee benefit through the employee's medical insurance. Police unions can provide tremendous assistance with this process during contract negotiations and assist in the proper vetting of practitioner qualifications. The union's buy-in at the front end also greatly reduces any suspicion about confidentiality, encourages officers' utilization, and presents a united front about valuing employee wellness by both the union and the organization.

Chaplains

There is a long and rich history of chaplaincy in law enforcement. Today, there is a significant increase in police agencies opening their doors to or enhancing the use and exposure of their chaplains. With increased representation among today's law enforcement agencies, it is important for there to be more spiritual and religious diversity among chaplains available to officers. As valuable as psychological care is after a significant critical incident, some officers prefer to seek spiritual or religious support. It is imperative that religious and spiritual counselors working with officers understand the occupation and have been trained in the department's critical incident stress management protocol. Their level of participation following an incident may vary from being available to provide emotional support to actually responding to the scene. Some departments have chaplains serve as co-facilitators in formal debriefing or diffusing sessions, depending on their level of training and, perhaps, based on officers' wishes. Many departments have police chaplains imbedded in the field, riding with officers for entire shifts. In office environments, chaplains attend team meetings, team building forums, and freely roam in the workplace where appropriate and invited. They often maintain relationships with supervisors and command staff and are called upon to assist after significant incidents, which may impact the entire department, as well as after particularly traumatic internal events like an officer death, extraordinarily traumatic accidents and investigations, or during and after any event where employees may benefit from having spiritual support. When officers are unable to leave secure posts during extended traumatic incidents, chaplains can be used as roving support and go to the officer or be available at the command post. This spot intervention can be as simple as providing a bottle of water to the officer or as elaborate as providing emotional support and counsel. Both are needed services and are almost always appreciated. And for some smaller agencies, the chaplains may be the only resource available for a critical incident absent support from other agencies. For this reason, it is imperative for smaller agencies to establish a volunteer program with interested local chaplains who become familiar to officers long before their services are needed.

Larger departments often have chaplains assigned to divisions or units, and some have chaplains that ride exclusively with officers assigned to a division. Their role, described by chaplains as "a ministry of presence," is not to proselytize or preach but to be available for the officer as a second set of eyes and as a companion, with discussion during the shift dictated by the officer. Many chaplains ride entire shifts with officers without discussing religion or spirituality at all. Chaplains are viewed as part of the team and, as a result of the bonds made with the officers during their time spent together, officers are more inclined to reach out when they do struggle with issues and would like spiritual or religious support at a later time or on a more formal basis away from work. The San Diego Police Department has three chaplains that work full-time in this capacity and spend the bulk of their time riding in police cars with officers.

Many chaplains are missionaries and financially supported by donations or funded by their home church. Most chaplains have primary responsibilities with a home church and serve as part-time volunteers for police departments. In some cases, smaller agencies have leveraged an existing relationship with a nearby military base to include those military chaplains to serve their police agency. Chaplains spend a mandated minimum number of hours, as determined by the department, and primarily serve in an on-call status. Typically, departments have a lead or designated chaplain who receives immediate notification when significant incidents occur so that, if appropriate or when officers ask for a specific chaplain, they are deployed directly to them. When an officer is involved in a shooting or is injured on-duty and requests a chaplain, it is common for some departments to allow the chaplain to remain with the officer in a supportive capacity throughout the investigation. Most departments publish information about all clergy serving as department chaplains and provide officers with direct access to them. Regardless of a station or division assignment, the chaplains are available to any officer seeking a particular religious or denominational affiliation. The chaplains typically also offer other services to officers and their families, including officiating marriages, funerals, personal counseling, and other clergy functions, at no cost.

The selection process for determining chaplains' eligibility should be well thought out and stringent. Minimally, chaplains should be ordained, represent the community in good standing, and possess training and experience in counseling. Ensuring that their motivation aligns with the Department's mission and values, that they understand the necessity to be objective, and that they have the capacity to be non-judgmental is also important. It is imperative for each potential chaplain to pass the department's volunteer level background investigation process prior to beginning any volunteer activities as they will have access to sensitive and confidential information. They will also potentially be called as witnesses if they partner with officers in the field. Both large and small agencies should consider leveraging their community's spiritual resources.

It is also recommended that chaplains should be required to attend specialized and certified chaplaincy training offered by their State's Peace Officer Standards and Training (POST), or some equivalency, to ensure their suitability and willingness to work within the confines of a police department. They will need to agree to limit conversations about religion or spirituality as dictated by the officers in their presence. This may be a challenge for some clergy members and should be thoroughly assessed by adding questions to their initial selection interview, and strongly addressed in standard operating procedures provided to them before they begin serving. This issue and other reminders about any limitations of confidentiality imposed by the department should be discussed and updated at continuing department chaplain training provided at regular intervals. While clergy are afforded a high level of confidentiality by statute, some police leaders limit the level afforded the chaplain while serving as an agent of their department.

Departments looking to enhance their chaplaincy program are encouraged to recruit chaplains who offer religious and denominational variety and to encourage networking with other chaplains specifically serving in law enforcement. These networks are growing throughout the country and allow chaplains from smaller agencies to participate in quality training and to receive emotional and spiritual support from others who are already doing the work and understand this unique population. Chaplains are not immune to compassion fatigue and burnout. Any opportunity to acknowledge their service goes a long way in counteracting the disproportionate cynicism and negativity they may develop when dealing with officers who are suffering or when personally exposed to traumas in the field.

Peer support

Peer support is the most commonly used help resource by police officers. Whether through a formal or informal process, most officers will turn to a peer to discuss problems or issues they are having rather than seeking out a psychologist or a chaplain. Knowing this, departments would do well to build a healthy peer support program, create a thoughtful process for selection, and develop quality training that allows only the best-suited peers to serve as peer supporters. Officers selected should be emotionally intelligent, credible, trustworthy, and free from any residual issues from their own past traumas. While having navigated through a similar significant incident might provide for relatability, unhealthy and negative feelings about either the supporter's own incident or resolution, or their opinion about how they were treated by the Department, can undermine the healing of the officer they intend to support.

Police officers are problem solvers who are conditioned to quickly recommend solutions. The necessity to be an objective and patient listener is very important and often difficult for officers when dealing with peers. Training is essential to assist the supporter in understanding the distinction between providing limited counseling and the tendency to problem solve for the officer. Active-listening, honed through role playing and practice, is essential for any peer support training. Peer support members should also be active participants at patrol line-ups, briefings, and team meetings. Checking in with peers after significant incidents, initiating team discussions about the psychological aftermath of traumatic incidents, and recommending available help resources are important tasks for peer support officers. Most police departments assign a peer supporter to all officers, including those who were witnesses, involved in an encounter when deadly force is used and a criminal investigation will be conducted. These investigations are often perceived as invasive, lacking compassion, and, even, unintentionally adversarial. The assignment of a peer supporter throughout this process allows involved officers the benefit of emotional support from someone who has been through a similar process and can provide context, explanation, and support throughout.

The selection of peer support officers for a smaller agency can provide unique challenges. The decision to form a peer support team will be based on the size of the department and then based on the number of officers with experiences and the temperament needed for a successful team. For some of these departments the solution lies in collaborating with adjacent agencies to form a suitable peer support team. It is better to rely on capable resources from another agency than to form a team that cannot provide competent or enough support for your officers and staff. In fact, this is not always just a staffing issue. The ramifications of many critical incidents reverberate through a smaller agency's entire workforce, including those who may be serving as peer supporters. At these times, when peers are urgently needed to provide support, it is advisable to bring in peers from another agency, with whom a relationship is already established, who were not directly impacted by that critical incident.

Peer supporters provide a breadth of services including providing limited counsel to peers about work and personal issues. The ability for an officer to select others with similar experiences and a willingness to share their journey and successes is important. This opportunity can be enhanced by having peer supporters create a profile containing a brief summary about themselves and their personal contact information. Profiles can be accessible through the department intranet and allow compatibility matching through key word field searches. This enables officers to search any issue such as, elder parent care, child custody issues, injury or medical issues, lawsuits, personnel investigations, and any area that a supporter advertises as his or her experience. For workgroups that do not have personal computers assigned, notebooks should be available to officers in areas frequented by them, such as in the workplace briefing and dining areas, where they can easily access the list of peer supporters.

Certified peer support training is essential for all supporters so that they understand their mission, limitations of their scope and expertise, and the level of confidentiality they can promise based on department policy and the law. Comprehensive training for new peer support officers is critical and sets the stage for the success of any peer support program. All trainers should be carefully vetted and appropriately certified. Many large departments develop and certify their own training course, using their own psychologists and senior peer support officers as trainers. This provides for a level of expertise about trauma exposure and other potentially common themes and issues in the department to be specifically addressed in the training. This method is preferable as it provides the peer supporter an opportunity to develop rapport with and understand the capabilities of the psychologist, who may be the more appropriate resource for the officer. The relationship with peer support officers and psychologists is also important because they work collaboratively during critical incident debriefing forums but also separately prior to and potentially after a crisis.

Consideration should also be given to include chaplains in the peer support training, since they also may regularly participate in debriefings. The peer supporter's trust in and confidence referring to a psychologist or chaplain are important components in the ability to best serve the officer. When developing internal peer support training is not feasible for a department, there are many other available training classes from which to choose through the Peace Officers Standards and Training regulatory commission in every state. Most states have Peer Support Associations that offer annual conferences. These conferences offer great training by specialists, highlight best practices, and offer networking opportunities for officers to share ideas and provide support to each other.

Accessibility

As police departments create and add help resources for their officers' use, careful consideration should be given to how to promote them so that officers know about all available resources without having to ask. Posters should be prominently displayed in every workplace, and an easily accessible list of resources should be placed on the department's intranet. Brochures for the officer and their family should also be available. All supervisors should be required to have immediately accessible resource lists for their officers and to regularly review them with their officers. This could easily be a performance anchor incorporated into supervisors' performance evaluation. All help resource providers should be accessible to officers, recognizing shift work schedules often interfere with routine service provider hours. Location is also very important. Multiple location options are optimal, including the option that service providers agree to come to the officer or a neutral location that works for both parties. Careful thought about the location of established and stationary service providers is also crucially important to ease officers' concerns about their privacy and anonymity. All help resources offered by the department should either be free of cost to the officer or available through their insurance, and readily accessible without the need for a referral.

Role of the family

Success in acculturating new officers to a healthy career in law enforcement requires early and frequent education about the stressors inherent to the occupation. There must be a strong emphasis on the necessity for proactive self-care. Prior to starting the police academy recruits should be thoroughly educated about the mental, emotional, and spiritual vulnerabilities intrinsic to a job in law enforcement. During this indoctrination, executive leaders assure recruits that they understand and expect that officers will occasionally struggle with their experiences in the occupation. A simple acknowledgment about the impact of cumulative and traumatic stress on officers and their families can go a long way in normalizing the utilization of help resources and in maintaining proactive self-care. A comprehensive offering of resources needs to be available for officers and family members very early in the recruit's training to affirmatively reinforce effective communication and healthy habit building.

It is not unusual for an officer's most significant stress to come from family members who are concerned about the dangers of the occupation. Heightened negative media coverage has no doubt increased resistance from loved ones about the recruit's selected career choice. As soon as it is practical, departments should include family members in the acculturation process. Some departments immediately, upon hiring, provide access to department help resources to family members. They can obtain help to assist their loved ones in the early transition into the occupation. And, most importantly, services are made available as a way to assist family members in understanding how the occupation will impact their loved one and the family unit. Departments that recognize the need to facilitate everyone's adjustment to a law enforcement career provide this family assistance, which helps in navigating through inevitable lifestyle changes and the demands placed on the family. Through providing family members with a better understanding of why changes may occur, departments show their commitment to promoting wellness.

Many departments offer forums for family members to learn more about what to expect while their loved one is in training. They also describe the resources available to recruits, as well as to any family member, who is struggling to adjust. Access to psychologists and chaplains while the recruit is in the academy can assist by encouraging or facilitating important discussions about expectations, allaying unrealistic concerns, and assisting in the development of healthy communication habits early in the career. Providing access to these and other important resources from the beginning creates a sense of normalcy about the utilization of help resources and contributes to destigmatizing their use.

A family forum utilized by the San Diego Police Department since 2012 is facilitated by the Chief Psychologist of their contract services. New officers are mandated to attend, and family members are encouraged to participate. Family Day is offered the Saturday after academy graduation to provide for maximum attendance of out of town family members who attended the graduation ceremony. The forum includes several of the Department's contract psychologists, chaplains, and staff members assigned to the Department's Wellness Unit. It is a casual forum where the new officers are introduced (or reintroduced) to the care providers who explain what each has to offer. It also provides for a candid discussion about the next phase of training and beyond for the new officers. Testimonials by senior officers who overcame adversity and successfully worked through significant issues are given, highlighting the use of available Department resources and how family members were impacted. The new officers are encouraged to ask questions. Speakers include officers who were involved in significant critical incidents involving the use of deadly force, line of duty deaths of coworkers, medical retirements, substance abuse, injuries and significant illnesses, family illness and tragedy, and many other incidents that an officer might encounter during the career. Speakers offer their stories to encourage the utilization of services before problems progress beyond the point of no return.

Family members arrive at noon for a shared lunch with their loved ones and a casual opportunity to meet members of the Wellness Unit, including the psychologists and chaplains. After lunch, family members are offered an introduction to the psychologists, chaplains, and Wellness Unit staff without their loved one present. This allows for family members to ask questions of the professional staff, which they may not be comfortable asking in front of their loved one. This also is when the family members are reminded that they have direct access to the professionals at any time they have a concern about their loved one or need assistance themselves. Brochures, including detailed descriptions of what services each resource provides, the names of providers, and 24 hours access phone numbers are provided with the encouragement to call with any concerns. Parents and spouses are encouraged to call and offered anonymity if they want a department member to check on their loved one if they have any concerns.

The afternoon session continues with a married couple who offers their suggestions for navigating through a police marriage. They provide first-person details about ways in which families might be impacted by the occupation. Topics include shiftwork, working on holidays and other special occasions, on-call status, impact on non-law enforcement friends, hypervigilance, and others related to the family dynamics associated with the career. Recommendations are given to couples about establishing agreed upon expectations about what their spouse and children want to know about the details of their work, how they want to be notified if a major incident occurs involving them, and how public they wish to be about their law enforcement affiliation. Questions by all family members are encouraged and plentiful.

Many agencies have spousal support groups. These include maintaining a social media presence (e.g., Facebook page), scheduling informal social gatherings, and, more formally, having regular meetings and sponsoring events. The emotional support provided by these groups to other law enforcement spouses cannot be understated. These groups can be an excellent source of information for families about childcare and other trusted and vetted family support resources. They are also, oftentimes, the first support mechanism for law enforcement families in need of assistance during critical incidents, including officer deaths, significant injuries or illness, and other personal tragedies. Including spouses in this very important function serves as a force multiplier to already overwhelmed departments and provides spouses with a greater sense of contribution to the occupation in a very meaningful way. To the greatest extent possible, police departments should support and embrace these groups, recognizing the value of inclusivity of the family unit.

Training

It is critical that officer wellness and resilience training starts in the academy and receives regular and frequent reinforcement throughout an officer's career. Many departments provide basic stress management training in the academy and inconsistently through in-service classes, time and priority permitted. Limited training hours, staffing, competing state mandated priorities such as emergency vehicle operations, firearms, first aid, and defensive tactics often eliminate additional training time for meaningful and necessary training in stress management and resilience building.

Often, training is an immediate response to a catastrophic event such as an officer suicide, line of duty death, or significant traumatic incident, which impacts department members and causes leaders to react by mandating crisis response training. When training is reactive, in response to tragedy, its delivery is not often well thought out, and it does not necessarily bring in the most qualified instructors who know the culture of the organization and speak the wellness language. Reactive training is usually perceived as boilerplate, impersonal, and merely a band aid.

Fortunately, several models and programs have been vetted and tested. These are available in a "train the trainer" style, which can be easily adapted for the needs of a given agency. One such model, *Emotional Survival* (Gilmartin, 2002) is relatable to officers because it was created by a practitioner in both psychology and law enforcement. Departments can modify and present this model to their officers or consider having the author, Kevin Gilmartin, Ph.D., address officers, either in person or via his video series. The *Emotional Survival* book is accessible, affordable and a quick read. Many departments provide the book to all recruits and use *Emotional Survival* as a starting point to discuss how the occupation changes officers and how they can protect their emotional and mental health. Many also recommend it to family members for a better understanding of how the job will likely impact their officer.

San Diego police department

The San Diego Police Department begins wellness programming for recruits during their orientation prior to their academy. They are provided a brief overview of department resources; a brochure containing descriptions and contact information for each provider and granted immediate and direct access for themselves and family members living in their household. At the mid-point of the academy, recruits attend the first of two classes introducing the *Emotional Survival* model (Gilmartin, 2002). Their final class is offered closer to the end of the academy and introduces the concept of "hypervigilance" as a perceptual set, the associated physiological impact, and tendencies toward cynicism and the impact on the family and friends. The second class occurs just prior to academy graduation and assignment into the field where the new officers will be under the supervision and close scrutiny of a training officer.

Out of necessity, training received in the academy and during new officers' field phase training is often disproportionately focused on officer safety, sometimes to the detriment of important interpersonal skills. Some new officers have little life experience and have never been physically attacked nor ever fired a gun, let alone considered the possibility of ending a life. The sad truth is that an officer's next interaction could potentially be with a person who values his own freedom more than the officer's life. The limited duration of training and the necessity to teach and test for effective officer safety utilizing appropriate defensive tactics and force options, tends to condition recruits toward a worst-case scenario mindset. After the academy their field training officers tend to focus on the trainee's ability to make quick decisions and to take immediate action while optimally maintaining officer safety. This disproportionate focus is often at the expense of rapport building and other highly desired social skills, which the new officer demonstrated during the hiring process.

To reinforce and reintegrate social skills compromised through necessary worst-case scenario training, the San Diego Police Department collaborated with psychologist Daniel M. Blumberg, Ph.D. to develop training for the new officers. This training is scheduled immediately following field training and just prior to the officers being certified to work on their own. It strongly reinforces a de-escalation mindset and allows the officers to integrate their own personality into the way they police. The two-day training, entitled *Effective Interactions*, is built on the theory of emotional intelligence and integrates psychological job dimensions for police officers.

Training focuses on the application of techniques to enhance officers' emotional regulation and emotional competence in their interactions with the public as well as with fellow officers, superiors, and all members of the Department. The course emphasizes how officer safety is enhanced when these techniques are mastered. Following brief explanations and didactic modeling of each primary skill, officers practice target skills through class exercises and role-playing scenarios. The class also includes a component that includes community members, allowing for shared learning and relationship building. Each skill builds on the previous skill and provides officers with a clear understanding of how they are fundamentally responsible for making each and every interpersonal interaction more effective (Creighton & Blumberg, 2016, p. 23).

The class also includes case studies about officers from their own department, about whom they may be familiar. The new officers hear examples of officers who were ineffective at coping with job stress or personal issues. The examples highlight career ending illegal substance abuse and officers who were criminally charged with domestic violence, sexual assault, and driving under the influence of alcohol. These case studies promote discussion about what can happen when officers are unable to navigate the stressful challenges of the job and are not proactive in maintaining self-care or reaching out early for some help.

Closing thoughts

Like other life-saving skills training, stress management and resilience building skills should be viewed as perishable. Unless reinforced and practiced at regular intervals, an organizational culture of wellness is not sustainable. Fortunately, most states mandate update training every two years where line officers and supervisors can focus exclusively on training. It is absolutely essential for officers' wellbeing for this training to include an instructional block that addresses current barriers to officer wellness. Resilience tools and specific skill-building techniques should be provided.

Officers in the State of California are required to attend 24 hours of continuing professional training, every two years. "Advanced Officer Training," as it is referred to by the San Diego Police Department, was extended by the Department to 40 hours so that important organizational issues could be addressed and reinforced with all officers and sergeants. Starting in 2009 wellness and resilience building classes were added to the week-long training. Initially wellness classes were heavily focused on resource familiarization and access. After the first two-year cycle, the class hours increased from two to four, allowing for class discussion on a variety of important issues. Over the years, the following topics have been included based on current events and trends in the Department: ineffective coping (substance abuse, gambling, overspending, excessive exercise), police suicide, cognitive biases such as catastrophic thinking, "Emotional Survival," emotional hijacking, burnout and compassion fatigue, sleep hygiene, post-traumatic stress, and a variety of others intended to educate officers and promote wellness and resilience building. Classes are co-facilitated by peer officers and psychologists. They consist predominantly of discussions about current wellness obstacles, which are trends in the department and within the occupation. They also focus on training and practicing resilience strategies. These classes reinforce language and concepts introduced during the academy using the *Emotional Survival* model (Gilmartin, 2002) and other concepts previously introduced during in-service training.

Additional optional training opportunities are offered by the Department and through the County Wellness Group and have included many guest speakers and experts within the law enforcement wellness community. Topics include: police suicide, nutrition, money management, home and work balance, mindfulness, shift work and sleep habits, and physical fitness. Because San Diego has a robust county wellness group, all county agencies attend when speakers are brought in and any costs can be shared. Frequently churches offer their sanctuary as a venue at no cost, allowing for maximum attendance. This county partnership allows for shared responsibility in training and for the opportunity to share resources. In the end, beyond the responsibility of police executives to foster a culture of wellness, it is up to members of the whole community to support efforts at promoting police officer wellness.

References

Creighton, S., & Blumberg, D. M. (2016). Officer wellness is fundamental to officer safety: The san Diego model. In *Police Executive Research Forum, Critical issues in policing series: Guiding principles in use of force* (pp. 23–24). Washington D.C: Police Executive Research Forum.

Gilmartin, K. M. (2002). *Emotional survival for law enforcement: A guide for officers and their families.* E-S Press.

12

The role of compassion satisfaction

Detective Beth Milliard
YORK REGIONAL POLICE, AURORA, ON, CANADA

Introduction

There are many different reasons why people choose the policing profession. Some people are considered Type "A" personalities and therefore adjust well to the command and control structure of a paramilitary organization. Others are considered adrenaline junkies and enjoy the rush of high risk situations and the thrill of high speed chases, foot pursuits and executing search warrants. However, when speaking with officers at a police service in Ontario, Canada, the majority of people said that they joined the profession because of their desire and passion to help others. In this chapter, risk factors such as compassion fatigue and burnout will be discussed and how they have the potential to affect the lives of police officers. Also, the term compassion satisfaction will be explored as well as strategies police officers can utilize to enhance their compassion satisfaction which is important in a profession that is exposed to a lot of negativity.

Police officers risk their lives every day in order to protect the community they serve. As people are running away from threatening situations, police officers are running toward these situations in an effort to stop the threat. In addition, they are dispatched to a variety of calls for service and are expected to portray many different roles. This includes being direct, authoritative and commanding in one instance and then being compassionate, consoling and empathetic in the next. It is also important to mention that the context of policing today is very different with social media and other technological advances. In other words, police officers are not just exposed to traumatic incidents but they are also faced with a variety of stressors, which if left unresolved, have the potential to affect one's mental health.

These role dichotomies and the consistent responsibility of dealing with human suffering and negative situations make police officers vulnerable to suffer from burnout and/or compassion fatigue. Collins and Long (2003) "speculated that compassion satisfaction may fuel people's will to work and protect against compassion fatigue and burnout" (as cited by Thompson, Amatea, & Thompson, 2014, p. 61). The opposite of compassion satisfaction is compassion fatigue. Compassion fatigue is recognized as an indirect, secondary form of trauma exposure that can lead to post-traumatic stress disorder, work dissatisfaction, depression, burnout, self-criticism and destructive coping strategies (Radey & Figley, 2007; Cicognani, Pietrantoni, Palestini, & Prati, 2009 as cited by; Tuttle, Stancel, Russo, Koskelainen, & Papazoglou, 2019).

The majority of the studies to date focus on the prevalence of compassion fatigue and burnout among the policing community with very few studies related to police officers and compassion satisfaction (e.g., Grant, Lavery, & Decarlo, 2019; Papazoglou & Chopko, 2017; Turgoose, Glover, Barker, & Maddox, 2017). Most research on compassion satisfaction has looked at nurses, doctors, and other professionals who work with vulnerable populations such as children and the elderly (e.g., Bae et al., 2019). Therefore, it is prudent to look to studies among other professions and the few studies that have been conducted among police officers to explore the importance of educating police officers on the effects of burnout and compassion fatigue, as well as the positive aspect of helping others, which can result in compassion satisfaction. At the same time, police organizations should be exploring the role of self-transcendent emotions and how it is through these emotions that police officers can remain resilient and healthy throughout their policing career.

Effects of good and bad stress

There are many studies that speak to the stress associated with police work (e.g., Andersen, Papazoglou, Nyman, Koskelainen, & Gustafsberg, 2015; Griffiths, Murphy, & Tatz, 2015; Karaffa et al., 2015). This includes everything from life and death situations to the cumulative stress that builds up over the years. The Working Mind First Responders (TWMFRs), which was originally termed Road to Mental Readiness (R2MR) was developed for the Canadian Military and then tailored for first responder audiences, compares reactive stress and cumulative stress by using the analogy of a car (The Working Mind First Responders, 2019). Reactive stress is similar to quickly slamming on the brakes, whereas cumulative stress is the damage caused over time by routinely hitting the brakes. Both reactive and cumulative types of stress are not good, however, there are protective and preventative factors that one can implement to decrease the wear and tear of stress.

Stressors in policing are complex and are not created solely from the nature of the job. Types of stress in policing can be classified as organizational, operational and personal. Organizational stressors are anything where decisions are made at a high level that can have a negative effect on the officer. In the world of policing this can be seen as inflexible supervisors, not getting a promotion or job position, budget cuts, lack of communication, little to no training opportunities, unplanned transfer, lack of support from supervisors or co-workers, harassment, bullying and other bureaucratic decisions.

Operational stressors are stressors that are inherent in the job. These include: high level of risk and low level of control; shift work; overtime; staffing issues; organizational policies and procedures; social media; making life or death decisions in a spit second; discretion; levels of oversight; moral injury and the effects of not being able to help others.

Personal stressors are numerous. Some of these stressors reported by police officers include family dynamics (sandwich generation, two working parents, and issues with children), financial strains, physical health issues, and one's regular commute. Coupled with the organizational and operational stressors, which can result in missing important time and significant events and holidays with family, these personal stressors also contribute to high levels of stress among police officers.

Let's face it, what police officers hear, see and do on a daily basis is unfathomable for most. However, having some type of stress (optimal stress) is also important. Craig and Sprang (2010) explain, "optimal stress, which can produce exhilaration, high motivation, mental alertness, high energy, and sharp perceptions is the ideal, however, too often the levels of stress become excessive and threaten to overwhelm the professional's self-efficacy" (p. 322). This optimal or good stress is the type of stress that police officers strive for in order to do their job well. In other words, optimal stress is that heightened awareness to be able to respond to high risk calls in a proficient and safe way. The concept of an optimal amount of stress arose from the Yerkes Dodson Law (1908) that indicates that increasing stress is beneficial to performance until some optimum level is reached, after which performance will decline. This optimal level or good stress is also described as eustress, which is a term coined by Hens Selye in 1936. In short, eustress is determined by one's perception. What might be stressful for someone may not be stressful for someone else. Think of professional athletes who thrive in competitions; for them, this is the eustress or that perceived stress that allows them to perform at their optimum levels. Importantly, there are techniques that police officers can learn to manage their internal levels of distress and maximize the experience of eustress.

Burnout

In some instances there is confusion when it comes to burnout and compassion fatigue. The words are sometimes interchanged and used in the same context. Although both represent an overall exhaustion, they have well-defined meanings. Thompson et al. (2014) explain that "burnout is defined as a psychological syndrome that develops in response to chronic emotional and interpersonal stress and is characterized by three features: emotional exhaustion; depersonalization (a defense mechanism for caregivers and service providers to gain emotional distance from clients); and feelings of ineffectiveness or lack of personal accomplishment" (p. 58). Further, strong contributors of burnout in policing can be described as the mental fatigue police officers experience from job responsibilities and other factors, such as organizational dysfunction (Maslach, 2003, p. 189).

The concept of burnout then not only encompasses the emotional exhaustion of helping others but it also includes other stressors that are in police officers' lives. Again, it is important to distinguish that there are different stressors for everyone and not everyone is affected by the same stress. For example, when looking at stressors faced by a police officer, most outsiders would infer it is because of what they see on a daily basis and whom they deal with. However, stress in policing is more than just traumatic events. Stress can include operational, organizational, personal and/or a combination of one or more.

Another area that should not be ignored when looking at burnout is the effects of moral injury. The term moral injury originated in the military but is now being used and even seen as more of a stressor than operational stress injuries. Litz et al. (2009) explain moral injury as "the impact of perpetrating, failing to prevent, or bearing witness to acts that transgress deeply held moral beliefs and expectations and violate assumptions and beliefs about right and wrong and personal goodness" (p. 697, 698). Symptoms of moral injury with police officers after specific events (officer involved shootings) have resulted in officers feeling shame and guilt for their actions.

What is compassion fatigue?

In order to understand compassion fatigue, it is prudent to first define compassion. Stellar et al. (2017), explains that "compassion is a feeling of concern for another's suffering accompanied by the motivation to help and is experienced toward a variety of targets ranging from others who suffer emotionally to those in immediate danger" (p. 202). Compassion is different from empathy as empathy is the ability to understand what someone is going through by being able to put yourself in someone's shoes. The main difference between the two is how they affect one's overall well-being. Empathy has the potential to lead to burnout as one feels the pain of another where compassion is feeling the pain of another but, in a position where they can help.

According to Burnett and Wahl (2015), compassion fatigue was "first identified by Joinson (1992) among nurses who exhibited feelings of anger and helplessness or turned off their own emotions in response to watching their patients suffering from major illnesses or trauma" (p. 318). As the role of a police officer has changed over time to more of a helper role as opposed to strictly being a crime fighter the chances of getting compassion fatigue increases. Police officers are now being trained to spend more time listening to their victims and establishing a rapport instead of just getting the facts. These responsibilities now require officers to be more engaged in their investigations, which contributes to compassion fatigue or, as Figley (1995) described it, the "cost of caring." This comes from dealing with victims of crime and those who have gone through traumatizing and life altering events. One example is my work with sexual assault victims who tell their story. In one case, I remember a victim who was reluctant to speak to a male officer. So, when I volunteered to speak with her privately and she disclosed very intimate and humiliating details, I got shivers down my back. I convinced her to re-tell her story on video but she said she would only do it if I was with her. Through her interview she was physically sick when she talked about certain details and, being a very new officer I had doubts of my role but knew that I had to help her. Looking back now, I became aware of the physical signs of caring and how it took a toll on my emotional and mental state.

The issue with compassion fatigue it that it is typically not explained to police officers at the beginning of their career as something that can happen to them over time. Unfortunately, in most cases, compassion fatigue can result in negative feelings toward the job and subsequently these feelings may result in negative behaviors with co-workers and members of the public. Grant et al. (2019), "demonstrated that new recruits to policing usually enter the profession highly committed with visions of making a difference in the world, however, over time, a cynicism has been shown to set in with many that could be the first signs of compassion fatigue" (p. 2). These signs of compassion fatigue often get dismissed as the officer having a bad attitude or a low performance which can result in a performance improvement plan or even *Police Service Act*[1] charges.

One interesting study regarding Child and Youth service providers of traumatized children and adolescents stated that "risk factors for developing compassion fatigue include: younger age, female gender, greater caseload, higher number of traumatized clients on caseload, personal history of trauma and occupational stress" (De Figueiredo, Yetwin, Sherer, Radzik, & Iverson, 2014, p. 287). Although the data were collected from individuals in Child and Youth Services and the medical profession, the same factors can be applied to those in the policing profession. Throughout their careers, police officers are exposed to many different types of victims, with limited training and education on the effects of these calls.

As an example, police officers are called to horrific situations, traumatic events and scenes where they are dealing with people of all ages, ethnicities and socio-economic status who may have just suffered a loss, been injured, or victimized in a number of different ways. It now may be up to that same officer to have to be responsible for notifying family and/or friends about the incident and the condition of victim. So police officers not only have to hear and live the story first hand with the victim, they may have to re-tell the story, which opens them up for further traumatization. The problem is further exacerbated if the police officer does not have education or training on the effects of these calls and what they can do to alleviate the effects.

Compassion satisfaction

As stated above compassion satisfaction gives police officers the fuel to continue in a profession that is plagued with human suffering. How police officers arrive at feeling compassion satisfaction is different is for every officer and could be felt at many stages during one's career. Usually during the first few years, police officers are preoccupied with just trying to learn the job. It is when they start to become familiar with their role and begin to understand the meaning of their work. For example, ways in which an officer can derive compassion satisfaction is through supporting a victim through a statement, consoling families of deceased loves ones or saving a child from an online pornography ring. It is through these acts of caring and compassion they achieve an adrenaline rush or good feeling knowing that they have made a positive difference in

---

[1]*Police Service Act* - is the law governing the conduct of police officers in the province of Ontario, Canada. In addition to regulating the conduct of police officers, the law also established the Special Investigations Unit, a civilian oversight agency which conducts independent investigations where police actions have resulted in the death or injury of a civilian.

someone's life. Kulkarni, Bell, Hartman, and Herman-Smith (2013) explain that "providing energy, insight, or strengthened resolve for helping and service, compassion satisfaction is most commonly seen in heightened performance, positive attitude toward work, enhanced value, or greater hope for positive outcomes that resonate among successful social workers" (p. 115). Therefore, when looking at the effects of compassion satisfaction, it is also prudent to look at overall job satisfaction. In other words, people tend to thrive in their work environment when they are generally satisfied with their work and the role they play. For example, Brady and King (2018) explain that "understanding the underlying mechanisms of job satisfaction can not only help with officer retention but also boost officer morale and commitment to their profession by reminding them of aspects that bring them satisfaction" (p. 251).

Of course, this is different for everyone as people's motivations for work and work ethic varies. For example, money and promotion may motivate some people, where working in a supportive environment, having a flexible supervisor and being able to contribute in a meaningful may be motivational factors for others. Regardless, it is important to further explore compassion satisfaction in the policing community as a way for officers to deal with negative aspects of policing. According to Miller, Mire, and Kim (2009), "compassion satisfaction can be pivotal in helping law enforcement appreciate the value of their services in their communities" (p. 421). One of the ways this can be fostered in police organizations is consistent feedback from supervisors regarding officer's performance. In most organizations, feedback mostly came in a yearly or bi-yearly performance appraisal. In other words, if there were issues this often catches the officer off guard.

Further, Ahmad, Islam, and Saleem (2019) addressed the retention of employees and how to reduce members from leaving the organization. They found that Human Resource managers and policymakers should "focus on employees' job satisfaction as it negatively relates to leave intention. Particular to the public sector, employees' job satisfaction does not depend upon compensation, but career growth and grooming" (Ahmad et al., 2019, p. 9). They further suggest that one of the ways to retain employees is to provide them with an environment to learn, encourage the sharing of ideas and promote teamwork. These opportunities increase an employee's confidence and allow them to feel valued and to take pride in their work.

In police organizations, job satisfaction was reported in high functioning units or teams (Milliard, 2010). For example, at York Regional Police in Ontario, Canada, the Hold-Up Unit consists of a close-knit group of people who share the same work ethic, drive and ideas. There is also a high level of trust among the group which ultimately helps with their success and overall job satisfaction.

In policing, job satisfaction was described among officers working in the Internet Child Exploitation (ICE) Unit (Milliard, 2010). These individuals are considered hard working, goal driven, passionate and determined to not only saving innocent children but to bring those responsible to justice. Most times officers selected for these Units know what they have signed up for and understand that they will be seeing and hearing heinous details of the worst things being done to children. However, their compassion satisfaction is derived from catching the "worst people in the world and saving children" (Milliard, 2010).

What works?

Kobasa (1979) looked at high level executives who worked in stressful situations. She primarily focused on the hardiness of workers in general when it comes to stress. Hardiness is defined as a personality style that allows individuals to overcome stress in a proactive and constructive way through the use of goal setting and personal values to adjust to a new environment. Fyhn, Fjell, and Johnsen (2016) further explain in their research with police officers that hardiness is the trait whereby one's worldview or self-awareness determines how they will control their own circumstances and stress-related outcomes and that hardy individuals assign meaning to circumstances that for others may be perceived as stressful. For example, officers can allow themselves to express their emotions after a traumatic call and take solace in the fact that they have done their best and that they cannot control the outcome.

In addition to having a hardy personality, police organizations are realizing the benefits of providing training for police officers to learn techniques to help them through stressful situations and to improve their resiliency. For example in TWMFR course listed above there are four strategies to help first responders get through stressful situations which include: goal setting; visualization; positive self-talk; and, tactical breathing.

These strategies that are promoted on the TWMFR course were adopted from the United States Navy Seals training that promotes the "Big Four". In an effort to increase the number of recruits to successfully get through the Navy Sea, Air, and Land Teams (SEALs) training, the creators of the program looked to neuroscience. In other words, Navy SEALs are confronted with life-threatening situations and in order to get through these situations they must learn to manage their fears. It has "been shown that humans can minimize the time before the fear stimulus reaches the frontal cortex so that the decision is more conscious. It basically means that the response from the frontal cortex should be as close as possible to the response from the amygdala" (Vlad, 2015, para. 11). For police officers, this includes understanding the flight, fight and freeze response and knowing that there are automatic physiological symptoms that occur in one's body during high stress situations. During these high stress situations, our brains are hijacked and the ability to make rational decisions is sometimes difficult. However, practicing and applying the "Big Four" can help officers work through these situations.

The first is goal setting. The idea is that when a person is going through a stressful situation, they can calm the amygdala by setting goals and focusing on important things in their lives. Goal setting is also encouraged through the SMART principle – specific, measurable, attainable, realistic and time – bound. The second is visualization. This includes a mental rehearsal of your actions in your mind so when a real situation occurs you will be ready. Visualizing stressful situations in your mind over and over again will help someone when they encounter it for real. The third is self-talk. Positive self-talk can help override signals to the amygdala. Using positive cue words such as, "I am going to win", "I got this", "I will succeed" can help when faced with threatening and stressful situations. The fourth is tactical breathing. The idea is to breathe slowly in an effort to reduce the effects of panic and to promote relaxation. The goal is to use the Big Four in tandem and to practice on a regular basis to be most effective.

In addition to having a hardy personality, looking at the self-transcendent emotions in relation to stress and resiliency can also explain how people can experience greater compassion satisfaction. Self-transcendent emotions are a set of positive emotions that "have the capacity to encourage individuals to transcend their own momentary needs and desires and focus on those of another" (Stellar et al., 2017, p. 201).

The self-transcendent emotions are important because they have the ability to increase one's compassion satisfaction. As police officers, being aware of these emotions is important in a profession that is plagued with negativity, heartbreak and human suffering. Finding opportunities to be able to express self-transcendent emotions is important for the promotion of resiliency in police work, but it is also a reminder that within so much turmoil there are moments when officers can take satisfaction knowing that they have made a difference in someone's life.

Gratitude

One of the ways to encourage self-transcendent emotions in police officers is to first educate officers on their meaning and their importance. For example, gratitude or a "grateful disposition is the tendency to acknowledge the positive values, benefits, and experiences in daily life" (McCanlies, Mnatsakanova, Andrew, Burchfiel, & Violanti, 2014, p. 406). Similarly, gratitude is associated with positive emotions, satisfaction and optimism (McCanlies et al., 2014).

Gratitude can be expressed in many ways. However, police officers should be taught about the importance of gratitude and how it offsets the negative aspects of the policing profession. Some strategies of gratitude can include "checking your complaints at the door." In a lot of situations police officers like to complain about stuff that is really out of their control. This constant complaining fills one with negative feelings and attitudes. These negative feelings and attitudes then are often projected onto others. Instead of dwelling on the negative, police officers should try to focus their energy on what is positive in their life. If there is a specific issue about which the officer is upset, the focus should be on trying to find solutions to solve the issues, rather than just complaining about them.

Another strategy of gratitude is to acknowledge positive moments throughout the day. Officers can write in a journal or on sticky notes to document each, even small, positive moment and how it made them feel. The positive experiences to keep track of can be as minor as a "thank you for your service, officer" or a wave from a child or as significant as a victim crying in an officer's arms. This gratitude ritual serves to train officers to pay attention to the small successes even in the midst of a day filled with lots of strife and tragedy.

Lastly, gratitude can be expressed by recognizing or thanking someone. Although this small act of gratitude tends to be very sparse in most police organizations as we are quick to point out faults or to criticize, focusing one's attention on appreciation is a key strategy to prevent compassion fatigue. For example, officers can tell co-workers and supervisors that they appreciated the assistance or guidance on a particular call. They can tell a witness or a victim that they value and respect their willingness to come forward. And, officers can remember to thank their spouses, children, and loved ones for their support and sacrifice. These small acts of gratitude are inexpensive ways to express positive feelings toward others, which benefit both the officer and the recipient of their gratitude.

Gratitude is often portrayed by police officers who become Peer Support Team members within their organizations. It is through a traumatic event, a life altering incident, or a mental health struggle where these officers use their own experiences to help fellow officers. They learn to view their own struggles through a lens of self-growth and discovery rather than one of self-stigma or career ending. It is a courageous form of gratitude that they want to share their story in an effort to help others. A study by McCanlies et al. (2014) found that individuals who scored high on gratitude scales are also generally satisfied with life, and have greater self-esteem which is an important indicator of how police officers will cope with a traumatic events. In other words, higher levels of gratitude have been found to increase the resiliency of police officers who encounter stressful situations and traumatic incidents.

Appreciation

In addition to gratitude, appreciation is an emotion that can help people see the positive and not focus so much on the negative. Appreciation has been defined as "acknowledging the value and meaning of something—an event, a person, a behavior, an object—and feeling a positive emotional connection to it" (Adler & Fagley, 2005, p. 81). In my own experiences as a police officer, appreciation tends to fade as one goes through their career. Whether it is through cynicism or general dissatisfaction for the job, it is sometimes hard to remember why someone decided to become a police officer. Instead of appreciating the benefits and opportunities of the policing profession, police officers tend to get wrapped up in the political bureaucracy whether this is failing to get promoted, not getting a desired job or the consistent change in organizational process. As a result, police officers forget to appreciate the positive aspects of their job and in some cases end up dwelling on the negative. This negative loop can be broken through support from supervisors, co-workers, family and friends. Being appreciative for what is important in one's life can help one get through all of the adverse experiences that come with being a police officer.

Awe

Being inspired in any position generates positive emotions and overall job satisfaction, which explains the next self-transcendent emotion called awe. Awe can be explained as the overwhelming feeling of wonder and admiration. In some cases, a person does not immediately understand feelings of awe, which can lead to admiration and inspiration. Police officers who experience awe explained the emotion as what one feels when they remember the reason why they became a police officer. In other words, police officers recognize and focus on the higher purpose of their calling and nobility of their profession. Another example of awe is when police officers see the fruits of their labor and know that they are making a difference. This sense of awe can be immediate or come years later through communication from a victim who tells the officer how they changed their life. Knowing this as an officer revitalizes our career decision and builds our compassion satisfaction.

Role of the police organization

In an effort to increase officer retention and maintain officer wellness, police organizations are starting to make mental health a priority. One of these ways is to educate supervisors on the importance of knowing their people. Police supervisors who are trained to recognize signs and symptoms of when officers may be suffering and to provide supports early will assist in fostering an environment to promote compassion satisfaction and prevent compassion fatigue. For example, Andersen and Papazoglou (2015) suggest that teaching police about the importance of compassion satisfaction can help to shield the officer from compassion fatigue and to promote officers resilience.

Policing was originally based on a reactive model. A call came in and the police were dispatched. Through the years, other models of policing were introduced to keep up with changing societies and social needs. The same is true for the training and education of police officers. Typically, police training relied on physical fitness and forms of strength and endurance however, psychological and social supports are just as important. Encouraging officers to be proactive in maintaining their overall health and to put mechanisms in place to encourage their mental and physical health throughout their career is just as important as their physical fitness. Therefore, education on the signs and symptoms of when one's mental health is declining and the importance of social and professional supports is also required.

In addition to educating police supervisors, it is also important for mental health professionals who treat police officers to understand the police culture and the unique stressors faced by police officers. Although the TWMFR course is mandatory in police services in Ontario, topics such as burnout and compassion fatigue are rarely discussed.

Self-awareness

Self-awareness is the general understanding of one's personality, emotions, strengths, weakness, thoughts and beliefs. In the policing profession, it is important to have this self-awareness as an indicator of a sense of empowerment to know where you want to go in life and what you want to succeed. There is internal self-awareness in how you see yourself and external self-awareness in how others see you. Being self-aware is another aspect that can assist officers to achieve a level of compassion satisfaction. For example, in a study by Wagaman, Geiger, Shockley, and Segal (2015) they found that there is a "relationship between self-awareness and compassion satisfaction, and that self-awareness training may help to prevent burnout by increasing compassion satisfaction" (p. 202).

When working with police officers and liaizing with psychologists, the biggest issue that comes up in maintaining good mental health is self-awareness. Unfortunately, the police culture and the old school mentality regarding mental health or reaching out for help is one of the biggest barriers in allowing one to be self-aware. Instead, as police officers we make excuses when we are suffering and in most cases take care of everyone else before we take care of ourselves. Knowing when we are stressed and taking the time for our own self-care is another aspect that should be encouraged during police training as recruits and at many intervals in one's career. Examples on how to achieve self-awareness as police officers include: writing down goals and assessing where you are in your life and where you want to go. Also, seeking out feedback from others regarding your behaviors is important to assess if people see you as you see yourself.

Conclusion

Burnout is more closely related to stressors at work where compassion fatigue has been associated with the amount of time interacting with traumatized clients. Both can be managed and prevented with the appropriate awareness, education, training and self-care. However, everyone has a role to play. Policing is a stressful occupation but at the same time a rewarding one. In order to experience compassion satisfaction, one has to be part of a supportive environment that allows and encourages growth and for police officers to come forward when they are affected by aspects of the job. It also includes a deeper understanding of self and emotions, which are aspects that police officers are not educated about when starting their career. There is research to suggest that emotions such as gratitude, appreciation and awe are positive feelings that lessen stress, make people feel good, and can help increase police officers' resilience. However, similar to the "Big Four," compassion satisfaction needs to be acknowledged and practiced in order to achieve its benefits.

One way is to educate police officers on the importance of their role and how they can positively affect so many lives. It is easy to get lost in the bureaucratic negativity of the police environment; however, police officers need to be reminded of the reason why they became police officers in the first place. Conducting research with investigators in the Internet Child Exploitation Unit, it was clearly evident that one officer who was flourishing and felt compassion satisfaction had the ability to not internalize the work. Although this sounds easy, it comes with years of experience and being self-aware. What was also interesting is that there was also a sense of doubt because he was questioning "why" he was not affected by this type of work and was actually excelling. In a sense, he almost felt guilty for doing so well. He needed to understand that yes, some officers may be affected by certain types of police work but, others may not and this is OK. So making officers aware that it is fine to achieve this level of compassion satisfaction, in the face of human suffering, is normal.

When asked about compassion satisfaction in one of my courses, a student and serving police officer wrote:

> Compassion satisfaction is the pleasure and benefit you experience while on the job. As a first responder, there are several emotions that are encountered throughout any given shift due to the nature of the work. These emotions range from the negative to the positive and in no particular order as it depends on the type of calls that you attend to. As a first responder, there is no greater or more positive experience or emotion than that of helping another in need and to see the benefit of your actions to reach that result (M. Wise, personal communication, March 16, 2019).

As a serving police officer, educator and student, I was unfamiliar with compassion satisfaction but clearly knew about burnout and compassion fatigue. It was not until my role in the Peer Support Unit that I fully understood and embraced compassion satisfaction. It was through mandatory mental health training where police officers would come up to me after class and explained they were not doing well. Being able to peer support them, provide them with resources for getting help and later learning that these simple steps prevented them from going off work and actually enjoying their job again was very rewarding. For me compassion satisfaction was the joy of being able to look after the well-being of our officers and their families. Knowing that I have had a part in assisting police officers (in my organization and other police services) to remain healthy at work at the same time assisting those to recover and return to work from a mental or physical injury has been the greatest reward of my career.

References

Adler, M. G., & Fagley, N. S. (2005). Appreciation: Individual differences in finding value and meaning as a unique predictor of subjective well-being. *Journal of Personality, 73*(1), 79–114. https://doi.org/10.1111/j.1467-6494.2004.00305.x.

Ahmad, R., Islam, T., & Saleem, S. (2019). How commitment and satisfaction explain leave intention in police force? *Policing: An International Journal, 42*(2), 195–208. https://doi.org/10.1108/PIJPSM-12-2017-0154.

Andersen, J. P., & Papazoglou, K. (2015). Compassion fatigue and compassion satisfaction among police officers: An understudied topic. *International Journal of Emergency Mental Health and Human Resilience, 17*(3), 661–663. https://doi.org/10.4172/1522-4821.1000259.

Andersen, J. P., Papazoglou, K., Nyman, M., Koskelainen, M., & Gustafsberg, H. (2015). Fostering resilience among the police. *Journal of Law Enforcement, 5*(1). Retrieved from http://jghcs.info/index.php/l/article/view/424.

Bae, J., Jennings, P. F., Hardeman, C. P., Kim, E., Lee, M., Littleton, T., et al. (2019). Compassion satisfaction among social work practitioners: The role of work−life balance. *Journal of Social Service Research*, 1−11. https://doi.org/10.1080/01488376.2019.1566195.

Brady, P. Q., & King, W. R. (2018). Brass satisfaction: Identifying the personal and work-related factors associated with job satisfaction among police chiefs. *Police Quarterly, 21*(2), 250−277. https://doi.org/10.1177/1098611118759475.

Burnett, H. J., & Wahl, K. (2015). The compassion fatigue and resilience connection: A survey of resilience, compassion fatigue, burnout, and compassion satisfaction among trauma responders. *International Journal of Emergency Mental Health*. Faculty Publications. 5. https://digitalcommons.andrews.edu/pubs/5

Cicognani, E., Pietrantoni, L., Palestini, L., & Prati, G. (2009). Emergency Workers' Quality of Life: The Protective Role of Sense of Community, Efficacy Beliefs and Coping Strategies. *Social Indicators Research, 94*(3), 449−463. https://doi-org.ezp.waldenulibrary.org/10.1007/s11205-009-9441-x.

Collins, S., & Long, A. (2003). Too tired to care? The psychological effects of working with trauma. *Journal of Psychiatric and Mental Health Nursing, 10*(1), 17−27. https://doi.org/10.1046/j.1365-2850.2003.00526.x.

Craig, C. D., & Sprang, G. (2010). Compassion satisfaction, compassion fatigue, and burnout in a national sample of trauma treatment therapists. *Anxiety, Stress and Coping, 23*(3), 319−339. https://doi.org/10.1080/10615800903085818.

De Figueiredo, S., Yetwin, A., Sherer, S., Radzik, M., & Iverson, E. (2014). A cross-disciplinary comparison of perceptions of compassion fatigue and satisfaction among service providers of highly traumatized children and adolescents. *Traumatology, 20*(4), 286−295. https://doi.org/10.1037/h0099833.

Figley, C. R. (1995). Compassion fatigue: Toward a new understanding of the costs of caring. In B. H. Stamm (Ed.), *Secondary traumatic stress. Self-care issues for clinicians, researchers and educators* (pp. 3−28). Baltimore, MD: The Sidran Press.

Fyhn, T., Fjell, K. K., & Johnsen, B. H. (2016). Resilience factors among police investigators: Hardiness-commitment a unique contributor. *Journal of Police and Criminal Psychology, 31*(4), 261−269. https://doi.org/10.1007/s11896-015-9181-6.

Grant, H. B., Lavery, C. F., & Decarlo, J. (2019). An exploratory study of police officers: Low compassion satisfaction and compassion fatigue. *Frontiers in Psychology, 9*, 2793. https://doi.org/10.3389/fpsyg.2018.02793.

Griffiths, C. T., Murphy, J. J., & Tatz, M. (2015). *Improving police efficiency challenges and opportunities*. Ottawa, ON. Retrieved from https://www.publicsafety.gc.ca/cnt/rsrcs/pblctns/2015-r021/2015-r021-en.pdf.

Joinson, C. (1992). Coping with compassion fatigue. *Nursing, 22*(4), 116−121. https://doi.org/10.1097/00152193-199204000-00035.

Karaffa, K., Openshaw, L., Koch, J., Clark, H., Harr, C., & Stewart, C. (2015). Perceived impact of police work on marital relationships. *The Family Journal, 23*(2), 120−131. https://doi.org/10.1177/1066480714564381.

Kobasa, S. C. (1979). Stressful life events, personality, and health: An inquiry into hardiness. *Journal of Personality and Social Psychology, 37*(1), 1−11. https://doi.org/10.1037/0022-3514.37.1.1.

Kulkarni, S., Bell, H., Hartman, J. L., & Herman-Smith, R. L. (2013). Exploring individual and organizational factors contributing to compassion satisfaction, secondary traumatic stress, and burnout in domestic violence service providers. *Journal of the Society for Social Work and Research, 4*(2), 114−130. https://doi.org/10.5243/jsswr.2013.8.

Litz, B. T., Stein, N., Delaney, E., Lebowitz, L., Nash, W. P., Silva, C., & Maguen, S. (2009). Moral injury and moral repair in war veterans: A preliminary model and intervention strategy. *Clinical Psychology Review, 29*(8), 695−706. https://doi-org.ezp.waldenulibrary.org/10.1016/j.cpr.2009.07.003.

Maslach, C. (2003). Job burnout: New directions in research and intervention. *Current Directions in Psychological Science, 12*(5), 189–192. https://doi.org/10.1111/1467-8721.01258.

McCanlies, E. C., Mnatsakanova, A., Andrew, M. E., Burchfiel, C. M., & Violanti, J. M. (2014). Positive psychological factors are associated with lower PTSD symptoms among police officers: Post hurricane Katrina. *Stress and Health, 30*(5), 405–415. https://doi.org/10.1002/smi.2615.

Miller, H. A., Mire, S., & Kim, B. (2009). Predictors of job satisfaction among police officers: Does personality matter? *Journal of Criminal Justice, 37*(5), 419–426. https://doi.org/10.1016/j.jcrimjus.2009.07.001.

Milliard, B. (2010). *Project S.A.F.E.T.Y. A leadership strategy for promoting the psychological well-Being of police officers* (Unpublished master's thesis). Ontario, Canada: University of Guelph.

Papazoglou, K., & Chopko, B. (2017). The role of moral suffering (moral distress and moral injury) in police compassion fatigue and PTSD: An unexplored topic. *Frontiers in Psychology, 8.* https://doi.org/10.3389/fpsyg.2017.01999.

Radey, M., & Figley, C. R. (2007). The social psychology of compassion. *Clinical Social Work Journal, 35*(3), 207–214. https://doi.org/10.1007/s10615-007-0087-3.

Stellar, J. E., Gordon, A. M., Piff, P. K., Cordaro, D., Anderson, C. L., Bai, Y., et al. (2017). Self-transcendent emotions and their social functions: Compassion, gratitude, and awe bind us to others through prosociality. *Emotion Review, 9*(3), 200–207. https://doi.org/10.1177/1754073916684557.

The Working Mind First Responders. (2019). Retrieved from https://www.mentalhealthcommission.ca/English/working-mind-first-responders.

Thompson, I., Amatea, E., & Thompson, E. (2014). Personal and contextual predictors of mental health counselors' compassion fatigue and burnout. *Journal of Mental Health Counseling, 36*(1), 58–77. https://doi.org/10.17744/mehc.36.1.p61m73373m4617r3.

Turgoose, D., Glover, N., Barker, C., & Maddox, L. (2017). Empathy, compassion fatigue, and burnout in police officers working with rape victims. *Traumatology, 23*(2), 205–213. https://doi.org/10.1037/trm0000118.

Tuttle, B. M., Stancel, K., Russo, C., Koskelainen, M., & Papazoglou, K. (2019). Police moral injury, compassion fatigue, and compassion satisfaction: A brief report. *Salus Journal, 42*(1), 42–57. Retrieved from http://www.salusjournal.com/wp-content/uploads/sites/29/2019/04/Tuttle_Salus_Journal_Volume_7_Number_1_2019_pp_42-57.pdf.

Vlad, C. (2015). *US Navy SEALs conquer fear using four simple steps.* Retrieved from https://qz.com/450517/us-navy-seals-conquer-fear-using-four-simple-steps/.

Wagaman, M. A., Geiger, J. M., Shockley, C., & Segal, E. A. (2015). The role of empathy in burnout, compassion satisfaction, and secondary traumatic stress among social workers. *Social Work, 60*(3), 201–209. https://doi.org/10.1093/sw/swv014.

13

Community Relations & Community-Oriented Policing

POLICE TRAINING INSTITUTE OF THE STATE OF ILLINOIS, CHAMPAIGN, IL, UNITED STATES

Introduction

I have been in the field of law enforcement for 35 years. In my career, I have spent 20 years as a police officer and 15 years as an academy instructor, director, and researcher. During my time as a police officer, I considered myself to be a community policing officer. This was not a title or designation suggested by my department. This was based on my personal ideology of what a police officer should do. However, although I use the job title "police officer" throughout this chapter, I feel a better moniker is "peace officer." Like the majority of officers coming into the field of law enforcement, I felt my job was to protect those that cannot protect themselves, help those that cannot help themselves, and become a part of the community.

During this time, I was mostly referred to by community members as "Officer Mike." Hence, throughout this chapter I will share personal experiences as Officer Mike. For the past 15 years, I have taught new academy recruits about community policing, presented on the topic of community policing, and researched community policing. I briefly discuss community policing initiatives and philosophies globally; however, because of my efforts and studies, the focus of this chapter is on community policing in the United States.

What is community policing?

Community safety and quality of life cannot be the responsibility of the police alone. It is necessary for law-abiding citizens to take some responsibility for their neighborhoods and communities. Therefore, the police need the citizens they serve to participate in the police process and police need to participate in the citizen process. Such a partnership between law enforcement and the community allows for broader solutions to neighborhood issues that arise rather than the police having a narrow focus on simply enforcing the law. An important aspect of community policing is to first understand it is a philosophy rather than a set of specific activities, meetings, or programs. According to the Office of Community Oriented Policing Services (2003), "Community policing is a

Power. https://doi.org/10.1016/B978-0-12-817872-0.00013-6

219

philosophy that promotes organizational strategies that support the systematic use of partnerships and problem-solving techniques to proactively address the immediate conditions that give rise to public safety issues such as crime, social disorder, and fear of crime" (p. 2). The three key components of community policing are organizational transformation, community partnerships, and problem solving (Lawrence & McCarthy, 2013). Although community policing must be accepted as a philosophy, it could not be successful without concrete initiatives and activities.

Organizational transformation means that a police agency's structures, policies, and practices can promote community policing. For example, officers must be assigned to specific areas or beats to ensure they develop relationships with the community and better understand local issues (Lawrence & McCarthy, 2013). Community partnerships include any combination of residents, schools, churches, businesses, community-based organizations, elected officials, government agencies, and so on in a neighborhood who work cooperatively with the police to resolve the problems that impact or interest them. Problem solving involves the police and community sharing ideas and brainstorming on how to tackle local issues and concerns.

So how do the police become proactive in building these imperative partnerships? First, the department needs to use critical thinking to identify partners within their community. The more partners, the better. Anyone can be a partner. It is important to brainstorm and be creative to identify and find partners as well as understand the makeup of the community based on the community profile (e.g., population, income levels, educational levels, ethnic make-up, unemployment rates, and crime statistics). After identifying potential partners, the police must initiate dialogue and begin organizing community meetings. The initiation of dialogue means more than just having a conversation; it means asking questions, explaining what you are doing and why you are doing it, and, most importantly, listening to others. Neighborhood meetings must be planned and well organized to simplify and ensure good attendance. To host a user-friendly meeting, choose the location carefully and provide the proper equipment to create a positive police presence. Facilitating discussion and listening are imperative in these collaborations. At these meetings, the issues within the community must be identified and recognized by everyone as true concerns. Together, the community and police can then formulate a plan and decide what actions to take. However, it does not end with the list of actions: identify those you can do something about and those you cannot. Formulating a plan means setting objectives, getting volunteers to step forward, and formalizing the plan itself. Taking action (implementing your plan) is the most important step. It is important to find out if we are getting results together. There must be a way to evaluate and assess any progress or lack thereof in solving the identified issues. If progress is being made, then it is extremely important to monitor and maintain this progress. Conversely, if there is no progress, or not enough, it is important to re-evaluate and try new ways to attack the issues. Therefore, it is important to maintain and sustain the partnership.

Beyond individual citizens collaborating with the police, participation in community policing must also involve groups within the community. For example, communities must consider how governments, schools, businesses, churches, social service agencies, and other community organizations can work with law enforcement and with each other to create a safe community and solve crime- and non-crime-related issues within a neighborhood or the larger community by creating community partnerships. Specific crimes may be prevalent in the community or a specific neighborhood or non-crime-related issues may need to be addressed.

However, community policing must go beyond crime reduction and crime prevention. It must also involve helping improve and/or sustain quality of life. While physical safety and crime reduction/prevention are naturally important factors in improving quality of life, it also considers living conditions, productive activities, health, education, leisure and social interactions, economic well-being, governance and basic rights, the natural and living environment, and overall life experience (Eurostat, n. d.). Community members and organizations must be empowered. All ideas and strategies must be considered and everyone must be given a voice.

Once the issues and concerns are uncovered, solutions must be proposed. An early trendsetter was Henry Goldstein, whose theory of problem-oriented policing argued that community policing called for "analysis, study, and evaluation" to ensure and sustain positive outcomes (Goldstein, 2003, p. 14). This is a commonsensical approach to assisting both law enforcement officers and the community they serve. One problem-solving method that has evolved from Goldstein's theory is the SARA model, which is an acronym for Scanning, Analysis, Response, and Assessment (Office of Community Oriented Policing Services, 2003). Scanning involves recognizing and prioritizing community issues, problems, and concerns; Analysis involves researching the details of the problem; Response involves developing solutions to eliminate or at least reduce the problem; and Assessment involves evaluating the success of the response (Office of Community Oriented Policing Services, 2003). The reviews of numerous studies show mixed findings on the effectiveness of problem-oriented policing; however, there are well-documented cases of success (Goldstein, 1990; Reisig, 2010).

One of the most important and proactive community policing efforts remains the day-to-day patrol, or *daily community policing*, which can be summarized in two sentences: (1) police officers need more non-enforcement contacts and (2) they must get to know citizens on a personal level and let citizens get to know them on a personal level. An important benefit of successful community policing is its effect on the public's perception of police officers. These positive interactions and collaborations raise the sense of police legitimacy, as citizens are more likely to be satisfied with and trust the police (Gill, Weisburd, Telep, Vitter, & Bennett, 2014).

Officer Mike Anecdote

Whenever I was on patrol, as well as during my off-duty time, I got to know the people in the community I policed. I got to know them on a personal level and they got to know me on a personal level by removing myself from my squad car. I got to know their families,

I got to know their personalities, I got to know their interests, I got to know their views on life, I got to know their concerns, I got to know their hobbies, I got to know their views on local, global, and national issues, I got to know their favorite sports teams, I got to know and understand their concerns with the police, and I got to know so much more. However, the getting to know was reciprocal. They got to know me in the same ways. This is how I gained their trust. Someone would often call the department with a problem and say, "I only want to talk to Officer Mike." This was a great feeling, and such trust allowed me to help the citizens of my community in many ways. Such daily community policing, if practiced by the entire department, raises the trust and legitimacy of the policing profession.

Sir Robert Peel

Although most argue that the community policing era in the United States began in the 1970s, Sir Robert Peel's beliefs on law enforcement 190 years ago coincide with the ideology of community policing. Sir Robert was responsible for leading the Metropolitan Police Force in London, England, in 1829. He understood the importance of an ethical and legitimate police force and recognized that the police need to be part of and work with the public, not against it. His nine principles of policing are as follows (Nazemi, 2009):

1. To prevent crime and disorder, as an alternative to their repression through military force and severity of legal punishment.
2. To recognize always that the power of the police to fulfill their functions and duties is dependent on public approval of their existence, actions, and behavior, as well as on their ability to secure and maintain public respect.
3. To recognize always that to secure and maintain the respect and approval of the public also means securing the willing cooperation of the public in the task of securing the observance of laws.
4. To recognize always that the extent to which the cooperation of the public can be secured diminishes proportionately to the necessity of the use of physical force and compulsion for achieving police objectives.
5. To seek and preserve public favor, not by pandering to public opinion, but by constantly demonstrating absolutely impartial service to law, in complete independence of policy, and without regard to the justice or injustice of the substance of individual laws, by ready offering of individual service and friendship to all members of the public without regard to their wealth or social standing, by ready exercise of courtesy and friendly good humor, and by ready offering of individual sacrifice in protecting and preserving life.
6. To use physical force only when the exercise of persuasion, advice, and warning is found insufficient to obtain public cooperation to the extent necessary to secure observance of law or to restore order, and to use only the minimum degree of physical force which is necessary on any particular occasion for achieving a police objective.

7. To maintain at all times a relationship with the public that gives reality to the historic tradition that the police are the public and that the public are the police, the police being only members of the public who are paid to give full-time attention to duties which are incumbent on every citizen in the interests of community welfare and survival.

8. To recognize always the need for strict adherence to police-executive functions, and to refrain from ever even seeming to usurp the powers of the judiciary to avenge individuals or the State, and to authoritatively judge guilt and punish the guilty.

9. To recognize always that the test of police efficiency is the absence of crime and disorder, not the visible evidence of police action in dealing with them.

Police Executive Research Forum report

In 2015, the Police Executive Research Forum gathered 150 participants including police chiefs and community members for a one-day brainstorming effort to improve police–community relations and build trust. The police chiefs were asked to bring along one community leader from their community to participate. These community leaders had to be respected in the community but not necessarily pro-police. Although several ideas and suggestions were discussed, the following 18 suggestions and insights from the selected police chiefs and community leaders were deemed to be necessary to ensure effective community–police partnerships (Police Executive Research Forum, 2016, pp. 5–8):

1. Don't be afraid to apologize
2. Create and enforce a duty to intervene
3. Be open to hearing people's negative experiences with the police
4. Understand the roots of mistrust
5. Reach out to local business owners who know their customers
6. Encourage officers to mentor youths
7. Encourage officers to volunteer in the community
8. Measure officers' performance in building relationships
9. Police must acknowledge that mistrust is legitimate
10. Strive for diversity in police-community panels
11. Work for mutual respect
12. Police should approach community members, not wait to be approached
13. Tear down stereotypes by engaging with youths
14. Take action immediately when you see that something is wrong
15. Acknowledge mistakes
16. Include community members in recruiting and hiring
17. Reach out to each other during non-stressful times
18. Recognize that young officers and community leaders face big challenges

The benefits of community policing to the officer

Many stressors can be placed on police officers including political pressure, a lack of time for one's family, a negative public image, low salary (Bano, 2011), organizational stress (Shane, 2010) and of course danger of the job. Several initiatives and efforts aim to manage these various police stressors. However, in this chapter, we focus on how officers participating in community policing have greater job satisfaction and less cynicism as well as tend to be more resilient, more able to rebound from adversity, more motivated, and enhanced work/life balance.

Torres, Reling, and Hawdon (2018) found that community policing has many positive effects on police officers. Officers show increased job motivation, decreased cynicism, and lower apprehension (Torres et al., 2018). Additionally, they showed that the positive outcomes for officers spilled over onto community members as well. Community policing efforts can reduce crime and public fear (Braga, Welsh, & Schnell, 2015) as well as increase citizen satisfaction and help restore police legitimacy in the eyes of the public (Gill et al., 2014). In the same vein, there is little evidence to show that aggressive enforcement strategies significantly reduce crime (Braga et al., 2015). It is simply common sense that the lower the crime level, the fewer instances officers have to interact with criminals, thus lessening the need for officers to use force as well as the likelihood of injury to either the officer or the arrestee. This will therefore reduce the number of risks during criminal encounters for officers, making the job safer. Additionally, when police gain the trust of the citizens they serve and protect, the safety of both the police and citizens rises. When citizens trust the police, they are more likely to comply, even during arrest situations, again increasing both officer and citizen safety.

Officers who reach out and get to know citizens develop strong relationships with them and a better understanding of the local community. These interactions are likely to lead officers to become more culturally competent and have greater respect and empathy for community members. The forming of these relationships and trust instilled helps create a partnership between the community and police to collaborate to solve current or emerging concerns. Further, community policing allows for more discretion, raises the ability to make decisions, and increases officers' control of their work environment (Rohe, Adams, & Arcury, 1997).

The attitudes of police officers toward the community and their sense of accomplishment, and thus job satisfaction, can be influenced by their involvement in community policing (Greene, 1987), and officers who emphasize service to the community demonstrate higher job satisfaction than those who focus on controlling crime through the enforcement of the law (Halsted, Bromley, & Cochran, 2000). This increase in an officer's job satisfaction trickles down to improving morale, as the officer will feel more worth in helping citizens solve community issues. Accordingly, this becomes an important factor in increasing police officers' resilience and overall wellness. The public's image of the police contributes to officers' job satisfaction, too (Yim & Schafer,

2009). If an officer's perceived public image is poor, this may lower his or her job satisfaction (Yim & Schafer, 2009). Officers working for police agencies aggressively implementing community-oriented policing report higher job satisfaction than officers in other agencies (Brody, DeMarco, & Lovrich, 2002). Another example of community policing efforts that contribute to officer wellness is the involvement of School Resource Officers (SROs) with young people. SROs' duties emphasize less law enforcement and more positive engagement young people in the community. Rhodes (2015) found that SROs report higher levels of job satisfaction than those working the streets, partly due to the lower levels of role ambiguity and conflict, which results in better job performance and overall well-being.

Job satisfaction is an important factor in the health of any employee regardless of occupation (Faragher, Cass, & Cooper, 2005) and continued improvements in job satisfaction can prevent people from further health deterioration (Fischer & Sousa-Poza, 2009). In the current context, job satisfaction is associated with improved psychological well-being for police officers (Violanti & Aron, 1993). Indeed, the meta-analysis of around 500 studies of job satisfaction presented by Faragher et al. (2005) found a strong correlation between job satisfaction and both mental and physical health.

In summary, the benefits to police officers infused in community policing are encouraging. And not only are there benefits to the community; officers who immerse themselves in community policing experience greater job satisfaction and less cynicism, and they are more motivated, are safer, and have greater overall well-being, which contributes to their improved resilience. These are just some of the reasons why police agencies should engage in community policing practices.

Officer Mike Anecdote

Getting to know citizens and treating them with respect can be extremely valuable. Throughout my career, I made every effort to treat everyone with respect, even when arresting someone. This came in handy one time during a bar fight. While on patrol, if I saw citizens outside, I would stop and talk to them regardless of their race, class, or criminal history. On one occasion, I noticed a large group of people cooking out and drinking beer in the backyard of a house. As I drove down the ally, I rolled down my window and asked how things were going. I received a few cop jokes and I laughed with them. I recognized most of the group, who were members of a motorcycle gang. They already knew me through various enforcement and non-enforcement encounters, and I often climbed out of my car and chatted. I spent about 45 min simply hanging out and joking with the group, some saying things like, "Hey, Officer Mike, remember the time you arrested me for …" A few nights later, I was dispatched to a fight in a local bar. It was a busy night and although backup was en route, I knew I would arrive first. When I entered the bar, two men were fighting; they did not stop on command. As I was trying to break up the fight, I heard a voice saying, "Officer Mike, want some help?" It was a prominent leader of the motorcycle gang. He grabbed hold of one man while I restrained the other. The leader then yelled at the two men who were fighting and said, "Listen to Officer Mike ... break it up!" The fight was over immediately and both subjects complied as backup entered the bar.

Global initiatives

Similar community policing efforts have been initiated by law enforcement agencies globally. For example, Canada, Sweden, France, Germany, Australia, and the United Kingdom are just a few countries that have developed community policing concepts to help prevent crime as well as gain community trust. Although there is no one agreed-upon definition of community policing, most are wrapped around the idea of preventing crime, creating partnerships within the community, and changing the philosophy of law enforcement agencies from traditional functions to law enforcement to an emphasis on community-oriented policing.

Sweden has created Crime Prevention Councils nationally and invited community groups to meet periodically. Those invited include the local police chief, local politicians, religious organizations, medical services, social service agencies, those within the court system, counselors, those in education, business members, and willing community members (Jones & Wiseman, 2006). Outreach teams visit certain neighborhoods at least twice a month. These teams can consist of any of those groups mentioned in the Crime Prevention Council such as police officers, paramedics or nurses, and counselors (Jones & Wiseman, 2006). This community policing initiative has proven successful in crime reduction and prevention (Jones & Wiseman, 2006).

In Germany, community policing is a philosophy used to solve problems at the local level. In other words, states, towns, and cities can apply the tactics of their choosing to their specific issues (Jones & Wiseman, 2006). Crime prevention is considered to be the duty of society as a whole, not just the police (Jones & Wiseman, 2006). Like other community policing initiatives, in Germany this involves collaborations with social services, housing departments, health care providers, business leaders, schools, and teachers (Jones & Wiseman, 2006) At the national level, Germany has created the Commission on Police-Based Crime Prevention that conducts research and shares with state and local police agencies best practices for specific issues in "how-to" manuals (Jones & Wiseman, 2006).

In 2002, England and Wales began using police community support officers, who are civilian staff that wear uniforms and patrol the streets (BBC News, 2012). The aim is to increase the number of representatives of the police visible to the public to reduce crime and antisocial behavior (BBC News, 2012). These community support officers are granted certain powers and take responsibility for many of the lower-level duties the police normally handle including foot patrol, traffic control, crime prevention advice, guarding crime scenes, and taking care of other minor offenses and community issues (BBC News, 2012).

Positive community policing efforts in the United States

Many police departments are making innovative community policing efforts. A number of agencies have developed positive initiatives that are improving police–community relations. There are too many positive initiatives to discuss in one chapter; however, the following are positive examples.

> *Positive Changes in Camden, New Jersey – Minimize harm and try to save lives.*
> Goldstein (2017).

Camden, New Jersey is a poor community in which 40% of its citizens live below the poverty line and the rates of murder and other crimes are extremely high. However, it is seeing positive effects from interesting community policing ideas. One simple change, which has nonetheless been a paradigm shift in police officer expectations, has involved adopting a philosophy under which writing traffic tickets is no longer a measure of productivity. The department understands that forcing poor individuals to pay high fines for traffic violations only serves to make their lives even more stressful and leads to even more negative outcomes. Officers in Camden are receiving more training in areas such as tactics and de-escalation techniques. For example, when interacting with someone showing signs of mental illness, even if the subject is holding a knife, officers are trained to create a safe distance. Then, rather than yelling out commands, they use de-escalation techniques to avoid the use of deadly force. Further, if deadly force is necessary, officers are instructed to rush the subject to the hospital rather than wait for an ambulance, if an ambulance is delayed.

Camden Video:

In what has become a famous video, Camden officers interacted with a man wielding a knife while walking along a sidewalk. The man did not stop for the police and kept walking away, while swinging the knife around. Rather than use deadly force or make an aggressive response, officers kept a safe distance and surrounded the man. Officers ahead of the man made sure there were no citizens on the path. Eventually, the man dropped the knife, and he was taken into custody with no injuries to the subject or officers.

Officers also go on foot patrol in neighborhoods, knock on doors, and introduce themselves. In 2012, there were 67 homicides, and this dropped significantly to 47 in 2016. Although this community continues to have a high crime rate on average, citizens report feeling safer than before this community policing initiative.

Officer Mike Anecdote

While on patrol, I initiated a traffic stop on a vehicle with a broken taillight, loud muffler, and expired registration. The driver also had no insurance. When I share this story with our recruit officers at the academy, I ask them what citations and warning tickets they would write. Most say they would write the expired registration and no insurance. I then tell the class that I knew the subject I stopped and invite questions about her. Through the questioning, they learn that this is a grandmother raising four children because their father is not around and their mother is incarcerated. They learn that I have had interactions with her involving minor juvenile delinquency with two of the children. They learn that she is concerned about the children's well-being and welcomes my suggestion to work as a mentor for them rather than enforcing the law. They learn that she has a full-time job at a factory during the day and a part-time job at an IGA grocery store in the evenings to help support the children. They then ask, "What citation(s) did you issue?" I reply, "None." She needed every penny to support her and her grand-children and worked hard to do this. I simply told her to renew her registration and insure her vehicle when she had the funds. I shared this information with other officers so they knew she planned to do so as soon as possible. And she took care of all the issues: registration, insurance, the taillight, and the defective muffler. The lesson here is to get to know community members on a personal level and help them succeed.

Beyond the Badge: Columbia, South Carolina.
Columbia's Beyond the Badge — Community Engagement through Community Service (2016).

The Columbia Police Department's Beyond the Badge program is an excellent example of such an initiative at work. It aims to help new Columbia police officers not only connect with the community, but also create meaningful relationships with the citizens that they will serve. This program gives training academy graduates an opportunity to help those in need in their own community. What makes this an exceptional idea is that these are new officers just beginning their careers. They have not yet developed the cynicism seen in many veteran officers. Most young recruits join the police to help those that cannot help themselves and protect those that cannot protect themselves. This initiative is thus likely to develop in them an understanding and empathy toward the citizens of their community that can be carried forward into their careers. These new officers, even before regular duty, spend a week doing things such as serving food, assisting at a food bank, reading to students, preparing food for the homeless, playing bingo with the elderly, and mentoring children. This requires the department to collaborate with several service locations in the area to set up the opportunities. The advantages are manifold: they not only gain an understanding and empathy toward those in their community, they learn about the community's needs and create mean-ingful relationships. Overall, they learn that there is more to policing than enforcing the law, including the positives of public service, compassion, and goodwill.

Police Athletic League (PAL) Watts Bears in Los Angeles — Working with Youth.
Harrison (2015).

The PAL exists in numerous cities across the United States. The organization not only strengthens police–youth relations; its positive interactions can reduce juvenile delinquency and youth violence, help keep young people on the right track, build character, enhance young people's leadership abilities, and give them a place in which they feel safe. The PAL provides many programs to enhance the lives of young people while promoting these positive relationships. For example, officers may help young boys and girls with homework, coach them in sports, and assist with other school-related activities.

U.S. Department of Justice statistics document that juvenile crime triples between the hours of 3 p.m. and 6 p.m., which shows the need for young people to be involved in positive after-school activities during this part of the day. For example, the report shows that 97% of youth participants of the Philadelphia PAL feel safer when they are at a PAL center.

The Los Angeles Police, through their PAL, has created the Watts Bears, which includes an athletics team, a youth football team, and a track and field team. The Watts Bears focus on education and community service. This program was created for the young people living in the most violent and gang-affiliated communities in South Central. Officers thus serve as coaches and mentors for the most oppressed and marginalized youth in the city. After just two years of this program, there was just one shooting death in Watts' largest housing projects compared with 43 murders in the previous six years.

Officer Mike Anecdote

I ran my own martial arts dojo for many years. The purpose of my business was not to make money, which it did not, but rather to offer an opportunity to the young people in the community to participate in a structured activity that would promote self-confidence, the importance of community involvement, respect, and empathy. My fees were so reasonable that everyone in my city could afford them. The city in which I worked was a relatively poor community where most citizens worked in service jobs and factories. I mentored and instilled important values in my students. We would also stage charity martial arts tournaments, the proceeds of which would be donated to various charities, such as those focusing on fibromyalgia. We earned enough money to extend the youth center, including buying a new water fountain and building a climbing wall. Each year, we sponsored youth baseball and softball teams, which my wife and I would coach. These examples helped demonstrate the importance of community and charity to all my martial arts students.

Redefining the Role of the SRO: Bridgeport, Connecticut Police Department.

Rosiak (2016).

The use of SROs has been a debated issue. Whereas some feel schools are safer when the police are present, many sense that this police presence has a negative impact on young people, especially racial minorities. Some assert that the presence of an SRO contributes to the school-to-prison pipeline (Heitzeg, 2009; Mallett, 2016). For this program to be successful, all collaborators must agree on the role of the SRO. Schlosser's (2014) case study found that even when the SRO wanted to take on the role of educator and counselor, law enforcement became the primary responsibility due to the expectations and pressure of the principal and teachers.

A fairly new approach being taken by the Bridgeport Police Department involves collaborating with juvenile probation officers, a juvenile review board, and other community agencies. In Bridgeport, one in five citizens are below the poverty line and the city has a high rate of violent crime. Officers were finding themselves getting called to schools because students were fighting at dismissal time almost every day. The Chief of Police and School Superintendent worked together to derive a new approach that redefined the roles of both the police and school staff. To start with, SROs and security guards both report to the Bridgeport Police Department and are trained not to make an arrest; however, students are still held accountable by providing a variety of consequences, including mediation and a juvenile review board that includes a diversion program providing proper resources.

Additionally SROs have an educator role by presenting on topics such as laws, sexting, and bullying. SROs and school security personnel thus serve as informal counselors/mentors, while attempting to build relationships every day. They are trained in areas such as crisis intervention, active shooter training, de-escalation, first aid, preventing cyberbullying and texting, social media, and cultural awareness. Most importantly, SROs are not responsible for student discipline or the enforcement of school rules.

This program by the Bridgeport Police Department has had some outstanding results. There has been a large decrease in arrests at school due to the strong partnership and consistent support for diversion. The number of arrests in public schools dropped from 207 in 2010–11 to 43 in 2014–15 (a nearly 80% decrease) and suspensions were reduced by close to 600.

Social workers within the department.

Dalton (2018).

While social workers often work with police departments, Salt Lake City Police Department took this concept to a new level in 2015. What started with a social worker being hired to research a possible program resulted in the police department having an entire social work team as department employees. The team consists of a program manager, three licensed clinicians, four case managers, two front desk staff, one sergeant, two HOST (Homeless Outreach Service Team) officers, and three CIT (Crisis Intervention Team) officers. The benefits of this program have been numerous, including the department dictating assignments without the need for outside agency approval, those requiring services obtaining a timely response, streamlined communication, and relationship building between social workers and officers. The program has been shown to help citizens in need by providing services as well as reducing repeat calls for those who never receive all the help necessary to solve their problems. The social workers are trained to work with struggling individuals that may need counseling, empowerment, and services from other social service agencies. They are also encouraged to follow up on their cases to better ensure success.

Utilizing social media

Police agencies' use of social media for community policing initiatives is improving. Agencies can use social media to post positive stories of their department's activities as well as positive police—citizen interactions. They can also use it to provide important information to the public about crimes as well as any issues within the department, thereby raising transparency. Some police agencies are even hiring public relations companies to help them market themselves in a positive light. Social media can thus ultimately increase public trust in the police.

Road blocks: us versus them mentality and cynicism

The police often see people at their worst. Nobody calls the police and says, "Hurry, send the police! We are all getting along and cooking out in the backyard!" The police get called when that family picnic turns into an argument and a domestic disturbance. People simply do not call the police when things are going well, even if that is most of the time. But since the police mostly interact with citizens when there is trouble, it is difficult for them to get a true picture of people's lives. Over time, the constant dealing with the public in times of trouble and even danger results in many police officers becoming cynical, developing a view that the world is negative and even unsafe (Stone, 2004). Although police cynicism is attributed to many issues, including negative views of the justice system, poor management, and police bureaucracy, negative citizen contact and thus negative views of citizens are a factor in stimulating police cynicism (Gilmartin, 2002; Stone, 2004).

We have all heard of the "us versus them" mentality in policing. The police are a family within themselves and often feel that only other police officers can truly understand how they feel. What officers need to realize is that good people go through bad times. Good people have to deal with issues involving financial difficulty, alcohol and drug addiction, relationship problems, mental health issues, employment concerns, and so on. So how do we encourage officers to understand that although they are interacting with someone in a negative context, most people are good and simply going through "bad" times? One logical solution is for police officers to get to know their community members as "people" and allow them to get to know the officer as a "person" as opposed to just a cop. This can be achieved through more non-enforcement contact (i.e., interactions with citizens in "good" times).

Another contributing factor to this mentality is related to the media, whose role is to cover the most impactful stories. When an officer is involved in a shooting, uses excessive force, or is found to be corrupt in some fashion, this makes the news. It is thus easy to see that citizens could begin to think that officers are always aggressive or involved in shootings or use-of-force situations. However, the facts tell us something different, and the police hope for coverage that conveys the realities of police work. The truth is that no force is used in 99% of all police–citizen contacts (International Association of Chiefs of Police, 2001). Similarly, in over 82% of arrests, no force is used (Garner & Maxwell, 1999). The vast majority of police officers serve their entire careers without ever firing their weapon in the line of duty, and officers involved homicide are exceedingly rare (Morin & Mercer, 2017; Schlosser & Gahan, 2015).

Officers' views of whether a use-of-force incident is reasonable differs from the public's view (Rojek, Alpert, & Smith, 2012). Officers typically find the use of force to be reasonable, whereas citizens find it excessive (Rojek et al., 2012). Everyone wants to confirm their pre-existing beliefs. This is where the simplest form of community policing comes into play. Officers are encouraged to be proactive to fight crime, and I agree with this. However, I would argue that officers need to be proactive in getting to know community members on a more personal level. Under this simple proactive approach, police officers might start realizing that not everyone is a bad person and citizens might start realizing that police officers are not just crime fighters. The importance of gaining citizen trust cannot be overstated, as this is an important aspect of community policing. Indeed, this should be reciprocal: officers must also gain the trust of citizens to increase the safety of both those citizens and the police.

Many police officers interact positively with the public, including young people, on a daily basis. However, whenever someone captures on video a police officer playing catch with children or shooting baskets with them, it appears that the public make a big deal about this because they think it is rare. Police officers have been doing things like this for years and citizens do not seem to realize. In fact, I have heard citizens say things like "That officer is only doing that because it is on video." This cannot be further from the truth. Police officers are citizens, used to be children, and many have children of their own. Although it may seem self-fulfilling, police officers and agencies need to work harder at marketing themselves. The scenario described above occurs much more often than a police officer being involved in a shooting, and society needs to know this. With the emergence of social media, police agencies and organizations should be proactive in showing this side of police work. Simply said, share the truth.

There have been many setbacks in police–community relations in the United States, including the 1991 beating of Rodney King by police officers and the 1992 acquittal of those same officers. One of the most recent incidents was the 2014 death of Michael Brown, an African American, by a white officer, Darren Wilson, in Ferguson, Missouri (Schlosser, Cha-Jua, Valgoi, & Neville, 2015). This increased the divide between citizens and the police, as most officers stood by Officer Johnson, while many, especially the African-American community, were outraged (Schlosser et al., 2015). This and other high-profile incidents of white officers shooting African-American men have greatly diminished citizens' trust in police officers, especially in the African-American community. This has subsequently fueled a more prominent "us against them" mentality. For instance, it has played a role in fostering the Black Lives Matter movement, later countered by the Blue Lives Matter movement, again further contributing to the "us against them" mentality.

In light of these incidents, in December 2014, President Obama formed the President's Task Force on 21st Century Policing to help improve the trust between the police and community (President's Task Force on 21st Century Policing, 2015). This proactive initiative helped police agencies implement several important philosophies to first build trust and legitimacy because "[p]eople are more likely to obey the law when they believe that those who are enforcing it have a legitimate authority to tell them what to do" (President's Task Force on 21st Century Policing, 2015, p. 9). A second important initiative to reduce crime recommended by this task force was to adopt community policing, which "requires the active building of positive relationships with members of the community" (President's Task Force on 21st Century Policing, 2015, p. 41).

Officer Mike Anecdote

I received many commendations from my police department for acts of valor. However, my greatest commendation was when I received our city's volunteer of the year based on my citizenship, not my police work. I was always involved in the community both on duty and off duty to help any way possible. I cannot emphasize enough how important it is for officers to be involved in their community while off-duty. Such activities are extremely rewarding and allow officers to become a part of the community as a citizen.

Conclusion

We all want to live in a safe and just society, although achieving this goal is difficult. So what can we do to work toward this goal and what are the benefits? Community policing is a great proactive approach to helping foster both a safe and a just society. There are certainly difficulties in reaching the overarching goals, including gaining officer/community buy-in and changing the predominating biases in our society. We all have certain assumptions, biases, and stereotypes about gender, race, occupation, social status, sexual orientation, and so on. The best way to reduce these biases is to develop relationships with people that are different than us. Community policing is an excellent approach to getting to know such "others." And when we get to know others and understand "their world," we often realize we have the same goals.

Examples of successful community policing initiatives abound both in the United States and around the world. While there is no one-size-fits-all initiative, a common thread is simple effort that can be made by virtually every officer: having more non-enforcement contacts with citizens when it is not a call for service, criminal encounter, or vehicle stop. Getting to know the citizens you serve and letting them get to know you as not only an officer, but also a person will increase respect, empathy, and trust between the police and the public.

Finally, community policing can have positive effects on the well-being of officers. Officers engaged in community policing have greater job satisfaction and a more positive attitude, and they are more motivated and resilient. Moreover, they even show increased health benefits, both physically and mentally, compared with officers who emphasize the law enforcement role of policing.

References

Bano, B. (2011). Job stress among police personnel. *IPEDR, 4*, 290–293.

BBC News. (2012). *What is the role of police community support officers?*. Retrieved from https://www.bbc.com/news/uk-17702622.

Braga, A. A., Welsh, B. C., & Schnell, C. (2015). Can policing disorder reduce crime? A systematic review and meta-analysis. *Journal of Research in Crime and Delinquency, 52*(4), 567–588.

Brody, D. C., DeMarco, C., & Lovrich, N. P. (2002). Community policing and job satisfaction: Suggestive evidence of positive workforce effects from a multijurisdictional comparison in Washington State. *Police Quarterly, 5*(2), 181–205.

Columbia's Beyond the Badge – Community Engagement through Community Service. (2016). Retrieved from https://theiacpblog.org/2016/09/16/columbias-beyond-the-badge-community-engagement-through-community-service/.

Dalton, L. (August 2018). Social workers embedded in law enforcement. *The Police Chief Magazine*, 44–47.

Eurostat, (n.d.). (February 28, 2019). *Quality of life indicators - measuring quality of life*. Retrieved from https://ec.europa.eu/eurostat/statistics-explained/index.php/Quality_of_life_indicators_-_measuring_quality_of_life#B1_dimensions_of_quality_of_life.

Faragher, E. B., Cass, M., & Cooper, C. L. (2005). The relationship between job satisfaction and health: A meta-analysis. *Occupational and Environmental Medicine, 62*(2), 105–112.

Fischer, J. A., & Sousa-Poza, A. (2009). Does job satisfaction improve the health of workers? New evidence using panel data and objective measures of health. *Health Economics, 18*(1), 71–89.

Garner, J. H., & Maxwell, C. D. (1999). *U.S. Department of Justice, Office of Justice Programs. Use of force by police: Overview of national and local data. National Institute of Justice, Research Report, jointly published with the Bureau of Justice Statistics. Chapter 4, Measuring the amount of force used by and against the police in six jurisdictions.*

Gill, C., Weisburd, D., Telep, C. W., Vitter, Z., & Bennett, T. (2014). Community-oriented policing to reduce crime, disorder and fear and increase satisfaction and legitimacy among citizens: A systematic review. *Journal of Experimental Criminology, 10*(4), 399–428.

Gilmartin, K. M. (2002). *Emotional survival for law enforcement: A guide for officers and their families.* Tucson, AZ: E-S Press.

Goldstein, H. (1990). *Excellence in problem-oriented policing.* New York, NY.

Goldstein, H. (2003). On further developing problem-oriented policing: The most critical need, the major impediments, and a proposal. *Crime Prevention Studies, 15*, 13–48.

Goldstein, J. (2017). *Changes in policing take hold in one of the nation's most dangerous cities.* Retrieved from https://www.nytimes.com/2017/04/02/nyregion/camden-nj-police-shootings.html.

Greene, J. R. (1987). Foot patrol and community policing: Past practices and future prospects. *American Journal of Police, 6*, 1.

Halsted, A. J., Bromley, M. L., & Cochran, J. K. (2000). The effects of work orientations on job satisfaction among sheriffs' deputies practicing community-oriented policing. *Policing: An International Journal of Police Strategies Management, 23*(1), 82–104.

Harrison, N. (2015). *Establishing a DC Police Athletic League: A road to reduction in youth violence* (Doctoral dissertation, Johns Hopkins University). Retrieved from https://jscholarship.library.jhu.edu/bitstream/handle/1774.2/39412/HARRISON-CAPSTONE-2015.pdf?sequence=1&isAllowed=y.

Heitzeg, N. A. (2009). *Education or incarceration: Zero tolerance policies and the school to prison pipeline.* Urbana, IL: Forum on Public Policy Online. Oxford Round Table.

International Association of Chiefs of Police. (2001). *Police use of force in America.* Retrieved from https://www.theiacp.org/sites/default/files/2018-08/2001useofforce.pdf.

Jones, A. A., & Wiseman, R. (2006). *Community policing in Europe: Structure and best practices (Sweden, France, Germany).* Retrieved from http://www.lacp.org/Articles%20-%20Expert%20-%20Our%20Opinion/060908-CommunityPolicingInEurope-AJ.htm.

Lawrence, S., & McCarthy, B. (2013). *What works in community policing: A best practices context for measure Y efforts. The Chief Justice Earl Warren Institute on Law and Social Policy.* Retrieved from https://www.law.berkeley.edu/files/What_Works_in_Community_Policing.pdf.

Mallett, C. A. (2016). The school-to-prison pipeline: A critical review of the punitive paradigm shift. *Child and Adolescent Social Work Journal, 33*(1), 15–24.

Morin, R., & Mercer, A. (2017). *Police officers who have fired a gun on duty: A closer look.* Retrieved from http://www.pewresearch.org/fact-tank/2017/02/08/a-closer-look-at-police-officers-who-have-fired-their-weapon-on-duty/.

Nazemi, S. (2009). *Sir Robert Peel's nine principals of policing.* Retrieved from http://lacp.org/2009-Articles-Main/062609-Peels9Principals-SandyNazemi.htm.

Office of Community Oriented Policing Services. (2003). *Community policing defined.* Washington, DC: U.S. Department of Justice.

Police Executive Research Forum. (2016). *Advice from police chiefs and community leaders on building trust: 'Ask for help, work together, and show respect'.* Retrieved from https://www.policeforum.org/assets/policecommunitytrust.pdf.

President's Task Force on 21st Century Policing. (2015). *Final report of the president's task force on 21st c1entury policing.* Retrieved from http://www.cops.usdoj.gov/pdf/taskforce/TaskForce_FinalReport.pdf.

Reisig, M. D. (2010). Community and problem-oriented policing. *Crime and Justice, 39*(1), 1–53.

Rhodes, T. N. (2015). Officers and school settings: Examining the influence of the school environment on officer roles and job satisfaction. *Police Quarterly, 18*(2), 134–162.

Rohe, W. M., Adams, R. E., & Arcury, T. A. (1997). *Community oriented policing: What it is, why it works, how to get started.* Chapel Hill, NC: Center for Urban and Regional Studies, University of North Carolina at Chapel Hill.

Rojek, J., Alpert, G. P., & Smith, H. P. (2012). Examining officer and citizen accounts of police use-of-force incidents. *Crime and Delinquency, 58*(2), 301–327.

Rosiak, J. (September 2016). Forging a school-police relationship to decrease student arrests. *The Police Chief*, 58–63.

Schlosser, M. D. (2014). Multiple roles and potential role conflict of a school resource officer: A case study of the Midwest Police Department's School Resource Officer Program in the United States. *International Journal of Criminal Justice Sciences, 9*(1), 131–142.

Schlosser, M. D., Cha-Jua, S., Valgoi, M. J., & Neville, H. A. (2015). Improving policing in a multiracial society in the United States: A new approach. *International Journal of Criminal Justice Sciences, 10*(1), 115.

Schlosser, M. D., & Gahan, M. (2015). Police use of force: A descriptive analysis of Illinois police officers. *Law Enforcement Executive Forum, 15*(2), 1–12.

Shane, J. M. (2010). Organizational stressors and police performance. *Journal of Criminal Justice, 38*(4), 807–818.

Stone, V. (2004). *Cops don't cry: A book of help and hope for police families.* Ontario, Canada: Creative Bound.

Torres, J., Reling, T., & Hawdon, J. (2018). Role conflict and the psychological impacts of the post-Ferguson period on law enforcement motivation, cynicism, and apprehensiveness. *Journal of Police and Criminal Psychology, 33*(4), 358–374.

Violanti, J. M., & Aron, F. (1993). Sources of police stressors, job attitudes, and psychological distress. *Psychological Reports, 72*(3), 899–904.

Yim, Y., & Schafer, B. D. (2009). Police and their perceived image: How community influence officers' job satisfaction. *Police Practice and Research: An International Journal, 10*(1), 17–29.

14

Closing thoughts

Daniel M. Blumberg[a], Konstantinos Papazoglou[b]

[a]DEPARTMENT OF UNDERGRADUATE PSYCHOLOGY, CALIFORNIA SCHOOL OF PROFESSIONAL PSYCHOLOGY, ALLIANT INTERNATIONAL UNIVERSITY, SAN DIEGO, CA, UNITED STATES; [b]YALE SCHOOL OF MEDICINE, NEW HAVEN, CT, UNITED STATES

Police officers' wellness is fundamental to law enforcement agency effectiveness and to the very wellbeing of the communities in which they serve. For decades, many of us have been championing this cause from within the ranks of police departments as officers, executives, and psychologists. Consequences of deficits in officer wellness were ever-present (and, sadly, continue to be prevalent). In those days, it was common for front-line supervisors and police executives to expect officers, simply, to be tough. By this, they generally meant to remain steely and unshaken when encountering the grim realities of the job. Any sign of psychological struggle was viewed as weakness, a character flaw, and an indication that the officer just was not cut out for the profession.

Fortunately, just as tactical procedures and safety equipment have improved over the years, the concept of toughness also has evolved. Mental toughness is no longer seen as an innate, fixed trait, which one either possesses or not. It is now commonly viewed as a skill, which can be learned and, with ongoing training and support, strengthened. This perspective recognizes that police officers should utilize a repertoire of stress management techniques and will benefit from periodic wellness programming and ongoing efforts to boost resilience. Moreover, growing attention has been paid to the array of challenges that officers differentially experience throughout the career cycle. For example, the psychological needs of two officers at the scene of a traumatic death of a child may be quite different for the early career officer with young children at home than for the late career officer with grown children. Officer wellness, therefore, just like body armor, is not one-size fits all and needs to be tailored to meet the specific challenges faced by various officers within a given organization. Similarly, officers from different organizations may encounter dissimilar stressors, so wellness programming should be adapted based on the particular needs of officers in each organization (e.g., PERF, 2018).

The increased attention on police officer wellbeing has led to an explosion of wellness programming. Millions of dollars have been allocated for officer wellness grants (e.g., COPS, 2019; Matthews, 2018; POST, 2019). Although it would be nice to believe that all grant recipients have benevolent intentions, it may be naïve to assume that there are no charlatans among wellness providers. This is where police executives need to develop

Power. https://doi.org/10.1016/B978-0-12-817872-0.00014-8

greater expertise in officer wellness, better awareness of their employees' specific challenges, and a more discerning ability to select the most impactful programming. Moreover, when police executives adopt the skill-based perspective, they will require two important dimensions in the wellness programs that they offer. First, they should never accept a one-off training that is not fully integrated into the organization's larger culture of wellness. Every specific wellness program should complement and/or enhance ongoing wellness efforts. Second, police executives should expect the programs that are offered to leave a positive, lasting effect. This requires evidence of efficacy; how well did the programming work? Each program should contain a method to measure its impact. At the same time, police executives retain some responsibility for ensuring that officers continue to demonstrate the benefits provided by the programming. It does little to put on a program without measuring its efficacy or instituting some mechanism to verify that officers are practicing what they learned.

The present volume highlighted the complexity of police officer wellness and demonstrated the need for a multidimensional commitment to wellbeing. Although there may be value in, for example, a mindfulness workshop, sustained wellness requires a much broader approach. For example, one innovative program (Romosiou, Brouzos, & Vassilopoulos, 2018) included "... four 4-h sessions over a 5-week period with a 10-day interval between the sessions" (p. 6). Moreover, rather than addressing a single dimension, this training recognized the transactional relationship between wellness variables and provided detailed instruction in and practical application of emotional intelligence, empathy, resilience, and stress management (pp. 6 & 10). Their statistical analysis showed how beneficial the training was; significant improvement was observed on all four variables, which was sustained at the three-month follow-up assessment (p. 11). In part, this can be attributed to the adult-learning theory model whereby participants actively engage the material, which is far more useful for police officers than passively sitting in a lecture on some wellness topic.

Forward thinking police executives can utilize a variety of training modalities to deliver wellness programming. This is especially salient in the age of social media. One such innovative, preventative program to boost officers' resilience was developed by Dr. Alex Thornton (Thornton, Blumberg, Papazoglou, & Giromini, 2019). The HEROES Project is delivered virtually. Officers access the self-paced training in the comfort of their home. The program includes six online sessions designed to develop and strengthen officers' positive psychological skills, such as self-efficacy, optimism, and empathy. Each session includes video lectures and clips, projects, and access to a variety of resources, e.g., podcasts (p. 6). A preliminary pilot study showed promising results that the impact of the training was not only significant in boosting psychological capital (Luthans, Avolio, Avey, & Norman, 2007), but these improvements continued at subsequent post-test assessments at six-months, one-year, and two-years after completion of the training (Thornton et al., unpublished manuscript, p. 10).

Beyond even the most impactful wellness programming, the present volume demonstrated the essential importance for police agencies to establish a comprehensive, multidimensional culture of wellness. Such a perspective will guide recruiting and hiring efforts (including extensive pre-hire preparation and socialization activities). Officers' health and wellbeing will be seamlessly integrated into academy training and continuing professional education throughout the career. This includes frequently emphasizing the relationship between wellness and ethical decision-making. Supervision will preemptively focus on detecting early warning signs of distress, so that problems can be addressed when they are small and manageable. Promotional practices will require strict adherence to the agency's wellness priorities. Officers' health and wellbeing will receive appropriate career-stage interventions, which consider officers' developmental needs, such as work-life balance, leadership development, and retirement planning services. And, just as importantly, disciplinary procedures will be implemented, which continue to treat officers as valued members of the organization even after they have made a mistake that requires some form of punishment. This whole-person perspective recognizes that an organizational commitment to employee health requires flexibility, fairness, and consistency.

When police executives recognize the relationship between officers' wellness and their ability to withstand and, even, thrive following adversity, resilience becomes central to police training. This should be incorporated into basic academy training. Resilience is strengthened when training in the academy is as realistic as possible, and recruits are repeatedly exposed to situations that they will encounter in the field. For example, there are numerous benefits to virtual reality training. Harding and Orth (2019) discussed how virtual reality training can address unconscious biases. This technology has been around for years and can provide trainees with lifelike exposure to intense situations that would be otherwise impossible to recreate in a training environment. In one such product, "When police officers duck, their avatars duck. And when their avatars are shot, the police officers feel pain" (Ungerleider, 2012). Through exposure and repetition, officers can reduce their fear of the unknown and build more confidence in their ability to competently handle critical incidents.

Officer wellness is not something that occurs in a vacuum. In addition to the establishment of an internal culture of wellness, police executives are encouraged to make good use of available community assets. The relationships among the police department and other local, state, and federal agencies as well as among various community organizations can become a valuable source of support and shared resources. For that matter, police executives can partner with local psychologists, universities, and other organizations to obtain research funds and grant opportunities, which would bring wellness programs and initiatives to their officers without charge. Along these lines, police executives are encouraged to listen to their employees in order to learn about the various specific sources of stress that they experience. This will help target wellness initiatives to the most important areas of need. In the end, police officer wellness is an individual endeavor that requires a strong, concerted organizational commitment.

This book provided a detailed look at police wellness and its challenges from a variety of perspectives. It was not surprising that some overlap of content occurred among a few of the chapters. The material presented represents the current state of the research in this field. However, there is a great need for more exploration into police wellness, since so much of the data on topics covered in the book come from outside of law enforcement. Frankly, police wellness research should still be considered to be in its infancy. Although there is general consensus of the overall stressors in policing and their effect on officer wellness, there is still much to be learned. For example, it will be quite informative when more empirical attention is paid to individual factors regarding which police officers are most vulnerable to experience reactions like moral injury, compassion fatigue, and burnout. Clinical and organizational psychologists can investigate what police executives can do to mitigate these and other deleterious conditions. Additionally, police unions should not be ignored as a potential partner in the officer wellness movement. Likewise, community groups and corporations have a vested interest in police wellness and may be a viable source for funding research in this area.

Research findings cannot reside only in books or academic journals. The data must be interpreted and translated into practical applications to benefit police officers, their families, and their law enforcement agencies. Wellness programming must reflect the evidence-based, best practices gleaned from the valid results of relevant research projects. The outcome will be a far more integrated and comprehensive approach to improving and sustaining police officer wellness, ethics, and resilience.

Finally, although this book has suggested a variety of prevention and intervention strategies, there is still much to be learned and much that can be done to assist police officers. To be continued…

References

California Commission on Peace Officer Standards and Training (POST). (2019). *Innovations grant program. State of California.* Retrieved from https://post.ca.gov/Innovative-Grant- Program.

Community Oriented Policing Services (COPS). (2019). *Law Enforcement Mental Health and Wellness Act (LEMHWA) Program.* U.S. Department of Justice. Retrieved from https://cops.usdoj.gov/lemhwa.

Harding, C., & Orth, B. (April 2019). Virtual reality training: New technology opens up new training opportunities for law enforcement. *The Police Chief, 86*(4), 48.

Thornton, A.R., Blumberg, D.M., Papazoglou, K., & Giromini, L. (unpublished manuscript). *The HEROES project: A wellness intervention.*

Thornton, A. R., Blumberg, D. M., Papazoglou, K., & Giromini, L. (2019). The HEROES project: Building mental resilience in first responders. In C. A. Bowers, D. C. Beidel, & M. R. Marks (Eds.), *Mental health intervention and treatment of first responders and emergency workers.* Hershey, PA: IGI Global.

Luthans, F., Avolio, B., Avey, J., & Norman, S. (2007). Psychological capital: Measurement and relationship with performance and job satisfaction. *Personnel Psychology, 60*(3), 541–572. https://doi.org/10.1111/j.1744-6570.2007.00083.x.

Matthews, T. (2018, Sept. 13). *Improving officer wellness: Funding initiatives for mental health support.* Police One.com. Retrieved from https://www.policeone.com/health- fitness/articles/480394006-Improving-officer-wellness-Funding-initiatives-for-mental- health-support/.

Police Executive Research Forum (PERF). (2018). *Building and sustaining an officer wellness program: Lessons from the San Diego Police Department.* Washington, DC: Office of Community Oriented Policing Services.

Romosiou, V., Brouzos, A., & Vassilopoulos, S. P. (2018). An integrative group intervention for the enhancement of emotional intelligence, empathy, resilience and stress management among police officers. *Police Practice and Research*, 1–19.

Ungerleider, N. (2012). *Virtual training world for law enforcement inflicts real pain.* Fast Company. Retrieved from https://www.fastcompany.com/3000383/virtual-training- world-law-enforcement-inflicts-real-pain.

Index

Note: 'Page numbers followed by "f" indicate figures, "t" indicates tables'.

Biography

Dr. Konstantinos Papazoglou, PhD is a postdoctoral scholar at Yale University School of Medicine. He completed his doctoral degree (PhD) in psychology (clinical – forensic area) as Vanier Scholar at the University of Toronto (U of T). He is a former Police Major of the Hellenic Police Force and European Police College and he holds a master's degree in applied psychology from New York University (NYU) as Onassis Scholar. Currently, he is involved in community policing trauma-focused programs aimed to support victims of violent crimes. In addition, he is affiliated researcher with the Loss, Trauma, and Emotion Lab at Teachers College, Columbia University of New York. His research work focuses on stress, trauma, and resilience promotion among police officers. Towards this direction he has established research collaboration with many law enforcement agencies in US, Canada, and Europe (e.g., Police Training Institute – Illinois State Police, State Police of Kentucky, National Police of Finland).

Daniel M. Blumberg, PhD is a licensed clinical psychologist who has spent the past 33 years providing all facets of clinical and consulting psychological services to numerous local, state, and federal law enforcement agencies. He specializes in employment-related psychological evaluations, psycho-educational training, and management consultation. In addition to his expertise in workplace stress prevention and trauma recovery, Dr. Blumberg is an authority on the selection, training and supervision of undercover operatives. His training program on successful hiring of public safety personnel has received widespread praise. He is an Associate Professor in the California School of Professional Psychology at Alliant International University's San Diego Campus where he teaches a variety of psychology and forensic psychology courses. His research interests include police integrity, the moral risks of policing, and programs to improve relations between the police and the community.

CPSIA information can be obtained
at www.ICGtesting.com
Printed in the USA
LVHW101955191220
674545LV00009BA/143